PROMISE
AND
DELIVERANCE

PROMISE
AND
DELIVERANCE

S. J. De Graaf

Volume Three
Christ's Ministry And Death

Translated by H. Evan Runner and
Elisabeth Wichers Runner

PAIDEIA PRESS

2012

First published in Dutch
as *Verbondsgeschiedenis,*
© J. H. Kok of Kampen.

This edition published by special arrangement with Paideia Press
and the publisher of the original Dutch edition.

© Copyright 2012 PAIDEIA PRESS
2123 Godwin Ave. S.E. 49507
Grand Rapids, Michigan
USA
refpubproject@sbcglobal.net
REFORMATIONALPUBLISHINGPROJECT.COM

ISBN 978-0-88815-008-0
Printed in the United States of America

TABLE OF CONTENTS

MATTHEW: KING AND PEOPLE

MATTHEW: THE ROAD TO POWER

LUKE: THE MERCIFUL HIGH PRIEST

LUKE:
THE DISCLOSURE OF LIFE'S NEED

LUKE: THE LAMB THAT WAS SLAIN

TRANSLATOR'S INTRODUCTION

The publication of Volume Three of S. G. De Graaf's *Promise and Deliverance* launches a new phase of this remarkable undertaking. It brings us to the New Testament, where the proclamation of the Kingdom of God's grace in His Anointed (the Messiah, the Christ) comes into full view.

It is only natural for Christians to want to turn immediately to the New Testament portion of Holy Scripture. And in a work like De Graaf's, they will be eager to read what the author has to say about the New Testament. There is, of course, ample justification for this inclination. In his Introduction to the whole work De Graaf writes: "The entire Scripture is God's revelation of Himself . . . " and, "As a result of sin, there is no revelation of grace other than in the Mediator" and further, " . . . the Mediator [is] also the Head of the covenant, the second Adam" (Vol. I, pp. XX, XXIII). From this we see that it is in the New Testament that we find the fullest, clearest revelation of all these things. It is in this light that we are to understand Jesus' somewhat puzzling statement that the least in the Kingdom of heaven is greater than John the Baptist (see p. 75 below).

Indeed, since all of us live in the period of history that comes after the full revelation of the grace of God, it is only natural that any man—whether a believer or a seeker—who wants to learn the meaning of the Christian religion will turn automatically to the New Testament.

Undoubtedly, then, there will be people who begin reading De Graaf at this point. And that is well and good—except that they will discover almost immediately not just that "Scripture is a unity" but that God's revelation of Himself in the Mediator and in His covenant with His people has a long history, a history which is presupposed in the New Testament and which simply must be understood by readers of the New Testament if it is to light up for them fully as the revelation that it is. Even the Kingdom of grace that John the Baptist announced and Jesus came to proclaim is firmly grounded in the covenant God established with man in the beginning.*

In this connection De Graaf warns against seeking simple stories about "Jesus and the soul" in the New Testament. This is to remind us that neither individualism nor mysticism—which are both widespread interpretations today—represents a correct understanding of Biblical revelation. As for individualism, he writes: "In the covenant God always draws near to His *people* as a whole— never just to individuals. Because of the covenant, the entire people rests secure in God's faithfulness, and every individual member of the covenant shares in that rest as a member of the community. We need not always use the word *covenant*—the beginning of the Bible does not—as long as the children are told about the covenant relationship" (Vol. I, p. XV).

At the beginning of this third volume, he explains: ". . . the New Testament places much more emphasis on the individual life of the believer than the Old Testament. But this emphasis must be seen in the proper perspective. It does not mean that the fellowship of the people in the covenant as revealed especially in the Old Testament is neglected. Here, too, divine revelation follows pedagogical lines. After the communion of the people in the covenant has been sufficiently established in the Old Testament, the value of each individual life within that community becomes the focus of attention in the New Testament" (p. 1 below). Nevertheless, to quote Herman Ridderbos once more, ". . . the thing of special importance for the entire structure of Jesus' preaching of the kingdom [is] that the

*On this important point the reader may wish to consult the very illuminating discussion, so sorely needed in our time, that Herman Ridderbos offers in his magnificent book *The Coming of the Kingdom* (translated by H. de Jongste and published by Paideia Press, of St. Catharines). The reading of just one page of that book (p. 192) will surely be sufficient to whet the appetite for more. Let me quote a single paragraph: "It is the reality of God's covenant and of his theocratic relationship to Israel as his people which is the basis of the description of the gospel as the gospel of the poor. It is this true people of God which is addressed in the beatitudes and to whom the salvation of the kingdom is granted as their lawful right. And it is this special relationship which from the outset codetermines the contents and the structure of the gospel of the kingdom of heaven."

coming of Christ, the salvation given by him, and the community of those who believe in him, *remain qualified* by God's covenant and the relationship to Israel established therein."* At the very end of the present volume, De Graaf, in accordance with this principle, raises an interesting question: "Why did Jesus [after being recognized by the two men from Emmaus] disappear so suddenly?" (p. 448). His answer is: "He did not want to give Himself here and there to isolated individuals, but He wanted to gather together His own circle, the community of His people" (p. 449).

Mysticism—the second widespread error De Graaf warns against—is at least as serious a misunderstanding of the gospel of Christ as individualism, and the two are frequently encountered together. While there is indeed a mystical union or communion between Christ and His people, mystic*ism* derogates from the written Word of God as it fixes the believer's mind on his own inner experience. The believer's certainty of faith is made to reside exclusively in some inner consciousness of a spiritual experience ("Jesus and the soul") instead of being attached to the prophetic Word of God. And when adherents of mysticism do study the Bible, it is more to reinforce this innate religious sense.

The Scriptures themselves teach otherwise. Peter says: "We heard this voice borne from heaven, for we were with him on the holy mountain," referring, of course, to the spiritual experience of the inner circle of disciples (Peter, James and John) on the Mount of Transfiguration. But he immediately continues: "And we have

---

The Coming of the Kingdom, pp. 197-8. Especially to the point is what Ridderbos writes about Jesus' words about the Savior, in which He indicates that the purpose of His coming was to search for "what was lost," i.e. the one sheep, the prodigal son, and so forth. Ridderbos observes: . . these pronouncements . . . have been quoted to prove that Jesus broke through the particularistic idea of Israel's election as God's people. He is then supposed to have insisted on a kind of religious individualism and on the infinite value of the separate and single human soul (the *one* sheep, etc.). But this is incorrect. The 'lost state' of the publicans and sinners that Jesus sought to save consisted just in their complete estrangement from the totality of the flock, i.e., of God's people. And this is why they run the risk of losing the salvation promised to this people of God" (p. 196).

the prophetic word made more sure" (II Pet. 1:18-19). The spiritual experience is not denied, but the assurance of its validity is linked to the Word of prophecy as the fulfillment and confirmation of that Word. The rest of the passage exhorts us to pay attention to the Word. Similarly, the women at the tomb on Resurrection Sunday were told to relate their personal experience of the empty tomb to what Jesus had said back in Galilee, where He had foretold His suffering, death and resurrection. As a final illustration of the point, consider the two followers of Christ from Emmaus, who did finally recognize Him when He broke bread but were kept from recognizing Him until then by God. De Graaf comments: "They should not believe that he was risen only on the basis of His appearance but they should acknowledge that God had said it. They were to believe the Word of God. God's Word is the ground of all our certainty" (p. 449 below). "Belief in Christ's resurrection must not depend on His appearing to us but in the Word of God, or, which is the same thing, in the Word of Christ. It is noteworthy how often we are referred to the Word of Christ in this chapter [Luke 24], and to the Word of God in the Old Testament" (p. 445).

Mysticism by-passes this Word of God that came prophetically in the past. It ignores God's mighty acts in history by which He revealed Himself to His people in the Mediator and in His covenant, and thus it completely overlooks the fundamental importance in the Christian religion of the *historical unfolding* of that self-revelation and of the covenantal relationship and community it brings into being. But these things constitute the essence of the uniqueness of the Christian religion. They also give us a Biblical basis for dealing seriously with the world religions, but this is a subject we cannot enter into here.

Since God's revelation of Himself can only be understood in the light of the precious accumulation and preservation of revelation within the covenant community, readers who begin with the present volume will want to go back to the first two volumes repeatedly. Often De Graaf's discussions will suggest fruitful ways of doing so. And this is also the place for me to express my conviction that it is highly desirable to refer back to De Graaf's own Preface and Introduction (Vol. I, pp. 15-26) time and again when using any of these four volumes.

Strikingly, the New Testament announces the full liberation

of life. This is the meaning of the proclamation of the Kingdom in which God's grace reigns, the Kingdom of which Christ, the one anointed by God, is King. The *promise* of the Old Testament has become the actual *deliverance* of the New. This speaks to our deepest human need.

Right down through almost the last five centuries, "Freedom" has been the rallying cry of modern Humanism, of which Rousseau is one of the major prophets. At the time of the French revolution, people danced around the "tree of liberty," and since then progressive liberalism and Marxist socialism have successively promised them what they wanted most—freedom. "Liberation" is still the key term, as when people speak of "struggles of national liberation" and "liberation theology." But the promised freedom continues to elude people because it is wrongly conceived from the start.

At one time, the effort to achieve freedom was directed against the medieval church, which had become something of a totalitarian threat to the free development of the several spheres or sectors of life. At other times it has been directed against a monster state that has taken away from the other areas of life the freedom to develop in accordance with their own nature, or against a capitalistic society in which the economic sector has taken over and has begun to lord it over the non-economic sectors in a way that runs contrary to their nature. But all these efforts of man to save himself, to be free, that is, to be free from whatever threatens the sound development of his *whole* life, in order to realize and develop all of his potentialities— all these efforts have failed, and they will continue to fail because the human agent in all these efforts at liberation is enslaved to sin himself.

The church as such was not the villain. Neither was the state. Church, state, marriage, family, the business world—these are all various spheres or sectors of life which together make up God's one creation order. There is no life here on earth without them; they constitute the very structure of the creation, which is a many-sided splendor. When people, in these various sectors of their lives, function in accordance with the order of creation which gives every sphere its limited mandate, the result is a Kingdom of peace (shalom) and blessedness, a temple holy to the Lord. There is no part of the creation structure that is evil. Every bit of the creation order proceeded from God, and there is *no dark side of God*.

The culprit in every situation is sin, and sin is a matter of the direction of the human heart relative to the order of creation and the covenant relation that characterizes all religion. Sin resides in our inmost being; it is man himself, in the unity of his selfhood, responding disobediently to the creational-covenantal conditions of our life. Sin is our personal rebellion against God's order, the order of His good creation. God, however, remains sovereign; He maintains His Word, in which the creation order is grounded. Sin, as a way of relating to that order, makes its presence felt whenever we act within that order. It is the sinfulness of the human heart that leads to attempts to build a *totalitarian* church or a *totalitarian* state or a *totalitarian* economy, and it is the sinfulness of the heart that drives man to try for an independent existence in which he looks out only for Number One. The word *totalitarian* here refers to man's stubborn attempts to substitute one or another of the *limited*, delegated spheres of authority that go to make up God's creation order for the Kingdom of Christ, where the Word of God's grace that calls men (back) to order holds sway over the *whole* of the creation. Only Christ has been given all authority, that is, the fullness of authority.

It is of the utmost importance to distinguish between *structure* and *direction* and to see that the disobedience of our fall into sin and the obedience of our new nature, redeemed in Christ, presuppose a creation order and the conditions of the covenant, from which obedience and disobedience, as ways of relating to that order and to those conditions, acquire their meaning. When "flesh" and "spirit" are contrasted in Scripture, these terms refer to two possible *directions* of our lives in all the sectors of the one creation order, not to a supposed *structurally* lower world of matter and body and a superior world of soul or spirit, as we sometimes see it in systems of thought—even theological thought—that have been influenced by the pagan Greek philosophers.

Since it is the sinfulness of our hearts that threatens our existence, victory over sin is the way to real freedom. That victory was wrought by Christ. Christ is the Savior, the Redeemer, the one who made atonement for sin. Not only are our sins forgiven in Christ, but we are delivered from bondage to sin. We are given a new nature; we are born again.

Real freedom, freedom in the meaning opened up for us in God's revelation, is more than a freedom *from*. Here we see the superiority of true freedom to all the contemporary talk of "liberation" among revolutionaries, who fail to see what they are left with after the revolution—sinful man. The freedom Christ gives is a freedom from our bondage to sin (by the renewal of the heart), in order that we may live by *every word that proceeds from the mouth of God*. That is true freedom—to live in accordance with the will of God. This includes the (law-) words, often called ordinances or decrees, by which God gave structure to His creation in the beginning (see Ps. 119:91; Prov. 8:29). Through the Spirit of Christ, who is a Spirit of holiness, we receive a new heart on the basis of Christ's work, a heart that loves God for His own sake and is therefore submissive to every word of God spoken for our redemption and well-being. Through such submission we come to be at one with the will of God, and that brings peaceful harmony everywhere in the creation. Only then do we enjoy shalom, blessedness, freedom.

To understand this point and what De Graaf has to say about it, two aspects of Christ's work call for brief comment here. Both recall the covenantal character of Biblical religion, thus reminding us again to look upon the New Testament as the newest portion of the Book of the Covenant. The fact that the word *covenant* occurs less frequently in the New Testament means little, for the covenant relationship continues. Moreover, the word does come up in some crucial passages, such as Matthew 26:28 and parallel passages (compare Exodus 24:8 and Hebrews 10:29), I Corinthians 11:25, Ephesians 2:12, and Hebrews 8:6. *Diathéké*, the Greek word used to translate the Hebrew word *berith* (covenant) points to God's initiative in the covenant (see Vol. I, p. 311 and notes, and p. 118 below).

De Graaf tells us that one reason the word *covenant* is used less often in the New Testament is that "the gospels are concerned with the Christ, the Head of the covenant. All the light falls on Him" (p. 1 below). Christ came into this world as the Mediator of our redemption. He is the second—and last—Adam. He was the new Representative of His covenant people. He bore the judgment of God upon sin for all who are in Him by believing in Him. But He also lived a wholly righteous life. That life of righteousness, which the covenant conditions demanded, He offered to the Father on behalf of His people. Although He was born of Mary, He was capable of living a wholly righteous life because He was begotten of God. Listen to what the angel said to Mary: "The Holy Spirit will come upon you, and the power of the Most High will overshadow you; therefore the child to be born will be called holy, the Son of God" (Luke 1:35).

Christ was the Holy One, subject in heart and life to every word of His Father. He came, as He said at His baptism, to fulfill all righteousness, to meet all the demands of the law, to keep all the conditions of the covenant, and thus, as a man, to earn eternal life. But He did that as Head of the covenant; He did it as our Representative and Substitute. On the basis of His covenant faithfulness as our Mediator, His Holy Spirit gives us a new heart, uniting us by faith with Christ in His holiness. Our lives here and now are to be in all things a growing up into the One who is our Head, that is, Christ (see Eph. 4:15). Thus He is our righteousness, and we are free men, subjects of the Kingdom where God's Word *and* grace reign. Revolutionaries of the world, unite! Unite in giving heed to Christ's Word of liberation and in submitting to the gracious *and righteous* rule of the Word of God! It is a sounder Word than Rousseau's, or Marx's, or Lenin's, or Che's, because the Word of the Mediator of our salvation is the Word of one who is also the Word of creation.

A second point we should note is that Christ is also the one anointed by God. *Christ* and *Messiah* are titles rather than names. The former is Greek for *the anointed*, and the latter, which has the same meaning, is Hebrew. In Acts 10:38 we read that "God anointed Jesus of Nazareth with the Holy Spirit and with power." This title, then, points to the idea of office as it is found in Scripture. Ephesians 4, to which I referred above, speaks of a number of offices, although the word itself is not used. In the Old Testament we read of men being anointed to be prophets, priests and kings. Although we are all more or less familiar with the idea of ecclesiastical offices and we all speak of holders of political office, the Biblical meaning of office is not widely understood in our day. Therefore a word about this matter is in order here.

The Latin word *officium*, from which our word *office* is derived, means "an obligatory service, obligation, duty."

Although we may think at first of an office as a room or a building where one's work is done, English dictionaries also list such meanings as "a service done toward someone, duty towards others, duty attaching to one's station or position." In these meanings something of the Biblical conception of office is retained.

To get at that Scriptural meaning, we must go back once again to the Old Testament. When man was created, God established a covenant relationship with him. In the context of that relationship, He assigned him a task, a task that only man could perform. It was a rather comprehensive task. What it amounted to, essentially, was that man was to serve God in the world by administering God's love and solicitude to the creatures (not just to his fellow men). He was to do this in God's name and to His glory, which meant that he would have to carry out his duty in accordance with every word of God by which the creation had been constituted. In short, man's duty would have to be performed in accordance with the conditions of the covenant. Thus Adam was given a charge or mandate, and he was also given the delegated authority to carry out the mandate. Furthermore, since he would be performing this task as the covenant head, the heart-direction of his work would be decisive not only for himself but also for his posterity and for the whole world he administered.

Thus "office," in Scripture, implies that God assigns to man, as His servant, a task that comports with his position as the creature who bears God's image. It also means that man is granted the authority or right to perform this service in God's name and in freedom. Man is charged with preserving order, an order that was already laid down in the creation. Within the framework of that order, he is to freely develop the potentials in the creation.

When Adam fell and was thus deprived of his office, the office itself did not disappear from human life. It was immediately reinstated, because in the counsel of God, Christ was found ready to accept the office of Mediator and of covenant head. These were tasks God gave Him, which He voluntarily accepted and for which He received authority, John 10:18, for example, speaks of the authority (Greek: *exousia*) that Christ received from the Father as His commissioned representative to lay down His life and to take it up again.

Christ came into the world on a mission. "Lo, I have come to do thy will, O God," He said. As the new Office-bearer, Christ did everything the first Adam ought to have done and suffered everything Adam ought to have suffered because of his desecration of his office. United to Christ as members of His Body, our entire life is to be service of God and an administering of God's love and solicitude (which in a fallen world requires pronouncements of judgment, because God is a holy God and is jealous of that holiness) to the creature.

What we have been discussing is often called the general office. Sometimes people speak of three offices when discussing this general office, but actually there are only prophetic, priestly and kingly aspects to the one office. At a particular moment, either in the ministry of Christ or in our own lives, one of these aspects will stand out. When the head of a household prays with and on behalf of his family, as Job did (see Vol. I, pp. 144-5), the priestly aspect stands out. But at the same time, such prayer is a prophecy pointing to the foundation of the believer's life, and also a form of kingly rule. Not one of the three aspects can ever be separated from the others.

As people multiplied and relationships became more complex, the general office that every man possesses as man, with its three aspects, became particularized or specialized. And though the three aspects cannot be separated, the special offices of prophet, priest and king developed. These special offices are grounded in the general office. In a great variety of ways, a man's general office as man becomes particularized or takes on a more specialized form in his life by reason of the experience, training and particular historical calling that determine in what area of life he renders his more specific service (without losing his whole-hearted service). This particularization also has to do with the various sectors or spheres of the creation order. Thus we get ecclesiastical offices, political offices, and so forth. Offices imply the limitation of delegated sovereignty. Only Christ, as the Mediator, has been given *complete* delegated sovereignty.

Through a great variety of ministries, God is reconciling the world to Himself. At Pentecost His covenant was opened to all the nations. The very first chapter of the Bible, writes De Graaf, reveals "first and foremost.... the Kingdom of God.... This Kingdom was a Kingdom of Peace. The world was like a great temple which God chose to inhabit and favor with His blessing" (Vol. I, pp. 1, 7). It is a constantly recurring theme in De Graaf's work that because of the redemption accomplished by Christ, the whole creation, groaning now under the burden of sin, is in the process of being restored to a holy temple.

In these volumes De Graaf is concerned with how Biblical history is to be told to children. Many reviewers have naturally mentioned this. But I should like to call attention to a sentence in De Graaf's Preface: "These outlines are thus meant for people who are looking through the Scriptures for an understanding of the Word of God *before* they begin telling the story" (Vol. I, p. 17). This, I think, indicates the wider significance of these volumes.

When I introduced Volume I just a brief two years ago, I suggested that because of the author's perspective, this work would be helpful to new Christians and to young people in Latin America and the rising nations of Africa and Asia, who may often think of themselves as social revolutionaries but are actually crying out in anguish of soul for righteousness and justice, for social and economic peace (Vol. I, pp. 14-15). How thankful I am to the God who keeps His covenant not just that in a mere two years more than 25,000 copies have been sold but particularly that the work is already in the process of being translated into Spanish and Chinese. I can only hope and pray that we shall soon be hearing of efforts to produce translations into Japanese, Korean, Arabic, French, and the languages of Africa, India and Indonesia.

My wife and I would like to dedicate this stage of the work we have done jointly to our precious grandchildren, of whom there are an increasing number, with the fervent prayer that they, too, in the midst of our evil times, "may grow up into Him in all things, who is the Head, that is, Christ."

H. Evan Runner

MATTHEW: CHRIST'S COMING INTO THE WORLD

CHAPTER ONE
GIVEN BY GOD
MATTHEW I

The New Testament is just as much a book of the covenant as the Old Testament. True, the word *covenant* is used less often in the New Testament, but the covenant relationship continues. Initially Christ was sent only to the lost sheep of the house of Israel. Whenever Gentiles came to Him, He first demanded an acknowledgment of the Lord's covenant with Israel. On the day of Pentecost the covenant was opened up so all could share in it. Israel as a people became one among many nations—no more, no less. Believers of all nations were added to the covenant community. Like wild branches the Gentiles were grafted onto the cultivated olive tree, the Old Testament covenant people. The old covenant, then, truly flowed into the new. (On this point, see especially the Letter to the Hebrews.) Moreover, whenever the Bible speaks of Christ and calls Him our Head, or whenever it mentions God's concern for us in Christ (which is the sole content of Scripture, both Old and New Testament, it is drawing attention to that covenant relationship.

There are other reasons why the word *covenant* is used less frequently in the New Testament. In the first place, the gospels are concerned with Christ, the Head of the covenant. All light falls on Him. This fact must govern our treatment of the gospel stories. Everywhere the self-revelation of Christ confronts us.

In the second place, the New Testament places much more emphasis on the individual life of the believer than does the Old Testament. This emphasis does not mean that the fellowship of the people in the covenant as revealed in the Old Testament can be neglected. Divine revelation follows pedagogical lines: after the communion of the people in the covenant has been sufficiently established in the Old Testament, the value of each individual life within that community becomes the focus of attention in the New Testament.

The third reason why the word *covenant* appears less frequently in the New Testament is because the emphasis has come to fall on the Kingdom of God, now proclaimed by both John the Baptist and Christ Himself. This Kingdom, foreshadowed in the kingdom of Israel and present in Old Testament prophecy, is now expressly announced. Its coming is bound up with the dispensation of the new covenant and the outpouring of the Holy Spirit. Part of the significance of that outpouring is the opening up of creation to man's use in the name of the Lord and to man's dominion over it. That dominion permits man to catch a glimpse of the Kingdom which has finally come. When the Kingdom is proclaimed, the covenant is not abandoned. Through their fellowship with one another and with Christ, their Head, and through Christ with God, people exercise dominion over creation.

I will not attempt to construct a harmony of the gospels. Each gospel tells a particular story with a specific purpose, a purpose bound up with the aim of that gospel. When telling the story of each gospel we must preserve that specific purpose. Also, it's not useful to deal with Christ's work by geographic areas. The procedure adopted here is to deal with a series of events from each gospel. As much as possible, I have tried to avoid repeating stories. This method offers a distinct advantage in that a different gospel can be dealt with each year.*

The focus of Matthew 1 is on the genealogy of Joseph, who, like Mary, was of the house of David. Joseph's line was the line formally recognized by the Jews. The child Jesus was formally registered as Joseph's son and, as such, a son of David. This brings us closer to the meaning of the genealogy.

The child Jesus was not the son of Joseph, David's descendant. Yet Joseph (and, through him, the house of David) would receive this child as his own. On the other hand, through Mary this child was truly of the house of David.

This indicates Christ's twofold relationship to us. On the one hand He is of the flesh and blood of Mary and therefore one of us. On the other hand, He is without human ancestry for He is conceived by the Holy Spirit. He is the Holy One, a stranger to sin. Because He is a stranger to our sinful nature we must receive Him

---

*Here the author is referring to his original purpose in writing these story outlines. He explains that purpose in the Preface, which appears in Vol. I, pp. 15-16. —TRANS.

in faith in order that He may sanctify us, just as Joseph had to take in his arms the child that was not his own.

In the story of the genealogy, the light falls not so much on Mary as on Joseph. Christ was known in Israel as Joseph's child. This fits in with the purpose of Matthew's gospel which was written for the Jews, who recognized Joseph's Davidic ancestry.

Main Thought: *The Savior is given by God.*

Son of Abraham, Son of David. In Volumes 1 and 2, I dealt with the history of the old covenant where everything pointed to the Redeemer who was to come, the Redeemer who was promised long ago. According to the promise He would come forth out of Israel, a son of Abraham. Later it was indicated that He would be of David's house. Everything promised to Abraham and David would be fulfilled in Christ.

God had promised Abraham that in his seed all the peoples of the earth would be blessed. Christ, the great Son of Abraham, would be the blessing of nations. He would bring freedom to all peoples, a freedom from sin and freedom to have communion with God. He would do this by atoning for sin.

David had received the kingdom in Israel. With it he received the promise that his son would sit forever on his throne. That promise, too, could only be fulfilled in Christ, since no other man would reign forever. Christ would be king forever and would reign over this life to sanctify and restore it to God.

In the course of history, the splendor of David's house had been darkened by its sins and those of the entire people. It had gone so far that both king and people were carried away into captivity. They became strangers on the earth.

After 70 years the people did indeed return to Canaan, but their restoration was temporary and provisional. The house of David was never restored to honor during Old Testament times. Israel never regained full control of its own land but served foreign tyrants.

Christ would restore possession of the earth to His people. Only, Christ wanted to consider all nations as His people, not just Israel. By nature we are strangers on this earth and serve foreign tyrants, such as the devil and sin. Christ came to restore complete possession of the earth to us.

Genealogies were kept up to date in Israel thus providing accurate records of Christ's lineage as a son of Abraham. We can also trace His lineage through a certain branch of the house of David.

In the lives of many of Christ's ancestors we find types of Christ and living prophecies pointing to Him. In the case of His genealogy, the usual pattern is reversed. Contrary to other genealogies, the offspring, Christ, was preeminent over His ancestors, not the other way around.

Conceived by the Holy Spirit. Finally, after many centuries of waiting, the time had come for Christ to be born. His coming was not preceded by intense expectation, otherwise the house of David would not have fallen into oblivion as fully as it had.

There lived a man named Joseph in Nazareth of Galilee. He was of the house of David but was not especially honored because of it; in the little town of Nazareth he was only a simple carpenter. Perhaps he had come from elsewhere and had taken up residence in Nazareth and found his trade.

Joseph was engaged to a local girl, Mary, to whom the Lord wished to give a child. An angel of the Lord had told her so. But that was such a miracle she could not tell anyone about it—not even Joseph. Who would have believed it? The child was going to be born by a miracle of the Holy Spirit!

It had to happen that way, for if the child came into the world in the normal way, He would be just as sinful as we are. Then He could not be our Redeemer but would Himself be overcome by sin. Hadn't all the leaders and kings of Israel failed to redeem the nation because they were sinners?

The child would have to be able to do what not one of His forebears had managed: He had to be the Holy One, born by a miracle of the Holy Spirit.

Joseph perceived that Mary was going to have a child. But it was not his child; he was not the father. Joseph and Mary weren't yet married and Joseph knew nothing of what the angel had said to her. He did not know about the miracle that had happened through divine conception.

Joseph thought that Mary had disgraced her name and honor, but he did not want to accuse her publicly. He was a man who kept the commandments of the Lord. Because he could not cope with this disgrace, he decided to break the engagement quietly and leave town.

Mary must have guessed something of what was in Joseph's mind. Even then she did not dare tell him the secret. It was too wondrous and too unbelievable. How she must have prayed to the Lord for help and light, especially for Joseph! And the Lord answered her prayer.

A divine command. An angel of the Lord appeared to Joseph in a dream after he had already appeared to Mary to foretell the birth of her child. The Lord was beginning to speak to the people again. For four centuries He had kept silent. Now that the Redeemer was going to be born, He began to speak again. The angel revealed to Joseph the secret that the child had been conceived by a miracle of the Holy Spirit. The angel also commanded Joseph not to be afraid to take Mary for his wife. Mary's pregnancy was no disgrace, but a miracle. And once the child was born, Joseph was to accept Him as his own child.

Joseph was to call the child Jesus, meaning savior or redeemer. Jesus, the angel said, would redeem His people from their sins. He would gather them from all nations and would atone for their sins, thereby freeing them to serve the Lord. The name and the angel's explanation of its meaning made it clear to Joseph that he was dealing with a miracle. The Redeemer was going to be born, as God's gift, in mysterious fashion.

Yet Joseph must have been puzzled by the angel's command. He was supposed to accept the child as his own. He was to take Mary, together with the unborn child into his house, despite the fact he was not its father. Would he be able to accept the baby as his own with his whole heart? If only he could see the baby as a gift from God, the greatest gift in his life! If only Joseph could recognize the child as a gift for the house of David, to which he himself belonged, and also for the people of Israel and ultimately for the whole world, then he would joyfully accept it.

We must accept the gift in the same spirit. The Redeemer had to be born by a miracle. He could not be born like any other human being, for that would have made Him just as depraved as we are. The fact that He had to be born in this way implies a condemnation of our entire sinful life. Yet that is the way we must receive Him, for only as the Holy One can He redeem our lives and reconcile us to God. The world, too, will have to receive Him in this way.

The obedience of faith. Joseph obeyed the word of the angel who brought him God's message. He took Mary into his home as his wife whereupon the child was born. He accepted Him as his own child and gave Him the name Jesus. He did so by faith in the word of the angel.

Just imagine Joseph standing there with the child in his arms. To him the child was the greatest treasure of his life—dearer than everything else. It was such bliss to receive the child into his home and to acknowledge Him as the Redeemer! Joseph, together with Mary, was privileged to be the first one to recognize Him.

That's how Jesus was brought into the world by God and given to mankind. We must do what Joseph did—take the child in our arms, acknowledge Him in faith as the Redeemer, and call Him Jesus. He is our Redeemer too.

CHAPTER TWO
EPIPHANY
MATTHEW 2

The Feast of Epiphany has often been linked with the coming of the wise men from the East. Popular tradition often portrays three wise men seeking the newborn king. The story would have us believe that, following a successful search, they *appeared* before Christ. After all, doesn't *epiphany* mean appearance? But that's not what happened! It was Christ, or rather God's grace, which appeared to them! It was Christ's epiphany, not theirs! It was God who initiated the call which brought them to the stable.

We should not attempt to reinforce the first two verses of Matthew 2 with assumptions such as the idea that the east had received a special revelation, or that the east was acquainted with the expectation of the Messiah because of Israel's stay in Babylon. Scripture tells us nothing about such matters.

We have to work with the facts that the Bible gives us. The wise men saw a special star or a special phenomenon in the starry heavens. As true heathen astrologers they started calculating and concluded that a special king must have been born among the Jews. They went to Jerusalem to find out whether their calculations were correct. To a considerable extent, the wise men were pursuing their own interests by making this journey; they wanted to confirm the accuracy of their science. From their words: "for we have seen his star in the east," we can read tension between the lines.

I will not deny that the Holy Spirit guided the wise men in spite of themselves. Divine love, which was eager to reveal itself to the heathen, used a stratagem.

Not until they came to Jerusalem and talked with the Israelites were the wise men given further guidance. They discovered that nothing was known about the birth of the king, until they heard about the promise of the Messiah. This brought about a change in their thinking. Their heathen wisdom had not led them to Christ. Their own line of reasoning was interrupted and the Word of promise in Israel began to guide them.

When the wise men saw the star again on the way to Bethlehem, it took on a different meaning for them. It became a sign accompanying the Word of promise. When the star stood still above Bethlehem it was not to point out the place, which was still uncertain. Rather, it was the wise men who stood still. The Word of promise told them they had arrived. Of course the star stood still also. To their eye of faith, the movement of the star had guided them; its sudden stop confirmed that they were in the right place.

The wise men came to Jerusalem as astrologers. There they came to believe the Word of promise. Scripture makes the fact that they came to see the star in a different light clear to us when it speaks of their great joy. At that point they no longer trusted their own calculations but believed in the Word. They took their stand in that Word. The star was only a confirmation of the Word.

Their faith, though weak at first, grew steadily. When they found the child in circumstances very contrary to what they had probably expected, they still opened their treasures.

The concealment of Christ in Israel, which must have been a stumbling block to the astrologers at first, undoubtedly gave further direction to their faith. Christ was not a king like any other; He was not known by everyone but was a gift of God and known only by faith. He was an "epiphany," an appearing. The wise men became even more convinced of all this by the divine revelation that came to them in a dream, telling them to return home by a different route.

The concealment of Christ in Israel is explained more fully in the rest of Matthew 2. He had to flee from Bethlehem. All the wonderful things that had happened and had been reported about His birth were suddenly cut off in a bloodbath. A curse hung over this child which prevented everyone from discussing Him.

After the return from Egypt, Joseph did not settle in Judea, where the horrors of the past might recur. Instead Christ grew up in Nazareth, in complete concealment. The name *Nazarene*, derived from the Hebrew for *shoot*, (Is. 11:1) points to this humble concealment, a gift of God which only faith can see.

Main Thought: *Christ, hidden to the flesh, is revealed by God to the people of His choice.*

Heathen science used by God. The child promised to Mary

and Joseph was not born in Nazareth, where Mary lived, but in Bethlehem. In Bethlehem the angels announced that the child was the Savior, but the news went no farther. There were no heralds to proclaim it throughout the land and it did not spread by word of mouth. The spirit of men was simply not capable of receiving and transmitting that marvelous message for what it was. Like seed in rocky soil, this gospel did not take root.

At some point there came to Jerusalem a group of Eastern astrologers who said they had seen a special star from which they had concluded that a king must have been born among the Jews. They had come, they said, to worship him, to kneel down before him, for it was their custom to kneel before every prince. This king had to be someone special if his birth was announced by a star.

At Christ's birth, the Lord had provided a special sign in the starry heavens. That in itself was not necessarily a miracle, for God's grace, which governs all things, controls even the course of the stars. The Lord caused this special sign to coincide with the birth of the Christ.

The wise men were accustomed to calculating the destiny of men from the course of the stars. That was heathen wisdom which more often than not, was foolishness. But is there anything the Lord can not use to lead His people where He wants them to go? Their calculations had led the astrologers to the conclusion that a special king had been born among the Jews. Without their knowledge the Lord had guided their minds in this matter. That was how they came to Jerusalem.

The wise men's line of reasoning interrupted. If the wise men had wanted to find Christ, (the Savior of the world and the gift of God's grace in His covenant) their hearts would have had to change because Christ is found only by faith. They had come to Jerusalem looking for a wonderful confirmation of their studies, but Christ cannot be found by proud human wisdom.

They encountered their first disappointment in Jerusalem: nobody knew anything about this birth. An Edomite by the name of Herod, a cruel, arbitrary and suspicious man, reigned over Israel. When he heard about the astrologers' arrival, he was troubled. He knew about the promise of the Messiah. Could it be, he wondered, that this Messiah had been born? Herod knew that his whole godless reign was in conflict with the Messiah's reign of grace. If it was true that the Messiah had come, Herod's reign would come under judgment. Along with Herod, all official Jerusalem was agitated. Could it be true that the Messiah was born while they knew nothing about it? If the birth had taken place in such secrecy, it could only mean a condemnation of their way of life. Therefore, the arrival of the astrologers threw all Jerusalem into an uproar.

How strange it must have seemed to the wise men! If this king was really born, people's reactions were certainly different from what they had expected. Something inside them began to change; God would lead them even further.

Herod summoned the Sanhedrin, the assembly of the leaders of the people. To him the matter was very serious. He asked them where the Christ was to be born. They were able to tell him the exact place: according to Scripture He would be born in Bethlehem.

Once Herod knew the location, he had a secret message sent to the wise men, telling them to come to his palace. There they would be able to get more information about their destination. He pretended to have a hearty interest in their message. He informed them that this could possibly be the fulfillment of the promise the people of Israel continued to believe, the promise that the Redeemer would be born among them. Herod informed the wise men that the Redeemer would be born in Bethlehem. He encouraged them to look for Him there. He urged them to come back and tell him, should they find anything.

Herod sent the wise men away as soon as possible, eager to get them out of Jerusalem. He feared that their presence might spark a popular uprising. And if the rumor about the Redeemer was true, Herod would have to take all necessary precautions.

The wise men departed. Nobody from Jerusalem went with them. Herod did not have the faith to expect anything good from the Messianic promise; he only knew fear but thought he had taken adequate measures to protect himself. The leaders of the people soon regained their self-control. The report of the astrologers could not be true, they believed, for if the Christ had been born, they would certainly have known about it.

Because of their pride, they, too, were incapable of receiving the gospel of redemption. Is anyone capable of receiving it? No one, surely! God Himself must always show it to us.

Revealed to the heathen. The wise men must have had a strange sensation when leaving Jerusalem that evening. They would surely reach their destination seeing Bethlehem was only eight kilometers south of Jerusalem and the journey was not difficult. Yet how different things had been when they left Jerusalem! Until they had come to Jerusalem, they had been guided by their own reasoning; now they were guided by God's prophetic revelation to Israel. Earlier they had traveled in the hope that Jerusalem would receive them with joy; now they realized that nobody there knew anything about the new king or was really interested. Belief in the Word of God began to take hold of them, but the struggle of faith also began.

When evening fell, they saw in the southern sky, directly in front of them, the star they had seen in the east. When they moved on, it was as though the star went ahead of them, showing them the way. How differently they looked upon the star now than they had in the east! There they had been busy calculating the possible meaning of the star on the basis of their own heathen wisdom; now they looked upon it as something the God of Israel was showing them to confirm their faith.

Had it not been foolish to continue their journey after their shock in Jerusalem? But now, when they looked at the star, they traveled with great joy and a faith which made them eager and curious. What would they find? Did God want to show them something that remained concealed from Israel itself? Faith also grows by way of longing.

They soon reached Bethlehem. There they stopped, while the star, which confirmed that their desire would be fulfilled, also stopped. The people of Bethlehem knew more. They directed the astrologers to the house where Mary and the child were. In that house they found a very simple mother with an ordinary child. Had God not prepared them for this and had He not awakened faith within them, they would never have acknowledged the child as King of Israel and Savior of the world. But they were able to recognize Him. They knelt before the child as they would kneel before no other sovereign. To them the child was the gift of God's grace to the world. Why would God have led them by a star along such a surprising route all the way from the east to this place if the gift had been for Israel alone?

The wise men had brought treasures of considerable value. How differently they had imagined their presentations to the royal child!

However, they opened their treasures with hearts full of believing adoration and offered their gold, frankincense and myrrh. How small their gifts were compared to the immensely great gift which God had given! But they offered their gifts in sincere gratitude to the Lord.

During the night God revealed to them in a dream that they should not go back to Herod but should return to their own land by a different route. This made them see even more clearly that many in Israel were not familiar with this salvation and even chose to reject it. It was to strangers that God had revealed the salvation of the world.

Indeed, not everyone in Israel would reject it. God would not forsake His people, but would extend His covenant to all peoples in order that all nations could acknowledge Christ as Head of the Lord's people. Of those nations, not all would acknowledge Christ, but in the believers those nations would be saved. Believing in the grace that had appeared, the wise men returned to their own country.

Bethlehem's expectation smothered in blood. Soon afterward Joseph received instructions in a dream that he was to flee to Egypt with Mary and the child, for Herod wanted to kill the child. Herod felt his reign threatened by Christ's reign of grace, just as we are threatened by Christ in all that we attempt to possess outside of Him, all that we do not use in His service. Herod hated the promised One. Although he was not at all sure that the expectation of the wise men was correct, when they did not return he felt deceived by them although they had never made him any promises.

What was behind all this? Herod feared the unknown. He would have to do something about it. However, before he could do anything, the Lord put the child beyond Herod's reach in Egypt.

When the wise men did not return, Herod slaughtered all .he children two years old and under in Bethlehem and surroundings. What a murderous deed! How were Herod's men able to carry out such orders? How the mothers of Bethlehem wept! Once before, when Israel was led away into captivity, it was as if Rachel, mother of Joseph and Benjamin, had cried for her children as they were taken away from her. That was how Scripture talked about that event. And now it was as if history was repeating itself. Would covenant people always be beaten down so mercilessly? How, then, could they still hold on to God's grace?

They could only hold on if they saw that God led the enemies of salvation to hate and oppress God's people, and that the resulting damage was God's punishment for their sins, a chastisement that would lead them to prepare a place for Christ in their hearts and embrace the grace found in Him. We are all like dead men under God's judgment. At this point before Christ's flight into Egypt, the sword struck His people. One day He would experience judgment within His own heart and then His people would be free.

Would anyone in Bethlehem still think of these things? It was as if they had been led by the shepherds' message to dream a beautiful dream. The arrival of the wise men had strengthened their expectations. But the birth of that little child had become a curse. Nobody dared or wanted to mention it anymore. Under such circumstances, who could still summon the courage to boast that the grace of God had appeared to them? Faith can and does so. But how many in Bethlehem had such a living faith? From then on, everything connected with the child would be passed over in silence in Bethlehem. God's grace would be forgotten there.

Christ would be revealed by other means. That revelation often follows a course that interrupts our faulty human expectations. Yet there was grace even for Bethlehem.

From Egypt to Nazareth. Joseph had fled with Mary and the child to Egypt. During the journey and their stay in Egypt, the family must have lived off the gifts the wise men had brought. But the very necessity of the flight had been terrible. Christ had become an outcast; He had been banned from His own people and country and had been forced to flee to Egypt. By nature we are all outcasts and strangers, but Jesus became one because of our sins! The people of Israel had once been strangers in Egypt, but the Lord had adopted them as His people and had brought them into their own land because of the atonement which Christ would one day accomplish. Christ, too, was rejected because of our sin, but He will be accepted as Head and Redeemer of His people because of His own righteousness. Following that, His people will receive their own place on earth again.

Not long after, Herod died. Again Joseph was informed by

divine revelation in a dream that he could return with Mary and the child. He made ready for the journey, and left for Judea. Upon arrival Joseph learned that Archelaus, who was very much like his father, had succeeded him as king over Judea. Joseph did not dare settle in Judea where the child might be threatened by Archelaus' sword. Again God gave Joseph instructions. Following God's instructions Joseph settled in Galilee, governed by yet another son of Herod who, however, had a somewhat different nature.

Joseph settled in Nazareth, his original home. No one in that little town knew anything about the wondrous things that had taken place in Bethlehem. It seemed as though the thread had been completely broken.

Completely forgotten, Christ grew up in Nazareth. Accordingly He would later be called a "Nazarene." This word calls to mind the Hebrew word for shoot. Prophecy had promised that another living shoot would come forth from Israel, specifically from the house of David. The shoot was there, only very small and forgotten. In time God would reveal Him, together with the salvation that is in Him, to the people.

How strange are the ways of the Lord! Just when human expectation breaks down, the miracle of God's grace appears

CHAPTER THREE
HEAD OF HIS PEOPLE
MATTHEW 3-4

In this chapter I shall deal primarily with the baptism, anointing and temptation of Christ. The ministry of John the Baptist will be mentioned only in passing, to be discussed more fully in connection with the later gospels.

The unity of baptism, anointing and temptation lies in Christ's function as our Head. He is our Head in accordance with His divine calling. The divinity of His mandate is clear from His words that it is fitting to fulfill all righteousness, and even clearer from the Father's description of Christ: "In whom I was well pleased, whom I called in My counsel according to My good pleasure."

As Head of His people, Jesus was baptized. Even in sin He was one with His people; as their Head He went down into the water of baptism and rose again, thus making His baptism a prophecy of His death and resurrection.

It is an open question whether anyone besides John was present when Jesus was baptized and the heavens were opened. In any case, the descent of the dove as the sign of His anointing was witnessed only by John.

As our Head Jesus was also tempted. His temptation stands in contrast to that of the first Adam. Not only did the second Adam do what the first should have done, He also justified and reconciled what the first Adam had done wrong. Christ's temptation took place under circumstances which differed from Adam's. Satan tempted Him indirectly through God's love in which Christ shares. Satan prefaced his challenge to Christ with the taunt: "If You are God's Son," that is to say, "If You share in the Father's love . . . ." Satan was careful to agree with what God had said about Jesus: "This is My Son, My Beloved." Satan was in effect saying, "If You are God's Son, You can take chances, for then all things are Yours." Through this temptation, Christ, as our Head, learned obedience; better perhaps: He learned to show obedience (Heb. 5:8).

Main Thought: *In accordance with the calling of the Father, Christ functions as Head of His people.*

His baptism. Some months before the Lord Jesus was born there had been another birth in His family, that of John, forerunner of the Lord. John was to announce Christ's coming and prepare the people of Israel to receive Him.

When John was 30 years old, he began to preach in Israel. The place of his ministry was the wilderness of Judea, near the Jordan River. He proclaimed that the Kingdom of heaven was at hand. That was the Kingdom of grace, the Kingdom where all things are given to believers again by grace.

As the Kingdom was close at hand, the people were told to repent. They were to have no illusions about themselves anymore, but expect everything from the grace which is the hallmark of the Kingdom. They were to believe that God's grace would give them all they needed without exception. Only through repentance and faith could they enter the Kingdom. A complete change would have to come about in their lives.

We also sin by trusting in ourselves, thereby ruining our lives. We must also renounce our misplaced trust and misguided expectations in order to live as new creatures. That's why John baptized those who believed the tidings of the Kingdom of heaven. They went down into the waters of the Jordan as a sign that the old man in them had died. Their sins were washed away. They rose from the water as a sign that they now enjoyed the privilege of living as new men, as believers.

Little by little, John the Baptist gathered a following. But they still lacked a Head in whom they were one. That Head was to be the Lord Jesus Christ; God had chosen Him to be their Head. The Lord Jesus knew that. And now He heard that John was baptizing and gathering a people around him. At 30, He also went to the Jordan in Judea and asked John to baptize Him.

At first John did not want to baptize Jesus. Wasn't Jesus Head of His people, he reasoned, and he only one of its members? Wasn't it necessary for him to be baptized by the Lord Jesus instead? But God had sent John to baptize and, through baptism, to gather the people who were to inherit the Kingdom. Therefore, he would also have to baptize the Head if the Head was to be truly one with the people. Accordingly, the Lord told him that His baptism was the will of God.

We are also inclined to ask: Why did the Lord Jesus have to be baptized? Wasn't He without sin? Surely He didn't need to go down into the waters since He had no old man to lose and therefore no new man to gain!

The Lord Jesus, the Bible says, made Himself one with His people in their sins in the sense that He took their sins upon Himself. As a result He also deserved to be rejected by God. For that reason He had to die and rise again. His baptism was a prophecy of His death and resurrection. His baptism was the sign of His oneness with His people as their Head, reflecting their need to die unto sin and rise unto glory.

Today when we are baptized we receive the sign that we are also privileged to belong to that people whose Head is Christ. The sign indicates that we may also enter the Kingdom of heaven. At the same time we must believingly surrender to the grace of that Kingdom.

His anointing. Once the Lord Jesus climbed up out of the water, the heavens were opened to Him. A dove descended and alighted on Him and then disappeared. This vision only the Lord Jesus and John saw. It signaled that the Holy Spirit had qualified Him for His public office in Israel. Everything He did—His preaching, His suffering, His victory over sin and its consequences—He did by the power of the Holy Spirit. It was the Spirit who bound Him constantly to the Father and enabled Him to work in obedience to the Father.

God gave Him the strength and Spirit to do the work to which He had been called, for it was God Himself who had called Him. At the very moment the dove had descended, God had spoken from heaven, "This is My beloved Son, whom I was pleased to appoint to redeem My people."

Only faith can hear God's call. It was wonderful for the Lord Jesus to hear His Father's call and realize that, because of His obedience, He shared in the Father's love and good pleasure. He knew that the Father would continuously give Him strength through the Holy Spirit to do His work.

That's how Christ was called and anointed and, because we're

His people, the mandate and office were extended to us. True, we have not been called to all the work to which He was called. Still, with Him we are called to serve God in all things and relate all things to Him. If we have been called with Him, we also share in His anointing and our whole life will be a life of communion with the Lord, through the Holy Spirit.

His temptation. Adam was once our head. He was put to the test to determine whether he truly wished to devote his whole life to the Lord. Adam became unfaithful and rejected the Lord's favor. When the Lord Jesus took Adam's place as our Head (of the covenant), the temptation had to be renewed since satan was bent on destroying the covenant. In this temptation Christ not only had to show obedience but also had to justify and reconcile what Adam had ruined. Therefore the temptation came to Him under different circumstances than it had to Adam.

After Jesus had been baptized and anointed, the Holy Spirit led Him out into the desert to be tempted by the devil. The desert was quite a different place from the paradise in which Adam had lived. In Paradise everything had testified to God's favor and communion, while the desert betrayed that everything had been forsaken by God and man because of our sins. Everything had been in Adam's favor, while Christ had everything against Him. Despite the isolation of that forsaken place, Jesus had to hold on to God.

Forty days and forty nights God left Jesus in the desert. During that time He had no thoughts for food or drink. His work possessed Him. His sorrow for sin was His daily bread; thoughts of the cross His daily drink.

At the end of forty days He was overcome by hunger. That's when satan came to tempt Him. The Holy One had to suffer the sacrilege of the tempter. God delivered Him up to that suffering for our sakes. Satan said to Jesus: "Aren't you the Son of God, and don't You share in Your Father's love? Well then, isn't everything at Your disposal? Surely You may do whatever You wish! Tell these stones to become bread, so that You can satisfy Your hunger."

Satan's language was full of lies. Christ shared in the Father's love precisely because of His obedience. He never did anything for Himself but acted only for God and for His people. He could only use His power in God's service, for only then would He Himself be blessed. If He had changed stones into bread against the Father's will, no deliverance would have been possible and the bread would not have served Him. After all, we do not live by bread alone but only by the blessing which God graciously bestows upon it. That was Christ's answer to satan, an answer that came straight from Scripture. He defeated satan with the Word of the Lord. In resisting temptation Christ gained the victory over satan. In Christ we are victors; His strength enables us to go on winning. We also must refuse things we cannot have without God's blessing.

Satan thereupon took Christ to the pinnacle of the temple. The fact that he could actually force Jesus to do his bidding indicates his power over Him. In this respect God placed Christ in satan's hands. What suffering this must have caused Him! But because of our sins, it had to be!

On the pinnacle of the temple satan said to Him: "You are the Son of the Father and share in His love. Hence You must also long for proof of His love. That proof is easy to come by. Throw Yourself from this pinnacle, for then He will surely see that You are protected by angels, in accordance with His promise. This proof of His love will do You good."

There satan touched the most tender chord of all. If the Lord Jesus thirsted for anything, it was for His Father's love and for proof of that love. But would He willfully conjure that proof, and compel the Father to give it to Him? Wouldn't that be a sign that He did not trust the Father's love? That was exactly what His people kept doing in their unbelief. Once more He turned satan aside by quoting Scripture: we are not to put the Lord our God to the test.

Twice Jesus had resisted the temptation to unbelief. He did this for us. We triumph only through Christ, our Head. Are we prepared to wait patiently for the Lord and believe in His love, as Jesus did? Are we content with the miracle of His love or do we still need "special miracles" as evidence of His love?

Satan next took the Lord Jesus to a very high mountain. There he showed Him all the kingdoms of the world and their glory. Satan even had power over Christ to force Him to look at all the kingdoms passing in review. When the Lord Jesus saw them, His heart must have mellowed. Had He not come to regain them for His Father?

Satan had already made two attempts at seducing Jesus by appealing to God's love. Now he tried yet another approach and said: "Break with that love. Worship me, and I will give You all those kingdoms which are now, as You see, in my hand."

Satan was right; because of sin all those kingdoms were indeed in his hand. But Christ only wanted to reclaim them for the Father. Christ valued His relationship to the Father above all else. Without the Father He could never completely claim them. Satan had shown Him the outward splendor of those kingdoms but not the misery that consumed them as a result of sin. Christ wanted to restore them to their true glory. He turned satan aside with yet another quotation from Scripture: the Lord alone is to be worshiped as the God who gives Himself to man through His covenant. At that point Christ knew He had struggled enough and told satan to depart.

Where do we stand now that Christ has triumphed for us? Since the victory has been won there's nothing we need but to follow the Lord in faithful obedience!

After His triumph the angels ministered to Him. It was proof of His Father's love which He had always known was there. That's what faith is all about. The evidence of God's love is in our life of faith.

His revelation to the people. After His temptation, the Lord Jesus began His public ministry, mainly in Galilee at first. He did not choose Nazareth as His base but settled in Capernaum by the sea, a center within easy reach of the rest of Galilee. It was indeed a great privilege for Galilee that the Lord Jesus first revealed Himself as the Redeemer there. Galilee was farthest removed from Jerusalem and the temple and it was the poorest part of the country. Messianic hopes had suffered most there, yet that's where the Lord first appeared as had been predicted by Scripture: the people who sat in darkness would see a great light.

In Capernaum Jesus called His first disciples to follow Him and to help Him with the work. He had already asked some of them to join Him right after His baptism in Judea. They wanted to see something of His work. Now He definitely called them to be His disciples and co-workers.

One day as He was walking along the seashore, He saw Peter and his brother Andrew busy fishing. He promptly called them away from their work to follow Him. He would make them fishers of men. They would be allowed to help Him win people for the

Father and for His Kingdom. Such honor! In faith they saw the glory of that calling and followed Him immediately, leaving their work where it was. The same thing happened with John and James who were busy mending their nets with their father Zebedee in the boat.

This was a happy day for the Lord Jesus. He was privileged to call people who would be busy with Him in the work for God's Kingdom!

From Capernaum He went throughout Galilee, teaching in the synagogues. He brought the same message that John the Baptist had preached, namely, that the Kingdom of heaven was at hand and that the people should surrender themselves in faith to the grace of that Kingdom. He confirmed His preaching by the miracles He performed, healing many sick. By healing the sick He meant to say: Don't you see that in the Kingdom your sins are overcome and removed? Aren't the effects of sin such as disease and death also conquered? Believe in the grace which has come! Surrender and be saved!

MATTHEW:
THE KINGDOM

CHAPTER FOUR
THE REIGN OF GRACE
MATTHEW 5-7

In Matthew 4:23 we read: "And he went about all Galilee, teaching in their synagogues and preaching the gospel of the Kingdom and healing every disease and every infirmity among the people." These words recur in Matthew 9:35. In between these two passages, Matthew gives us an example of the Kingdom's message, the Sermon on the Mount. He also records some instances of healing.

The Sermon on the Mount does not give us the complete teachings of the Kingdom of heaven. In this address Christ speaks of the reign of grace and the effects that reign has upon our lives in the Kingdom.

Main Thought: *Grace reigns supreme in the Kingdom of God.*

The citizens of the Kingdom. John the Baptist had already declared that the Kingdom of heaven was at hand. The Lord Jesus used the very same words when He preached to the people in Galilee. The Kingdom would come with the imminent outpouring of the Holy Spirit. But the spirit or life of that Kingdom could already be understood, for it was a life of faith in God's grace, a God-given faith through which He forgives our sins. In that Kingdom grace reigns supreme. Each Kingdom citizen must believe in God's favor and live by it. That's what the Lord Jesus wanted to say to the people and why He talked so much about the Kingdom.

One day a great crowd gathered to listen to Him. Jesus wanted to speak to them so He climbed up the slope of a mountain and sat down. Then He called His disciples close to Him. They were to listen very carefully to the preaching of the Kingdom, for they would have to carry its message abroad. The people stood somewhat lower on the mountain so they all could see and hear Him.

When Jesus began to talk about the Kingdom, He first wanted

to tell who its citizens were. Like every other kingdom, this one too has its own citizens. Grace, His favor that forgives sin, reigns supreme in the Kingdom. The citizens of this Kingdom are those who submit in faith to His grace, who do not trust in their own wisdom or rely on their own virtues but are wholly dependent on the grace of God, accepting that grace and making no excuses for unbelief. People who live by God's grace in such a way show that they take after their Father in heaven and resemble Him.

Citizens of this Kingdom, the Lord Jesus declared, are the poor in spirit who thank the Father for all they know, have nothing of themselves but daily hold out their hands to have all their needs supplied by the Father. They do not pretend to have lived according to God's will; on the contrary, they know they are unrighteous sinners whose lives conflict with the will of God. Their hunger and thirst for righteousness will surely be satisfied, for what they lack in themselves will be given to them by Christ. Because they do not trust in themselves, they are allowed to see God. We are able to see God only if we see everything in the light of God's grace and nothing in our own light, believing that God gives us His complete favor.

Kingdom citizens also reflect the image of the Father. They know that God shows them His mercy and, in turn, they show mercy to others. Thus they share more and more in God's mercy.

There was once enmity between God and us but God made peace by giving Christ as a propitiation for our sins. Because believers want to be children of that Father, they also make peace. They do not seek their own rights.

The spirit motivating citizens of the Kingdom is different than that of unbelievers. Those hostile to God's grace are also hostile to those living by that grace. Therefore the citizens of God's Kingdom will be hated and persecuted by others. This should not surprise believers, for in former days the prophets who witnessed to God's grace were also persecuted. Unbelief always actively opposes faith.

The citizens of the Kingdom, however much they may be hated and persecuted, are still the key to the world's preservation, for if they were no longer in the world, the Spirit of Christ would no longer be in the world either. God's grace would no longer be present in the world. Hence believers and their descendants must be sure to retain what they have received from the Lord. Otherwise they no longer serve a purpose in this world.

Neither may they hide the gospel of the Kingdom. Instead they are to preach it everywhere so that others may come to understand and glorify the Father in heaven.

The law in the Kingdom. In the Kingdom of heaven as in every kingdom there are certain laws. What law but the law of God should be in effect in the Kingdom, a law God first gave to His people at Creation and later codified in the form of the Ten Commandments? Unfortunately, rabbinic tradition had later given a superficial and deeply mistaken explanation of the Mosaic law. The Lord Jesus had to uncover the meaning of the law to show what God really wanted.

The rabbis had said that it was sinful to kill, but they had failed to point out that abusive language, hatred and unjust anger were just as sinful. This the Lord Jesus now proclaimed. We must seek forgiveness for the sins of our heart. Only then can we have peace with God. Though we may suppress a desire to sin, we are still guilty before God because the existence of the desire proves the sinfulness of our heart.

We are to love God and ourselves but only as God's children, never apart from God. Therefore we may never subordinate God's cause to our own interests. We may never use God's name to serve our own interest, as the Jews so often did when they swore by the name of the Lord in their business affairs. We may never assert our own rights; if we defend ourselves, it must be for God's sake only, on the grounds that God's name and rights are being violated through the attack on us. If only our rights are at stake, we should not fight back: if someone strikes us on one cheek, we should simply turn the other.

The law of the Kingdom goes quite a bit further than the law of unbelievers which implies that we should love only those who love us and hate our enemies. But the Father in heaven doesn't even ignore His enemies, let alone hate them. He is good to them, for His sunshine and rain are for them too. Therefore we should also love our enemies.

We can't get away with partial obedience to the law of the Kingdom. The citizens of God's Kingdom have to be perfect, just as the Father in heaven is perfect. Even though they will never be perfect while on earth, they may not rest until they are perfect. It's a never ending struggle in which they must be guided by the Father's perfection.

The inner life of man. The purpose of life in the Kingdom is also not to bring public recognition. Its purpose is the hidden life of communion with God. Our inner life, our heart, must seek the riches of that communion. At the return of the Lord Jesus Christ, God will publicly crown that which now remains hidden.

Thus we are not to give to the poor for the sake of men's approval. That's what the Pharisees did. Man's approval was all they lived for, and they received it too. They had everything they wanted; they had reached their goal. For them there was no glory in the future because they had no hidden life with God.

The Pharisees often prayed long prayers at the street corners for the benefit of others. Similarly we, too, want to appear pious in the eyes of others. It's not hard to get a reputation for piety, but then we also have our reward. He who knows the hidden life with God will pray in secret to be strengthened in communion with Him. One day God will reward him with true honor.

We must not, like the heathen, pray with a great many words either, thinking that we must talk God into doing something for us, as though He were alien and remote. Those who join in the hidden life with God know that God, as our Father, is aware of all our needs and will supply them. In a believing, childlike prayer of few words, we will receive from Him what He has already prepared for us.

The Lord Jesus gave us an example of such a childlike prayer in the one He taught to His disciples: "Our Father, who art in heaven . . . ." If we have this hidden life with God in which we receive forgiveness, we will also be able to forgive others their wrongdoings, as taught in "The Lord's Prayer." But if we are proud of our own piety, we will not be able to forgive our fellow men.

The Pharisees were also proud of their fasting by which they thought they were doing God a favor. Therefore, on days of fasting they walked about with drawn, emaciated faces to impress people with their "piety."

For those who have hidden fellowship with God, life is a continuous feast. Even then God sometimes withdraws Himself from them because of their sins. They should then feel the need to confess their sins to the Lord and show sorrow for their sins by fasting. But fasting is not a ploy to score merit points with God. True fasting is a confession of sin, the awareness that all is lost. That's a matter between God and the sinner. In fasting he does not seek approval from men, for he sees the shame of his sins more and more, something that does not directly concern others. A person who fasts in this way must therefore anoint his head and wash his face before going out into the street and not broadcast his repentance in cheap exhibitionism. God knows what is in his heart and will one day publicly reward him with true honor because of the hidden communion he sought.

Trusting in the Kingdom. There will also be deep trust among the citizens of the Kingdom of God. After all, God is their Father and He takes care of them. If only they would recognize that! If only their eyes would focus on that fact. If only they would stop trying to concentrate on God's Kingdom and their self-interests simultaneously. If we trust in God, then we must trust in Him alone. And if we are single-minded about this, our whole life will be full of light.

We should not gather huge amounts of treasure on earth hoping to ensure our life. All such treasures will fade. There is another treasure which we receive only by putting our trust in God: the treasure of hidden communion with Him. That treasure will never fade away, but makes our life secure.

When children are grown up and have their own jobs, they contribute their share to the family income until they leave home. They should not think they are carrying the burden of their family. The father does that. Similarly, living like children in our Father's house, we must do whatever our hands find to do, but we should not think that we carry the burden of our lives. What would we gain by all that anxiety? We should learn from the birds who fly hither and yon in search of food. Still God takes care of their lives. Neither are the lilies responsible for their splendid colors. It's God who adorns them, and their glory exceeds even that of Solomon. Won't God clothe us as well? If only we were not so lacking in faith!

There's just one thing we should seek: the Kingdom of God and its righteousness. This means living in communion with the Lord. Within that communion we are to give to each his own. To God we give what is properly His, namely, our whole heart and life; to our neighbor we also give our heart. We needn't worry for God will care for us. We may be carefree, knowing God looks after us each day again.

Reflecting God's love. The blessings we receive in communion with God in His Kingdom we must pass on for we are to be a blessing to others. We should condemn the evil others do but not in a spirit of pride, for then we run the risk of being judged ourselves. Our attitude towards ourselves must be especially critical. And since we do so much evil ourselves, we will no longer have the heart to look down upon others. We should humbly look for God- given opportunities to be a blessing to others.

We should not try to scatter the blessings of the gospel like pearls before the swine, for the contempt which men would show could consume our own faith. Rather, we should look around for constructive opportunities so that God's chosen people may be saved.

Or do we have nothing to pass on? Do we ourselves often lack the joy of communion with God and fail to see the riches of the gospel of the Kingdom? What, after all, is necessary but the just faith that God grants us, His full favor in Christ? If we pray, we will receive; if we seek, we will find; if we knock, it will be opened to us. And then we may sit at the table of God's full communion. Certainly, our heavenly Father will give good gifts to those who ask, even more so than an earthly father does.

But then we must go to God in faith, not in doubt. Faith is like a narrow road leading to a narrow gate through which we must pass. When we believe in God, we lose our trust in everything else. If we trust in ourselves, we will not be able to pass through the gate. Many people do not see and cannot find that narrow road because they don't want to see it. They go down the broad road of self-reliance which leads to destruction. The narrow road and the narrow gate lead to life in communion with God.

Living securely in the Kingdom. How wonderful the proclamation of this Kingdom is. We learn that only by faith in God do we have eternal communion with Him. Those who live by faith and proclaim God's gospel seek nothing for themselves but everything for the Lord; they seek to bring people to God. The honor the believer gives to the Lord makes the sinful heart jealous because it seeks everything for itself.

It should not surprise us that false preachers will appear, pretending to be very pious while denying eternal life by faith. They find ways to subject the Lord's flock to themselves and seek their own glory. They will be known by their fruit, for a good tree does not bear evil fruit. From their outward display of piety they look like gentle sheep, but inside they are ravenous wolves.

Those false preachers abuse the name of the Lord. They loudly proclaim, "Lord, Lord," in order to invoke power. They have made a magic formula of the Lord's name to impress the man in the pew. But they will not enter the glory of the Kingdom of heaven when the Last Day comes. Yet there are other prophets who have acknowledged God in faith as their heavenly Father and who, like children, have .sought to do the will of their Father. They will surely enter the glory of the Kingdom.

There are people who believe the gospel, who see that they are saved by grace alone and whose hearts are not at rest unless they can trust in that grace. They are safe, like the man who dug in the sand until he struck the rocky ground beneath. On that rock he laid the foundation for his house and then proceeded to build. When storms and severe weather came, his house did not fall. There are others who trust in themselves and their own piety, like the man who built his house on the sand. When the storms of winter came, his house collapsed with not one stone left upon another. They will be destroyed.

When the Lord Jesus had finished this sermon, the crowds were astounded, because He spoke in God's name and with authority. By comparison, what was there to the preaching of the rabbis who relied solely on their own authority?

CHAPTER FIVE
POWER TO SAVE
Matthew 8:1-13

Christ taught as one having authority, but He also revealed His power or qualification through the miracles He performed. He had been sent by the Father, something which believers could see for themselves. The leper confessed it unequivocally, as did the centurion. At the beginning of the Sermon on the Mount, Christ said that He had not come to abolish the law and the prophets but to fulfill them. This becomes evident from these two distinct acts of healing involving the leper and the centurion. Jesus told the leper to show himself to the priest and to offer the sacrifice of purification. The law already reckoned with the possibility of healing. In fact, the law was a signpost pointing to the coming salvation. Christ fulfilled the law. The fact that Jesus told the leper to go to the priest is important and should have proven to the Jews that Christ in no way opposed the law but rather fulfilled it.

The centurion was a Gentile, although probably not a Roman since he was in the service of Herod Antipas. At that time Christ had not yet come to the Gentiles; He was sent only to the lost sheep of the house of Israel. The house of Israel enjoyed the privileges of the covenant. Not until this Gentile acknowledged the privileges of the covenant with the words "I am not worthy to have You come under my roof" did Christ offer His help.

Perhaps we should read verse 7 as a question: "Should I come and heal him?" In other words: Should ƒ go to a Gentile? In the original Greek, the "I" is emphatic. But even if it is not a question, verse 7 expresses Christ's awareness that He was crossing the boundary between Israel and the Gentiles. When the Gentile asked in faith, Jesus could see that the Father wanted Him to help the man. Then, in the spirit, He saw the covenant opening up, and He prophesied that many would come from east and west and would sit down at the wedding feast with Abraham, Isaac and Jacob in the Kingdom of heaven. The healing of the Gentile's servant is a prophecy of the salvation of Gentiles. Here, too, Jesus fulfilled the law and the prophets, because adoption of the Gentiles had already been foretold in prophecy.

Jesus' amazement shows how completely human He was. He did not expect such faith from a Gentile. Thus, when Jesus spoke of the centurion's great faith, He was not congratulating him. He was amazed at the Father, who had given such faith to Gentiles. By great faith Jesus did not mean that the centurion showed quantitatively more faith than normal. Faith is not a power of the soul to be measured by size, weight or volume. The power of faith is not in faith itself but in its focus. Not even in Israel had Jesus found such a faith, a faith that was so ready to believe, enabling its possessor to see clearly that Christ had the power to redeem.

The faith Jesus expected people to have, and that enabled Him to perform miracles was not always a true faith in Him as Savior. Sometimes it was just faith in miracles. But that need not make any difference when we tell such stories to children, because that faith in miracles represented faith in Christ, just as the healings pointed to the complete salvation of the whole man.

We sometimes ask whether leprosy was thought to be contagious. It was not because it was thought to be contagious that lepers in Israel had to live in isolation, but because they were unclean in an allegorical sense. The ugliness of the disease clearly illustrated the vileness of sin. A leper was banished from the community as a sign that we all deserve to be banished from communion with God because of our sin. Christ touched the leper, thereby identifying Himself with our sinful nature. But the real purpose of His entry was to build the new community of which He is the Head.

Main Thought: *Christ reveals Himself as the one who has the power to save.*

Law and Prophets are fulfilled in the purification of Israel. After the Lord Jesus finished His Sermon on the Mount a large crowd followed Him. They were all amazed at His teaching because He didn't discuss irrelevancies as the scribes did. Jesus taught with authority, as one directly sent by God. Most people were duly impressed by His way of teaching, but this didn't mean they believed He had received power from the Father to do the Father's will.

A few saw something of this and believed. For instance, there was a leper who had heard the words of the Lord Jesus. Perhaps he was there in person, or he may have heard Jesus' words from others.

If he was standing there himself, he must have been at a distance from the others, for a leper was banned from the community in Israel. Leprosy was a horrible disease. It showed most vividly how vile we have become in God's sight because of our sins. A person with leprosy was cut off from society to illustrate that we by our sins deserve to be cut off forever from communion with God. A leper would experience double suffering. By being cut off in his personal life, he served as a witness to the curse that is upon us all.

The leper had heard the words of the Lord Jesus and now believed that Jesus was sent by God for salvation. Christ was privileged to show, in both word and deed, the grace and love of God for the salvation of His people from sin and its consequences. The leper saw that. He submitted in faith to the mission of the Lord Jesus.

When Jesus was there, he may well have rushed forward, pushing his way through the crowd. People fell back before him, for he was unclean. He knelt before Jesus and said: "Lord, if You wish, You can make me clean. You have the power to deliver me from this curse. Will You do it?" In such cases the Lord Jesus is always willing to grant our request. If, in faith, we acknowledge His power to save, He will always give deliverance. If we have heard His Word and it has taken hold of us, His will to save is always there.

Then something happened that must have filled the crowd with horror. The Lord Jesus did not recoil from this unclean man, as they had all done, but bent over him and touched him. He was not afraid of this man's curse, nor was He afraid of the curse that is on us all. He took that curse upon Himself and suffered it upon His cross. That was how He would conquer the curse and bring His people, who are cut off, into communion with Him and with the Father. That was why He touched the leper.

Jesus said: "I wish it. Be clean!" He used the same words the man had used in making the request. Not only did the leper have to be healed but the uncleanness, the curse, also had to be removed. He would have to be restored to the blessed communion in God's grace.

It all happened in a moment. One word from Christ, and all was well. Such is His power. One word from Christ, and everything in our life, too, is well forever. Then we have eternal communion with God. May we all acknowledge His power! For that purpose the Father sent Jesus into the world.

The Lord Jesus thereupon said: "See that you say nothing to anyone. You must not make any fuss about this, for then the people will see Me as a miracle-worker and not as sent by the Father with the power of His love. Rather, ponder these things in your heart so that you may know Me even better and grow in the knowledge of the Father's love unto salvation."

The Lord Jesus also commanded the man to go to the priest. That was what the law required. The priest had to make sure that he had indeed been healed. After that he would have to offer a sacrifice of purification. In that sacrifice communion with the Lord would be renewed; the man would accept the fact that the Lord received him again into His fellowship.

The Lord Jesus commanded the man to do everything prescribed by the law. From this the Jews were supposed to learn that Jesus did not act contrary to the law but rather fulfilled it.

The fact that a leper was cut off by the law was intended to teach the whole people of Israel that they deserved to be cut off forever from fellowship with God. But the law had already shown that there was a possibility of cleansing. Christ came bringing that blessing. He wanted to bless Israel and grant Israel God's fellowship forever. The Jews had to learn this and so must we.

Fulfillment in the calling of the Gentiles. One day when the Lord Jesus entered Capernaum again, the elders of the synagogue came to Him with a request from an officer, a centurion belonging to the army of King Herod. Would Jesus, they asked, please come to heal the centurion's servant, who was paralyzed and suffered much pain?

That officer was a Gentile, but he loved the Jewish people. He had even built a synagogue in Capernaum because he had learned to worship Israel's God. That was like "worshiping from afar," for he did not belong to the covenant, to the people claimed by Israel's God as His own. The centurion admitted this openly; he did not approach the Lord Jesus directly. Instead he requested the elders of the synagogue to speak for him. He had heard about the Lord Jesus and also understood something of the fact that Jesus had been sent by God and had received power from God unto salvation. Still, he acknowledged that this blessing was for God's people and not for the Gentiles.

Even so the centurion sent a message to the Lord Jesus. Wouldn't this God, the message read, who was so tremendous for His people, want to give something of His blessing to the Gentiles as well? By now the centurion had come to know the grace of Israel's God better. Yet, he acknowledged the covenant; he recognized that this salvation in the first instance was for the people of Israel.

The centurion's attitude was better than the attitude of the elders. The elders said to the Lord Jesus: "He is worthy to have You do this for him, for he loves our people and has built us a synagogue." They were proud of their privileges and understood very little of the fact that all benefits they received were gifts from God, gifts of His grace, gifts which they, just like the Gentiles, had forfeited.

The centurion's request made the Lord Jesus very happy. He saw that the eyes of the Gentile had been opened to His mission. That was God's doing. And this Gentile, the first one to be permitted to see something of the Messiah's mission, represented a prophecy anticipating the many Gentiles who would later believe. Therefore, with great joy, Jesus said: "I will come and heal him. With gladness I will go the way the Father points out to Me."

In the meantime, the officer had had second thoughts: "Can I," he wondered, "rightly ask Him to come to the house of a Gentile? Is that even necessary for one sent by God? All He has to do is say the word and it will be done. Such is the power given to the One commissioned by God. And isn't it the same with me?" he continued. "Herod has given me power and my servants obey my every word."

The centurion had his messengers tell this to the Lord Jesus. Jesus was amazed: a heathen who so clearly sees My calling and the power I have received from the Father! How wonderful is the work that the Father has given Me! No one in Israel has insight like this man!

The Lord Jesus began to tell the crowd what He saw in the centurion's deed. The covenant, presently limited to Israel would be extended. Many people from all nations, united by the same faith, would have fellowship with God, just like Abraham, Isaac and Jacob. They would have this fellowship here on earth but also eternally in the new world. That was the glorious Kingdom unto which Jesus had received the power to save. That power extended even to the Gentiles.

At the same time the Lord Jesus warned that there would be people born within that Kingdom who would not acknowledge His authority. Such people would be thrown into outer darkness where there would be weeping and gnashing of teeth. There, cut off forever from fellowship with God, they would have to acknowledge Christ's authority against their will.

Jesus gave a demonstration of the power that was His in the Kingdom. He spoke one word and the servant was healed. That Kingdom is the Kingdom of salvation, of peace and joy, of God's eternal favor. If in faith we acknowledge Christ's authority, then we, too, are included in the Kingdom.

The Kingdom is still open for many people. But even now there are people born within the Kingdom who will be cast out because they did not acknowledge Christ's authority.

CHAPTER SIX
WEDDING GUESTS
MATTHEW 9:9-17

There seems to be some difficulty with the saying: "I desire mercy, and not sacrifice." Didn't the Lord order those sacrifices? Or course He did! But we must not forget that the Lord did not order sacrifices in the same way Israel and the Pharisees often brought them. Their sacrifices were burdensome sacrifices by which people tried to get something for themselves, sacrifices for personal gain. The Lord desired sacrifices that signaled joyous acceptance in faith of His grace in His covenant.

The acceptance of the Lord's grace makes wedding guests out of believers. During the Old Testament period, the full liberation of life had not yet come. Hence the command to fast. Also, we should not forget that only a few commands for fasting have been given in the law. Those commands were substantially enlarged in later times, especially by the Pharisees. Once you have introduced the idea of buying and earning, the burdens must of necessity be extended.

Even in the New Testament, fasting may sometimes be in order if the Lord withdraws His fellowship and reveals anger. But with the coming of Christ, God's full favor has been given to us, and with the outpouring of the Holy Spirit, the creation has been given to us for our use. Now believers are wedding guests sitting down at the table of God's love. One way they do this is by enjoying everything He gives them on this earth.

Our place as guests at the wedding of God's love on earth is not compromised by the calling we have received to be merciful; the calling to give ourselves to our neighbor, especially to those who are miserable; the calling to engage in social work. If we do not gladly enjoy the Lord's communion in everything He wishes us to have, we will not be able to proclaim the joy of the gospel of the Kingdom, nor will we be able to show mercy. Having communion with the Father, Christ sat down at the table in Matthew's house.

For the same reason Jesus rejected the reproach of the Pharisees. People who, like the Pharisees, do not know the freedom and joy of the Kingdom of grace are not able to give. They are afraid to get into a compromising situation by associating with "tax-collectors." But Christ was able to give Himself at Matthew's table. At that table mercy reigned because Christ had communion with the Father.

Main Thought: *Because of Christ's coming, believers have become wedding guests on earth.*

Matthew called to the wedding feast. At the very beginning of His ministry in Galilee, the Lord Jesus had called a few disciples who were to follow Him. Those men He wished to prepare in a special sense to become His co-workers. There were just a few of them, and He looked for more until the group of twelve was complete. They were to live by trusting in God's grace rather than in themselves. That's the norm for life in the Kingdom.

In Capernaum the Lord Jesus found another disciple, someone we would never have thought of. In that city there was a customs office where taxes were levied on goods that were imported and exported. Capernaum was a frontier town. The job of collecting taxes was farmed out by the hated Herods. There were some Jews who performed those services on lease and got rich by demanding too much tax. But the worst thing was that such tax- collectors placed themselves in the service of the foreign tyrant and betrayed their own people.

One day the Lord Jesus was passing the customs office when He saw a certain Levi or Matthew sitting there. He saw that the Father wished to give Him this man for a disciple. How strange God's election is! This tax-collector, this traitor, was a man God chose as a disciple for Jesus. The Lord Jesus called him and said: "Follow Me!"

Matthew stood up and followed Jesus. How strange that he could leave his work right then and there to follow the Lord. How did such a sinner dare to follow the Lord Jesus right away?

In all probability Matthew had heard a lot about Jesus before, because Jesus had often passed through the streets of Capernaum. But Matthew must have been of the opinion that the gospel of the Kingdom was not for him, for he had betrayed the cause of his people by selling out to the hated Herod.

Then, suddenly, the Lord Jesus was calling him! The grace of the Kingdom opened up to Matthew and he saw that by grace our sins are conquered and forgiven, as God adopts us as His children. With Jesus' calling came the revelation of grace. That was what conquered Matthew, and to that revelation he surrendered.

How marvelous it is in that Kingdom! Only God's grace reigns supreme there. The same Matthew later became an apostle and to him we owe the first gospel. He understood the happiness in the Kingdom of heaven and also preached about it.

The mercy that seeks. That Matthew understood the grace and joy of the Kingdom is evident from the fact that he hosted a dinner in his house to which he invited the Lord Jesus along with His disciples and also many other tax-collectors. What a joy that dinner must have been for Matthew! Now that he himself lived by grace, he was permitted to acquaint the other tax-collectors with the Lord Jesus so that they, too, might believe. A dinner party was a good occasion for this. What else is the life of a believer than sitting at the table of God's love to be fed by grace? This Matthew had understood very well.

The Pharisees in Capernaum saw that the Lord Jesus was sitting at the table with tax-collectors, those despised traitors of the national cause. How could He do such a thing? If He associated with such people, nothing further could be expected from Him. They did not dare say this to Him directly, but complained about it to His disciples. The Lord Jesus heard the complaints and answered them. "You do not seek Me; you do not need Me as your physician," He said to them. "Only people who feel sick call for the doctor. You close your hearts to Me because you think you are righteous. Your outward appearance of righteousness is the reason why My calling does not reach you. It will penetrate much sooner to people who are known as public sinners. Your pride is what especially stands in your way. That's how it always goes with people who think they are righteous, who think they are giving to everyone what is properly his, while withholding their hearts from God and their neighbors."

The Pharisees thought they could take care of their own righteousness and salvation. They only worked to earn something from God. With that in mind, they also brought their sacrifices, proud of their accomplishments. In their pride they despised the tax-collectors and would never sit down at the same table with them. It did not occur to the Pharisees to reach out to those tax-collectors. They themselves were not spiritually rich, even though they thought they were, and consequently had nothing to give to others.

The Lord Jesus, who understood the grace of the Kingdom, had so enormously much to give. That was why He sat down with tax-collectors and showed them the mercy of God who sought them. To the Pharisees He said: "It is written in Scripture that God desires mercy, and not sacrifice as you offer it out of self-will and in order to gain something by it. Learn what that means! "

The wedding feast. After they had finished eating, the disciples of John the Baptist came to Him. They had not understood their master very well, for John had always pointed away from himself to the Lord Jesus. John's disciples still wanted to honor their master more than the Lord Jesus. Therefore, looking disgruntled, they now came to Him with this question: "Why do we as well as the Pharisees fast a great deal, while Your disciples do not fast?"

John the Baptist had come to preach that we have forfeited all claims because of our sin. To make this point clear, he fasted often and had his disciples do the same. The Lord Jesus came with the message that by His suffering He would buy back everything for us. Through Him life could become a constant enjoyment of God's communion, and in that communion an enjoyment of everything God gives us. Thus life becomes one big wedding feast. And since fasting is out of the question at a wedding feast, the Lord Jesus taught His disciples not to fast.

In the Old Testament God had sometimes ordered His people to fast in order to teach them that because of sin they had forfeited everything. John the Baptist, with whom the Old Testament came to an end, brought this message once more, even more strongly than in the Old Testament. But John was to prepare the way for the coming of the Lord Jesus, with whom God would give us all things again.

The disciples of John wanted to accept the new order that Jesus brought (communion with God through Christ), but also hold on to the old order (communion with God under the Law). That's impossible. "You cannot put a piece of unshrunk cloth on an old garment," the Lord Jesus said, "for then the tear will become bigger. And you cannot put new fermenting wine in old, dried-out wineskins, for then they will burst."

42

The disciples of the Lord Jesus were allowed to enjoy the full happiness of the Kingdom. With the Lord Jesus they also received communion with God. After a while, when the time of His suffering and death came, He would be taken away from them. Then they would mourn and fast. But at His resurrection He would be given back to them. And after His ascension He would give them the Holy Spirit. In that Spirit He would remain with them forever.

This makes life in the Kingdom a wedding feast. That's what it is now for the believer. Sometimes it can happen that God withdraws Himself from us because of our sins and it is possible that we may have to mourn and fast, but if we confess our sins, God always gives Himself to us again. Then life becomes a feast once more.

CHAPTER SEVEN
THE LABOR OF HIS SOUL
MATTHEW 9:27—10:42

Here we see Christ at work. We see the needs He uncovered while engaged in His work and how He gave Himself to them. In the course of that work He found the cross, not only in the misunderstanding of the blind men He healed but also in the slander of the Pharisees. As a result of His work He looked upon the crowd as sheep without a shepherd. His labors had brought Him to this recognition. He began to long for coworkers and so He sent His disciples out to preach.

We should regard Matthew 10:1-17 as the actual speech with which He sent the disciples out. Then come some words which the Lord Jesus may have spoken on another occasion, words that describe the work in a much broader way. In the latter verses He is thinking not only of the immediate mission of the twelve disciples through Israel but also of their work after the outpouring of the Spirit. In an even broader sense, He was thinking of all the work that would have to be done before His return. That's how we are to understand the words: "You will not have gone through all the towns of Israel before the Son of man has come." This "coming" refers to the reign of His grace over all the nations. Rome will be reached before the last town in Israel. At that point it can be said that the Kingdom has come, although it will come in glory only with His return.

Main Thought: *In His Kingdom, Christ offers the labor of His soul.*

His work misunderstood. The Lord Jesus labored much in Capernaum. There He preached the gospel and performed many miracles. The work was hard and pressing. How much He often had to do in one day!

Did the people understand Him in His work? Did they understand what He was really after, that His object was to ensure that the grace of the Kingdom would have dominion over the hearts of men? That would indeed become clear.

One day when the work was very pressing and the Lord Jesus had already done much, two blind men called out to Him in the street, "Son of David, have mercy on us!" They wanted to be healed, but they called Jesus the Son of David, indicating that they already knew He was of David's house.

We are not certain whether these blind men knew that Jesus was the promised Savior of the house of David; in any case they understood that the honor of David's house came to light again in this man who went about healing people. But how could these blind men have understood this and how would the people understand it when they heard them? Would they think only of the glory of David's house, or would they understand that the kings of that house had really been called to bring the people under the dominion of God's grace? How often the people had been concerned only with outward splendor! Would they now honor the Lord Jesus only for His miracles, without their hearts being opened to His grace? In that case the goal of His labors would not be achieved.

How dangerous it was when those blind men cried out in the street! Therefore the Lord Jesus paid no attention to them. But when He entered the house, they followed Him inside. It was less dangerous there, for there were no people around. Jesus did not ask them what they meant by calling Him the "Son of David." Instead He asked: "Do you believe I am able to do this?"

Without faith on their part, He could not heal them. He first wanted to awaken that faith in them; they were to look solely to Him. He meant that they should not look to His power to work miracles alone; but should also see and believe that He had come to redeem all of life by bringing their hearts to God again in faith.

The blind men answered, "Yes, Lord." Although they believed in His power to work miracles, it is not entirely clear whether they understood what the Lord Jesus had really meant. But by the faith He had awakened in them, He could now heal them. He touched their eyes and said: "Be it done to you according to your faith." As was so often the case, He touched them. By that gesture He seemed to associate Himself with their suffering and take upon Himself the sin of the world, which is the source of all suffering. He took our sin upon Himself and wanted to make atonement. By so doing He was able to redeem life. Through His touch He was saying to the two blind men that He sought their hearts and wanted to save their lives for all eternity.

Their eyes were opened and they could see the One who had been good to them. But the Lord Jesus immediately told them not to let anyone know what had happened. He said this very sternly, almost angrily, for He feared that they and all who heard about it would misunderstand His work. He was struggling for them and for all Israel.

When the blind men left the house, they spread Jesus' fame all around. They forgot His command. They had not understood Him nor had they understood what He really wanted to do for their fellow Israelites. What a disappointment that must have been for the Lord Jesus! Would it prove impossible to save His people after all?

Now, we are not to look only at the two blind men. When the Lord Jesus seeks our heart and asks us to surrender to His grace in faith, we often don't understand Him either—because we do not want to understand Him. We reject Him. The Lord Jesus may do much for us, but when He asks for our hearts, we don't want to hear Him. It's fortunate that His suffering and atonement also covered our rejection of Him. Now He can continue to ask for our hearts and take possession of them.

His work slandered. As the blind men were going away, a man who was dumb and possessed by the devil was brought to Jesus. In those days, instances of possession were not uncommon. The devil had such people completely in his power so that his victims had no will of their own.

That demon possession could happen in those days was in accordance with God's intention. Over against this power of satan, the power of grace would stand out the more gloriously. It was indeed horrible to be so completely in the power of the evil one, but it is even more horrible when we surrender ourselves to his power of our own accord and do his will.

Here the Lord Jesus stood face to face with His enemy. Had He not come to destroy the works of the devil? Therefore He gave

Himself fully to His work. By making atonement for the sins of men, He would break the power of the evil one. It was granted Him to deny the devil his dominion over this person and to cast him out. What joy Jesus felt as He made the devil leave this man and enabled him to speak again! The man was at liberty to praise God once more after satan had held his mouth bound for so long.

Would His people now recognize Him and understand that He had come to gain the victory over the power of the evil one in their lives too? Alas, there was nothing of such understanding to be seen. The crowds were amazed, but they kept the miracle at a distance; it had no meaning for their lives. And the Pharisees slandered Him, saying: "He casts out demons by the prince of demons." Jesus is in league with the devil—that's what they were saying.

How badly He was misunderstood! How aggrieved He must have felt! It was as if the devil was laughing at Him and saying: "You may be able to cast me out of this man, but the hearts of the masses and of the Pharisees are in my power."

How fortunate that the Lord Jesus suffered for the slander of men and made atonement for such sins, enabling Him to break satan's power over the heart. If only we believe in that power of grace which is stronger than satan's power!

Catching sight of His task. How busy the Lord Jesus was preaching and healing the sick—not just in Capernaum but in all of Galilee. What was the result of all that work? Did the people believe in Him, and were their hearts healed by submission to His grace?

How little He was understood! As His work progressed, He increasingly learned to recognize the need of the crowds. He saw them as sheep without a shepherd. They were scattered and had wounded themselves on the thorns of sin. There were enough leaders who wanted to use the people for their own interests, but shepherds who sought their hearts to bring them to God, shepherds who gave their lives for the sheep—these He did not find. And the masses did not even desire such shepherds. The people and their leaders were united only in straying from the Lord.

That's how wretched the people really were. That Jesus viewed them in such terms was partly the result of His work. That was how He found them. This discovery on Jesus' part was no meager result. No one sees things as Jesus does. And no one wants another person to know that he is hurt and lonely. We all hide our inner selves from each other. How fortunate that there is One whose eyes are open, who wants to see us just as we are and find us in that same way. We may tell God everything there is to know about our misery, including the things we would never tell a fellow human being. He knows about it before we do.

His desire for co-workers. The work among the crowds was so extensive and the misery so great that anyone else would have lost heart. But not the Lord Jesus! Still, He did long for co-workers who would prepare the harvest in His strength. He knew they would have to be given to Him by the Father. He prayed for fellow laborers and also told His disciples to pray for them. The talents are there, but God has to call people to the work and qualify them for it by His Spirit.

At this early stage the Lord Jesus already chose to appoint disciples to be His co-workers. He gave them power to reveal grace, not only by preaching but also by healing the sick. They would go out two by two, not to the heathen but for the time being only to the people of Israel who were scattered and had completely lost their way.

The disciples were not to concern themselves with provisions; those who received the gospel would take them in. They were to let the Lord's peace descend on the house that received them. But for any house and city that did not receive them, their coming would be a judgment. In those cases they were to shake the dust off their feet as they left as a sign that they had had nothing in common with that place. The gospel always gives rise to a crisis. It brings us either peace of judgment.

Later, too, the Lord Jesus often spoke to His disciples about their future calling. When they preached the gospel in the world, they would not have an easy time of it. They would be as sheep in the midst of wolves. They would be persecuted everywhere. Yet they would see the dominion of grace come in all the world. They were not to be afraid but were to surrender their own lives to the grace they preached. Anyone who wished to save his life would lose it; his life would be empty and worthless. But anyone who was willing to lose his life and surrender it completely to the Lord's grace would keep it; his life would bear everlasting fruit. The disciples were not to fear men who could only kill the body but could not make their life eternally fruitless. They were to fear God, who can not only destroy their body eternally in hell but also their life, by condemning it forever as fruitless.

The disciples were to start their work immediately even though they had hardly been taught by the Lord Jesus yet. Even later, however, they were never fully ready for the work. Who is ever completely ready? We always must remain disciples. Only if we surrender completely to the Lord, will He speak through us and bless our work. Then, because we are co-workers of the Lord Jesus, our work is not without fruit.

CHAPTER EIGHT
THE KINGDOM FORCES ITS WAY THROUGH
MATTHEW 11

More than any other episode, the story about the doubts entertained by John the Baptist shows us that so-called objective doubt (doubt as to whether the things written in Scripture are true) cannot be separated from so-called subjective doubt (doubt as to whether *we* have a part in salvation). If we insist on this separation, John's doubt remains a puzzle. He himself pointed out the Christ after he had witnessed the sign from heaven (see John 1:32-4). If it were only a question of an objective observation of fact, no doubt would be possible. But that's not how one confesses that Jesus is the Christ. When John pointed Him out earlier, he disregarded himself completely and looked solely to Christ (see the discussion with the representatives from Jerusalem in John 1). That is the only way Christ can be pointed out.

In prison John began to look to himself. Then he could no longer hold fast the confession that Jesus is the Christ. We are only able to make this confession when we surrender to Him completely.

For John this self-surrender bore a very special character. With him the Old Testament came to an end. The law and the prophets had led up to him. By not eating or drinking, he brought the message that by our sins we forfeit everything.

John's behavior is not to be confused with asceticism. The background of asceticism is invariably a contempt for everything that is material or is of the body. Thus asceticism involves a heathen dualism. As a preacher of penitence, however, John the Baptist had brought the message that every benefit was corrupted by sin and that, as a result of man's sin, God had denied man access to the treasures of creation.

The laws of the Old Testament still spoke to this loss. However, the Old Testament was also a dispensation of the covenant of *grace*. Hence it foretold the opening up of the creation by Christ and by the outpouring of the Holy Spirit.

The prophets came to an end with John, who was privileged to point out the Christ. Christ came eating and drinking, bringing the joyful message that in His Kingdom we are entitled to all benefits. Those benefits have been earned for us again. John stood precisely on the borderline. His self-surrender meant that he was leaving behind the first dispensation of the covenant of grace for the second, which would surpass the first in the glory of the Kingdom.

From this vantage point we can see that the least in the Kingdom of heaven is greater than John the Baptist. As a person, John will surely rank above many in the New Testament dispensation, and John's place in glory will certainly be higher than that of many others. As for his calling on earth, John received the highest honor because he had seen the most and had the most to tell. Nevertheless, those who witnessed the outpouring of the Holy Spirit and the glorious Kingdom which accompanied that event had seen more and had more to report than John.

Verse 12 is probably better translated: "And from the days of John the Baptist until now, the Kingdom of heaven forces its way through, and men of violence take it by force."* The Kingdom forced its way through because many believed the message of John the Baptist that the coming of that Kingdom was at hand.

Main Thought: *The Kingdom forces its way through so that we may take it by force.*

Taking no offense at the Christ. John the Baptist had been privileged to point out the Lord Jesus and to proclaim Him to be the Christ, the promised Messiah who would establish the Kingdom of grace. But since that time events had not unfolded for John as he expected. Herod Antipas, who ruled over Galilee, put him in prison, and there was no prospect of John's regaining his freedom. Would his life end in prison? Was that to be the end of his glorious career?

John had known temptation while he was free. The people took him for someone of importance; they wondered whether he might not be the Messiah. John could have set himself up as a leader of the

*See, for example, Ned B. Stonehouse, *The Witness of Matthew and Mark to Christ*, pp. 245-8. —TRANS.

people, but in the face of those temptations he did not think of himself for even a moment. He pointed away from himself to the Lord Jesus as the Savior. At that time he was able to believe in the Lord Jesus with all his heart and surrender to Him completely. All his work and all of the Old Testament, of which he was the keystone, led up to the Lord Jesus and glorified Him.

What a glorious life it had been for John! Only in that spirit can we live in joy and peace. In prison, however, John began to think about himself; he began to feel sorry that his own life was ruined. Then he could no longer see the glory of the Lord Jesus, and he even began to harbor doubts as to whether He was really the Christ. As long as we see the glory of the Lord Jesus, everything is well with us no matter what happens; then we are always in His service. We must leave it up to Him in what manner He wishes to glorify Himself in us.

This was no longer the situation with John in prison. That's why he sent two of his disciples to the Lord Jesus to ask if Jesus was indeed the Christ. What an appalling question! John was entertaining doubts about the Lord Jesus! That's the worst thing we can do.

On the other hand, note that John took his question to the Lord Jesus Himself. This shows that he was still attached to Him and that there was another voice in his heart, a voice that was saying: "He is the one." If doubt has sprung up in us, we can do no better than to go to the Lord Jesus Himself. He will kill that doubt in us with His reproof.

That's what He did with John too but in a way peculiarly His own. He spoke no words of reproach; instead He said to John's emissaries that they should report to him what they heard and saw, namely, that the sick were healed, the dead were raised, and the good news of salvation was preached to those who by the Word had been made to feel the need for it and to long for it. The Lord Jesus made this point with words borrowed from the prophets. John had also used those words from the prophets and declared that their prophecies would now be fulfilled. The fulfillment had come: life was being freed from the prison in which it was now locked because of sin. Then why did John doubt?

It was indeed the Kingdom John had foretold, but it was costing him so much! All he had been called to do was announce it. Now that the Lord Jesus Himself had appeared, John had to withdraw into the background. Moreover, with the Lord Jesus and His Kingdom there dawned a dispensation of God's grace that was much more glorious than anything believers had known in the Old Testament. John had to recognize that the old dispensation was only temporary, that it was destined to pass.

How much John had to give up! But we, too, must surrender completely to the Lord Jesus and allow Him to determine the course to be followed. That's very hard for us to do, which is why He said: "Blessed is he who will take no offense at Me," that is, blessed is the one to whom I am not a stumbling block over which he trips and falls.

Elijah and John. The crowds had heard this reprimand of John. But they were not to think lightly of him because of it, for he was still a messenger from God. The Lord now wanted to explain what John's significance was.

To begin with, the people had to learn not to look at John in personal terms. Who had John been? Certainly he was not a wavering man to be compared with the reeds on the bank of the Jordan River, which are shaken by every breath of wind. Neither was he a flattering courtier who did not dare to tell the truth. Yet, even a man with great strength of character can fall prey to doubt. The glory and salvation of a man lies solely in God's calling.

What, then, was John's calling? The people took him for a prophet. But he was far more than a prophet, for he himself had been announced by the prophets of the Old Testament. John was the Elijah whose coming the prophets had foretold. This did not mean that he was Elijah returned from the dead; the point was that John ministered in the spirit and with the strength of Elijah.

His was the very special calling to point out the Christ. John had the highest task a man has ever had—higher than any of the prophets. Even so, his work falls before the coming of the New Testament. Anyone present at its appearance, anyone who saw the Kingdom come, will have seen more and will have more to announce than John.

And that Kingdom is coming! Even then, when it had just been announced that its coming was at hand, it was already a force to be reckoned with and was already bringing division among the people. There were those who gave themselves with all their might to possess it. They wanted to surrender to it and lose everything else for it. Such is the Kingdom's glory!

An arbitrary generation. Again the Lord Jesus seized an opportunity to speak to the crowds about the glory of His Kingdom. That Kingdom did indeed exercise force, and there were people who by denying themselves, forcibly entered the Kingdom. Yet the masses rejected it. They were not aware of the great turnabout occurring all around them now that the Kingdom was coming. They did not experience the great transition from the Old Testament to the New. They wanted neither the one nor the other. As the Lord Jesus said, they were like fickle children who want to play first this game and then another, complaining all the while that their friends do not want to dance to their tune. First they wanted to play wedding, and then funeral—and they complained when their friends did not yield to their whims.

The people of those days were a capricious, arbitrary generation, and John was unable to please them. He was a preacher of penitence who fasted a great deal. The Jews said of him that he was possessed by an evil spirit.

Jesus wasn't able to please them either. He stood in the midst of life and more than once accepted an invitation to a meal. He even sat at the same table with tax-collectors. But the Jews said of Jesus that He was a glutton and a drunkard. Neither John nor Jesus had pleased the Jews. What they really meant, however, was that God, who had sent them both, each with a different calling, had not done it right. God had not acted in accordance with their fancies. He had sent John, the preacher of penitence, with the message that all claims had been forfeited because of sin. And the same God had sent the Lord Jesus with the proclamation that He would reclaim everything again.

Neither John nor Jesus managed to please that generation. Neither the message of the Old Testament, which convicted men of guilt because atonement had not yet come, nor the message of the New Testament, which proclaimed complete remission of sin and complete liberation of life, pleased them. They preferred to do their own thinking. But God stuck to His guns and would be proved right by His works.

Because of the Jews' rejection, the Lord Jesus began to rebuke the cities where He had revealed the glory of the Kingdom by His miracles. He rebuked them for their unbelief. If Tyre and Sidon had been allowed to see what Chorazin and Bethsaida now saw, he said, they would not have remained indifferent. Yet, those two cities in Israel were apathetic. Capernaum, the center of Jesus' work, turned out to be just as apathetic. If Sodom had seen what Capernaum saw, it would not have remained indifferent and subsequently been destroyed. Israel's sin was greater than that of Sidon, Tyre and Sodom of old. Therefore Israel would be judged even more severely.

Christ's yoke. It was really quite amazing: the Israelites thought they were so rich and wise. They no longer rendered glory to God for the gifts He had given them nor did they confess their dependence on Him. Therefore, they were unable to receive the grace Christ's Kingdom offered them. Because they boasted in their own strength, they were cut off from salvation. Salvation was hidden from these "learned" Israelites and revealed instead to those who accepted their dependence on God in a childlike fashion. The Lord Jesus calls these simple believers to Himself and gives them the rest they can find nowhere else.

Also, Jesus Himself is dependent on the Father and therefore does not put on others a yoke that is too heavy to bear as the Pharisees did. He does not push His own beyond their limits but gives them rest. His yoke is easy and His burden is light. After all, it is the yoke of service in God's love, given to us in the Lord Jesus. To serve that love is never oppressive, for by that love we are blessed.

CHAPTER NINE
THE GOSPEL OF THE
KINGDOM IS LIKE SEED
MATTHEW 13:1-30

The Kingdom of heaven is hidden from the flesh but revealed in faith. This is evident from Matthew 13:11, where we read: "To you it has been given to know the secrets of the Kingdom of heaven." The Kingdom remains a secret for the flesh because it runs completely contrary to the expectations of the flesh. It is the Kingdom in which God's grace is all in all. Everything in it is a gift. The flesh does not understand what it means to live by the gift of grace.

We should understand the gospel of the Kingdom as seed in a field, the seed which is received by the earth and then brings forth new life. Many people cannot understand this comparison because they reject the gospel. There are some on whom the gospel of the Kingdom makes no impression at all. Others think they understand it but, in fact, do not. Christ spoke to these people in parables so that they might realize they do not understand. In other words, even the little knowledge they thought they possessed was taken from them. Using parables as a tool, Christ was preparing them to receive the message. Should they fail to become receptive, the Kingdom would close to them forever. By means of these parables, the disciples would have an even deeper understanding of the Kingdom's meaning. Because they have already, they will receive more still.

A parable is different from an allegory. John 10 is an example of an allegory. There the Lord Jesus Christ speaks of Himself and of the Kingdom, but He places the lesson within the framework of daily life: "I am the good Shepherd; the sheep hear My voice. I am the door of the sheep; I give My life for My sheep." Each feature of the allegory must then be dealt with and explained. A parable is a story from daily life in which many features have no spiritual significance at all but only serve to make the story come alive. With a parable we have to seek for the third thing which is common to the two things—one from daily life and one having to do with life in the Kingdom of grace—that are being compared, and not all the features need be explained. The first parable of this section of Scripture is explained by the Lord Jesus Christ, even down to the particulars, but when He interprets the second parable He omits things—for instance, the instructions to the servants, who want to separate the chaff from the wheat too soon.

It is definitely wrong to tell a Bible story first and then make an application. But with a parable we cannot avoid telling the story first and then in a stroke or two point out the meaning. In these outlines, of course, the story will be very short.

Main Thought: *The gospel of the Kingdom is like the seed falling on the earth.*

Different places in the field. The Lord Jesus had traveled all through Galilee, preaching the gospel of the Kingdom and performing miracles. In both word and deed Jesus told people that God wanted to give man everything since man really had nothing of himself, however rich he may have thought he was. That's how the Kingdom of heaven would be established. In that Kingdom all things are gifts from heaven.

Not everyone has understood the message. That was out of the question because we would prefer to be self-sufficient rather than admit bankruptcy and have God bail us out. We can't understand that everything is a gift of God's grace and that all we have to do is submit to that grace. Or sometimes we only think we understand while in fact we haven't grasped it at all.

The Lord Jesus Christ wanted to warn the people following Him. One day He left His house in Capernaum for the seashore. Immediately many people followed Him, whereupon He stepped in a boat and taught them from there.

He told the people a story. Once there was a sower who went out and scattered seed on his field. Some seed fell on the path beside the field. Immediately birds pecked at it and snatched it away. The field had been leveled but there were yet some spots where the soil only barely covered the rock beneath. Seeds that landed there grew well at first but were soon scorched by the sun for lack of a proper root system. The field had been weeded only imperfectly and in some places thistles sprang up with the grain and, being hardier than the grain, they choked it. The rest of the field, however, was good. One seed sometimes yielded as many as thirty, sixty, or even a hundred fold.

There is a special message in the parable. God made field and seed for each other. The field may receive the seed in which case the seed bears fruit—sometimes a hundred fold. God's grace controls the field. Each field is a miracle of God's grace. But sometimes there are obstacles which prevent the seed from bearing fruit. It may be said the field did not receive the seed properly, failing to provide the seed with essentials.

The secrets of the Kingdom of heaven. After the Lord Jesus had told this parable, He was silent. He wanted the crowds to think, to ask themselves: "What does He mean by this story? And if we don't understand the story, have we ever understood any of His words?" Anyone who had understood anything of Jesus' previous messages would also understand something of this story, while those who had understood nothing might now begin to wonder why.

The disciples asked Jesus why He spoke to the crowds in a parable without explaining it. He answered: "Because they have never understood My words. Let them now first see that they do not understand. Then perhaps their hearts will be opened to receive the gospel of the Kingdom. First whatever they think they have must be taken away from them, otherwise the discovery that they have nothing will come too late. Relying on their own wisdom, they have shut their ears and eyes to the Kingdom, as was predicted by the prophets."

We must all discover that our own wisdom is folly and that the Kingdom is different from what we imagine. We also pretend to know and to have something, but the Kingdom teaches and gives only to those who have nothing.

The Lord Jesus said to the disciples that they were blessed because of what they saw and heard of the Kingdom. Believers of former centuries had longed to see and hear news of the Kingdom. The disciples understood some of what the Lord Jesus had said, therefore He explained it to them further. Once we've caught glimpses of the Kingdom, we will understand it too.

Different attitudes. The gospel of the Kingdom, the Lord Jesus had said, is like seed. Many people hear the gospel but their hearts are not fit to receive it, because they overestimate their own strength. They think it's nonsense to say we have absolutely nothing, cannot gain anything but must be given everything, so they are indifferent to the gospel or scorn it. That explains their indifference or scorn to the gospel. The devil immediately takes the message away. Their hearts are like the path beside the field.

There are others who, for the most part, prefer to fend for themselves but who, when the going gets rough, like to be assured that God is willing to help. They have simply not been converted. God has not become everything to them though they may think they've understood the gospel of the Kingdom. And because they think God allows them to maintain their own way, they go along joyfully. Later, however, when oppression comes and God does not relieve them like the safety valve they had believed Him to be, they abandon Him. They had never understood the message. Their hearts are like rocks with a sprinkling of soil.

Still others seem to receive the message with gladness but continue to serve mainly themselves and their own interests. They also would like to serve God a bit, but in the long run they're too busy taking care of themselves. There is just no time left for God. They haven't understood the gospel of the Kingdom either. They are like the places where the seed is choked by the weeds. If we receive everything from the Lord by grace, we should give our whole lives to the Lord and to Him alone.

Finally, there are also people whose hearts are converted by the gospel of the Kingdom. They expect everything from God and are therefore prepared to serve the Lord with their whole life. They really see and believe in the Kingdom and go on bearing much fruit. As the gospel takes hold, God produces the fruit in their lives.

Step by step, God's grace oversees the entire growing process. First He prepares the soil; then He sows the seed; next He forms the roots; finally He produces the plant and its multiple fruit. How great is His sovereign grace! If only we wouldn't obstruct His grace with the many obstacles we throw in its path!

The necessary sifting. Unfortunately, the cause of the Kingdom will also be frustrated by intruders who are not citizens of the Kingdom. The Lord Jesus warned His own against intruders by means of another parable. A man had sown good seed in his field, but at night his enemy came and sowed weeds in the field and slinked away. When the weeds first started to grow, they looked very much like grain. The servants of the owner saw a great many weeds in the field they had carefully weeded. They couldn't understand it!

The master concluded that his enemy had deliberately sown weeds in it. The servants volunteered to pull out the weeds at once but the master was afraid they would damage the grain in the process. "The harvest will come," he said, calming them down. "I will tell the mowers to bind the weeds together in bundles and burn them. Then my grain will still be gathered and stored free of weeds."

Once again Jesus did not explain the parable to the crowd. The disciples later asked Him about it. They had understood enough of the parable to know that for a long time to come there would be weeds in the Kingdom. They now asked Jesus for a detailed explanation.

There are people, Jesus explained, who genuinely believe the gospel of the Kingdom. Such people belong to the Kingdom. They are the good seeds that grow in the field. But there are also people who play a role in the Kingdom but do not belong to it. They are brought in by the devil, having been deceived by him. They think they hear Christ's message and think they're following Him but are really in the service of satan. They have not been converted by the gospel of God's grace. They frequently obstruct the cause of the Kingdom with their simulated faith. They can be an obstacle to the true believer, as the disciples later discovered.

But we can't just look at those people! Satan, God's enemy, manipulates them—but one day he will be overthrown. On that day, at the end of time, the harvest will take place and God's children will enter glory. Fifth-columnists and obstructionists will first be gathered together and thrown into the fiery furnace where there will be weeping and gnashing of teeth.

Jesus repeatedly sounded the warning: "He who has ears to hear, let him understand!" What of our understanding through faith?

CHAPTER TEN
THE KINGDOM IS LIKE A TREASURE
MATTHEW 13:44-52

Once again we must remind ourselves that these stories are parables. Not every feature is meant to be taken in a spiritual sense. Neither may we ask the question whether it was right for the man who found a treasure in the field not to let the owner know about it before he bought the field from him. Christ takes examples from daily life without stamping those life situations as ethically correct.

The difference between the first parable and the second is that there was talk of searching in the second parable and not in the first. If that feature in the second parable is meant to be taken in a spiritual sense, we much point out that by nature we do not seek the truth. God's Spirit and Word make seekers of us.

Main Thought: *The Kingdom is like a treasure.*

Like a treasure in a field. The Lord Jesus had explained the parable about the weeds to His disciples. As He went on to speak to them, He used only parables. Through parables they were to understand better the things of the Kingdom that are hidden from the unbelieving mind. In this way He hoped to prepare them for their future task of spreading the gospel of the Kingdom everywhere.

He told them about a man who dug in a field and suddenly struck an urn containing a great treasure. Apparently someone from a previous generation had buried it there and died before he could dig it up. The finder put the treasure back in the ground, sold everything he had, and bought the field. That made him the owner of the treasure.

That's how it is with the Kingdom of heaven. God has revealed it, and its strength has become effective in the life of the world. Still, we all walk right past it. We do not know what a treasure God has given us in this life. We may often have heard about it without ever seeing it. If our eyes are opened to it in faith, we see it at once. Then the Kingdom is so valuable to us that we will give up everything for it. We find it so attractive that we do not want to possess anything except the Kingdom, for it alone gives our life value. All our possessions are sanctified by the grace of the Kingdom.

Like a pearl of great value. This same thought, that the Kingdom is totally fascinating and captivating once we have seen it, was made clear by the Lord Jesus in yet another way. Once there was a merchant of pearls, He explained, a merchant who was out to buy the finest and most expensive pearls. One day he saw one that was extremely large and expensive. He was so delighted that he sold everything he had and bought that pearl.

There are also people who search for the Kingdom of God. The gospel that they have heard and the Spirit of the Lord have made them restless. Therefore they can no longer find any satisfaction. Then, suddenly, their eyes are opened to see the Kingdom, and they surrender completely to the grace of that Kingdom. Anyone who has seen it cannot escape its charm.

Like a fishing net. The fascination of God's Kingdom is so great that it even draws people who do not "see" it. They do see something of the strength that the Kingdom has in the world. Because they cannot free themselves completely from the hold the gospel has on them, they participate in the activities of the Kingdom without belonging to it. There is a dynamic movement of the Kingdom in the world. By the movement of the Kingdom God wishes to recapture all of life and sanctify it to His service. That's why some people string along without "seeing" the Kingdom. The Lord Jesus cautioned His disciples against such people and told them that they would experience this in their work.

The Kingdom, He said, is like a fishing net that is dragged through the water. All kinds of fish are caught that way, including some that are inedible and unclean. When the net has been drawn up, those fish are thrown away. Likewise, when the struggle of the Kingdom here on earth comes to an end one day, the angels will come with the Lord Jesus to judge. They will separate from the believers those who drifted along with the movement of the Kingdom but did not "see" it. God's judgment will be hard on those who went along just for the ride. His anger will be kindled against them because they pretended to belong to the Lord while actually seeking their own interests. By so doing they offended the Lord's grace doubly.

Like a householder's treasure. After the Lord Jesus had said these things to His disciples, He asked them, "Have you understood all this?" They answered, "Yes, Lord!" Most likely they did not see through everything. Who could ever understand it all? But they had understood the secrets of the Kingdom of heaven, and they were also able to teach them. Now they were scribes in the good sense of the word, that is, people well versed in the Scriptures.

The treasure of the Kingdom of heaven is so great that they could see and say new things about it over and over again. It is like the owner of a big house with a large storeroom. Every day the man will be compelled to set the same foods before his family, but he will also often surprise them with dishes they have never tasted before and did not expect. In the same manner, the gospel of the Kingdom is our daily bread. The same things have to be said over and over again, but the Spirit of the Lord also teaches us to see and say new things. The wisdom of the Kingdom is inexhaustible. Every day the Lord Jesus revealed new things about it, thereby preparing His disciples for their calling.

MATTHEW: KING AND PEOPLE

CHAPTER ELEVEN
LORD OVER THE FORCES OF NATURE
MATTHEW 14:13-33

Adam originally exercised dominion over the works of God's hands here on earth, including the forces of nature. But we must not think of Adam apart from the eternal Word by which God's communion came to him. When that communion was broken, he also lost the dominion. In Christ the Word appeared in the flesh. That Word now has dominion.

We must remember that the eternal Word was the revelation of God's favor and is now the revelation of His grace (grace being the favor that forgives sin). *All* things are in subjection to the Word of grace, including the forces of nature, for they were made by the Word. We have here the same revelation as in Elijah's day. The Word of grace, of which Elijah was the bearer, rules over drought and rain. The forces of nature were not Baals. And now the Word has become flesh in Jesus Christ.

If Christ in His grace has authority over all things, through faith in Him we also have dominion in principle. Peter understood that, and we must follow him in this belief in Christ. True, we are still in subjection to the forces of nature (Heb. 2:8-9), but in the spirit we exercise dominion. Soon all things will be put in subjection under our feet as well. Here, too, it must be emphasized that all things are placed in subjection under those who share in the grace of the eternal Word.

Christ already exercised that authority on the basis of the work He would accomplish. Thus this exercise of His power was temporary. And we are justified in saying that He assumed that power at His resurrection.

Main Thought: *As the Word-become-flesh, Christ is Lord over the forces of nature.*

Alone on the mountain. In the days when the Lord Jesus spent a lot of time in Capernaum, He also crossed the Sea of Galilee more than once and preached on the other side. Now again He sailed across, this time to escape the crowds. He wanted to be alone with His disciples for once. But the crowds walked around the lake along the shore and so He ministered to them again. In a miraculous way He fed the multitude.

It was evening. Jesus and the disciples would have to return to the other side. But He told His disciples to go back in the boat alone. He Himself would take care of sending the crowds away. That evening He wanted to be completely alone.

When He was alone, He climbed up the mountain to pray. Apparently He spent many hours there in prayer. He was indeed God, but He was also human. While on the one hand the fullness of the Godhead was in Him, on the other hand, that is, on His human side, He had to hold on to His communion with God by faith and in prayer. Hence He struggled on the mountain. There He drank from the well of communion with God in order to strengthen Himself for the fulfillment of His calling on earth. But He struggled there as the Mediator, seeking to hold on to the communion with God for the whole world.

"For the whole world"—but this is not to say for all people. He struggled for those who believe in Him and in His victory.

It is I. Strengthened in His communion with God, Jesus went back to His work. During the night a storm had broken out on the lake. It was such a violent storm, with strong headwinds, that the disciples in the boat found themselves in desperate straits.

Between three and six o'clock in the morning, the Lord Jesus appeared right in the middle of the lake, walking on the water. It was still dark. All the disciples could make out was a figure. They said to each other that it was a ghost, and they cried out in fear. We would have done the same, for that's how little we are attuned to the truth. We believe that the world is controlled by dark powers which our imagination turns into ghosts. But we cannot quite bring ourselves to believe that all things, including the forces of nature and even the waves and the winds, are in subjection to the Lord Jesus.

Yet, it's true. Jesus wanted to reveal this in that situation. At once He spoke to the disciples and said, "Take heart; it is I. Don't be afraid." Then they were no longer afraid, for He was with them. They did not see any hostile powers arrayed against them. All they saw was the Lord Jesus whose grace was for them. Can it ever be different for us if we believe in Him?

With Him on the water. When they knew that it was the Lord, Peter asked, "Lord, if it is You, tell me to come to You on the water!" Peter had understood the situation correctly: if the Lord Jesus commands the forces of nature, then we may do the same by faith in Him. But it still depends on the Lord's will. That's why He asked the Lord to tell Him to come. Some day we will reign with the Lord Jesus over all things. He wanted to give a sign of that reign in advance. That's why He told Peter to come.

Peter walked on the sea to meet the Lord. It went all right as long as he looked to the Lord. But then he must have looked down at the water and been amazed at what was happening. At that point he was no longer believingly amazed at the Lord Jesus and the power of His grace. Instead he was amazed at what he was experiencing. Then things went wrong. Fear rose up, and he lost the bond with the Lord Jesus. At once he began to sink.

Fearfully he cried out, "Lord, save me!" The Lord caught his hand, saying, "O man of little faith, why did you doubt?" Looking to himself had made Peter afraid. At that point he began to sink because of his lack of faith.

If we continue to look to the Lord Jesus we are always in control. It may be that the forces of nature are not yet in subjection to us but nothing in the whole world will then be able to get us down. In the spirit we are more than conquerors.

Truly the Son of God! Once the Lord Jesus climbed into the boat with Peter, the wind quieted down. This showed once more that the forces of nature were subject to Him.

The disciples came to Him and worshiped Him, saying: "Truly, You are the Son of God!" In Him, they were confessing, the fullness of divine grace had come to them. The promise, which once was given and was repeated many times, had been fulfilled.

The fullness of divine grace had been opened up to them. It did not always remain that way. If we, by faith have an eye for that grace in the Lord Jesus Christ, we will see in Jesus the glory of God, the sovereign Master; that is, we will see grace's mastery over all things.

CHAPTER TWELVE
YOU ARE THE CHRIST
MATTHEW 16:13-28

Jesus is *the Christ*, that is the Anointed One. The fact that He was an office-bearer governed His existence as Son of man. It also governed the nature He assumed in His conception and birth. Because He was *the Christ*, He had to suffer. This was the purpose of His office, and it was to this end that He had been sent into the world by the Father. Accordingly, through His official capacity as *the Christ* He embraced all who are His. It was for them that He suffered.

Being an office-bearer Himself, He also gave the office to His disciples. It is by virtue of that office, the calling to proclaim *the Christ*, that Peter is the rock on which the Church will be built. Likewise, the names of the twelve apostles are written on the foundation of the wall of the New Jerusalem. The Church has been built upon their words, which they spoke in the name of Christ. By their words they opened and closed the doors of the Kingdom. By their words they bound and loosed; that is, they interpreted what was to be accepted as the truth and what had to be rejected as falsehood.

"Flesh and blood" is man as he lives here on earth. Because of sin, man is cut off from communion with God. Therefore "flesh and blood" becomes a contrast with "the Father who is in heaven." Frequently, words and phrases like *world, earth, children of men, flesh and blood,* and *natural (psychic),* which in themselves indicate nothing unfavorable, point to man's state as being cut off from God because of the fall.

The gates of hell in verse 18 are the gates of the realm of the dead. When we speak of the realm of the dead, we must not think of a particular place, as a sort of holding area, for we know that the separation between believers and unbelievers takes place immediately at death. Believers are with Jesus; unbelievers are under judgment. The realm of the dead is merely a collective term for the dead, just as we speak of the vegetable kingdom and the animal kingdom.

The realm of the dead is portrayed here as a power. For man the realm of the dead actually means oblivion, utter futility. The name of the godless will perish along with them. However, in His death Christ entered the realm of the dead. After all, He, too, belonged to the dead. At His resurrection He opened up that realm for Himself and for those who belong to Him.

At the resurrection the realm of the dead will give up the believer and his name will be restored. There will also be a resurrection for the unbelievers at the last judgment—but only so that they can be given over to more oblivion and futility.

The gates of the realm of the dead will not prevail against the Church. The Church, the believers, will not be subjected to oblivion and futility. When resurrection day comes, they will receive a new name.

The same word (*psyche*) is used for "life" in verse 25 and for "soul" in verse 26. What is meant here is life with its fruit. Anyone who seeks to save his life by living for himself will lose it. One day his life will be judged to be vain and fruitless. What will it profit a man if he gains the whole world and one day loses his life, that is, if one day his life is eternally rejected as having been vain and fruitless?

The Son of man has come into His Kingdom. He came to power at His resurrection, at His ascension, and at the outpouring of the Holy Spirit. Since then He rules in the power of His grace over all things. Today He still directs history.

Main Thought: *To His own, Jesus is known as the Christ.*

A profession under the Father's guidance. The people and their elders did not know the Lord Jesus; they did not accept Him as the one sent by God. A clash between Jesus and the people was unavoidable. Things were gradually heading in that direction. The disciples would also be involved in the conflict. Would they know Him, would they understand the meaning of His ministry on earth?

Jesus had to prepare Himself and the disciples for what was going to happen. They crossed the border and went to the district of Caesarea Philippi. Since the crowds did not follow Him there, He could be alone with His disciples.

There, for the first time, He asked them who the people said He was. When He ministered among them as a man, He had not kept it from them that He had come with a distinct calling. What was that calling, according to the people in Israel?

The disciples were well-informed about this matter, for they heard the talk that was making the rounds among the people. They replied that the people thought Jesus was a prophet, or perhaps Jeremiah or Elijah, for whose return they were hoping. Herod the tetrarch had killed John the Baptist; he feared that John had reappeared in the Lord Jesus, which to him explained why those powers were at work in Him.

The Lord Jesus asked this question of them at the outset in order to ask them later if they had seen something else in Him. Indeed they had. What the crowds did not want to acknowledge they now professed by the mouth of Peter: "You are the Christ, the Son of the living God. You are the Messiah sent to earth by God to do the work of the Father. You, as His Son, have been sent to give His people the grace revealed in the Old Testament. You are the Savior who was sent and who, for that purpose, received an office from God."

How did Peter and the other disciples come by this knowledge? They did not possess it of themselves. The fact was that there were a great many in Israel who had not seen this in the Lord Jesus. The Father in heaven must show it to us; He must open our hearts to it. Then we see it by faith, that is, by the faith that accepts the Lord Jesus Christ as the Savior sent by God. Accordingly, by that faith He is our Savior. Anyone who does not surrender in faith to Him cannot and will not see Him as the Christ. We are blessed if we see Him in that light; we have found happiness in life. That's what the Lord Jesus said to Peter, and in him to all the disciples.

The power of the apostolic office. However, the disciples also had to understand their calling. One day the Lord Jesus would be taken away from the earth. Everywhere they would then have to proclaim the truth that He is the Christ. That was the reason He had called them to be apostles. He Himself had been sent by the Father, and He in turn was sending them. Upon those men in their office as apostles, in their power to witness to His name everywhere, the Lord Jesus would build His Church. Their words would form the foundation for the Church of all ages. That's why Jesus called Simon, whom He had addressed as Simon son of Jonah, by the name Peter. Simon himself, as son of Jonah, was nothing, but by the apostolic calling he would become a rock. In great faithfulness and steadfastness, Peter would proclaim his profession everywhere. He would serve as a rock upon which the Church would be built.

Speaking God's words the apostles would open and close the Kingdom of heaven. All who accepted their words by faith would find the Kingdom opened to them. Whoever rejected their message would be condemned by it and excluded from the Kingdom. The Word they proclaimed was like the key to the gate of the Kingdom of heaven. If we believe that Word, we are already inside the Kingdom; we are citizens of it. One day we will share in its glory. In the Word they proclaimed, the apostles would state what the truth is—what is to be accepted and what is to be rejected. Fortunately, we still have that Word as preached by the apostles. Let us believe it in all simplicity! Then for us, too, the gate of the Kingdom will be open.

The disciples might well have become enthusiastic because of the wonderful calling they had received. Right then they might have wanted to proclaim everywhere that Jesus is the Christ. But the work of the Lord Jesus had not yet progressed that far. First He Himself would profess His calling and die for it. The disciples were not ready yet either. They had seen a lot, but they still had much to learn. The people, too, were not yet ready for it. They would want to make a Messiah of Him according to their own conception—and misjudge the Father's calling in the process. For these reasons Jesus forbade His disciples to tell anyone that He was the Christ.

The necessity of Christ's suffering. Did the disciples themselves understand what it meant that the Lord Jesus was the Christ? Not by any stretch of the imagination. But now He began to reveal it to them. He was the Christ who had received an office from the Father, who was called to fulfill the Father's mandate. What was that mandate? As office-bearer, as the Head of His people, He embraced all who belonged to Him. All their guilt became His guilt. God's judgment would be transferred to Him. He would bear God's anger and curse. And when He suffered the curse, all who belonged to Him would be included in His Kingdom. He would liberate them from sin and its judgment. That suffering had to come. For that purpose the Father sent Him; for that reason He was the Christ.

He would finally have to suffer the anger and curse of God when men rejected and killed Him. The leaders of the people would do this to Him; they would fulfill that sad service. They would vent their own hatred on Him but they would not understand that their action was the means by which Christ would suffer God's judgment on the sins of His people. God would surely visit their crime on the elders of the people. Yet precisely by means of the suffering inflicted on Him by the elders, Christ would save His people.

The Lord Jesus began to speak of His suffering to His disciples. He also added that He would rise again on the third day, but they didn't understand that. They did not even hear it. That was because they did not listen to all those words in faith. They didn't hear that all this had to happen, that God delivered Jesus up to it, and that it was for this purpose He was the Christ. They didn't recognize God's hand in all this for that involves seeing and hearing in faith. Therefore they were unable to hear that God would raise Him from the dead on the third day. They only saw what people would do to Him. Because of this, Peter, again speaking for all of them, said that God would be merciful to Him and that this would surely not happen to Him.

How horrible those words of Peter were! In those words Jesus heard a temptation, an effort to make Him doubt the Father's mandate. Had He indeed been sent into the world for that purpose? Did the Father not love Him then? How He dreaded that suffering! But still, He was the Christ, the Head of His people. Therefore He could not help but suffer for that people.

Hence He did not want to hear such words from Peter. They sounded like satan talking. Peter was being manipulated by satan. That's why He turned away from Peter and said to him, "Get behind Me, satan!"

Peter was a stumbling block to Jesus to make Him fall. Peter did not see what God's calling involved for Jesus and he sought to obscure it for Jesus too. How fortunate that the Lord Jesus remained faithful to His mandate and rejected Peter's words so vehemently! He wanted to save His people and be obedient to the Father.

Fellowship in Christ's suffering. Anyone who wants to see Christ in the light of His suffering must be prepared to serve the Father as He did and hear His calling. Also, he must live not for himself but for God. Whoever lives for himself will lead a vain and fruitless life. Nothing will be left of his life; it will perish under God's judgment.

But anyone who surrenders his life to God will keep it, for it will bear fruit that will abide forever.

This means conflict even for the believer because we want so much to live for ourselves! Everything in this world stimulates us to possess it all for ourselves alone. If we want to take the same road that the Lord Jesus took, that is, to live for God, we must deny ourselves and take up our cross. Then we will truly be following Him. He went before us on that road and therefore we can be assured of His favor and communion. Then following that road will be easy for us.

What else is there to live for? What would it profit a man if he should gain the whole world for himself? He would live a fruitless life, a life that would come under God's judgment. He would lose his life and from all the treasures he possessed he would not be able to give anything to redeem his life from judgment.

Someday Jesus is going to return as the Judge of heaven and earth. God's angels will surround Him as a sign of His power and majesty. On that day He will judge every one of us. Did we live for ourselves or for the Lord? It is true that we are not able to change ourselves but Christ can change us by the power of His grace so that we will begin to live for the Lord. That's the power He received at His resurrection and ascension. And He exercises that power through the Holy Spirit whom He has sent. When He poured out the Spirit, the believers witnessed His power in His Kingdom. Hence He already prophesied then that some of His disciples (most of them, in fact) would not die before they had seen Him come in His Kingdom. He now reigns in that Kingdom. Do we believe in the power of His grace, by which He can also change us? And will we see to it that we, too, live unto the Lord?

CHAPTER THIRTEEN
THE PEOPLE OF THE LORD
MATTHEW 17:24—18:35

Gradually it was becoming clear that not all Israel would choose for Christ. The true Israel, the remnant, would be saved. Together with the believers from among the Gentiles, the remnant will form the New Testament people of God.

The principles of life in the new community begin to take shape in the gathering of the disciples from Israel. Christ was already giving orders for the life of God's new people.

Main Thought: *Through the gospel of the Kingdom, the new community will be formed.*

Like sons who are exempt. Little by little it was becoming clear that not all in Israel were going to choose for the Lord Jesus. Out of Israel and from among the nations the Lord would gather to Himself a new people. He began to prepare His disciples for the task that awaited them. On various occasions He spoke to them about the life of His new people.

One day, the Lord Jesus, with His disciples, came to Capernaum again. It was customary for every Israelite over nineteen years of age to pay a temple tax of two drachmas. Because of His long absence, the temple tax had not yet been paid that year for the Lord Jesus, and apparently not for Peter either. As soon as they arrived in town, the men who collected the tax spoke to Peter about it, asking whether Peter's master, who had so many peculiarities, would refuse to pay the tax. Peter answered that his Master was used to paying the tax and that therefore this matter would surely be taken care of.

When Peter returned home, the Lord Jesus brought up this issue by asking him from whom the kings of the earth collect taxes—from their own children and the members of their family, or from aliens? Peter answered: "From aliens." The Lord Jesus then said: "Then the sons are exempt."

In the Kingdom of heaven Jesus and His followers were like sons who are exempt from paying taxes. In Old Testament times Israel was still in a state of bondage. Therefore a tax was levied on the Israelites for the temple service. For the New Testament people of God there are no such taxes. But sons who are exempted will voluntarily give of their possessions in the service of their king.

Nevertheless, the Lord Jesus and His disciples submitted to the Old Testament laws as long as the old covenant still was in existence. Not paying the temple tax might give the Jews excuse to turn away from Him. Therefore Jesus sent Peter to the sea with a fishing line. The first fish he caught would have a silver coin in its mouth—the equivalent of the temple tax for two persons. It would be just enough to pay the tax for the Lord Jesus and Peter. Peter did as the Lord commanded and paid the tax. As sons who are exempt from paying taxes the Lord Jesus and His disciples had everything at their disposal. For them there was this lost coin and a fish that held it in its mouth. If by faith in the Lord Jesus we have become sons who are exempted in God's Kingdom, all things are for us even though sometimes it seems as though things are against us.

Like little children. At this time the disciples disputed who would be the greatest in the Kingdom of heaven. What would a person have to be or do to attain that honor? That such a question kept them busy showed that all were eager to be recognized as the greatest.

Such a desire is not in the spirit of the Kingdom of grace. Therefore it may never arise among the Lord's people. Whoever is a citizen of that Kingdom simply receives and passes on what he has received but he does not pride himself on his position in that Kingdom. He knows that God takes care of him and has determined his position in the Kingdom so that it brings the most glory to God.

The disciples did not see anything wrong with their dispute. Hence they decided to place their question before the Lord Jesus. Jesus took a little child and put him in their midst. Then He told the disciples that they had to become like a little child who is not yet concerned about his own position but trusts that his father will take care of him. If the disciples did not live that way, they did not belong to the Kingdom. There is no other way to be a citizen of the Kingdom. The one who becomes as dependent and trusting as a little child will be the greatest in the Kingdom.

The value of children. People who have thus become like children are of great value in the sight of the Lord. Anyone who receives such a child receives the Lord Himself. Jesus meant it when He talked about a little child—but as a likeness of people who have become like children before God. We are pleased to receive people of standing and prestige but despise those who are small before God and little in the world. The Lord Jesus was saying: Woe to us if we do that! That's how things are done outside His Kingdom. There the little ones are trampled underfoot. In His Kingdom that may never happen. If anyone is prejudiced against little ones it would be better for him to be drowned in the sea with a millstone fastened around his neck, so that even his corpse would never be found.

If we ourselves belong to those little ones before God, we must be careful not to become proud. If there was something preventing us from being humble before God, we would have to give it up, even if it meant a great deal to us. It is better to be poor and maimed in this life and saved hereafter than rich and healthy now and lost forever.

Despising little ones on earth seems unimportant, but it really isn't. They have their angels in heaven who are sent out by God to serve them. That's how great God's care for them is. And what settles the whole matter is that the Lord Jesus came to save those who were lost. What great joy there is in heaven over every one of them who is saved! It's like the joy of a shepherd who had lost one of his hundred sheep and searches until he finds it. Every sheep is precious to him. Just as precious to God—even more precious, in fact—is each little one who is saved. Should we then despise one of those little ones and cause him to sin?

Holy communion. Sin may not be tolerated in the Church, the community of the saints gathered by the Lord. If sin is seen there, it has to be punished. And if the sinner does not heed the punishment and break with his sin, he must be banned from the circle of God's people. We may not despise such a person even though he stands outside the Kingdom of God. We must try to win him back again.

There has to be discipline among the people of God. The Lord Jesus gave His disciples power to state what is in accord with the spirit of the Kingdom and what is not. If God's people are of one mind and heart in exercising discipline and prayer, God will bless them and give them their hearts' desire. If people, no matter how few, are gathered in the name of the Lord Jesus Christ, He will be in their midst, He will bear their prayers up to the throne of God and bless their actions.

Infinite mercy. The topic of discipline led Peter to ask the Lord Jesus how many times he should forgive his brother in Christ if his brother sinned against him. Should he forgive him seven times? The Lord Jesus answered: "Seventy times seven." In other words, over and over again. That's the rule in the Kingdom of heaven because it is the Kingdom where God forgives over and over again and is infinitely merciful. In this matter, too, we must show that we are children of the Father.

The Lord Jesus made this plain by way of a parable. A certain king settled accounts with his servants. One of them, who apparently had been in a prominent position, was millions short. His master was thinking of selling him with all his possessions to pay for his debt, but the man begged him on his knees for patience. The master then forgave him his entire debt. That same servant went out and put one of his fellow servants in prison because he owed him fifty dollars he was unable to repay. When the master heard about this, he became very angry. He withdrew his pardon and sentenced the servant to hard labor for as long as he did not pay up, which would mean life imprisonment.

How can God forgive us if we do not heartily forgive those who have wronged us? If we do not forgive we only show that we do not accept in faith the forgiving grace of the Lord. And if we do accept that grace in faith it will change us into the image of the Father. Then we will also be happy to forgive. Just as God forgives infinitely, so should we.

CHAPTER FOURTEEN
THE FIRST AND THE LAST
MATTHEW 19:13—20:16

The obedience called for within the Kingdom of heaven is different from the obedience we find outside of it. Within the Kingdom any thought of merit is out of the question.

Kingdom obedience is obedience of faith. It is granted to us along with the Kingdom. Because this is so, the Kingdom can belong to children. That explains how the first can be last and the last first.

Main Thought: *In the Kingdom of heaven, many of those who are first will be last, and many of the last will be first.*

To such belongs the Kingdom. The work of the Lord Jesus in Galilee had come to an end. Now He was going up to Jerusalem to suffer. But first He worked in Judea for a while. He even crossed the Jordan River and worked in a district of Transjordan that was still counted as part of Judea.

Some mothers brought their children to Jesus. The mothers asked Him to lay His hands on their children and pray for them. Bringing the children to Jesus was the best thing they could do. If He would lay His hands on them, the children would surely be blessed.

If only those mothers with their children would receive that blessing in faith! They must have done so, for they also asked the Lord Jesus to pray for their children. Thus they did not connect the blessing with magic. They certainly did not fully know who Jesus was. If they had known that He was the Mediator and the Son of God they would have valued His intercession all the more. But they did acknowledge Him as sent from God, as a prophet pleasing to God, a prophet whose prayer had much power.

How much joy this display of faith by these mothers must have caused the Lord Jesus! But along came the disciples who pushed the mothers and their children aside and rebuked them. The Master certainly had better things to do than concern Himself with children, they thought. The Kingdom He was proclaiming was surely not for children!

But why shouldn't it be for children? After all, it was a gift! And why wouldn't God be able to give it to children? Why wouldn't God accept even very small children in His Kingdom?

If the Kingdom is a pure gift, then children can receive it just as well as grownups. It is very well possible that children might take precedence over adults, even over the disciples who pushed the children aside. The disciples did not fully understand yet that the Kingdom is purely a gift.

But there was more. Here were children to whom God had promised the Kingdom. The fact was that they were children of covenant parents. The boys had received the sign of the covenant. How, then, could the disciples push them aside? Did they still not realize that the Kingdom was the fulfillment of the covenant promise? That was why the Lord Jesus said that the disciples should let the children come to Him, for to such belongs the Kingdom.

He laid His hands on the children and blessed them. By doing this He made it clear that the children belonged to Him and to His Father in heaven and that the blessings of the Kingdom of grace were for them. If only they would accept this in faith—then and later! In the same way, the Lord Jesus has laid His hands on the children in baptism to bless them. In baptism the children receive the same seal of the promise as in circumcision, namely, that to such belongs the Kingdom of heaven. Children who have been baptized must accept that in faith. It would be terrible if they rejected it in unbelief. And unbaptized children will long for baptism.

Righteousness and the law. When the Lord Jesus left for another town, a rich young man came up to Him. From his youth this man had lived modestly; his entire life had been exemplary. Yet he had no peace. It seemed to him he still lacked something. He had to do something more to gain eternal life. To him eternal life was a reward he felt he had to earn on his own merits. That was what the scribes had taught him. And our own ignorant hearts tell us the same thing. The man wanted to ask the Lord Jesus about it and so he said: "Good Master, what good deed must I do to gain eternal life?" He considered the Lord Jesus as another of those teachers who performed good deeds and taught good things so that people might earn eternal life by them.

The Lord Jesus had to reject this approach first. No man does good of himself and no man can earn anything by doing good. It must be granted to him because only God is good.

The Lord Jesus wanted to instruct this young man further. Therefore He told him that he should keep the commandments if he wanted to gain eternal life. If we keep the commandments and do God's will we show that we are God's children. We then have eternal life. But keeping the commandments is something that must be given to us by God, a fact the young man did not understand. He thought that he had already accomplished a great deal in his own power and only had to add a little more. Therefore he asked what those commandments were. And when the Lord Jesus mentioned the well-known commandments of the second table of the law, emphasizing that love for one's neighbor was basic, the young man answered that he had kept those commandments from his youth. With a certain feeling of disappointment about the answer the Lord Jesus had given, he asked what he was still lacking.

That young man was still outside the Kingdom in which everything is a gift, the Kingdom in which we see God's love and grace and from which we receive everything and for which we sacrifice everything. That's what the Lord Jesus wanted him to discover. Therefore He told him to sell all his possessions and give to the poor. Then he would have treasure in heaven. After that he was to follow the Lord Jesus as a disciple.

This the young man was not able to do. He had always trusted in his riches and he loved the independence which he thought they guaranteed him. He had always been independent and had lived for himself. His seemingly virtuous life had been proud and selfish. His eyes had never been opened to God's love. He still stood outside the Kingdom.

The young man went away sorrowful. A demand had now been made on him which he would never be able to meet because he loved his many goods. That demand he would never be able to meet by himself, but if in faith he had seen God's grace in His Kingdom, he would gladly have sacrificed his own goods for it. Thus the only thing that mattered was for him to see the Kingdom. But in all his pride and selfishness he was still restless, suggesting he had not found peace in his wealth and was very near the Kingdom. If it was a restlessness that the Holy Spirit had awakened in him, he would come closer and be converted. We don't know if that actually happened. We only know that the Lord Jesus sadly watched him go away, because He loved that restlessness in him. "How hard it is for a rich man to enter the Kingdom of heaven!" the Lord Jesus said to His disciples. It is easier for a camel to go through the eye of a needle than for a rich man to enter the Kingdom of God. Thus it is impossible and absurd, we often conclude, that a rich man would ever enter.

The disciples drew the same conclusion. Dismayed, they asked: "Who, then can be saved?" We all possess something in this world and thus we cannot be saved. Indeed, if we still possess anything at all, we cannot be saved. Christ meant this: as long as we still possess something of ourselves; as long as we still have something to which we think we are entitled; as long as we have anything outside of God in which we put our trust; as long as we do not see everything as a gift of God's grace, we cannot be saved. This the disciples had to understand. That's why the Lord Jesus looked right at them while answering, so that they would not misunderstand Him: "With men this is impossible, but with God all things are possible."

It's not necessary to give away everything we have. The Lord Jesus demanded this of the young man only to show him that he was still outside the Kingdom. But we all have to learn we own nothing in order to learn that all our possessions are gifts of God's grace. After all He alone is entitled to them. We then have a place and a name in the Kingdom forever.

The obedience of faith rewarded. The Lord Jesus declared that obedience has its reward. He said this in answer to a question from Peter, who had pointed out that the disciples had left everything to follow Him. He declared that at the renewal of heaven and earth the disciples would sit on twelve thrones, judging the twelve tribes of Israel. For what they did all of Israel should have done, namely, follow the Lord Jesus and sacrifice everything for Him because they saw God's grace in Him. The disciples' conduct would therefore be a judgment on all Israel. The disciples could not boast in this because it was God who had opened their eyes to grace. God's calling in them became so strong that they followed Jesus.

Such honor will be the reward of anyone who has followed the Lord Jesus, who has given himself completely to Him and sacrificed everything for Him. That which we must sometimes relinquish for His sake He repays a hundred times over. Yet the decision to reward is the Lord's. We must not think that if someone sacrificed a great deal for the Lord Jesus he would then have a claim to a place of honor. The Lord judges differently than we do. Besides, all that we are privileged to do for Him, He has given us to do. Thus He can reward our service in whatever way He sees fit. We will receive eternal life out of grace by faith, but what He wishes to grant us by way of honor and position we must leave to His judgment. We will never be able to fault Him for honor and position He may or may not give-us. Many who are first will be last, and who are last will be first.

The Lord Jesus taught this in yet another parable. He talked about the owner of a vineyard who on a certain morning hired some day laborers to work for him. He promised them one denarius for the day's work. Several times during the day he hired additional laborers who were unemployed. Even one hour before quitting time he hired another gang. At the end of the day he paid them the same wages. This greatly upset the workers who had worked a full day. When they grumbled, the owner of the estate pointed out that they had been paid the wages for which they had agreed to work. In a certain sense he had given the other workmen a gift. Wasn't he entitled to do that? Couldn't he do as he wished with what belonged to him? So the Lord Jesus is also free to give His gifts to anyone He chooses. Never will any one of us have any just reproach to make on that score. Whatever we receive, it is all a gift of His grace.

CHAPTER FIFTEEN
LOOKING FOR FRUIT
MATTHEW 21:18-46

God looks for fruit in our lives, the fruit of faith, but does not find it. Therefore His judgment and curse descend upon us. But when Christ pronounces judgment, He at the same time takes the curse upon Himself. Hence there is hope after all. On the one hand, it's all over when Christ pronounces the curse and says: "From you there will be no more fruit for all eternity! " but on the other He creates fruit bearing again.

The disobedient Israel of the old covenant is passing away, but the new Israel is being preserved and renewed in its elect. Life is redeemed because Christ Himself stands in the midst of the curse.

According to Mark it was too early for figs. In the case of fig trees, the fruit appears first and then the leaves. The Lord Jesus found a fig tree that was in leaf unusually early. He expected to find figs, but, there was no fruit. As is so often the case in nature, the leaves grew rank at the expense of the fruit. It is the same in the life of man.

Main Thought: *Christ Himself bears the curse of our fruitlessness in order that we may bear fruit.*

Disappointing fruitlessness. The Lord Jesus had come to Jerusalem. On Friday He traveled as far as Bethany and spent the sabbath there. On Sunday He entered Jerusalem amid the jubilant shouting of the crowds. Before that week was over the people would turn against Him. Nevertheless, He taught openly in the temple. Each evening He went back to Bethany to spend the night there.

On a certain morning, as He was returning again from Bethany to Jerusalem, He saw a fig tree standing by the side of the road. That fig tree was in leaf unusually early: it was just before the Passover feast. Jesus took special notice of the tree because He was hungry. Apparently He had not eaten anything that morning. Ordinarily the fig tree produces its first edible fruit as soon as it is in leaf. Hoping to find something He could eat, Jesus went over to the tree. But He was disappointed; there was no fruit on the tree.

The Lord Jesus saw in this a reflection of human life. God looks for fruit in our lives and we have much to show for ourselves. Our lives are fully developed and seemingly productive—we are, so to speak, in full leaf—but all men are self-seeking and there is no fruit for God.

The Lord Jesus pronounced a curse on this fig tree and declared that it would never bear fruit again. By that He meant to say that the curse would come upon the fruitless life of men in the same way, including fruitless Israel. His work in the midst of Israel appeared to have been without fruit. The people had not let Him gather them together. In the heart of Israel and its elders the decision to kill Him had already been made. That same week they were going to deliver Him up. Therefore the curse would strike Israel.

Yet the Lord Jesus Himself stood in the midst of the curse He pronounced. After all, He had come to bear the curse. Thus He represented the fig tree that was cursed. He would exhaust that eternal curse and thus save His own, including Israel. Israel will also be among the nations as they praise the Lord one day for their salvation.

Our life is also cursed by the Lord; better perhaps: our old man is cursed. But by faith our life will also be preserved. The Lord will see to it that this life here on earth bears fruit.

The next morning the Lord Jesus passed the same spot with His disciples. The fig tree had already withered, miraculously. The disciples were amazed at this and drew Jesus' attention to it. They should not have been amazed because the same power was available to them if only they would believe. If they would speak out of faith they would be able to say to the mountain on which Jerusalem was built: "Be taken up and cast into the sea," and it would happen.

Of course this did not mean that they would be able to perform all sorts of magical feats. Faith is always occupied with the coming of the Kingdom of God. In the service of that Kingdom the disciples would be able to pronounce the curse to remove all obstacles to the coming of the Kingdom. And the curse they pronounced would be effective. Whatever they desired in accordance to His will they would receive.

Believers will also exercise great power, provided they surrender to God's will. Whatever does not bear fruit will suffer the curse and make room for what is fruitful.

Closed hearts. When Jesus arrived in Jerusalem, the scribes and elders came up to Him and asked Him by what authority He did all those things. Who had given Him that authority? This was not an honest question. They didn't really want to be instructed about the Kingdom of God. They didn't want to hear about His authority in the Kingdom because they didn't believe God had given Him any power. They hoped to trick Him into incriminating Himself. Under such circumstances the Lord Jesus could not give Himself to them in His grace. However much He wanted to give them His grace, He would not give them an answer if they did not desire His grace.

Thus He asked a question in response to confront them with their unwillingness to listen and the prejudice of their hearts. He asked them whether John the Baptist had been sent by God to baptize or whether he had baptized on his own.

The question put them in an embarrassing position. If they said that John had been sent by God, Jesus would ask why they hadn't believed him. If they said that John's ministry was his own invention they would have had the people against them because the people considered John a prophet.

It was not the Lord Jesus' intention, however, to checkmate them. He only wanted to point out that they didn't care to listen or want to surrender. Thus they had forfeited the right to an answer about divine grace. To save themselves from embarrassment they answered that they did not know, whereupon Jesus declared in that case He wouldn't reveal the source of His own authority.

Thus He judged the hardness of their hearts. God's Word became a closed book to them. But for this Israel, which was now condemned thanks to its leaders, there was salvation, because Jesus had come to bear the judgment. We, too, ask a great deal—not humbly and submissively, not out of a desire to listen to God's grace which preserves, but to pass judgment on God. Then we deserve to have the secret of God's grace forever closed to us. Still, God will reveal it to us and open our hearts to that secret. Are we listening?

Lip service. The Lord Jesus wanted to penetrate even more deeply into their consciousness to have them discover themselves. They were always quick to appeal to their many good works and their obedience to the law. He wanted to teach them that this was lip service, that they did not perform these works for God's sake. They had never known God in His gracious love. Everything they did was for themselves. In their hearts they were disobedient to the Lord.

Jesus wanted to teach them this again in a parable. Once there was a father who had two sons, He told them. The father said to the older son that he was to work in the vineyard that day. The son didn't feel like it and said right out that he would not do it. Yet this young man knew his father. He was attached to his father and in his heart he acknowledged that his father had the right to ask this of him. Therefore he began to feel sorry for his rebellion and he went to the vineyard to work there that day.

In the meantime the father went to his younger son and told him to go work in the vineyard. He agreed. From all appearances he submitted to his father's will but in his heart he wondered what right his father had to order him around. He did not know his father and was not attached to him. He ignored his promise and did not go.

In the family circle there is also a covenant relationship in which each child has his own place and the father has the authority. This covenant relationship is a reflection of the relationship in which we live with the Lord. That's why the Lord Jesus could use this comparison in talking to the elders of Israel.

He asked them which of the two sons had done the will of his father. When they said that it was the older son, He replied that many of the tax-collectors and public sinners in Israel were like that older son. They rejected the Word of the Lord and ignored His covenant. But then John the Baptist came, who himself held strictly to God's law, and said that this law anticipated the coming of the Kingdom of grace. And when he preached that this Kingdom was now at hand, tax-collectors and sinners turned to the Lord and became obedient to Him in faith.

The elders of the people, however, had been deaf to John's words and were not now moved by the example of the tax- collectors and sinners. This showed that their obedience to the law was lip service. They had not become obedient to the Father who also came to them in His grace through the law. That's why they had neither been able nor willing to hear the words of John.

How wrong we are if we flatter ourselves with the idea that we're obedient when in fact we are not! We often pretend to obey, but do not submit to grace. We still live for ourselves. Yet Christ had atoned for this judgment which He pronounced. Even for such people there is salvation. The power of grace to convert is great enough even for that sin. Do we believe that?

The fruits refused. The Lord Jesus told another parable to the elders of the people. Once, He explained, an owner planted a vineyard. He took excellent care of it, put a fence around it to keep out the thieves and wild animals, dug a winepress in it, and built a tower in which the tenants could stay. Then he hired laborers to work in the vineyard.

The owner himself traveled abroad. At harvest time he sent servants to get the fruit. But the laborers in the vineyard refused to pay up. They wanted to keep all the fruit for themselves. They beat the servants, killed some of them and drove the others out of the vineyard with stones. The same thing happened when more servants were sent.

Finally the owner sent his own son. Surely they would respect him! The son would be able to deal with them with greater authority. But they took the son and cast him out of the vineyard and killed him, with the intention of keeping the vineyard for themselves. The owner would probably not be able to look after it anymore. Besides, he no longer had an heir for it.

"When the owner comes," the Lord Jesus asked, "what will he do with those laborers?" "He will kill them in turn," the elders answered, "and lease the vineyard to others who will deliver the fruits at the proper time."

With that answer they pronounced sentence on themselves. The Lord had given Israel the promise of the Kingdom and the covenant of His grace. Then He sent out the prophets with a calling: they were to tell the people to give the Lord the fruits of faith and conversion.

The Lord looks for fruit from the faith He has planted in His grace. Israel, however, had beaten and killed the prophets; Israel wanted to live for itself. Finally God sent His own Son who asked the same thing as the prophets, namely, that Israel should believe and turn to God in grace. They were going to kill the Son. Wouldn't God avenge that?

Yet, the Lord Jesus would suffer for their rebellion, their refusal to deliver the fruit. He would suffer in order to atone for all their sins. Then there would come others who would be taken up in God's covenant and Kingdom and would not refuse the Lord their fruits.

The stone that was rejected. God would perform a miracle which would bring judgment *and* salvation. The Lord Jesus Christ would be rejected. Precisely because of that rejection He would suffer and remove that rejection. Thus He would become a blessing and save people who once rejected the divine grace in Him. But Woe to those who continued to reject Him! To them He would become an everlasting judgment.

This was what the Lord Jesus wanted to say to the elders of the people. To make this point, He referred to an Old Testament saying with which they all were familiar. In Psalm 118 we read that there would be a stone that the builders rejected because they thought that it was not suitable. But God would make that stone the most important one in the whole building—the cornerstone. That stone was the Lord Jesus Christ. The elders of Israel would reject Him as harmful for the people. However, on Him God would build the whole spiritual temple of which believers are the living stones.

But this Israel under these leaders would then be rejected. God would call out for Himself a people from among all the nations of the world, including Israel. To that people He would give the Kingdom. Woe to those who took offense at the Lord Jesus. That stone would crush them to pieces.

The chief priests and Pharisees understood very well that the Lord Jesus was speaking of them in these parables. But they did not listen to the warning and didn't submit to the Word of grace. They hated Jesus all the more because of the warnings. And they plotted together as to how they would trap Him.

There had to be an end to this business with Him, for that grace He talked about, the grace they did not want to know about, was undermining their position among the people. At that time they did not dare arrest Him for fear of the crowds. The people all regarded Him as a prophet.

CHAPTER SIXTEEN
CALLING AND ELECTION
MATTHEW 22:1-14

The king was giving a marriage feast on the occasion of his son's wedding. It was a joyful occasion. In his joy the king looked for people who would share in his joy. And when the invited guests refused to come, his servants had to go out and bring people in off the street to fill the wedding hall.

God desires fellowship in the joy of His love. He wants that fellowship and looks for it. He insists on it.

Why did the invited guests refuse to come? They were people of the privileged class, people who fully counted on being invited. They thought they had a right to the invitation. They regarded themselves as equal with the king, and this gave them the idea that it was up to them whether or not to accept the invitation. They did not see the invitation as an honor for which they had been chosen, an honor that precluded a choice to accept or not.

Calling can only be viewed as election. We only hear God's calling if we see the great honor in being called or elected.

The man who did not find it worth his while to put on a wedding garment had not understood his calling as election any more than those who were initially invited. He did not understand the honor of the calling. Therefore the king could no more have fellowship with him in his joy than with the others who refused to come. So it is that Christ can conclude this parable, which appears to deal only with calling and with human responsibility to the call, with the words: "Many are called, but few are chosen."

Calling can only be understood as election. Here we have a curious interlocking of calling and election. If election is preached in this way, it cannot possibly give rise to the fatalistic attitude that says: "If I have not been chosen, I cannot believe anyway." It is in our calling that our election is revealed to us. Then we see how completely unworthy we are of that honor. At this point we are made captive, and it is impossible for us to refuse.

In this connection we read that the privileged class, the people who did not see it as an unusual privilege to be invited by the king, refused, whereas the people off the street filled the wedding hall in great numbers. We must allow that to stand in its generality: the people who see themselves as unworthy are precisely the ones who receive the honor. However, we must be sure to remember that seeing ourselves as unworthy is not a prerequisite. The calling, after all, goes out to "many," to the privileged classes as well as people off the street. Seeing ourselves as unworthy does not come until the calling goes out to us and we see the honor of the calling.

Even when we allow the calling to stand in its generality, namely, that people who consider themselves unworthy are precisely the ones who receive the honor, we can still wonder whether Christ had certain groups in mind when He drew a contrast between the privileged class and the people off the street. Was He thinking of the Pharisees in contrast to the tax-collectors, or of Israel in contrast to the heathen nations? When we bear in mind that in this section of his gospel Matthew is often thinking about the calling of the Gentiles and about the gathering of the Church from among both Jews and Gentiles, the latter contrast seems the more likely.

If we start from the fact that the king is determined to find companions to share his joy and that it is an honor to be a part of that joy, we can also understand his radical act of sending his troops to wipe out the murderers and burn down their city. In this way the king avenges the scorn inherent in the rejection of the privilege of sharing in his joy.

Main Thought: *Calling can only be understood as election.*

Invited but not worthy. The elders of the Jewish people looked for ways to trap the Lord Jesus, but they still feared the crowds. Yet the crisis was coming closer. Before long the people with their elders would reject Jesus. They would reject the grace of God in Him, just as they had rejected it time and again through all the centuries of their history. The decisive moment was coming.

How did it happen that the people rejected the grace of the Lord? They did not see that they were just as unworthy to be God's people as every other nation. They did not see that by His gracious election God had adopted them as His people. They were proud of being His special people. They thought they had a right to God's favor. That was why they could not understand God's grace as it came to the people again in the Lord Jesus Christ.

They did not understand the calling as coming from God. Such a calling can only be understood as a great privilege for which God has chosen us. Those who think they are worthy of God's Kingdom are outside of it. If God calls us to His Kingdom, it is not for us to wonder whether we should accept or not. What arrogance that would be! If we see the calling as a great privilege we cannot but accept it in great humility.

That was what the Lord Jesus wanted to try to teach the people and their elders. He still worked on their hearts. Again He did this by way of a parable. He told them that once a king prepared a great wedding feast to honor his son. He had his servants invite guests to come to the wedding. But the guests, people from the most privileged class of the kingdom, refused to come.

That was a gross insult to the king. He wanted to honor them with the privilege of sitting at his table, but they despised that honor—and that at a wedding feast to honor the king's son! The guests did not see it at all as a privilege to share in the king's joy. They imagined themselves the king's equals. Shouldn't he now punish those people?

The king was long-suffering and therefore he had them invited once more, emphasizing the abundance of the food by which he showed his favor to those who were invited. But they went about their business as usual. Some of them even seized the king's servants and killed them.

Now the king no longer suppressed his anger. He sent an army, wiped out those murderers, and had their city burned down. They had rejected the honor of sitting at the king's table, the honor of fellowshipping with the king and sharing in his favor! They did not understand how great an honor it was to be summoned for fellowship by the king. Thus they showed themselves to be unworthy of that honor.

That was the story the Lord Jesus told. He had the people of Israel in mind, the people who for many centuries had been called by the Lord to His fellowship. Although they had rejected the Lord's calling repeatedly, they had again been called to the grace of the Kingdom, this time by John the Baptist and Christ Himself. Yet they continued to despise that grace. They did not see communion with the Lord as a favor that God granted at His pleasure. They did not recognize the great honor involved in the fact that God had chosen this people to be His people. They thought it was completely up to them to accept or reject the invitation. That's why they were impervious to grace.

Now the great decision would be made. God would cause His judgment to come upon this people. The people would be driven away and Jerusalem would be destroyed. The same thing will happen to us if we do not humble ourselves before the fact that grace is a free gift of God which He grants according to His gracious election.

Without a wedding garment. The Lord Jesus continued with His story. The king was determined to find companions to share in his joy. Therefore he told his servants to invite to the wedding feast all the people they found out in the streets. Such people were not among the privileged by any means. Some were very poor; others had always obeyed the king and his laws; still others had often broken his laws. To all such people the king now wished to show his favor, so that they might yet be won for the king and his reign.

Those people did indeed appreciate the fact that the king had invited them. In general, they thought of themselves as completely undeserving of such honor. They hardly dared to come. But because the king invited them in a friendly way to share in his joy, they came. At last the hall was full and every seat at the dinner table was taken. Then the king entered. His eyes scanned the rows to see who these people were who would have the honor of dining with him. His eye fell on someone who had not put on a white wedding garment. Apparently he had failed to do it because he simply did not regard it as much of an honor to sit at the king's table. This was another case of despising the king's favor. Unlike those who were initially invited, he had indeed come, but he did not appreciate the invitation.

The king went over to him and asked him what had prompted him to come to the wedding feast when he obviously had little appreciation for the invitation. The man was dumbfounded. He had come inwardly opposed to the king's authority, and now he was totally disarmed by the king's majesty. At the king's command he was bound hand and foot and cast out of the wedding hall. He encountered the judgment of the king whom he had despised.

By way of this story the Lord Jesus was making it clear that the kingdom of Israel, as it existed up to that moment as the peculiar people of the covenant, would be removed. The grace of God's Kingdom would be preached to all nations. God would call another people to the feast of His favor, a people that was gathered together from among all nations, including Israel. God was determined to have people share in the joy of His love. The Kingdom of God's grace, in which we experience His favor, would be on earth.

God wants to conquer all peoples by the Word of His grace. But among those who will be caught up in that Word will be some who do not see the honor of being invited to the wedding feast of God's fellowship. When the invitation arrives, their hearts do not rejoice that they were deemed worthy of being invited. In fact they despise the king's favor. They will eventually be cast into the outer darkness where they will be in eternal rebellion against the judgment which they nevertheless cannot escape.

Then it will be evident that God never chose them to the honor of His fellowship. They never saw it as an honor for which one must be chosen. They thought of it as an offer which they could either accept or reject. God's everlasting anger will be upon them.

CHAPTER SEVENTEEN
FOR THE BRIDEGROOM'S SAKE
MATTHEW 25:1-13

The parable of the wedding feast already showed us that we may not treat a parable as an allegory and may not try to spiritualize its every feature. The wedding garment did not stand for faith or sanctification or some such thing. Not putting on a wedding garment was simply an indication of disrespect for the honor of the invitation.

Likewise, in the case of the parable of the ten bridesmaids, we may not ask questions like: What does the oil in the lamps represent? Does it stand for faith? Or for the Holy Spirit? That's not what the parable is getting at. Five girls just wanted to go to the wedding party. Hence they did not stop to consider what they would need to meet the bridegroom. The object of five of the girls was to honor the bridegroom. Therefore they gave careful thought to what they would need. Forgetting is proof that you don't have your mind set on the real goal.

Therefore we may not draw from the parable the admonition: *Examine yourself*, whether you really have oil for your lamp. Or: *Examine yourself*, whether your mind is really set on the coming of the Bridegroom. At the end the Lord Jesus Christ offers quite a different admonition: Watch therefore! Have your mind set on the coming of the Bridegroom; let your concern be with the Bridegroom, not self-examination! He is worth waiting for.

We are probably to picture the situation as follows. The bridegroom comes to the bride's parents' house for the celebration of the wedding. In that case the bridesmaids are not far from the house of the bride's parents.

Main Thought: *The Bridegroom is worth waiting for.*

Different intentions. One day in the last week before His suffering, the Lord Jesus left the temple with His disciples. One of the disciples drew His attention to the beauty of the temple. Pride in that beautiful building played a role even with this disciple. Didn't he realize that the favor by which God had given the temple to Israel as a sign of His indwelling among His people had been rejected and forfeited? The judgment of destruction would come upon Jerusalem and the temple.

This destruction the Lord Jesus then pictured for His disciples. At the same time He pointed out that the destruction of Jerusalem was a prophecy pointing to the end of the world. Just as Jerusalem would pass away, so would the beauty of the world, the beauty that people take such pride in.

Towards the end of the world, the Kingdom of grace will be rejected by the nations to which it has come. A similar judgment will then come upon the nations as first came upon Israel. Then when the Kingdom comes in its full glory, there will be a sifting among the people who said they were waiting for its glory. Some will enter into that glory and others will not. The Lord Jesus wanted to express this again in a parable.

Once there were ten girls who were invited to a wedding by the bride and her parents. Apparently they were friends of the bride. When the wedding feast was about to begin, they were to wait near the house of the bride for the coming of the bridegroom. When he came, they were to go and meet him with festive lamps and so usher him into the house of the bride with honor.

On the day in question they all took their lamps and left their homes to go to the place where they would wait for the bridegroom together. But those ten girls were not all alike. Five of them danced and leaped because of the party that evening, but they did not think at all that their primary duty was to honor the bridegroom. That's why they did not remember to bring sufficient oil with them when they took their festive lamps. The other five did think about the fact that they were to usher the bridegroom inside with honor. Therefore they saw to it that in addition to their lamps they also took along a flask of oil.

In our day, too, when history hastens towards its end, there will be people who say that they long to share in the glory of the Kingdom. Yet they do not think about the Lord Jesus Christ. They are not compelled by love to give Him eternal praise or to direct the whole of their lives toward Him.

All asleep. The girls waited and waited, but the bridegroom did not come. It became late in the evening. The five girls who were thinking only about the party were tired from the excitement. And the five girls who were thinking about going forth to meet the bridegroom and honoring him were tired from the strain.

All ten dozed off to sleep. That was really too bad, for now there was no one to wait for the bridegroom. That was a dishonor to him. Now there was no distinction between those who wanted to honor the bridegroom and those who only looked forward to the party.

Will there be a similar situation towards the end of the world? Here the Lord Jesus already hinted that it might well take a long time before the end of the world comes and He returns in the full glory of His Kingdom. Will the situation in the Church in all countries, among all who bear His name, be such that there is no one with his mind set on His coming? That would be a dishonor to Him. If so, those who are genuinely concerned with Him would no longer be able to remind the others to await Him and to have their minds fixed on His honor. Would the churches no longer be concerned with Christ and His honor?

Different judgments. Suddenly someone called: "Look! The bridegroom is coming! Go and meet him." The girls all woke up with a start. They took their lamps and lighted them to go and meet the bridegroom.

The lamps of the foolish girls flared up for just a second because the wicks were still damp, but immediately they went out again. The foolish girls could not fill them up with oil. They asked for some oil from the other girls, but those girls had just enough to keep their own lamps burning during the procession.

On the advice of the others they went off in haste to the store, but while they were gone the bridegroom came and went. The five wise girls accompanied him with honor and went with him into the wedding feast. The door was locked behind them. Then the others came—and found that they were too late. They knocked and asked to be let inside, but the bridegroom declared that he did not know them. They had not taken part in the procession and hence could not take part in the wedding feast either.

The same thing can happen to us if our minds are not set to honor the Lord Jesus at His coming in the glory of His Kingdom. He is worthy of our honor.

We do not know when He will come. That doesn't matter—provided we are ready every moment to receive Him, provided our whole life is directed towards Him, provided we long for Him in love.

Israel was not set for His coming when He came the first time. How will it be with the churches now that we are waiting for His second coming?

CHAPTER EIGHTEEN
THE MASTER'S GOODS
MATTHEW 25:14-30

The third servant in this parable had no enthusiasm for working with his master's goods. He longed for work for himself instead, for his own profit! His master was not worth enough to him that he thought he should work with his property. Inwardly he was not attached to his master; on the contrary, he lived in spirit of antagonism to him and in reaction to his own situation as a slave.

This parable does not legitimize slavery. In fact, at times there was an excellent relationship between master and slave. But the relationship between God and us is such that we belong to Him with body and soul, that is, with our entire life, with all of our strength and with all the fruit of our life. That's the relationship as it is laid down in the covenant. Because this is so, Christ can use the relationship of master and slave as an example.

The condition for using this example as it occurs in this parable is that the relationship between master and slave must be a favorable one. Therefore the picture the third slave draws of his master cannot be correct. It is true that the master himself takes over the slave's words, but only in speaking in the spirit of his slave. The servant believed that in being obliged to work for his master he was being exploited.

That the master is not the kind of man that the third slave suggests he is becomes apparent from the praise he gives his other slaves, and also from his words: "Enter into the joy of your master." Those words point to a personal relationship between master and slave.

Main Thought: *The Master deserves to have us work with His goods.*

Different attitudes. In the parable of the wise girls and the foolish girls, the Lord Jesus had spoken of different judgments that would strike the people because their attitudes toward Him, toward the

Bridegroom, were so different. Now He wanted to talk about the differences in the judgments in yet another way. But this time He wished to relate the different judgments to the different attitudes people have towards the goods He has entrusted to them—their talents, their strengths, their possessions. Did they see all those things as their Master's property? And did they consider it a great honor that the Master had entrusted those gifts to them, so that they would exert themselves for His sake to make the best possible use of them? They would do so if they loved Him and knew that they owed everything to Him and realized that He looked out for their well-being.

But there will also be people who do not want to admit that everything on earth belongs to the Master, people for whom the sovereign reign of Christ is an offense, people who would like to have everything for themselves alone. There will indeed be people who rejoice in the fact that they belong to Him with body and soul, but there will be others who only want to belong to themselves. It was that way in Israel and it would be the same way among the nations to whom He would give His Kingdom after that.

Again the Lord Jesus taught them in a parable. Once there was a rich man who had many goods and many slaves, He told them. Usually this rich man managed his possessions himself and traded with them, but now he had to go abroad on a business trip. In the meantime his business had to go on. Therefore he divided his goods among his slaves so that they would be able to develop them and make profit. To one he gave five talents, for that slave had an aptitude for trading and business affairs. To another he gave two talents, and to a third slave only one. Then he went off on his trip.

It was a great honor for those slaves to be allowed to trade with their master's goods. They would see it as an honor if they loved their master and were attached to him. Two of the slaves did see it that way—the ones who had received the five talents and two talents respectively. They understood their master and knew that he had their best interest at heart. But the third one was antagonistic towards his master and thought that the master was only interested in enslaving and exploiting him. When we are hostile towards someone, we do not understand him in anything.

The first two slaves went to work immediately. The one gained five talents in profit, and the other two talents. Thus they both made one hundred percent profit. But the third slave had no appetite for working for his master. Exert himself for a stranger? That would be crazy! Therefore he buried his master's money. When the master returned, he could give it back to him and there would be no problem. The master would not be able to complain, for he would have back what belonged to him. The master did not have a right to his slave, to all his strength and labor.

In telling this parable, the Lord Jesus did not mean to say that the master/slave relationship, a relationship in which the slave with his whole life and strength is the master's property, is a good one. However, the relationship between Christ and us is like that. We belong with body and soul to our Lord. That relationship was laid down in His covenant.

There are people who are willing to acknowledge this and gladly work for Him with all they have, which really all belongs to Him. There also are people who do not want to belong to Him and do not want to work for Him their whole life long. They are antagonistic towards Him and do not understand Him in His love. They do not understand that He has our best interest at heart—also when He entrusts us with His goods, whether He gives us much or only a little.

Different judgments. The master stayed away a long time. Finally he returned and settled accounts with his slaves.

The first slave was praised because he had worked with his master's goods and had made a one hundred percent profit. "Share in my joy at finding my estate in such good order!" the master said to him. Such was the communion between this master and his slaves. He said exactly the same thing to the second slave.

The third one came to his master and uttered his rebellious thoughts: "You are exploiting us, your slaves, and you appropriate that to which you have no right. Imagine for a moment what would have happened if I had lost money trading with your goods. You would have felt that you had been short-changed. That's what I was afraid of. So I buried your talent in the ground. Here it is. Now there's nothing you can say."

But his master did have something to say. He called him a wicked and lazy servant. "If I appropriate what I am not entitled to," he said, "then out of fear you should have put my talent in the bank. Then it would at least have yielded some interest. Your whole attitude betrays a rejection of me and a lack of regard for the honor I paid you when I entrusted some of my goods to you."

At the master's command, the one talent was then taken away from him and given to the slave who had ten talents. Whoever has something and actually possesses it for what it really is, as property of his master, and puts his heart into working with it, will find himself entrusted with more and more responsibilities. But whoever has something that he does not want to consider as his master's property, something he does not want to work with, actually possesses nothing. Even what he has will be taken away from him. The slave was cast out to undergo his punishment.

That's how people will be judged when the Lord Jesus returns. Those who have possessed their lives, together with all that was given to them, as belonging to the Lord and have worked with their possessions for Him will receive His praise and share His joy at the redemption of life. The Lord will give them great responsibility. But those who lived in rebellion against Him will be cast into the outer darkness, completely deprived. For all eternity they may utter their rebellious complaining.

Israel did not possess the covenant of the Lord and all the covenant entailed with thanksgiving, as a gift; Israel did not use that gift for the Lord. How would it go with the nations of the world, to whom the covenant now came? And how would it go with the individuals who made up the various nations?

MATTHEW:
THE ROAD TO POWER

CHAPTER NINETEEN
READY TO BE SACRIFICED
Matthew 26:1-16

People everywhere are to speak of the love of Mary of Bethany. Christ Himself pays tribute to her memory. But we should be aware that the love of Mary was awakened by Christ's love. Especially now that He spoke of His suffering, that love was prompted to express itself. In Mary's love there was an echo of the great love of Christ, the love that makes Him ready to suffer.

His love governs all things, even the deliberation of the Sanhedrin* and the hatred and betrayal of Judas. The revelation of Christ's great love in the response on the part of Mary's love, a response that Judas does not understand, leads him to the decision to betray Christ.

Main Thought: *Christ's love, by which He is ready to be sacrificed, is in control.*

The true Passover lamb. The Lord Jesus still had a great deal to say to the people and their elders during that last week in Jerusalem. Now the time of preaching to the people was past. The time of His suffering was approaching.

He was completely ready for that suffering. His love of God and of His own urged Him to it. He wanted to win His own, who were in the power of sin and death and the devil, back to God again. To that end He was willing to offer Himself as a sacrifice. He witnessed to that willingness in His words to His disciples. He said: "You know that the Passover will be celebrated in two days. Then the Son of man will be delivered up to be crucified." At the Passover feast He was to suffer and die. He would be like the Passover lamb that is slaughtered. That Passover lamb was once slaughtered in Egypt and

---

*The Jewish supreme court, which was also called "the council." Its members were ordinarily called "elders" and were generally selected from among the chief priests and scribes. —TRANS.

the angel of death whom God sent over Egypt passed by the doors whose posts had been smeared with the lamb's blood. In the same way the wrath and curse of God would pass by those people for whom the blood of Christ was shed. They would be privileged to share in God's favor.

The Lord Jesus was fully ready to die for His people. What wonderful love, a love the world does not know! He gave Himself not for a holy people but for a people that lived in sin, a people that by nature could only hate God's love. Such a people He wished to redeem. He was completely ready and willing.

He demonstrated this by showing Himself openly in Jerusalem in those days and by strongly opposing the leaders of the people. He walked into the lion's den, as it were. It had to be clear to everyone that He was prepared to seal with His blood His works of grace and the words He had spoken about God's grace. And that was what provoked the elders of the people to make their move. They were getting ready to become His executioners. They thought that their plan originated with themselves, but in all their calculations they were governed by Christ's love, for Christ was willing to be sacrificed.

This became clearly evident, for during those days the chief priests and scribes and elders of the synagogue at Jerusalem, who together constituted the Sanhedrin, gathered to consider how they might trap the Lord Jesus with a trick and put Him to death. Thus the goal was definitely premeditated. The only thing left to consider was the method of reaching the goal.

They decided that it should not take place during the Passover feast because there were many Galileans in Jerusalem celebrating the feast. Those Galileans might well side with Jesus and that could lead to an uproar.

Despite their planning, it was going to turn out differently than they imagined because the Lord Jesus had said that it would indeed happen during the feast. It had to be shown that He was the true Passover lamb slain for the redemption of His people. Even in their determination, the members of the Sanhedrin were being governed by His love, in which He was ready to offer Himself as a sacrifice. Truly, His love is in control!

Love awakened by love. Why did the Sanhedrin meet just at this time? Their long-nourished plan could now take on a more definite shape for something extraordinary had happened. Judas, one of the Lord Jesus' own disciples, had come to say that he was prepared to hand Him over to them.

What Judas contemplated was the worst thing anyone could do. He proposed to betray the love of God revealed in the Lord Jesus! What made him do this? For quite a while hatred of the Lord Jesus had brewed in his heart, but a few days before something had happened that settled the matter for him and made him decide to betray the Master.

In Bethany, perhaps on Saturday evening, a certain Simon had given a dinner. This man was called Simon the leper because he had once had leprosy. Perhaps he had been healed by the Lord Jesus. During the meal something had happened that drove Judas to his decision.

A certain Mary, sister of Martha and Lazarus, also lived in Bethany. Jesus often came to their home. Mary always listened whenever the Lord Jesus was at their house; her heart was receptive to His words. Thus she had come to understand more than the disciples. She had understood that in the Lord Jesus, God's love appeared to them. She also paid attention to the words He spoke about His suffering and death. What the disciples had not heard, because they did not want to hear it, she had kept in her heart. Knowing that His death was not far away, she wanted to show Him that she understood and decided to offer Him a token of her love.

While the Lord Jesus was sitting at the table in Simon's house, with Lazarus also at the table and Martha serving, Mary entered the room unexpectedly. She had in her hand an alabaster jar of expensive nard. She went over to the Lord Jesus, broke the neck of the jar, and poured the nard on his head and feet. The whole house was filled with the fragrance of the nard. Then she loosened her hair and used it to dry off His feet.

How she honored Him with this deed! What love and gratitude she showed Him! She made it clear that she understood the suffering He was facing. How her act touched and surprised Him! Would we have been able to do it? We should be grateful that at least one person in those days showed Him that she understood Him. How lonely and misunderstood He was!

The disciples should have appreciated what Mary had done for their Master because they loved Him too. Still, they did not understand anything of her deed. They did see that she had shown her gratitude and the love of her heart. Even then they had not yet reached the point where their love also was able to understand.

Surely they suspected that there was something between the Lord Jesus and Mary that they did not understand. That lack of understanding aroused anger and jealousy. Therefore they condemned Mary's act. That ointment should have been sold, they reasoned; it had almost the value of a laborer's wages for a whole year. Just think how many poor people it might have helped. But what really came through in their words was not a love of the poor but an unfavorable rejection of Mary's deed which they did not understand.

The Lord Jesus had to defend Mary's act. The disciples were not to trouble Mary; it was a beautiful thing she had done. She had demonstrated a love that understood perfectly. Such a love is rarely to be found. The poor, of course, were to be cared for, but if this was not done out of love of the Lord Jesus, out of gratitude for the love God shows us in Him, then it has no value. No one would be able to take proper care of the poor who now begrudged Him this gratitude and love that was bestowed upon Him. Mary had seen something of Jesus' approaching suffering and death; she understood what not one of the disciples wanted to understand. When she poured the ointment on His body, she was preparing for the anointing He would receive at His burial.

Mary's display of love was such pure bliss for Jesus that He said that wherever the gospel was preached, people would talk about Mary's deed. All believers are thankful that at least one person did what they all would have liked to do. Mary showed what love is awakened in us by Christ, in whom God's love has come to us. That love was a comfort to the Lord Jesus.

CHAPTER TWENTY
THE NEW TESTAMENT
IN HIS BLOOD
MATTHEW 26:17-29

I do not propose to take up the question whether the meal with which Christ instituted the Lord's Supper was the Passover supper. I will also stay away from the question whether Judas took part in the supper. Supposing for the moment that he did, no argument can be derived from that fact against the exercise of discipline in the church. Christ treated Judas as a true disciple up to the point when he admitted his intention of betraying his Master.

The main thing is that Christ here reveals the firm foundation of the covenant of grace. His words "One of you will betray me" dislodged from the disciples' minds all certainty they might have thought they possessed in themselves. The example of Judas showed that there is no certainty in man. Then followed the revelation of the firm foundation in the covenant of grace. That foundation is emphasized even more by the word that is translated here as "testament," for this term points to the covenant as a disposition of God's and thus brings out the original one-sided character of the covenant (the covenant as monopleuric—see Vol. I, p. 295 and note).

It is an established fact that a believer cannot fall away. God's favor continues to go out to him. God will not disavow the work He did in him. Nevertheless, the basis of certainty does not lie in the believer—not even in the new life God awakens in him through regeneration. It lies rather in the One who awakens it and maintains it.

In this New Testament sacrament Christ gave us the seal of His faithfulness. Not to see these things, not to look away from oneself, will most certainly bring the believer to the denial of his faith.

Main Thought: *The assurance of faith lies in God's faithfulness in His covenant.*

One of you. Shortly after the Lord Jesus told His disciples that He would suffer and die during the Passover feast, they came to Jesus and asked where they should prepare the Passover supper. They still had not understood; otherwise they would surely have waited for His instructions. He directed them to a certain house in Jerusalem which they would find by following someone in the street. The Lord probably indicated the house in this mysterious way so that Judas would not make plans of his own in connection with the supper.

In this way the disciples were led to the house of someone who acknowledged the Lord Jesus as his Master. That person would immediately be ready to put a room in his house at their disposal. All it took was a word from the disciples.

The disciples prepared the Passover meal. They did so unaware of what was going to happen there, or of what the Lord Jesus meant when He said: "My time is at hand." They did not yet know Him as the Passover lamb whose blood had to be shed so that the angel of death would pass us by.

That same evening Jesus sat at the table with His twelve disciples. In that circle around the table He gave Himself with all the love of His heart. Before leaving His disciples He wanted to show them that love and tell them that He was going to die for them and for all who belonged to Him and also that He would hold them securely in His arms forever by His Spirit. Many of the things He said to them during that supper both moved and saddened them. They were comforted, however, by the love that reached out to them and bore them up.

Suddenly, in that quiet fellowship of love, a terrible statement was heard: "Truly, I say to you, one of you will betray Me."

Would one of them betray this love? However little they understood of the suffering of the Lord Jesus, they did see that in Him the love of God that forgives everything had come to them. Would one of them be capable of betraying that love?

If *that* was possible, what, then, could be expected of man? It made them all feel uncertain. If *that* was possible, if any one of them was capable of it, then no certainty was to be found in any man. It was as though the Lord Jesus had removed the ground from under their feet. Therefore each one began to ask: "Is it I, Lord?"

The Lord Jesus had indeed meant to remove any and all certainty that they thought they had in themselves. If, after we have believed we do not fall away or betray God's love, that is due not to any faithfulness found in us but only to the faithfulness of God who makes us faithful. The ground of our certainty does not lie in ourselves but in God's faithfulness in His covenant. That's the certainty the Lord wanted to give them (and us) after He first removed whatever certainty they sought in themselves.

The traitor unmasked. The Lord Jesus wanted to show the traitor that He knew who he was. The traitor would have to carry out his plan in the awareness that Jesus knew all about it but did nothing to prevent it. Jesus would give Himself up voluntarily for His own. In this way, too, His love was to be shown once more to the betrayer. Wouldn't that put him to shame?

First the Lord Jesus repeated that the betrayer was one who was taking part in the fellowship at the table—a man to whom God's love was shown and who belonged to the circle that God was seeking. According to the counsel of God, however, the sin of mankind would bear fruit in that traitor, leading to the most awful rejection of God's mercy. That would indeed be the road by which the Christ would accomplish the reconciliation of His people. But in it all this man would bear his own responsibility. His life would be marked as the life of the betrayer of the love of God's Son. It would have been better for him if he had never been born.

Once again the Lord Jesus dipped bread in the sauce and offered it to Judas. It was as though the host at the table was once more offering His guest the honor of His full love. He still wanted to conquer him with love. Hypocritically Judas accepted the morsel and, like the others, asked: "Is it I, Rabbi?" Then Jesus answered that it was he.

The decision had been made. The Lord had now marked him as the traitor. At that moment Judas stood up and left the circle forever. All communion between Judas and the Lord Jesus was now broken.

The seal in the new covenant. Apparently the other disciples did not understand what was happening between the Lord Jesus and Judas, or why Judas now went away. They were in need of a certainty that could not be taken away from them, the certainty of God's faithfulness in His covenant. That covenant would now receive its new form.

Up to now the covenant had been sealed by the blood of bulls and goats. The blood of the One who was the fulfillment of all the promises given in the old covenant was about to be shed. Now it would be even clearer that the covenant originated with God alone and had been established solely by Him. Christ, who is the reconciliation of our sin, was given by God. The covenant is like a testament in which the inheritance is granted to us before we, from our side, are able to accept it. Thus it becomes all the clearer that the ground of our certainty lies only in God's faithfulness. This new covenant or new testament lasts forever.

The Lord Jesus wanted to assure His disciples of God's everlasting faithfulness. He took bread, gave thanks to God, asked a blessing on it, broke it, and gave it to His disciples, saying: "Take, eat; this is My body." After that He gave thanks for the wine and gave some to all of them to drink, saying: "This is My blood, the blood of the new covenant, which is poured out for many for the forgiveness of sins."

Through this ceremony Jesus instituted the sacrament of the Lord's supper. He commanded the disciples to keep this supper in remembrance of Him. Such a sacrament is like a wedding ring. Whenever a husband sees the ring he has given his wife his love goes out to her and she, looking at the ring, opens her heart to receive his love. This is what the Lord does when His children sit at His supper. His love goes out to them and they receive His love. In this way they are strengthened in their trust in the faithfulness of God who decreed that Christ was to be the atonement for their sins. Thus the disciples—and all God's people—received genuine assurance after all their false certainty had been taken away from them.

At this time the Lord Jesus also foretold that He would never again sit down with them for supper in this way. However, this supper, at which He maintained the communion of love with them, was a prophecy pointing to the perfect communion He would have with His people for all eternity after the Kingdom of heaven came in glory. He longed for that and all His people long for it too.

Scattered sheep. When He had said this He went out with His disciples to Gethsemane. He knew He would be taken prisoner there by a band from the Sanhedrin led by Judas. Judas now saw his way clear and wanted to get on with the plan; the betrayer wanted to get it over and done with. The Lord Jesus was ready and He surrendered Himself to suffering.

Were the disciples ready too? Had they found the ground for their certainty in God's faithfulness alone? Alas, this was not the case. They still trusted in themselves. Therefore Jesus had to tell them that they would all stumble because of Him that night; they would stumble because of His suffering, because of His readiness to suffer. They all would despair of Him and forsake Him. Only if they had completely looked away from themselves and looked to God's love in Him would they have been able to stand firm in that dark hour. But that they failed to do.

This, too, had been foretold by the prophets. God would strike the Shepherd and the sheep would be scattered. They could not believe that it would be through the downfall of Christ that God would prepare their redemption. The Lord Jesus had pointed this out to them by saying that when He was raised up He would go before them to Galilee. However, they were not ready for such encouragement. Because they were still trusting in themselves, they could not believe in the suffering or understand the reconciliation it would bring them.

Peter, in particular, declared that he would never be offended at the Lord Jesus for he was ready to die with Him. How Peter pushed himself to the foreground! This already showed that he did not live in dependence on God's faithfulness.

The Lord Jesus had to tell him ahead of time that he would deny Him that very night three times. The crowing of the cock would remind him of those words. Peter cast the whole thing far from him. He still had not seen the only ground of our certainty and thus he was also blind to the weakness of his own unreliable heart. We will be strong in times of temptation only if, in faith, we rest in God's faithfulness.

CHAPTER TWENTY ONE
THE FAITHFUL WITNESS
MATTHEW 26:57-75

Whether Jesus is *the Christ*, the Son of God—that's the crucial question. That was the question debated before the Sanhedrin. This question is the issue in the life of every person to whom the gospel comes. We may have many questions about the Bible and about the church and Christianity but we are personally confronted with Christ. I do not say this to separate Christ from the Bible. On the contrary, Christ appears to us in the garment of the Scriptures. Through the Scriptures we find ourselves face to face with Christ.

That's why the hearing before the Sanhedrin was of such tremendous importance. From the very outset the determining question for Caiaphas and the Sanhedrin must have been whether Jesus was *the Christ*. At first, however, they avoided this question and looked for false witnesses. When they were unsuccessful, they turned to the central question. Then they evoked from Christ His testimony, on the basis of which they would condemn Him.

That was terrible, we say, but by nature we all do the same thing. First we get around the central question with all kinds of excuses but afterwards we find ourselves face to face with Christ anyhow. Then comes the moment of decision.

Main Thought: *The Mediator undergoes substitutionary suffering in His rejection as the Christ*.

Looking for false witnesses. After the Lord Jesus was taken prisoner in Gethsemane, He was led to the house of Caiaphas, where the supreme council had gathered hastily. Normally this council met near the temple but this time they were in the house of the high priest.

Three groups of men were represented on the supreme council— the elders of the synagogue at Jerusalem, the scribes or rabbis, who devoted themselves to the study of the Scriptures and the chief priests, that is, the members of the most important priestly families. These three groups were divided into two parties, namely, the Sadducees and the Pharisees. The Sadducees believed they could know all things themselves and were not dependent on God's revelation in His Word. The Pharisees were of the opinion that they could take care of their own salvation, that they did not need God's gift.

However much these two parties differed they were equally fiercely opposed to the Lord Jesus. Jesus had said that God saves us by His grace which He reveals to us in His Word and bestows upon us in the Christ. The Lord Jesus had said that we are totally dependent on God's grace and must submit to it. He had preached the Kingdom of grace, the dominion of grace. That grace appeared in Him because He is *the Christ,* the one sent by God.

They all rejected Him because He said He was *the Christ,* in whom God's grace appeared. Still, at first they did not want to ask Him the crucial question yet—or even dare. It was as though they still shrunk from rejecting God's grace so expressly. Therefore they avoided the question. They had all sorts of false witnesses come in to see whether they could find a basis for condemning Him. That approach did not succeed for the law required that there be at least two witnesses who agreed. Two such witnesses could not be found.

All this time the Lord Jesus said nothing. He saw through their false game but He endured it in silence. He suffered this for us. We, too, bring many false accusations against God: God does this wrong, and for such and such a reason God is not just. But with these false accusations we are trying to escape the main question; we are unwilling to humble ourselves before His grace. How fortunate that the Lord Jesus suffered and atoned for this! Now He can reach out to men who accuse Him falsely.

The accusation about the temple. Finally two witnesses came forward and testified: "This man said, 'I am able to destroy the temple of God and build it up in three days.' " They were false witnesses because the Lord Jesus had not said that. What He had said was: "Destroy this temple, and in three days I will raise it up" (John 2:19).

Those words uttered by Jesus were prophetic. The temple would indeed be destroyed but Jesus did not mean the temple of stone in Jerusalem. That temple was a symbol of God's presence in the midst of His people. His indwelling was complete in the Lord

Jesus Christ. If they rejected and killed Him they would destroy the temple. However, He would rise on the third day. Filled with the Holy Spirit Himself, He would pour the Spirit out upon His people. Then God would have a dwelling place with His people forever. In that way Christ would raise up the temple again.

When the Lord Jesus said these things the people had not understood Him. Often we don't understand it because we don't want to understand. If He truly builds the temple all of life has to be holy to the Lord. Then we ourselves are no longer lords and masters here, which is what we don't want. That's why we do not understand this statement of the Lord Jesus. He has to teach us for us to understand it by faith. He *is* going to build that temple; in fact, He is doing it even now. He sanctifies the lives of all who believe.

Even this accusation brought no reply from the Lord Jesus despite the fact that it touched on His holy work. Behind what they were doing He saw their malicious intention and their hatred. He did not attempt to refute the accusation, not even when the high priest asked Him for an explanation. By suffering in silence He atoned for the hatred that all of us by nature direct against His work of sanctification. Through Him, we also receive the strength to suffer in silence for His sake.

The judgment of blasphemy. Even these two witnesses were not in complete agreement (see Mark 14:59). Therefore their charges did not provide grounds for a condemnation. The high priest now had to come forward with the real issue. He said: "I adjure you by the living God, tell us if you are the Christ, the Son of God!" He was requiring Jesus to testify under oath that He was the Messiah.

This was the terrible moment. The testimony was elicited from Him in order to condemn Him on the basis of it and then reject Him. At that point the people of God, by way of their public authorities, officially rejected the grace of God which had been given in the Christ. All flesh does likewise.

The Lord Jesus was officially being required by the Jewish authorities to testify under oath. Now He would not be able to remain silent. Moreover He would have to witness to who He was and to what God had given in Him. Therefore He answered solemnly: "You have said so." With that He took the oath and swore that He had been given by God for everlasting grace. He did so even though He knew what they would do with His testimony. Thus He was submitting willingly to suffering. That would be to the condemnation of the Sanhedrin. However, by His suffering He would atone for people who, by nature, all reject grace. For that purpose He surrendered Himself.

One more time He wanted to warn the Sanhedrin. Therefore He immediately added some words to His testimony about Himself: "But I tell you this, one day you will see the Son of man seated at the right hand of the power of God, and coming on the clouds of heaven."

Now they would see the reign of God's grace in Him. It actually happened. Soon after His death the report of His resurrection reached them. After the outpouring of the Holy Spirit the grace of God in Him was preached everywhere. The nations submitted to the reign of His grace. How that must have impressed them later! But they did not submit. On the contrary, the high priest tore his robes and accused Jesus of blasphemy. He was condemned to death unanimously on this charge. Now the grace of God was rejected. If Christ had not suffered and atoned for that, no one could be saved. By nature we all reject that grace.

The destruction of the temple. After this sentence the Lord Jesus was an outlaw for them. They spit in His face and struck Him with their fists. Others mocked Him as a prophet. Here they were destroying the temple. They were rejecting Him as the Holy One; they rejected God's indwelling in Him. Moreover, by carrying on as they did, they mutilated whatever remained in them of God's image. How human life was profaned by their hatred!

This, too, Christ suffered in silence in order that He might raise up the temple they were destroying. What endless mercy! And now He builds in the lives of so many. One day God's whole creation will be a holy temple again.

Peter's denial. While the Lord Jesus was testifying of Himself that He was *the Christ* and that God's grace had appeared in Him, one of His disciples was denying Him. At first Peter fled with the other disciples when Christ was taken prisoner in Gethsemane but then he went back. He was ashamed of himself. Hadn't the Lord Jesus warned him along with the other disciples? At the time he had said that even if all the disciples should take offense at Jesus, that would never happen to him. Peter said he was prepared to die with Jesus. Was he now going to flee?

Peter turned back and followed from a distance. John, too, had followed. Because John knew someone in the high priest's house Peter was able to gain access to the house. There he was, sitting in the courtyard by the fire the soldiers had made. He was not there by faith, in surrender to the Lord Jesus, expecting strength and faithfulness from Him; he was there because he was ashamed to flee. His self-confidence had been shaken.

When temptation came, then, he had to fall. And temptation came quickly. He was recognized as one of the Lord Jesus' disciples. First he was spotted by a maid and then, after she had drawn attention to him, by the people around the fire and after that by still another person as he was trying to get out. Peter's Galilean accent betrayed his identity. All three times he denied any association with Jesus; he even denied it with an oath. He said he would submit to a curse if he was one of them. He declared that he didn't even know Jesus. That man was a stranger to him. In all he denied His Savior three times.

That was terrible for Peter—and worse yet for the Lord Jesus who knew what was happening. Jesus endured that denial in suffering even while He Himself was confessing who God was in Him for His disciples. Wasn't His suffering before the Sanhedrin bitter enough in itself without this betrayal on the part of a disciple being added to it?

This suffering, too, the Lord Jesus endured in His atoning work so that He could offer grace again to disciples who denied Him and so that He could bring them to submit to Him in faith and thus be strong. For Peter, too, there was forgiveness. As he was going outside he caught a glimpse of the Lord Jesus looking at him. That look must have spoken to him of the suffering caused by disappointed love—but also of mercy.

As a result of the grace manifested to him again Peter did not flee from the Lord Jesus for good, like Judas. Instead he was brought to repentance. Then he was no longer ashamed of himself; rather, he felt shame at the Lord's love. He went outside and wept bitterly. For him, then, there was salvation. This, too, the Lord endured in suffering in order to atone for it.

CHAPTER TWENTY TWO
LIKE CLAY IN THE POTTER'S HANDS
MATTHEW 27:1-10

In this passage Matthew cites several words as those of Jeremiah, although we actually find them recorded in Zechariah 11:12-13. What Matthew had in mind, apparently, was a combination of ideas found in both Zechariah and Jeremiah. Zechariah writes about the potter and Jeremiah tells us what happens in the potter's house. Jeremiah 18:1-12 should be read in this connection.

Jeremiah saw a potter making a vessel of clay on his wheel. The potter broke the vessel in pieces and out of the clay he made another vessel that pleased him. The Lord could also do that with Israel. Israel might declare itself beyond all hope, but the Lord could transform His people into a vessel that was pleasing to Him.

That's what happened with Christ. In Him life was ruined, just as the potter ruined the vessel that failed to please him. Then life in Him and in His people was reshaped into a vessel of honor. The potter's field bought with Judas's betrayal money points to this idea.

The destruction of Judas is like clay that is not reshaped. It sheds light on the death of Christ. What happened to Judas is what would have happened to us all. Christ endured rejection, a rejection like that of Judas, in order that life might be transformed in Him.

Main Thought: *In Christ life is transformed just as clay is reshaped by the potter.*

The rejection of the covenant Head. In the night of betrayal, the Sanhedrin condemned the Lord Jesus to death. The Sanhedrin however, was not able or willing to carry out the death sentence itself. It chose to hand Jesus over to the Roman governor, Pontius Pilate, who happened to be in the city at the time, probably because of the festivities connected with the Passover feast. To arouse Pilate's interest an accusation had to be fabricated. That Christ had called Himself the Son of God would hardly concern a Roman governor. In a hastily called early morning session, the Sanhedrin quickly formulated such an accusation. It would say that Jesus had called Himself the king of the Jews. An act of insurrection was something with which Pilate would certainly have to concern himself.

Indeed, Christ *is* the King of His people—the people He is gathering out of all the nations. All kings and princes must bow before Him. Even the Roman emperor would become involved with Him. And as for Pilate, he would not be able to avoid pronouncing judgment on Him.

After the Sanhedrin bound Jesus, He was taken away and delivered to Pontius Pilate, the governor. In our minds we see Jesus walking in the midst of the Jews. They shoved Him forward through the streets of Jerusalem. There they cast Him out—the one who was their Head in God's covenant, the one in whom God's grace was given to the people. They rejected God's grace in Him.

This was not the first time they had rejected God's grace in Christ. The Israelites had been doing so throughout their entire history. They had already rejected the Christ of God when they served other gods. And in later times, in their efforts to save themselves by their own righteousness, they had rejected Him again. The delivery of Jesus to Pontius Pilate was but the culmination of that rejection.

Shouldn't God have abandoned Israel forever? But Christ wanted to be and remain the Head of His people. How He must have suffered when they pushed Him out before them! By His suffering He made atonement for the sin of His people. For that sin God rejected Him, and with Him all the people whose Head He was.

Christ endured that suffering willingly, thereby confessing that God's rejection of Him was just, because of His people's sins. In Him, the Head of the covenant, God destroyed life, just as a potter may destroy the vessel he was forming on his wheel. But the potter destroys to form anew. Similarly, God destroyed life in Christ in order to form it anew through Him, to create a people as a vessel for His honor.

Let us not look just at those elders of the people who pushed the Lord Jesus through the streets. Whenever we reject God's grace and refuse to have anything to do with it, we are actually following in the footsteps of those elders. We, too, reject the Head of the covenant, and we deserve to have God reject us. But He wants to transform our lives for the sake of Christ's suffering, so that we will become vessels of honor. Never are things beyond all hope. Let us believe in the grace that has appeared to us in the Christ!

The destruction of life through despair. Judas saw that the Lord Jesus was being led away by the elders of the people. He understood what had happened and what was going to happen. Jesus was going to be killed. That had been Judas's intention when he betrayed Christ, but now Judas was facing the fact. Now he saw the baseness of the Sanhedrin in contrast to the majesty of the Lord Jesus. Baseness had triumphed, and Judas himself had given support to its triumph.

Then Judas felt sorry for what he had done; that is to say, he came to his senses. Earlier he had lived in a whirl of conflicting emotions. He had been carried along by his passionate hatred and had allowed himself to be swept off his feet. Now he came to his senses. He saw what he had done and that he, Judas, bore the sole responsibility for this dirty trick. He could not bear this thought about himself. Thus the sorrow he felt was not repentance in humble confession of his guilt before God. He stood there in unbroken pride. He could not bear to think that he was guilty of such baseness. God's judgment awaited him. He did not think of God's grace or acknowledge the justice of God's judgment. Instead he continued to stand in his own power before God.

How had he ever come to such a deed? We say that Judas was a traitor, a criminal, a thief. True, but these were not his primary or most decisive traits. Judas was an unbeliever! Enthusiastically he had followed Christ as a disciple. He had even performed miracles in His name. Yet, he had closed his heart to what was essential in Christ, to the grace of God in Him, and therefore he had not been able or willing to believe in Him. Judas was unable to lose himself to Christ. Throughout his discipleship, Judas remained self-satisfied. How Christ had struggled, even at the last supper, for Judas's heart! But Judas had not allowed himself to be won over.

From the very beginning it had been amiss with unbelieving Judas. Thus he became a thief. A person who does not find the great thing in life, the great love, the great grace, grasps for scraps of apparent happiness. That was how Judas turned to thievery. Judas had seen Jesus' great love and the responding love of Mary when she anointed Him. But that love was beyond Judas; such bliss he did not know. And because it was alien to him, he hated that love.

That's why he had come to betray Jesus. Judas became the leader of those who took Jesus prisoner. He became the forerunner of the many who do not manage to surrender their lives to Christ's grace and who hate Jesus for this. Betrayal is rooted in unbelief. If we who follow Jesus do not surrender completely to Him, our failure is on a par with Judas's act of betrayal.

When Judas came to his senses and saw what had driven him, he still did not humble himself before God. Yet life for him was not worth living anymore. What he had done consumed his life. There was no turning back. God had delivered Judas up to his evil ways because he had surrendered himself to satan.

Judas went to the elders and told them that he had betrayed innocent blood. The elders, however, said that it was no concern of theirs. How could there be any compassion in those who lived in the same spirit? Filled with despair, Judas threw down the 30 pieces of silver he had received for betraying Jesus in the temple. Then he went out and hanged himself. He wanted to escape from himself— as though one could ever do that! When he fell into the hands of the living God, he realized the full horror of his act. This gives rise to weeping and the gnashing of teeth.

We must not forget Judas. It is indeed dreadful to stare into that hell. Yet we may not avert our eyes in order to continue in sin. As soon as we reject Christ in unbelief, we follow in Judas's footsteps.

When we have seen Judas, we must look to Christ. Only Christ's love could arouse the kind of hatred there was in Judas. How Christ must have suffered because of this betrayal and His disciple's sorry end! In that death Christ saw the hell which He had to enter to redeem us from it. Like Judas, He had to be rejected by God.

In Judas the words of the psalmist were fulfilled: "For lo, those who are far from thee shall perish; thou dost put an end to those who are false to thee" (Ps. 73:27). The Christ, too, is cursed by God because of our sins, in order to redeem us from the clutches of hell. Judas's life was ruined forever, but God would restore our lives to honor for Christ's sake.

The potter's field. Judas's silver coins were quickly picked up. Later the Sanhedrin deliberated about the money. The coins could not be returned to the collection box in the temple to be used to beautify the temple. It was blood money, even though it had originally been taken from gifts for the temple. By these deliberations the members of the Sanhedrin acknowledged their own dirty business.

But they had a solution. It happened from time to time that poor people from out of town died in Jerusalem. The responsibility for their burial lay with the city. With the betrayal money a field was purchased in which to bury these poor. In former days a well-known potter had used this field as his source of clay for the vessels he made.

Like so many events in the life of the Lord Jesus, the purchase of the field was a fulfillment of an Old Testament prophecy. It had already been foretold (Zech. 11:12-13). When it became known in Jerusalem where the money for the purchase of the land had come from, the potter's field was named "the field of blood."

Because these things had been foretold by the prophets and are expressly related to us in the Scriptures, the field acquires significance for *our* faith too. From then on the dead buried in the potter's field rested under the price of Jesus' blood. I do not know whether many who believed in Jesus were ever buried in that field. The field only functions as a sign: believers rest in this earth under the price of His blood. By that price they are redeemed from sin and death. Just as the potter can destroy a vessel and reconstruct it, so God, for Christ's sake, will transform the sinful and depraved into persons who serve Him in eternal glory.

All these things happened to reveal to us the grace conferred upon us in the Christ. Woe to us if we reject that grace in unbelief, for then we will perish, just as Judas perished.

CHAPTER TWENTY THREE
ARBITRARY TREATMENT
MATTHEW 27:11-31

Pilate dealt with Jesus in a way that was totally arbitrary. He allowed the elders to rail against Jesus and then waited to see whether He would clear Himself. Pilate placed Barabbas over against Jesus even before the sentence was determined. He washed his hands and shirked any responsibility in the case, leaving Jesus exposed to the ridicule of the soldiers. Matthew wishes to draw attention to this arbitrariness.

God does not deal with us arbitrarily. It is true that His strict justice has surrendered us to the arbitrariness of satan and of men. That's the result of our sin, in which we wanted to break away from justice and the law of God in order to exercise arbitrary power ourselves. Here Christ suffers that arbitrariness so that we may again find protection under God's justice.

The trial was conducted in the early morning. Pilate's wife had noticed something was happening. Perhaps she had even seen Jesus or heard about Him earlier. After first waking up, she had fallen back to sleep. In her sleep she was tormented by dreams. Her dreams need not be interpreted as revelation. Certainly we should not make her out to be something of a saint! It's true she called Jesus "that righteous man." But that may have been just an impression. Christ had become an obsession with her. She did not urge her husband to see that justice prevailed; she only told him to be careful not to burn his own fingers. Even in this appeal and course of action, there was arbitrariness. When Pilate washed his hands of the whole affair, it was in part because of his wife's warning.

Main Thought*: The Christ suffers arbitrariness so that we may find protection under God's justice.*

Arbitrary accusations. It was still early morning when the elders of the people came to Pilate's hall of justice with the Lord Jesus. Officially they presented Pilate with the accusation upon which they had decided: Jesus had called Himself the King of the Jews. Pilate took Jesus into the hall of justice and interrogated Him about this accusation. The Lord Jesus did not deny it; He confessed that He was the King of the Jews.

He is indeed the King of His people, and He had come to rule them in righteousness so that they might find protection under the shield of His justice. But we have all liberated ourselves from God and set ourselves up as leaders. We want to rule according to the arbitrariness of our power. That's the way the elders of the Jews wanted it too. That was why they could not accept the Lord Jesus and could not tolerate Him. He was their rival.

What could Pilate do with such a King who wanted to rule only in the name of God in accordance with justice? The entire dominion of the Roman empire rested on the arbitrary extension of power. Pilate, too, exercised his power arbitrarily. Christ's ministry was one long accusation against the Roman empire and against Pilate. But Pilate regarded Jesus as a fool not at all dangerous to the state. Even now anyone who acts in the name of the living God and on behalf of His Kingdom does not really have any influence on earth. Men prefer to bow before the arbitrariness of power. Thus Pilate could do nothing with Jesus. He led Him out of the hall of justice and set Him before His accusers. Surely Jesus would clear His name; then He would be let go.

When the people realized what Pilate had in mind, a stream of accusations burst forth. They did not confine themselves to premeditated accusations; their hatred showed in everything they now brought up against Him. The crowd of elders went wild. One arbitrary charge led to another.

But Pilate did not attain his goal, for the Lord Jesus replied to none of the charges. Pilate gave up his task as judge; he did not question the parties to arrive at a verdict but left the accused to clear Himself. And the Lord Jesus did not answer to the charges. In silence He suffered the arbitrariness of men.

Anticipating the sentence. From the hatred apparent in the many accusations, Pilate understood the Jews would not readily set the Lord Jesus free. Yet he wanted to release Jesus, for in Pilate's judgment Jesus deserved no sentence. Therefore Pilate looked for another solution. He remembered that it was customary to release a prisoner at the Passover feast and for the Jews to make the choice. We know nothing more about this custom. The Romans probably used it to give the Jews the impression that they were not a completely subjected people but still had a certain amount of freedom.

In prison at this time was a man named Barabbas, who had already been sentenced. He had committed murder in an insurrection. Pilate probably knew that this rebel was far from being congenial to the Sanhedrin. Therefore he placed Barabbas next to the Lord Jesus and asked which of the two he should release. Thus Pilate limited the Jews to two men between whom they could then choose freely. But that wasn't all. Much worse was that he treated the Lord Jesus as though He had already been sentenced. In doing so Pilate allowed the responsibility of judgment to be taken out of his own hands. The judge did not uphold justice but placed the accused at the mercy of his accusers.

Again the Lord Jesus suffered a violation of the law in the form of arbitrary treatment. It was as if there were no justice in the world. If it turned out there was no justice, under what shield would lives be safe?

A warning from Pilate's wife. While Pilate was occupied with this matter, he received a message from his wife. She had evidently been awake early and had seen something of what was going on. She had received a certain impression of the Lord Jesus and then fallen asleep again. In her morning sleep she had a bad dream about Him. Afterward her thoughts about this prophet of that strange people had become burdensome to her, and so she sent a warning to her husband: he should not get involved with Jesus but get rid of Him.

Here again there was no admonition to do justice. Both Pilate and his wife wanted to be rid of the Lord Jesus. What in the world can heathendom do when confronted with Jesus? What can unbelievers do with the King of grace? At best He becomes oppressive to them. By nature the whole world is embarrassed at the One who reigns in accordance with the justice of His grace. The One who wants to liberate life by that justice becomes a horror to unbelievers. Therefore men reject Him and will not have anything to do with Him. That has always been the essence of Jesus' suffering.

This does not remove the fact that in the message from his wife, Pilate received a divine admonition. It was clearly the time to act in accordance with the divine justice he was supposed to possess. If Pilate failed to do so in dealing with this man of whom both he and his wife had an extraordinary impression, he would never do it. Evident in that impression had been something of God's revelation to them. Nevertheless, they both arbitrarily wanted to dissociate themselves from Jesus. Where was justice for Him?

Pilate washes his hands. Little by little the people of Jerusalem, who had heard what was going on, congregated at the hall of justice. While Pilate was detained momentarily by the message from his wife, the elders had an opportunity to urge the people to ask for the release of Barabbas. Thus, when Pilate turned to the people again, they cried with one accord for Barabbas. And when he asked what he should do with Jesus, who was called "the Messiah," the people cried: "Let Him be crucified! "

The people's demand for Jesus' crucifixion was completely arbitrary. When Pilate asked what evil He had done, he got no answer. There was no answer possible. Jesus had only shown justice and the power of His grace. But that Kingdom the Jews would not tolerate.

Once we, too, were unwilling to endure the Kingdom of God. In fact, no one can accept it by nature. For no reason at all, we curse it. It brings the redemption of our lives, but we can only be suspicious of it and accuse it of making an attempt on our lives.

Now when Pilate did not get the expected answer to his question, shouldn't he have intervened? But he had lost control of the people because he had not allowed justice to prevail. A riot threatened. Hence he washed his hands before the crowd, saying, "I am innocent of this righteous man's blood. See to it yourselves!" He shook off his responsibility, even though he was the governor. Whereas God had placed him in this office, he was obliged by God to do justice. The protecting shield of justice was taken away from the Lord Jesus.

In all this arbitrariness, Christ suffered the consequences and punishment of our sin. We did not want justice and God's law to rule over us. Then God, according to His justice, gave us up to the arbitrariness of satan and each other. That arbitrariness now reigns on earth. But Christ suffered that arbitrariness so that His justice would rule over us again. Believers have been wrested free from the arbitrariness of satan and men and are in the hands of the righteous

Ruler. And God has also reinstated government and justice on earth to be a protecting shield for all men. This does not alter the fact that there is still a great deal of arbitrariness to be found on earth. Believers suffer from that too. But for them it is a chastisement and a trial aimed at strengthening their faith, the faith that they have passed into the hands of the One who judges justly.

The Jews were not afraid to accept responsibility for the death of Christ. They did not do it because they had sufficient reason; they did it purely out of hatred. They cried: "His blood be on us and on our children." They did not know what they were saying.

Later the guilt of that innocently shed blood did come upon them and their children when Jerusalem was destroyed and its people were scattered among the nations. God's judgment still rests on wayward Israel. This is not to say that Israel as a people has been rejected. The opposite is clear from all who have come to faith in Christ out of Israel. It was for Israel, too, that Christ suffered Pilate's arbitrariness. In its elect, this people will also be among the many nations that sing Christ's praise one day.

Having washed his hands, Pilate handed the Lord Jesus over to be scourged and then crucified, but he released Barabbas. When Barabbas was set free, perhaps to be received by the people with a joyful shout, that was a manifestation of the governor's arbitrary way of handling the situation. The Roman judge was not just. But because Christ suffered injustice, God will one day bring justice to Christ and to all who belong to Him.

Mocking the King. The soldiers who were present in the hall of justice, some of whom were charged with carrying out the sentence, wanted to get something out of this affair for themselves. They had heard that Christ was called the King of the Jews, and so they decided to make fun of that. They put a soldier's cloak on Him to represent the clothes of the emperor. They braided a crown of the thorns that apparently grew nearby and set the crown on His head. They placed a reed in His right hand to serve as a scepter. Then they kneeled before Him and said, mocking Him: "Hail, King of the Jews!" And when they had had enough of this cruel game, they began to spit in His face and hit Him on the head with the reed.

Nobody took Him seriously. They all laughed at Him. Even the soldiers dealt with Him arbitrarily. There was no legitimate execution of a sentence, only pure arbitrariness. Jesus stood completely outside the protection of the law. His whole appearance was an absurdity that everyone could poke fun at. The reign of grace of the Lord Jesus Christ is indeed an absurdity for anyone who does not believe. Who is the Christ, and what is His reign here on earth? Often power and its arbitrariness are the forces that rule in this world.

This mocking of Jesus, however, played a role in His atonement for that arbitrariness. Those who belong to Him are being redeemed from that sinful arbitrariness, of which even they are often guilty. Believers are arbitrary with respect to the Lord and His revelation and also their fellow men. Their guilt has been atoned for, and they learn to live a new kind of life. One day all the arbitrariness of which people who reject Him are guilty will become a mockery, for it will have had no effect. Such arbitrariness cannot interfere with Christ's reign of grace over those who belong to Him. That reign will then be revealed in all its reality.

CHAPTER TWENTY FOUR
CURSED BY GOD
MATTHEW 27:32-56

Matthew, who wrote for the Jews, portrays the Lord Jesus as the promised Messiah, as the fulfillment of the Old Testament prophecies, including the prophecy in the ceremonial services. Especially in His suffering on the cross, we see the curse. Christ is like the goat that was sent off into the wilderness laden with the sins of the people. Just as the goat was subjected to abandonment, so Christ was surrendered to abandonment on the cross.

This abandonment relates to Him as the Christ, the Anointed One, the office-bearer. As to His earthly ministry in His official position, God withdraws Himself from Him. This is not true of Jesus as God, or even as man. It is true of Him in the unity of His ministry on earth as the Christ.

By virtue of His office, that is, as the Christ, Jesus embraces all who are His. This is not a matter of His Person, or of His nature. It has to do with His office. If an office-bearer does something publicly, he involves all the people he represents in his action, if he in fact does it in the capacity of his office.

Christ suffered in being forsaken by God to the end. He reached the extremes of that suffering. He thereby exhausted or conquered eternal death.

Being forsaken by God, that is, being abandoned by God's favor, was a full reality for Him. For His people, therefore, abandonment is never a complete reality. They are forsaken by God in order that He may draw them closer to Himself. Even while God withdraws His communion from them, He holds them secure in Christ.

Main Thought: *Christ was cursed by God so that He might obtain God's blessing for us.*

The outlaw. At Pilate's command, some soldiers led the Lord Jesus through the streets of Jerusalem and finally out of the city gate. Outside the city Jesus was to be crucified. He was cast out of the city and separated from His people. He was banished. What suffering that must have caused Jesus, who loved His people with such great love and was bound to them with so many ties!

The act of being led out of Jerusalem fulfilled an aspect of the old sacrificial service. The goat on which the sins of the people were laid was sent out into the wilderness and abandoned to the curse. The Lord Jesus was similarly banned from the midst of His people and handed over to abandonment.

Jesus carried His own cross. He was already weakened by the suffering He had endured, and the soldiers evidently feared that He could not reach the place of crucifixion. Therefore they looked around for someone to carry the cross for Him. But everybody shunned the cross because there was a curse attached to it.

A man approached from the opposite direction, someone who had a field outside Jerusalem, possibly containing his own grave. He had taken a look at his field and was now walking back to the city. This man was Simon, who had formerly lived in Cyrene. The soldiers compelled Simon to carry the cross. He had to be forced to do it, for he also shrank back from the cross. How the Lord must have suffered when He saw Simon of Cyrene being forced to carry the cross! It made Him feel the shame of His cross.

Simon bore the cross behind Jesus. In his heart he must have cursed the foreign tyrants who forced this shame upon him. And think of how he must have glared at the Accursed One, whose cross he was carrying! Perhaps later he came to view it as an honor that he had been permitted to do that for Jesus.

In any case, Simon's carrying the cross behind Jesus speaks to us as only a picture can. The Lord Jesus did indeed suffer the curse for our sins, but we must still carry the cross after Him; that is to say, our sins have to die, and we have to deny ourselves for His sake.

Lifted up on the cross. When they came to the hill called Golgotha, they gave Jesus wine mixed with something bitter to drink. Once He tasted it, He refused it. Apparently the wine was intended to deaden the pain. But Jesus wanted to experience what He had to suffer in a fully conscious state. He gave Himself willingly for our sakes.

Then they lifted Him up on the cross. He was cast off the earth but was not accepted by heaven. Heaven and earth turned against Him. That's what it means to be cursed. To be involved in the curse means that everything is against us.

It was no coincidence that Jesus was crucified on a hill. The Romans did that whenever they could, so the criminals' shame would be visible to all. At Golgotha the shame of our sin was exhibited in the Christ. In that shame God cursed our sin.

This happened for all who believe in Him, for all who believe that Jesus, as the Christ, suffered for all who belong to Him. Those who know that their sin has also been stricken by God's curse and in principle has been destroyed must also die to their sin, by faith.

It was not His bodily suffering that was the worst for Jesus; what was worse, He was cursed by God. This realization was further strengthened in Him by what people did to Him.

His outer clothes were removed and the soldiers divided them among themselves by lot. That had also been prophesied about Jesus. They were already treating Him as someone who was dead. Men had settled accounts with Him. Had His life been fruitless then?

It was here that Jesus felt how God had rejected Him and wanted to have nothing more to do with His Son. Christ suffered that rejection for our sake, even though we fully deserve to have God settle accounts with us for all eternity.

If You are God's Son. Everyone who passed by saw it the same way. They all thought Jesus was dead. It was all the more mocking since the charge for which the Sanhedrin had handed Jesus over to Pilate was inscribed on a sign above His head. Moreover, He was crucified between two murderers. The one who had presented Himself as the King of the Jews ended His life between criminals! Wasn't it ridiculous? The people who passed by therefore shook their heads in mockery.

The leaders of the people still had one card up their sleeve. They pointed out how Jesus had always said that He was God's Son and shared in God's love. As the one claimed to have been sent from heaven and as the beloved of the Father, He had presumably redeemed men. Thus He wanted to be Israel's king. If all that was true, God would not abandon Him now in this way. With God's favor Jesus would now be able to save Himself. Didn't such an end mean a negation of His entire ministry? In the midst of the mockery the Lord felt this to be correct; He felt that God was now abandoning

Him. More and more the Father withdrew from Him, and Jesus became more and more lonely. His loneliness was intensified by this mockery.

Covered by darkness. How the Lord Jesus Christ must have yearned for His Father's love while on the cross! He was the one who could not live for a moment without God's love. Yet here this love was completely taken away from Him. During His life, too, He had suffered, but then there had still been a great deal of consolation for Him. Now all the light was extinguished. Star after star disappeared, until in His spirit He lived in a darkness in which He could no longer see a hand before His eyes. He was completely forsaken by God.

At twelve o'clock noon even the light of the sun was blacked out, as darkness covered the entire land. That could certainly have been expected. The one who is the Head of the world, the one through whom all grace and blessing come to us, was forsaken by God. Was it strange that the light of the sun, which also exists through Him, was removed? For Him this made the horror almost tangible.

The darkness lasted for three hours. It was the time of His greatest suffering. But because of the darkness, that suffering was hidden from the eyes of all men. Then a great fear took possession of Him. A world without God! He, the Head of the world without God! That meant eternal darkness, eternal death—hell itself. In His anguish He cried out: "My God, My God, why have You forsaken Me?" Didn't He know why God had forsaken Him? He knew better than we that it had happened because of our sins. But on the cross He had to live through that answer Himself, as it were; He had to discover the full breadth and depth of the guilt and punishment of our sins and feel their full extent. When would He reach the limit?

He felt the full weight of God's curse and suffered the ultimate horror. He died a thousand deaths as He suffered eternal death for us. That's what it means to be completely forsaken by God. As the Christ, He suffered in obedience for all who belong to Him. He still called God His God. Thus He destroyed the power of eternal death. He suffered for us, suffering what we deserve because of our sins. We all deserve eternal death; we deserve to be forsaken by God forever. By His suffering Christ covered us before God and atoned for us, removing that curse from us.

He did that for all who are His, that is, for all who believe. From all who believe, the curse has truly been removed. They have eternal communion with God and are never forsaken by Him. Because of their sins, God may indeed withdraw His communion from them, but only in part and for a time. For Christ's sake He holds onto them eternally and leads them through this temporary abandonment to a new, more intimate fellowship.

Everyone at Golgotha was deeply impressed by that darkness. But when the Lord Jesus uttered those words of abandonment, the crowd came up with words of mockery again. Ridicule was the only way to overcome anxiety. The people did not humble themselves before the judgment that was manifest in the darkness. Apparently the darkness had begun to lift. The Lord Jesus cried: "Eli, Eli, lama sabachthani." Now they mocked Him: "He is calling for Elijah." And when one of them sympathetically put a sponge filled with vinegar on a reed and offered Him drink, the others mocked: "Wait! Let's see whether Elijah will come to save Him." Their hearts were utterly closed to what was happening. Not only did they refuse Him all pity, they could see nothing of the sentence that was being carried out on Christ by God. We can see that only by faith.

If we see Christ's suffering in this context, we too have part in it, for it also happened for us. We then are freed from the curse as well. Christ had everything against Him: heaven and earth had turned against Him. But if we believe, we have everything with us: heaven and earth are then for us. All things work together for good to those who are called according to God's purpose.

Death under the curse. At last, after hours of suffering, the moment came when the Lord Jesus was to die. He suffered and died willingly for His people. He gave Himself in death. This was clearly revealed at the moment of His death, for He cried out with a loud voice and gave up His spirit. Still, it was death under a curse. He died as the Accursed One on the cross.

For His people it was a great blessing, for He bore their sins. He had identified Himself with their sins. God's curse was therefore directed at Christ only. Now it was as though He, as the Accursed One, still stood between God and His people. He, with the curse that rested on Him, had to be eliminated. Then God could again come to His people and give them His full fellowship.

That happened when Christ died. God also let it be known when at the moment the Lord Jesus passed away, the curtain in the temple, which separated the Most Holy Place from the Holy of Holies, tore in two from top to bottom. Up to that moment God had dwelt in the midst of Israel hidden behind the curtain. There had still been something between God and the people, for sin and the curse had not yet been removed. With Christ's death, however, the removal took place. Now God could come from behind the curtain and assume residence in the hearts of His people. Now He was no longer the hidden God who lived behind the curtain. He was fully revealed to His people in His favor, and His communion with His people was even more intimate.

In yet another way God made it known that the curse was now removed. The earth shook, the rocks split, and the graves opened. Many godly people who had died were brought back to life. After the Lord Jesus was raised from the dead, they appeared to the believers in Jerusalem.

This was a prelude to what God will do at the end of time: He will move heaven and earth. All the dead will rise, and God will make all things new. All the consequences of the curse will then be completely removed. God gave us a prophetic glimpse of that glory in what took place at the death of the Christ. It was then that victory was gained over the curse.

We do not know what happened to those people who had been raised to life. Perhaps they ascended to heaven like Enoch and Elijah. The purpose of this episode in Scripture is not to satisfy our curiosity. What we should do is give much thought to that resurrection of believers in Jerusalem and to the full communion with God that is apparent from the torn curtain. If in faith we see that communion as the fruit of Christ's death, we ourselves will share in it and partake of the new life.

The centurion and his soldiers were so deeply impressed by what happened at Christ's death that the centurion said: "Truly, this was God's son." In his heathen way he meant to say that the one who had died was a son of the gods. He did not properly understand the death of Christ. Neither did he know the gospel.

Christ's death must have made quite a different impression on the many women who had followed Jesus from Galilee to serve Him and were present at His death. His death brought despair to their hearts when it happened, but later, partly because of the signs that accompanied this event, they saw it as an atonement for their sins.

CHAPTER TWENTY FIVE
IN THE REALM OF THE DEAD
MATTHEW 27:57-66

According to Scripture, dying and being buried means entering the realm of the dead. We are not to think of the realm of the dead as a particular place because we know that death brings an immediate separation between those who are with Jesus and those who are under the curse. The kingdom of the dead is the dead taken collectively. Just as we speak of the animal kingdom and the plant kingdom, Scripture speaks of the kingdom or realm of the dead.

Entering the realm of the dead has first of all a negative meaning, namely, that we are no longer in the land of the living, no more under this sun. But entrance into this realm is the result of sin. What this means primarily is that we are forgotten, that our name perishes with us. Then our whole life becomes empty and ineffectual.

For believers that curse has now indeed been removed. Their names will not perish with them. One day their lives will be restored in glory; they will not have been in vain. But this does not alter the fact that believers, too, enter the realm of the dead, that they belong to the dead for a time. On the one hand, death is gain for them insofar as they enter the most intimate communion with Christ; on the other hand there is loss because their lives and names still await restoration in the light.

In connection with the burial of the dead, therefore, we are not to think only of the body. According to Scripture, *man* enters the realm of the dead. Unless we understand this we will not grasp the significance of Christ's death and burial. At His burial not only was something done with His body but He entered the realm of the dead. After all, Scripture usually does not say that He is risen from "death" but from "the dead." As man He also went to "the dead."

On the other hand, this does not rule out that Christ, in the spirit, went to the Father. It all depends on the side from which we view things. With a person's death and burial his presence in the body here on earth disappears; his name here disappears. That name calls for restoration. On the other hand, such a believer is with Jesus.

Christ, too, entered the realm of the dead. The curse fell also upon Him. Therefore He would be forgotten here for all time. His life would be ineffectual and His name would perish with Him. That was exactly the intention of Israel's elders when they sealed the stone in front of the tomb.

However, Christ suffered the curse upon sin *to the full*. He could therefore break open the gates of that Kingdom and rise from the dead. His name did not perish with Him. That victory was won for those who belong to Him.

Main Thought: *Christ enters the realm of the dead to open its gates.*

Buried by the hands of friends. Among the disciples of the Lord Jesus in the broader sense of the term there was a certain rich man of Arimathea named *Joseph*. This man believed in Him but had always stayed in the background. When he heard that the Lord Jesus was dead he went to Pilate and asked for the body in order to bury it. Friends of condemned persons or members of their family often did that. Pilate had no objection.

Joseph and some others with him went to Golgotha and together took the body down from the cross. With tender hands they touched it. It weighed heavily on their arms and shoulders. They wrapped it in pure quality linen and carried it to a new tomb nearby owned by Joseph. He rolled a great stone in front of the tomb and went away. Some of the women were witnesses of this burial.

It was wonderful that Jesus was buried by the hands of friends who continued to show Him love and respect. Still, they did so in the belief that it was now up to them to do what they could for Jesus. It was definitely Jesus' body they were burying and yet it was as though He was not really there. In their minds His life on earth was over and done with. He, too, was finished here. He had gone to the dead, that is, to those who are forgotten on earth. His ministry had aroused great commotion in Israel but now it all seemed to have been for nothing. After a while no one would think of Him anymore.

That is indeed the judgment that has come upon us because of our sin. Before long we die and are buried, and then forgotten. What remains of all our trouble and all our labor? Because of our sin it all turns out to be futile. But the Lord Jesus took upon Himself the curse of our sin in order to gain the victory over it. He exhausted the curse. Therefore His life would not be in vain. This was already forespelled in the way Jesus was buried—by the hands of friends. By this His friends seemed to express the hope that His life was not yet over and done with. Even in death they remained attached to Him with bands of love. His life was not in vain and the life of His people would not be in vain either—nor their love.

The tomb sealed off. The next morning, on the sabbath, the chief priests and Pharisees went to Pilate. To go to Pilate on the sabbath was not a step they would take lightly, especially not on the sabbath of a feast. There must have been something special that prompted them to do it. They were probably well aware of what had occurred after the Lord Jesus died and of how He had been buried. These things made them uneasy. The Lord Jesus was dead now; His life had ended. Their troubles with Him should be over, but now it had to be over for good. His life should not be allowed to have any abiding aftereffects.

They remembered that when He was still alive He had said that after three days He would rise again. They remembered this because it had made an impression on *them* even though it had made little impression on the disciples.

The chief priests and Pharisees did not believe that claim. In unbelief they kept that truth from their hearts. Such a statement can only be believed if we surrender to it and hope for our salvation through that resurrection. Still, that statement alarmed them. They imagined that His disciples might remove the body and then say that He had risen. That would give rise to even worse misunderstandings among the people. Then they would not be finished with Jesus yet. This was what they told Pilate.

Pilate gave them an armed guard and permission to seal off the tomb in whatever way they wanted. And that's what they did. They sealed the stone that had been rolled before the tomb and placed armed guards at the grave. Thereby any chance of deception was eliminated. Then their hearts could be at ease. Jesus was gone for good; His name would perish with Him. The Kingdom of grace which He preached and brought would not prevail. Instead, their idea of men's redemption by their own righteousness would continue to stand. Their seats of authority were well established again.

However, the Lord Jesus by His suffering made atonement for our sins which rested on Him. Accordingly, the judgment that His name would perish with Him was turned aside. He would rise again and live again and His Word and Spirit would move the world. Before long the elders of the people would say to the disciples in alarm: "You have filled all Jerusalem with His name" (see Acts 5:28). Then it would become clear how badly mistaken they had been. The tomb would not contain the Lord Jesus because He suffered and died as an atonement.

Those who belong to Him will not perish in death either. One day their presence on the earth will be restored. Then it will appear that their lives have *not* been in vain and that their names have not perished with them.

CHAPTER TWENTY SIX
THE ONE WITH AUTHORITY
Matthew 28

At the time of His resurrection Christ assumed all authority in heaven and on earth. He accepted this authority as *the Christ*, the Anointed, the Office-bearer. As both God and man, He came into the world as the one sent by the Father, as the Anointed, *the Christ*. As such all authority was given to Him and so He accepted it.

We can say that He assumed that authority at His resurrection although He already exercised it on earth before that by virtue of the work that He was to accomplish for the redemption of the world (see Chapter 11 above).

Thus it is the power of *grace* that He exercises. Temporarily that includes power over His enemies, over sin and death and satan, to conquer them and carry grace through into life and make it victorious. The control over all things is now in the hands of His grace in order that life may be liberated. At His return He will hand back this authority to the Father. Then comes the everlasting Kingdom of peace in which He will also have authority over the creation, together with all who belong to Him.

Belief in the resurrection of Christ involves belief in the liberation of life from sin and death. And if we believe that it also includes the salvation of our own life. On the basis of so-called historical faith we cannot accept the resurrection of Christ. All the disciples are proof of that—especially Thomas.

Main Thought: *The risen Lord has all authority in heaven and on earth.*

Assuming authority at the resurrection. The chief priests and Pharisees had sealed off the tomb and placed an armed guard before it. Jesus was gone and now there was no chance of His disciples' ever being able to spread the rumor that He had risen.

The chief priests and Pharisees certainly must have rubbed their hands together in self-congratulation about that. In all His words and deeds Jesus had said that with God there is grace for men. Yet they did not want any grace or any revelation of grace. They lived by their own wisdom and virtue. If there was grace, their own wisdom would collapse and they would have to account for their "virtuous" lives. But if *they* were in control, there was no room for Jesus. That's why they rejoiced that He would be forgotten in the grave. Their seats of authority were well established again.

The disciples were in Jerusalem too, not knowing what to do or where to go. For them it was just the other way around. If there was no grace, if the whole ministry of the Lord Jesus ended in disappointment, life was no longer possible. And He had indeed been crucified; it was as if God had pronounced a curse on His whole life.

In this frame of mind they spent the sabbath in Jerusalem. On Sunday at daybreak some of the women who had followed Him could no longer stand to stay in Jerusalem. The body of the Lord Jesus had been hastily taken care of on Friday evening. Now they wanted to take some more spices to anoint the body further.

As they went their way they didn't even think about the stone that sealed off the tomb. This shows that the spices were not the main thing on their mind. They wanted to be near the grave because they couldn't stay away from it. They did not think about resurrection. They had not listened to what He had said about His resurrection. That was still far beyond the horizon of their experience. If the Lord Jesus should rise, there would be total liberation of life and a basking in a renewed life in the favor of God. Then there would be a complete reconciliation and a new life—a new world in which they would live too.

No one can believe in the resurrection of the Lord Jesus without also believing in this redemption of life, a redemption in which he himself shares. The resurrection, this obtaining of God's favor, can only be believed by man with the heart. That's why they had not heard what He said about His resurrection. They had not listened in faith, and therefore His statements had made no impression on them.

When they were almost at the grave there was a great earthquake. What had caused it? Christ arose from the grave. Life was liberated from the shackles of guilt and death. Nobody saw it for the guards fled at the first rumblings. That we would have liked to see!

Think what the resurrection must have meant for the Lord Jesus! He had been weighed down with the guilt of our sins but then He entered into full and glorious communion with the Father. For us, too, He entered fellowship. For believers the guilt was gone and life was free.

But then He also accepted authority over all things. He would rule in the grace He had obtained. He now assumed authority in the Kingdom of grace. That would mean the renewal of the whole world. Hence the earthquake as a sign. And the angels would serve Him in His sovereign rule. So it was that an angel came from heaven to roll away the stone for Him. Right from the beginning the angels showed their eagerness to serve Him in the work of His Kingdom which He now undertook. And they still continue to serve Him in that work. In their service they exhibit the power of His grace.

The resurrection message. The women came to the grave and saw the angel sitting on the stone. His appearance was like lightning and his clothing white as snow. No wonder the women were afraid! But the angel said: "Do not be afraid, for I know that you are looking for Jesus, who was crucified." Those women, who were sinful women after all, did not need to fear the shining glory of the angel. It was the glory of God's favor obtained for us again by Christ that shone forth from the angel. Those women were attached to the Lord Jesus—that's why they were looking for Him. Because of the Lord Jesus we can stand in the light of God's countenance.

There before the tomb the women heard from the angel the message of the resurrection. "He has risen," that is, He has broken the power of sin and death. He now stands on the other side of guilt and death and reigns in the power of His grace. Because He redeems the world those women could now share in His glory. They could stand with Him on the other side of death because in Him they were conquerors.

That message was so tremendous that the angel gave them a sign: he showed them the empty tomb. Only for faith is that a sign. Where there is no faith signs have no value. Then one could question whether someone had perhaps removed the body. But faith is confirmed by the sign.

The angel sent the women away to bring the resurrection message to the disciples. They were to tell them to go to Galilee for the Lord Jesus would appear to them there. In Galilee! He had preached there so often and performed so many miracles! There

He had shown them how He redeemed life by His grace. That all seemed to have ended in failure but now He was going to establish a connection with His earlier ministry. Now the crown would be set on all that work. Now it would continue in full force and extend to all nations. By way of confirmation, the angel said, "See, I have told you." He said this so that the women would really believe it. The angel vouched for the things he had said in God's name.

Communion with the risen Lord. Quickly the women left the grave and went back to Jerusalem. There was fear and great joy in their hearts. It couldn't be true! It could not be true that they were living in a new world, and yet, it was true for the angel had said it and they had seen the sign. Thus they hovered between hope and fear as they struggled inwardly.

On the way the Lord Jesus suddenly stood before them and gave them His greeting. As He met them He spoke words of peace in which He extended His favor to them. Thereby He overcame the last bit of hesitation within them. It was true! The new world in which God's full favor shines on all things lay open to them. They went up to Him, touched His feet and worshiped Him. They had communion with the risen Lord and in Him they shared in God's full favor.

Although the Lord Jesus is now no longer on earth as a man, in His Word He still wants to appear to us. He meets us in His Word. He Himself wants to speak to us of His favor. Then, by faith, we have just as much communion with Him as those women. Then all hesitation disappears and the new world is open for us too.

The Lord Jesus gave them the same instructions as the angel. When we meet Him through faith in His Word we must also be messengers of salvation.

The power of the lie. The armed guard, meanwhile, had fled to the city and told the chief priests what had happened. The priests discussed the situation with the elders. Together they bribed the Roman soldiers and told them to spread the rumor that the disciples had stolen the body of the Lord Jesus during the night while the guards were asleep. The chief priests and elders guaranteed the soldiers that they would not get into trouble with Pilate if the rumor should reach his ears.

That's how hardened the chief priests and elders were. This was not only a deception of others but also of themselves. They would not allow it to be true that the Word of the Lord Jesus had triumphed after all, for in their minds there was no room for grace on this earth. They would not permit it to be true and therefore it could not be true. Thus they convinced themselves. They concocted a lie and passed it on.

The power of the lie which denies grace stood there over against the power of the truth of grace. Even the money was in the service of the power of the lie. These two powers still contest each other in the world. Today, too, everything is placed in the service of the power of the lie. But the Lord Jesus continues to claim everything for His service, for the service of the power of the truth. And the victory is His.

In the service of the One with authority. Later the Lord Jesus arranged with His disciples that He would appear to them at a certain time on a certain mountain in Galilee. The eleven disciples were not the only ones who gathered there; along with them there was a great crowd of people who believed in Him. Suddenly there He was in their midst! In those days after the resurrection He was still on the earth but He lived a wholly different life than before His death. We cannot form any idea of it.

All at once they saw Him. Although only believers were present there, there were still some who doubted whether it was really the Lord Jesus. They still doubted His resurrection. If they accepted it they would have to believe that God's grace had won out over guilt and death and that life and the whole world were now being renewed. It was fortunate that the others worshiped Him as God's Son, as the one who granted them the total victory of grace. As a result of their worship the doubters, too, were carried along.

There the Lord appeared to them as King with the majesty of His power. He said to them: "All authority in heaven and on earth has been given to Me." It was given to Him to rule over all things in His grace, to redeem all the nations and all relations among the nations. He was to redeem their whole life, grant them forgiveness of sins and lead them back to God.

To that end He sent His disciples into the world. Through the preaching of the gospel they were to make the nations His disciples so that all the peoples would learn of His grace. Baptism was to be the sign of the ingrafting of those peoples into His Kingdom. In baptism they were to give them the sign of their communion with God the Father and the Son and the Holy Spirit.

Not all the people in all those nations would believe and learn to live by grace. Many would become hardened. But the Lord Jesus would nevertheless accompany the forward march of the gospel with His Spirit. Thus the Word would have great power. The elect would be saved and in the elect the nations would yet be saved. The elect form the actual nucleus of the nations; they are like the cream of the milk.

Thus the entire life of the nations would still be influenced. And the exercise of that power of the Christ will not cease until the end of time. Today, therefore, when the gospel is rejected by so many we must go on proclaiming the Word of the One who rules over all things in His grace.

MARK:
THE KING APPEARS

CHAPTER TWENTY SEVEN
CHRIST AS KING
MARK 1:1-13

Mark describes *the Christ* as King. Here we think not only of the special temporal power that Christ obtained in order to bestow the benefits of grace and lead His Kingdom to victory, but also of the royal office that Adam had received. Just as Adam had been the first, the head, so Christ is now the first, in order that all may have a share in that power. After man fell into the slavery of sin, in Christ he appeared again as king. Christ, because of His obedience, obtained the power to lead His Kingdom to victory. Mark pictures *the Christ* for us in contrast with earthly kings and emperors who, far from ruling themselves, were often the slaves of their passions. Mark wrote for the Roman world. Thus, while the goods of the Kingdom receive greater attention in Matthew, Mark stresses the reign of grace.

John the Baptist appears here as the herald of the King. He preaches the baptism of repentance unto the forgiveness of sins. Repentance is always a turning away from sin—especially from the sin of trusting in oneself—in order to surrender to God's grace. Hence repentance is by faith and unto faith. Baptism by immersion was a sign of repentance which has its roots in regeneration. The old man by which we trust in ourselves goes down under the water; the new man by which we live out of God rises up. Because repentance is turning toward God's grace, it is also unto forgiveness of sins.

Christ proclaims: "The time is fulfilled, and the Kingdom of God is at hand. Repent and believe the gospel." Is there not first of all a threat of judgment in this proclamation? The Kingdom of grace is at hand: surrender in repentance to that grace! That this is the meaning is evident from the fact that attached to the "repent" is the "believe the gospel."

Main Thought: *Christ appears as King.*

The King's herald. At the time when the Lord was about to fulfill His promise to His people, the Romans, a people who had conquered the whole world, ruled over Israel. The proclamation that the Christ had come would also go to the Romans. But how would they receive that proclamation? They, too, recognized a man whom they revered and welcomed as their redeemer. That was the emperor, in whom all earthly power was concentrated. Through that power he was to redeem the world.

But was the emperor able to do that? Not only was he unable to remove the world's misery, he himself was far from being a king. He could not govern himself; like every other human being, he was a slave to sin and was in the power of the evil one. There would have to come someone who was truly a king, someone who in the name of God ruled himself. Only such a man would also be able to be king over others. That man was the Lord Jesus Christ who was proclaimed to the Romans as just such a man.

A king is often preceded by a herald who announces his arrival. Thus there was also a herald to precede the Lord Jesus when He was about to appear among men. That herald was John the Baptist who had been sent by God to announce that the Christ was coming. John would make preparations for His arrival.

The coming of this herald had already been foretold in the Old Testament. God would send His angel, or messenger to precede the royal Jesus who is also God. That messenger was John. In the desert he was to issue a call to the people. They were to prepare the way for the King because the King would come before long. That King was a spiritual king who wanted to reign in the hearts of men. Therefore, preparing the way for Him meant preparing hearts to receive Him. He is the King of grace and men prepare for His coming by turning away from sin, that is, by turning away from a life lived out of and for themselves to putting their hope in His grace instead. This was the message with which John came to the people.

He ministered in the desert of Judea near a ford in the Jordan River where many people passed by. There he summoned the people to prepare for the coming of the King by repenting or by turning away from sin to putting their hope in His grace. As a sign of their repentance they were to be baptized. This meant being immersed in the waters of the Jordan in order to rise from them again. That was a sign that the "old man," who lived out of himself and for himself, had died and that the "new man" had arisen, the one who put his hope in the King's grace. If they hoped in grace, then through that grace their sins were forgiven. The washing with water was a sign of this. John had been sent by God to baptize. That baptism was a sign given by God that He would grant conversion and forgiveness of sins.

Rumors of John's ministry soon reached Jerusalem and spread throughout the whole land. Large crowds came to see him. John spoke to all of them and many were baptized. By being baptized they were confessing their sins. They were saying that, because of their sins, they had forfeited God's favor. Now they believed that God forgave them their sins.

John spoke a great deal about the people living in sin. His preaching made a very deep impression, in part because it was done in the desert. Everything there spoke of abandonment. The image of the desert reminds us how alone we are because of our sins. This impression was heightened by John's appearance. He wore a rough coat woven of camel's hair and around his waist was a leather belt. Besides, he ate only grasshoppers and wild honey. Indeed, he was a strange herald of the King! By his appearance and his manner of life he wanted to say to the people that because of our sins we have forfeited all luxury, all favor in life—everything. Partly because of his way of life, many decided to confess their sins and ask for baptism.

But John did not forget to point constantly to the King. Someone mightier than he was going to come after him. That would be the man who would conquer sin and the devil and obtain God's favor for His people. That King would be both man and God at the same time. He is so exalted that John could never be His proper servant; John was not even fit to untie the thong of His sandals, for John, too, was a sinful man.

John stood so far beneath Him that he could only administer the sign, the immersion in the water. Christ, on the other hand, granted the conversion of the heart, of which immersion was the sign. This He did through the Holy Spirit. He would baptize with the Holy Spirit and through the Spirit He would later give many other gifts and powers as well.

The King's anointing. While John was baptizing, the King Himself, the Lord Jesus Christ, came from Nazareth where He had grown up. He came to the people whom John was gathering for Him. He would be their spiritual King.

He had to be there, for those people went down into the water and came up again as a sign that they went down as "old man" and came up again as believers. But could they ever rise up to a new life in their own strength? No, that they could never do. Someone would have to come who would go down into death for them and conquer sin, death and the devil in his own strength — and then rise again from the dead. Only such a one could truly be King and raise his people.

That was what the Lord Jesus was going to do. As a sign of what was to come, He was now baptized by John. He would go down into death, but then by His own power He would rise again. He could do that because He is both God and man. Thus He, too, went down into the waters of the Jordan and came up out of them again. In the same way He would go down into death on the cross and then arise, conquering death. That new life He would also give to those who were His own. For that reason they now could go down into the water and come up out of it again.

He would truly be King and would rule Himself and give His life to God. He would do this by the Holy Spirit, whom God gave to Him. Through that Spirit His whole life would be dedicated to God. As soon as He had climbed up out of the Jordan He saw the heavens being opened. He saw the glory of His Father's reign of grace, of which He wished to be a servant. And He saw the Holy Spirit descending upon Him in the form of a dove. That was His anointing with the Holy Spirit. Weren't kings usually anointed with oil? That was a sign to them that they were dedicated to God for a special service and that God would qualify them for their office through the Holy Spirit. This King was now anointed with the Holy Spirit. The Father would set His Son's life apart and the Son was privileged to give Himself to His Father. His whole life would come to its full realization even though He would have to surrender it to death.

Besides, the Father also told Him this from heaven, for a voice was heard, saying: "You are My beloved Son, with whom I am well pleased." Thereby the Father was saying that according to His eternal good pleasure Christ, as the King, would succeed in wresting life free from the domination of sin! Through the Son, God would show His great love.

Thus *the Christ*, even though He is the King, did not take on the work of redemption independently but was sent for that purpose by the Father. Therefore we may trust that He did everything in God's name and that His work is truly redemptive.

The King's victory. Immediately after the anointing with the Holy Spirit, the Spirit began to lead Him on into His work of redemption. First of all He would encounter satan, the enemy of God, who had the world in his power on account of sin. Satan was the one He would have to conquer. For this confrontation the Spirit led Him into the desert. In the desolation of the desert, He saw how men's lives were forsaken by God because of sin and how He, too, was and would be forsaken by God.

Satan saw his opportunity. Wasn't Christ thirsting for communion with God and with life itself? If only he could tempt Christ into seeking that communion along the wrong path! For 40 days satan tempted Him and tormented His spirit, but the King withstood him. He was faithful to His anointing. He withstood all of satan's attacks and broke his power.

Thus He was the royal figure who had His desires under control and directed them only to God. To such a royal personage belongs dominion. Once Adam fell and we fell in him. Therefore we do not have control over our desires anymore; we cannot rule ourselves and therefore are not fit to have dominion over the world in which God has placed us.

To Christ it was given to rule. In that desert He was surrounded by wild animals but they did not do Him any harm. They stood in awe of Him because He is truly King. Something of paradise returned there. In paradise even the animals were willingly subject to men. The angels, too, served Christ in the desert. By His obedience He obtained man's dominion over the angels so that the angels serve him.

The King won the victory for His people. If we believe in the one who triumphed, one day all things will also be made subject to us—even the angels. For now, however, we still have to struggle with satan. Yet, the army of satan is a defeated army and the King leads and strengthens us in our struggle. If only we, with the King, take God's side always in faith.

CHAPTER TWENTY EIGHT
THE HOLY ONE OF GOD
MARK 1:14-39

The devil in that possessed man in Capernaum's synagogue called Christ "the Holy One of God." The apostles and prophets, too, are called the holy apostles and prophets because God chose to use them in His service. All that God wishes to use in His service becomes holy. Thus all of life must be holy to the Lord. This is the result of the holiness of God which means that God is Himself and seeks Himself. By His holiness He puts His claim on all of life.

Jesus, as *the Christ*, received a special office from God which claimed His entire life and through which He became Redeemer of the world.

As the Holy One of God He is a strange phenomenon in this world full of self-interest. He collides with the self-interest of men—and especially with satan who has set himself over against God as the only ultimate starting-point. Here Christ appears in God's service to free life from the service of satan.

However, Christ does this by laying claim to this life in the name of God and setting it apart for God. This is what the name *the Holy One of God* expresses. He is not only devoted to God Himself but also claims all of life for God. He makes God's holiness felt here on earth.

Jesus also gave His disciples a special office: service to the gospel. Service to the gospel, however, is just one way among many in which they were to fulfill God's calling. All of life is called to be holy, that is, set apart to the Lord. However, the call to holiness separates us from sin only, not from any part of our lives.*

Main Thought: *As the Holy One of God, the Christ lays claim to life.*

---

*See the Translator's Introduction pp. 16-17.—TRANS.

Calling the disciples. Not long after John the Baptist baptized the Lord Jesus he was imprisoned by King Herod. John's main task was finished: he had announced the King. Now the King Himself took his place as the Lord Jesus began His public ministry in Galilee.

Jesus came with the same message as John. He, too, preached that the Kingdom of grace was at hand and that the people should surrender to that grace in faith. Thus He preached repentance as well. Even though He brought the same message as John He spoke with far greater authority than John, for Jesus Himself was the King.

That was immediately evident when Jesus called His disciples. He had already met several people from Galilee who were with John in Judea. He had drawn those men to Himself by faith. Now that He began His ministry He wanted them to be His disciples and co-workers. He knew that the Father had given them to Him.

He had to lay claim to their whole life and call them away from all other work. God knows what He is doing. When He calls us, we must follow immediately. Then it will also become clear that by this calling He saves our lives. Unlike the disciples, we are not called to abandon our ordinary work for the service of the gospel. Yet we are all called.

Because the disciples had to leave everything behind their calling implied a special testing. Yet the word of the Lord Jesus evidently took hold of them right away. As King His word had power.

One day He was walking along the Sea of Galilee. There He saw Simon fishing with his brother Andrew. He said to them: "Follow Me, and I will make you fishers of men." In that command lay an enormous promise and honor. They would be permitted to serve Him in spreading the gospel and winning people for His Kingdom. But there was also a tremendous calling and a great testing in that they were to abandon everything.

They did not hesitate for a moment. The Word of the King conquered them. It went exactly the same way with James and John, sons of Zebedee, who were busy mending their fishing nets with their father and the hired help. They, too, followed immediately.

It is true that *we* are called in a different manner but the Word of the King must take hold of our whole life also. It is the Word of the King in the Kingdom of grace and redemption.

Victory over the unholy or unclean spirit. Followed by His disciples, the Lord Jesus arrived in the synagogue of Capernaum by the Sea of Galilee one sabbath day. There He taught. In His teaching, too, He acted like the King, with authority. As such He was completely different from the scribes who tried to *exegete* Scripture.

There was so much power in His words that the people were astounded at His teaching. Unfortunately they never got farther than that. They were astonished at His words but they did not subject themselves to Him.

By His Word the Lord Jesus wanted to redeem the life of men so that it would be holy or set apart to God. It was obvious that satan would have to oppose that effort. In this synagogue there was a man who was possessed by the devil. In those days satan sometimes had people so completely in his power that they did not know what they were doing. Without a will of their own they were delivered up to him whereupon he would speak through their mouths. Thus satan thought he had man in his power for good. He had armed himself and made a fortress of human life in order to oppose the power of grace that appeared in the Lord Jesus.

How miserable was such a human life and how different God wants life to be in His redemption! When He fills us with His Holy Spirit, He does not manipulate us through our mouths but we learn to proclaim the praise of the Lord voluntarily.

Through that possessed man satan addressed the Lord Jesus in the synagogue. He said that Jesus should leave him alone and that he wanted nothing to do with Him. Satan knew he would have to lose out against Christ. He is no match for the power of grace. "Did You come," he said, "to destroy us devils?" Today God still grants satan a certain freedom to work but some day he will be bound under the curse. Satan calls that "destroying us." Had the Lord Jesus, he feared, come to bind them at that point? At first satan called Him "Jesus the Nazarene," that is, the man from Nazareth. He did it to mock Him. But afterward another confession was wrested from him. "I know who You are," he said. "You are none other than the Holy One of God, the one who is completely in God's service and who wants to bring all of life back to the service of the Holy God." Fear and panic were expressed in these words of satan.

The Lord Jesus rebuked him, saying, "Be silent, and come out of him." He did not want to be revealed by satan's words. The grace

He brought and the power of grace—that was what would reveal Him. At Christ's command, satan came out of the man, crying with a loud, terror-filled voice at his defeat. He also convulsed the man, tormenting his spirit.

Horror also filled the synagogue. The people were all amazed at the words that had been spoken to them, words that conquered even the devil. But they did not see what had really happened. They did not see that they were also in satan's power, though in a different way, and that Jesus had come to liberate them from satan. They did not believe in Him. This has been revealed to us so that we might believe in Him and be saved. The entire surrounding area in Galilee heard about it, but who believed in Him?

Blessing on Simon Peter's house. From the synagogue the Lord Jesus went with His disciples to the house of Simon Peter. Would all of them in that house, including Simon's wife and his mother-in-law, approve of Simon's leaving his house to follow the Lord Jesus as His disciple? After all, he also had a calling toward his own family. This was indeed true but the Lord Jesus had called Simon to something else. When He calls we must follow. And now He was going to bring peace to that house.

When He entered the house they told Him that Simon's mother-in-law was sick in bed with a fever. He went to her at once and took her hand in His. Perhaps she disliked this man who had torn her son-in-law from his family. But He took her hand, drew her near to Him and won her over. He does that often; He awakens faith in us. Simon's mother-in-law surrendered to Him. He lifted her up, and the fever left her instantly.

Now she knew Him as the Redeemer, who sets our lives free because He redeems them from sin. But He sets them free for the service of God. He is the Holy One of God who sanctifies our lives to God. He does that in different ways. He sanctified Simon's life by making him His disciple. Simon's mother-in-law had peace with that now too. This is evident from the fact that she got up and served them. Christ's peace had descended upon that house. They were one in God's service even though everyone had to serve Him in his own way.

His hand on the Lord's throne. In the meantime the sabbath had passed. When the sun went down and the sabbath was officially over for the Jews, they brought the sick and the possessed from that city to the Lord Jesus. It was soon crowded before the door of Simon's house. Jesus restored many sick people and set free many who were possessed. Just as He had done in the synagogue, He commanded the demons there to be silent. He wished to be revealed not by them but by the word and working of grace.

How this work must have wearied Him! He was actually fighting a battle against the devil, the enemy of God. And He was delivering life from the curse of sin. But He could not do this unless He took that curse upon Himself. He had to take the guilt upon Him and then atone for it later. How deeply human life lay under the curse and the misery of sin! How He must have suffered while doing all that work, seeing all that misery and guilt before God! Yet He would not hear of dropping the work or making peace with satan. In everything He wanted to belong to the Father. That meant that the conflict with satan was inevitable and irreconcilable.

In that communion with the Father, He had to be strengthened time and again. Therefore He got up while it was still night and went to a desolate place to pray. There He consulted with the Lord of hosts and admitted that the battle He was about to fight was God's battle. He asked the Lord for His help. What an enormous assignment the Father had given Him! But for God's sake He did not want it to be any different. Hence He was victorious. He won that victory for His people all alone, as the King. In faith we gratefully look up to Him who did not shrink from the fight nor give up.

The next morning Simon and the other disciples went after Him. When they found Him, they said: "Everyone is looking for You." But the Lord Jesus did not want to go back to Capernaum. The people honored Him because He healed them but they did not see God's grace which delivered them from their sins.

The people in Capernaum would have to learn to reflect upon His ministry. Therefore, He now turned with His disciples to the villages around Capernaum. There, too, He preached and cast out demons because He had been called by the Father to reveal the Kingdom of grace.

CHAPTER TWENTY NINE
POWER TO FORGIVE SIN
MARK 2:1-12

Christ has the power to forgive sins. Then we see Him not just as a kingly figure. Adam did not have this power, even though he was the head and king of creation. Christ has the power to forgive sin by virtue of His office as Mediator. But there is even something kingly in the way He opposes the scribes.

In His office as Mediator, He serves the Father. This is expressed in the words "seeing their faith." In the faith He discovers in the friends of the paralytic man, He recognizes that the Father is allowing Him to reveal Himself. We should not seek to explain these words in any other way. We should not say that He restored the lame man because of his friends' faith. Neither should we say *"through* his friends' faith," as though it is sometimes possible for one person to believe on behalf of someone else.

Apparently the lame man himself dreaded meeting Christ. Read the parallel section in Matthew 9, where Jesus says to him, "Son, be of good cheer!" (vs. 2). Accordingly, it is not without reason that Christ says to him: "Your sins are forgiven." The man may have been worried about his sins. What he had heard about Christ had made him realize what a sinner he was.

Here Christ seized on an opportunity to reveal Himself to the people as having power to forgive sins. How elated He must have been! The purpose was Christ's self-revelation *to all people*—not just the healing of one man.

Main Thought: *Christ reveals Himself as having power to forgive sins.*

Seeing their faith. The Lord Jesus preached in all of Galilee. Because of His miracles His fame became so great that it was difficult for Him to enter Capernaum openly. People crowded around Him. He spent most of His time in the desolate places outside the city. There they came to Him from all sides.

After several days He returned to Capernaum. When the people learned where He was staying, they not only entered the house but also gathered in front of the door.

Again He preached the Kingdom of God to them. How different His preaching was from that of the scribes! The scribes taught that men were to obtain eternal life by their own righteousness, while the Lord Jesus said that God *gives* everything freely. The scribes wanted to have nothing to do with such preaching because it subverted the whole way of their life and doctrine.

The people were surprised at His preaching and amazed at His miracles. But would they see that He had come to redeem life from its sin and thus restore it in God's sight? How He must have longed for an opportunity to reveal especially this to the people! And such an opportunity offered itself.

Four men came walking toward the house. They were carrying a lame friend. They very much wanted to see him well again. That's why they were bringing him to the Lord Jesus. *He* would be able to heal him. They believed that with all their heart. But when they came near the house they could not get through. There was a crowd in front of the door and nobody stepped aside to let them through. They discussed the situation together and came up with an idea. Using the outside staircase, they climbed up to the roof with their friend. Above the spot where the Lord Jesus was standing they removed some tiles and let their friend down through the opening. They lowered him right to Jesus. These were people who went out of their way to help others. They were determined to help their friend to the Lord Jesus.

How Jesus rejoiced at what these men did! He not only saw their love for their friend but also saw their faith in His power to heal. And He saw something else as well: the Father had given them that faith. Thus the Father wanted Him to reveal Himself in His power of redemption. That's what made Him rejoice. He wants so much to reveal Himself and to redeem us—also today! Do we believe that?

Freeing a prisoner. Would He now be able to reveal Himself clearly to the people as the one who redeems life from sin? He looked at the lame man and saw fear in his eyes. Clearly the poor man dreaded meeting the Lord Jesus. He did indeed long to be well again, but he had heard about the proclamation of the Kingdom of grace and God's

174

mercy in it. Through that proclamation he had been faced with his sins by which he had offended God's love and grace. For that reason he feared meeting the Lord Jesus. How would Christ receive him?

The Lord Jesus read all that in the man's eyes. How He rejoiced in it! Now He could tell the man that He had come to save people from sin. Therefore He said, "Son, your sins are forgiven you." In addressing him as "son," He was adopting him in the name of His Father as a disciple. And in the name of the Father He forgave him his sins.

The man must have soaked those words up. He was free, for he believed that Word! He knew that it had been spoken in the name of the Father, and that Jesus had the power to forgive his sins. He had received far more than he could ever have hoped for. For him everything was straightened out with God. Nothing was more glorious for him. That's the way it always goes. If we turn to Jesus, we always receive much more than we expect. Now the man saw clearly that Jesus' words about the Kingdom of grace were absolutely true: grace indeed reigned.

Refuting the scribes. The scribes were present when this happened. Some of them had even come from Judea to see if His teaching agreed with the law of Moses. And now they heard this and were appalled. Such blasphemy! Who could forgive sins but God alone? They did not know that He had been sent by God to redeem people from sin. The fact was that He would make atonement for sin on the cross. Therefore, as office-bearer, He had received the power to forgive sins and grant peace with God again.

Jesus knew what the scribes were thinking. He wanted to win them over by His words for they resisted His work in their hearts and they would also make the people resist. Therefore He said, "What is easier—to say to the lame man, 'Your sins are forgiven' or to say, 'Get up, pick up your mattress, and walk?' You think the harder thing is to say, 'Get up and walk'? People can see that, but I do not work to be seen by men. My task is to liberate the people for God, granting them forgiveness of sins and eternal peace. You cannot see that with your eyes and therefore you do not believe it. Your unbelief only asks for signs. Those signs are not the most difficult, but the liberation of the heart from sin is the thing of crucial importance." In this way Jesus opposed them with His words and showed them their unbelief.

But He also wanted to oppose them with His deeds and take all their excuses away. Therefore He said to the lame man, "I say to you: get up, pick up your bed, and go home." The man stood up at once because he believed that the Lord Jesus also had the power to heal him. Because he believed he was healed. He was able to roll up his bedding and go home by himself.

What a luxury for this man to be able to move around freely! But in this rehabilitation there was something else. To him it was a sign of God's favor, a proof that God had forgiven him his sins. Thus it was a confirmation of his faith. That man was truly redeemed. When we receive deliverance in our life and do not accept that deliverance as a proof of God's grace, then we are not really redeemed. This man was saved.

Through His healing power Jesus had silenced the scribes. But in the long run they did not allow themselves to be silenced for they did not believe in Him. They did not believe that He had been sent by God to redeem life from sin and its consequences. They felt they did not need forgiveness of sins. They came with another doctrine and were not about to let themselves be pushed from their position. It is marvelous to be pushed away from our position by the Lord Jesus but the scribes did not see that.

The astonishment of the crowd. Then the man who had been lame pushed his way through the crowd. The people stepped back, filled with amazement. God's glorious grace, which has sovereign control of life, had been revealed to them. They glorified God, saying, "We have never seen anything like this." They praised God's name. Undoubtedly there were people in the crowd who believed that God had come in the Lord Jesus to redeem life from sin and who, through that faith, were accordingly redeemed from sin themselves.

But many others were simply aghast at this mighty deed of healing. They kept their hearts far from the Lord Jesus and the grace that had appeared in Him. They did not seek forgiveness of sins with Him and did not acknowledge His power to forgive, for they were of the opinion that they did not need to be forgiven.

How many there are today who stay far away from Him! In spite of this, Christ is being revealed. That revelation will serve for the redemption of His people and the glorification of God.

CHAPTER THIRTY
LORD OF THE SABBATH
MARK 2:23—3:6

The Son of man is Lord of the sabbath. By themselves the words *Son of man* suggest nothing more than that Christ was a child of the human race. But when Christ calls Himself *the* Son of man, He is pointing back to Daniel 7:13, where we read that someone like a son of man would come with the clouds of heaven, that is, from heaven. These words imply that He was sent by the Father and point to Him as the Messiah. He is *the* seed of the woman.

The statement that the Son of man is Lord of the sabbath does not mean that man as such is above the sabbath or above the law in general. Man is subject to the law, including the sabbath commandment. However the one who fulfills the law—the ceremonial side as well as the moral side, yet each in a different manner—can reveal the correct intention of the law and bring it into play.

This coincides with something else. Even when it is said that the sabbath was made for man rather than man for the sabbath, this does not put man above the sabbath. The law serves to lead men to the true service of God. In that service the true freedom of man is found. As such the law exists for man, to give him freedom to serve God. The law is there for the sake of man because everything hinges on God. The same holds for the sabbath which blesses life and liberates people from bonds of slavery in order that man may serve God.

The Son of man has come to liberate life from sin, that is, to set it free for the service of God. He does this by making atonement for sin and by the rebirth and renewing of life by His Spirit. Yet this means that the original power of the law in the covenant of grace is restored. Christ brings out clearly the original intention of the law. In that sense He is Lord of the sabbath; He sets life free by the law. That this also entails the end of any ceremonial aspects that were still connected with the fourth commandment need not be discussed here any further.

Even the example of David eating the temple showbread does

not permit us to conclude in some general way that necessity is sometimes a ground for breaking the law. It would have been in conflict with the intention of the law—which is to set life free for the service of God—if David and his men had died of hunger while there was showbread available. This was especially true for David, who, as a type of *the Christ*, was supposed to redeem life in Israel.

The prohibition against plucking ears of grain on the sabbath since such activity could be viewed as belonging to the harvest had been issued by the scribes and was evidence of their misconception about the law, their failure to understand the law as serving the redemption of life. That's the reason why Christ released His disciples from that prohibition.

Main Thought: *The Son of man is Lord also of the sabbath.*

The sabbath for man. One day the Lord Jesus and His disciples were walking through the grainfields. It was the sabbath, the day of rest. How wonderful that God instituted the day of rest for us so that we may rest one day out of every seven. What grace He shows us in that provision! Through the sabbath commandment He proves that in His mercy He still remembers sinful human life. He does this for Christ's sake, because He wishes to reconcile human life. What a blessing this day of rest brings with it! True, many people reject that blessing, but for believers the sabbath is proof that God for Christ's sake will set life free from the slavery of sin. What a luxury that day of rest can be!

The Lord Jesus and His disciples must also have enjoyed that day of rest and God's favor in it. But the scribes and the Pharisees had turned it into something completely different. They had concocted many additional manmade commands. The people were not allowed to do this or that on the sabbath. Those commands became a heavy burden. Life on the sabbath had come to be tied down with restraints and the people did not enjoy the freedom with which Christ wished to set life free. This had to be, for if we try to earn our own salvation the burdens we place on ourselves and others become more and more heavy. But if we believe in God's grace, which sets us free, then everything God gives and commands leads to that freedom. The two conflicting views of the sabbath just had to collide. And collide they did, on that very day.

While the disciples were walking through the fields, they plucked some grain, rubbed the kernels from the ears, and ate them. There was nothing wrong with that. People walking along the fields were allowed to pluck from the edges. But suddenly some Pharisees appeared on the scene. Where had they come from so suddenly? They addressed the Lord Jesus and asked Him whether He realized that it was not permissible to pluck grain on the sabbath. That was one of those additional manmade commandments. Didn't plucking grain belong to the harvest? But harvesting was not allowed on the sabbath. They were watching the Lord Jesus continuously and were glad they could catch His disciples trespassing the law.

The rule they spoke of was not one of the Lord's commandments, the intention of which is always to set life free. It was a commandment made by the scribes, a commandment that put life in bondage. Therefore the Lord Jesus did not try to avoid their attack. Instead He tried to convince them that they had a mistaken idea about the sabbath and the law as a whole. He reminded them about a story from David's life. Once, when David and his men were hungry, they ate of the showbread, which was not to be eaten by anyone except the priests. And it didn't enter the minds of the Pharisees to disapprove of that deed on David's part. After all, David was Israel's king and deliverer. But if that was permissible then, wasn't it evident that the law had not been given to stifle and kill life but rather to be a blessing for life? The law existed to lead life to the love and service of God. In this way life becomes truly liberated.

It was the same with the sabbath. God had instituted the sabbath to bless man by it and to let him enjoy the freedom of serving the Lord. Man had not been created to fulfill the sabbath commandment as a heavy duty, the way a slave can be assigned a task without any enjoyment of his master's favor. What did the Pharisees make of the Lord anyhow? Did they think that the Lord did not sustain His people by His favor in the covenant of grace? Did they think He kept them far from Him and made them serve Him in unrelieved bondage?

It is indeed true that if we reject the Lord, the law becomes a curse to us. But that was exactly why the Lord Jesus had come—to remove that curse of the law from us by atoning for our sins. Thus He made the law to be a blessing for our lives again. By the law we now know the will of our Father in heaven, and in the way of obedience we live in communion with Him.

The Lord Jesus, who again brings us the blessing of the law, is the only one who understands the Father's will perfectly and can tell us about it again. He makes the sabbath a blessing and is able to tell us how God wants us to keep the day of rest. Thus He did not give in to the interpretation of the Pharisees and did not forbid His disciples to pluck the grain. It was not His intention to put our lives in bondage; He wanted to have His people understand the glory of God's law.

Doing good on the sabbath. The dispute on this sabbath day between the Lord Jesus and the Pharisees had not come to an end yet! God governed things in such a way that on that day it would become very clear what the purpose of the sabbath really was.

That same day the Lord Jesus went to the synagogue. When He entered, He saw a man whose hand had stopped growing and had withered. He also found the Pharisees there again, watching Him to see if He would heal the man on the sabbath. That was not permitted either, according to them, for healing was working. Didn't they see that by healing that hand and thereby making it possible for that man to do his work again, the Lord Jesus would be saving the man's life from depressing misery? And didn't they recognize this as a wonderful sign of His coming to redeem life from sin and all its consequences? What a wonderful fulfillment of the meaning of the sabbath if on that day the Lord Jesus would restore a human being!

That was one reason why He wished to heal the man, but He also wanted to oppose the Pharisees, who so badly obscured the will of God. He ordered the man to stand up in the midst of the people who were gathered in the synagogue. Everyone would see what happened and would realize the wonderful meaning of the sabbath.

Afterwards the Lord Jesus asked the Pharisees what was permitted on the sabbath—doing good or doing evil, saving people or killing them? *He* wanted to do good to someone and save his life, but the Pharisees wanted to do the Lord Jesus harm and were thinking of a way to kill Him. Who, then, was trying to do justice to the meaning of the sabbath?

When they did not want to answer that question because they would have had to condemn themselves, He looked around at them one by one with anger in His eyes. He raged against this distortion of the Father's will. At the same time, however, He was grieved at the hardness of their hearts. How could they oppose the grace of God? If only we could be angry like that! If only we could show our anger while at the same time being grieved at the sinful rejection of the Lord. Our anger would never turn into a passion that carries us away, and then our anger would never spring from a wrong motive either.

He said to the man with the withered hand: "Stretch out your hand!" Wasn't that a ridiculous command? How would this man be able to stretch out his hand? Because it was withered, it had lost its strength. Yet, the man managed to obey! He did it, and the hand was made well just like his other hand.

What happened? At the moment the Lord Jesus ordered the man to stretch out his hand, His healing power also went out to him. How fortunate that this man did not say: "But You know that I cannot stretch out that hand." On the contrary, he believed that at the Lord's command he would be able to do it. By means of that faith he was healed.

Nowadays so many people say, "I cannot believe and I cannot repent." Therefore they do not hear the Word of God. In unbelief they oppose the Word and the Spirit of the Lord, not accepting that the Word and Spirit are able to redeem them. How many there are who close their hearts in unbelief! If we listen in faith, we find the redemption of our life.

The Pharisees did not come to repentance by all this. They did not want to turn away from their conception of the law and from their thoughts about the Lord. They did not want to recognize that He was near with His grace. On the contrary, they left the synagogue and consulted with the people who sided with Herod, the foreign king of the land. What they talked about was how they might kill Him. Without those Herodians they would not get anywhere, for Herod would have to cooperate in this matter. Thus they began to plot a murder.

How easily people are brought to great sins by hypocrisy and willful worship! What keeps us from sin and gives us the victory over it is faith in the grace of God, who liberates life. This blessing the Lord Jesus Christ prepared for us by His coming.

MARK:
WHO IS THIS MAN?

CHAPTER THIRTY ONE
NOT KNOWN
MARK 3:7-35

Christ warns the Pharisees about the sin against the Holy Spirit. They would be committing this sin if they insisted on ascribing His work to an unclean spirit. The fact that they would go so far as to blaspheme the Holy Spirit shows that Christ was performing His work through the operation of the Spirit. That's how He reveals Himself here.

Driven by the Holy Spirit and working completely from, through and unto God, Jesus is unrecognizable. His friends think He is beside Himself. To man such a spirit-driven life is utter madness. In the judgment of the Pharisees He is possessed. They don't know the difference between being possessed by an unclean spirit and being inspired by the Holy Spirit. They don't know the difference because they don't want to know.

The sin against the Holy Spirit cannot be discussed here in detail. Yet, a couple of brief comments are in order. Christ revealed Himself in His work as inspired by the Holy Spirit. But even after the clearest revelation and declaration of the Lord, the Pharisees continued to look upon Him as one possessed. At that point their sin became satanic. It was clear that their aim was not just to maintain their position among the people; they appeared to be driven by a single-minded hatred of the truth of God's grace. In all human sins there are elements of foolishness and ignorance, for we think we can achieve something by our sins. But in satanic sin there is not a single element of foolishness left. Satan's sin is a premeditated expression of unmitigated hatred.

Main Thought: *Christ, driven by the Holy Spirit, is not acknowledged.*

A terrific commotion. The rumors about the Lord Jesus, about the miracles He performed and the words He spoke, went through the

whole country and beyond its borders. People came to Him from all
directions, even from Idumea, formerly known as Edom. Through
the Herods this country was closely connected with Israel.

One day the Lord Jesus was with His disciples on the shore of
the Sea of Capernaum. The crowd pressed around Him. The sick
pushed forward especially, just to be able to touch Him and thereby
find healing. This was dangerous. He had to ask His disciples to
keep a boat nearby at all times so that He could board it when the
crowd pushed Him too close to the water.

People possessed by unclean spirits fell on their knees before
Him and cried: "You are God's Son." They saw that He was the
one in whom the full grace of God has come to men. Immediately
He forbade those spirits to reveal Him. He was to be revealed not
by satan but by His own words and work so that He would have
personal contact with the people.

Yet He welcomed the terrific commotion among the people.
Through God's grace He wanted to win the entire nation—not just
a person here and there but the entire nation in its hidden life and
public life. Christ came to redeem all of life, to become King over
life as a whole.

Organizing the work. The situation was untenable, for He could not
throw His blessings around in general. He was especially interested
in a more personal sort of contact by which He could win people
for the Father. The conversion of life had to begin on the inside and
work itself out. Therefore He withdrew from the city to go to the
hills outside. There He called to Himself those whom He desired.
He could have His disciples bring the people to Him.

There must have been many people who spent unforgettable
hours with Him there, hours in which the light of the Kingdom of
grace dawned upon them. They were privileged people, but we may
be just as privileged since He still wants to speak to us through His
Word. When we hear the Word, it becomes just as intimate for us as
it was for those people among the hills of Galilee. Then we belong
to the people for whom He came and to whom He gave His Word.

On the other hand, He did not want to bypass the masses.
Everyone had to hear about Him and about the salvation that had
appeared in Him. Therefore He appointed twelve of His disciples
to be apostles, missionaries proclaiming the gospel of the Kingdom

everywhere in Israel. They were also to be with Him daily to learn a lot about the Kingdom of grace, first for themselves. And when He sent them out, He gave them power to heal the sick and cast out demons. By those signs they were to show that in the Kingdom of grace life is set free from sin and its consequences.

The twelve were to form the foundation of the new people of God, which He would gather to Himself from among all the nations of the world. Jesus would make them faithful by His Word and Spirit and also prepare them for their task. Woe to those who did not subject themselves to the gospel of grace! Unfortunately, there was one among those twelve who was not going to subject himself. That disciple was Judas, who later betrayed Him. Judas went along with the preaching and even performed miracles in the name of the Lord Jesus, but he shoved the yoke of the gospel from his shoulders, the wonderful yoke that the Lord Jesus had laid on him.

Beside Himself? After that it happened that the Lord Jesus and His disciples came into a house. Immediately a crowd gathered. He was so busy with that crowd that He and His disciples did not get a chance to eat. He gave Himself to the crowd uninterruptedly. The Holy Spirit urged Him on in this. Because of the Spirit His work for the Father and His Kingdom allowed Him no rest.

"What is the point of all this?" His friends asked themselves. "He will wear Himself out and it doesn't serve any purpose. He will not permit Himself to be made king. He is not becoming a leader of the people to liberate them from the Roman yoke, nor does He desire a position of honor like the scribes. Yet He does not stay in hiding either to have a religious conversation with someone or other. Instead He stirs up the whole people. This approach has no logical plan and is getting nowhere. It makes no sense." They thought He was beside Himself.

The fact is that this was a movement that proceeded from the Father and could only lead to the Father. The movement was of the Holy Spirit, who was working in Christ. Therefore the movement could not be compared with any other. That's why His friends thought it abnormal. And the movement is indeed senseless if we do not see God or know the Holy Spirit, who wants to lead all of life to God alone and sanctify it to God.

His friends tried to get through to Him and take Him with

them. They did not trust Him by Himself anymore. Isn't that awful? And yet, unless by faith we have received God's grace, our attitude cannot be any different toward Him and the Holy Spirit, who is presently in the world.

Possessed by Beelzebul? The scribes made it even worse. They had come down from Jerusalem to keep an eye on Jesus and to see whether He did anything contrary to the law of Moses. They could not deny the miracles He performed. And in those miracles they were at once confronted with the grace of God that sets life free. Now they would simply *have* to believe! But then they would have to submit to that grace, and with it they would have to deny their whole life and doctrine. They had no wish to do that. Hence they had to reinforce themselves against that revelation of grace.

There was only one way to do this: they would have to slander that revelation and credit His miracles to Beelzebul. That was the worst abomination. They said, "He is possessed by Beelzebul, and by the prince of demons He casts out demons." They wanted to squelch His movement by declaring that it was from the devil. They tried to make this blasphemy find acceptance among the people.

The Lord Jesus is so long-suffering that He even refutes this blasphemy. "How is it possible," He said, "for this movement to be from the devil? Wouldn't the devil be casting out the devil in that case? Do you think that devils oppose each other? If so, the kingdom of the devil would have been destroyed long ago. No kingdom and no house divided against itself can stand. The devils are not opposed to each other; together they oppose God and His Kingdom. There are but two principles in the world—the principle of grace and the principle of unrighteousness. And we live out of the one principle or the other.

"Don't you see that I have come to upset the kingdom of satan? That's clear from the fact that I cast out the demons. *You* were never able to do that with your doctrine and leadership, but *I* am stronger than satan. How can someone go into the house of a strong man and rob him of his vessels if he has not first conquered the strong man? I have conquered satan, and I will continue to conquer him. That's why I can snatch people from his power. In this the grace of God is revealed.

"Woe to you if you continue to deny this, if you blaspheme this work of the Spirit as a work of satan. You may blaspheme in many ways and still find forgiveness, but if the power of the Holy Spirit has been revealed to you and you blaspheme that power as a power of the devil, there is no forgiveness for you for all eternity."

His mother and His brothers. Jesus' friends, who could not persuade Him to come with them, had most likely warned His mother and His brothers. The latter now came to Him. But it was so full in and around the house that they could not pass through. Hence they passed along a message that they were there and called for Him. The people who were sitting around Him told Him that His mother and brothers had arrived.

What would He do? Would He let His mother and brothers disturb Him in His work for the Kingdom of God? Those blood relations and the bond of obedience to His mother were indeed of great importance to Him, but all those relationships have to be sanctified in the Kingdom of God if they are not to interfere with the coming of that Kingdom. It is, in fact, in those sanctified relations that the Kingdom has come.

The tie of faith in the Kingdom of grace is the most intimate one of all. All fellowship on earth stands in the light of that communion. Jesus looked out over those who were sitting around Him and said, "Here are My mother and My brothers. Whoever does the will of God is My brother, and sister, and mother." He spoke of that wonderful fellowship that we may possess by faith. There is no communion higher than this sanctified fellowship. And this communion abides forever. But at that time His mother and brothers did not yet understand. Only later would they understand.

CHAPTER THIRTY TWO
THE REVELATION OF THE MYSTERY
MARK 4:21-34

The Kingdom of God is a mystery to this world. In Christ it has been revealed—not to remain a mystery but to be known by faith. Despite the revelation, the Kingdom remains a mystery to the flesh. Therefore the flesh will bear the Kingdom's judgment. That judgment already appears when the revelation comes in the form of parables. By these parables faith will grow in its understanding of the Kingdom of God, while for the flesh the possibility of understanding is cut off. Rejection of the gospel already brought its own judgment in the form of parables.

These things are said in Mark 4:10-12. Perhaps Jesus spoke these words after His entire address in parables. For only after He had finished His address would His followers have asked Him for an explanation. In any case, these words may be connected with verses 33-34.

There is a difference in meaning between the parable of the seed which grows of itself and the parable of the mustard seed. The first one points to the hidden blessing that causes the seed to grow and the second to the phenomenal powers present in the tiny mustard seed.

Main Thought: *The mystery of the Kingdom of heaven has to be revealed.*

Like a candle. The Lord Jesus said much and did much in Galilee. There were indeed some who believed in Him and understood the grace of the Kingdom. But there also were many who closed their hearts to its grace, people who wanted to remain themselves and therefore did not understand His words. For this lack of understanding they would be judged. After all, the Kingdom did not come in order to remain a mystery.

He told them this in a parable. When someone brings a burning candle into a room, he does not put it under a bed; he puts it in the holder so that the whole room will be lit up. In Christ the grace of the Kingdom has appeared as a light in this world. Surely God does not intend that this grace should not be known. Grace must light up all of public and private life. Woe to anyone who thwarts this intention of the gospel by closing his heart to it!

Jesus therefore told the people to pay attention to what they heard. To the extent that they listened in faith and surrendered their hearts, they would continually receive more. But if anyone closed his heart in unbelief, even the knowledge he seemed to have would be taken away.

This judgment was already carried out by Jesus when He elected to speak in parables, because unbelievers understood nothing of what He meant. We, too, must heed in faith what we hear, in order that the gospel may light up our whole life.

Like seed that grows by itself. In yet another parable the Lord Jesus told the crowds that the fruit of the gospel is a miracle which God Himself effects by His hidden blessing. How was it possible that a word spoken bore fruit in converting the heart and redeeming life? That was certainly not the work of the man who spoke that word but was done by the hidden blessing of God, which became manifest in that fruit.

Isn't it the same with the seed in the field? Someone scatters it on the ground but the sower can do no more beyond that. Then come the rain and the sunshine, and with them the hidden blessing of God—the stalk and the ear and the full grain in the ear. There is nothing else for the farmer to do but harvest the grain. What a miracle right there on the field! There, too, the power of the Lord's grace works in that blessing. It is incomprehensible.

Isn't it the same with the gospel? God grants His hidden blessing upon it, and man is helpless with regard to the miracle. Do we believe in this hidden blessing? We will then see the fruit of the gospel becoming noticeable in our lives.

Like a mustard seed. The Lord Jesus aroused the curiosity of the crowds by asking: "With what shall I further compare the Kingdom of God? There are so many other things that can be said about it and so many comparisons that can be taken from life.

"You all know what a mustard seed is. The mustard seed is the smallest of all seeds. Think for a moment about the large plant that grows from it. It is larger than all other vegetables; it is a plant with large branches in which the birds build their nests." What a great power there is hidden in that tiny seed! God Himself awakens that power in the seed.

It's the same with the gospel. How insignificant it seems to be! Yet there is a power in that gospel, a power that conquers the world, a power that is going to redeem all the nations and bring them back to God. That has been seen in the great Roman empire, and if we believe, some day we will see the hidden power of the gospel revealing itself in the restoration of heaven and earth.

Speaking in parables. All these words Jesus spoke on the shore of the Sea of Galilee. Once, on an earlier occasion, He had already had to ask His disciples to keep a boat ready, for the crowds pressed all around Him. Now He took a seat in a boat. From there He addressed the crowds on the shore.

He constantly put His teachings in the form of parables. To the believers, the parables had to reveal more and more of the mystery of God's Kingdom. The believers often asked Jesus for an explanation of the parables and He would lead them further into the mystery.

To the unbelievers Christ's speaking in parables was a type of judgment which closed the Kingdom to them because of their unbelief. They understood nothing of it. Wouldn't some of them have sensed the judgment implicit in the parables? If they did, shouldn't they have put their own wisdom aside and begged Jesus to allow them to understand the mystery? In that sense the judgment became a blessing to those who accepted Jesus. We should always remember that our corrupted minds and sinful hearts will not understand the Kingdom of God. The gospel of that Kingdom also has to convert our minds. The glory of the Kingdom will then open up to us.

CHAPTER THIRTY THREE
SAFETY
MARK 4:35-41

Christ, sent by God, has power over the sea and the wind. By the power of God's grace He restrains the threatening powers in the world. He does this by virtue of His office. He is not just king over all the powers of nature as Adam once was, and He did not just shed His blood for the remission of sins so that He could restore that original kingship for Himself and for His own in communion with Him. There was more: He temporarily received power to redeem life from the threatening powers that entered the world through sin.

To these threatening powers belong first of all death, satan, and all slavery to sin, the slavery that came over us through our guilt. But the curse also belongs to it, together with everything else that threatens our life as a result of the curse. The powers that are in this world now have in many ways turned against us.

If the disciples had known Christ unmistakably as the conqueror of satan and the curse, they would also have known themselves to be safe with Him in the threat of the storm. However, it applies here, too, that whoever is without sin has the right to cast the first stone.

Main Thought: *With Christ, His own are safe in the world.*

Don't You care? For a long time Jesus addressed the crowds on the shore while sitting in a boat. Afterward He talked with His own, who surrounded Him. He must have been extremely tired from working so hard that whole day. Therefore He asked His disciples to cross over to the other side of the lake, where He could find rest with them in privacy.

The disciples sent the crowds home. Then, along with a few

other boats, they took off to sea. In the stern of the boat was a bench covered with pillows. The Lord Jesus sat down there and soon fell asleep from tiredness.

On this lake, however, it frequently happened that the wind would suddenly shoot out through the mountain gorges to the north and bring the water to a tremendous tempest. The storm would cause very high waves. That happened now too: suddenly a windstorm came up. It became so bad that the waves beat into the boat and the boat was filling up. It appeared that they would perish.

In the meantime Jesus slept on, overcome by fatigue. At first the disciples let Him sleep and tried to save the boat themselves. They must have felt that nothing harmful would befall them as long as the Lord Jesus was with them in the boat. But then they began to fear, their spirits let go of Him and they no longer surrendered to Him in trust. They became resentful that He was sleeping there so peacefully while they were fighting for their lives. Therefore they woke Him up with the words: "Teacher, don't You care if we perish?"

Because they did not yet see the greatness and fullness of the grace and salvation that had appeared in Him, their faith did not hold on to Him. If they had seen that in faith, they would have clung to Him under all circumstances. But they did not yet know Him sufficiently and therefore their faith was too weak for these circumstances. How often this is also the case with believers today!

Rebuking the wind. The Lord Jesus was so tired that He slept through the storm. But how unfair the reproach of the disciples was! How could they wonder whether He cared that they were perishing? He had come into the world to redeem life. Therefore wouldn't He be concerned about their need now? He was very much concerned about it, precisely because He was the Savior.

He saw the waves and heard the storm. In them He saw the threat of death and also the hostile power that had entered the world through sin. He had come to atone for sin and thereby conquer the power of death. One day death would be no more. Then all the powers in the world would serve man. Now they still attacked Him and threatened His life.

Jesus sensed the hostility in the storm. Therefore He rebuked the wind. His anger turned against the hostility that revealed itself in

the storm, and He rebuked it. To the sea He said: "Peace! Be still!" *
The wind ceased and there was a great calm.

How safe it is for believers in the world! Jesus wanted to atone
for sin and thereby He conquered satan and death. He has become
Lord over all things in heaven and on earth and He has received
power over all the hostile powers, power by which to restrain them.
All things are in His gracious hands. Is there anything, then, that
can harm the believer? Yet, it is far from true that we always think
of Him as possessing that power.

Why no faith? He had to reprove His disciples on this score too.
When the wind calmed down, He said to them: "Why are you so
afraid? How is it that you have no faith?" They had seen the distress
at sea but had they not seen the need in which the world found
itself, the need of a world that threatened to perish in its sin and
guilt? From that need the Lord Jesus would save the world. If they
believed that, they could no longer fear for the distress at sea.
Couldn't He save them from that distress?

Believers on earth so often act as the disciples did. They see this
or that particular need that frightens them. But sometimes they do
not see the need of the world from which Christ delivers us. Isn't
the particular need here or there insignificant in comparison with
the need of the world? Won't the One who rescued the world from
its depth of guilt also deliver us from that particular need? He will
do everything that serves our redemption. Do we believe in the One
who delivered the world from its guilt?

The disciples and those who were with them in the boats were
filled with awe after what had happened. They said to one another:
"Who is this, then, that even the wind and the sea obey Him?"
They still groped for the fullness of grace which had appeared in
the Christ, in the one sent from God, the one who was both God
and man.

Faith has to grope and search. Then it constantly finds greater
things and comes to see the glory of God, that is, the dominion of
His grace.

*The original meaning of the verb translated here as *be still* is *to muzzle.* In
other words, Jesus was saying: "Be muzzled." —TRANS.

CHAPTER THIRTY FOUR
BINDING THE STRONG ONE
MARK 5:1-20

The land on the other side of the Sea of Galilee is called the country of the Gadarenes (after Gadara) or the country of the Gergesenes (after Gergesa). In Mark 5:20 it is called the country of Decapolis, but then it is viewed in a much broader way.

This was no longer Jewish country. Here Christ was entering the heathen world which was still in the power of satan. Not until the outpouring of the Holy Spirit would the heathen world be liberated in principle, and with the return of Christ satan will be bound for good. The victory of Christ over satan in the country of the Gadarenes is a prophecy pointing to His complete victory.

The point, then, is not so much the liberation of that one man as the manifestation of Christ's power. This explains why satan's power in that man is pictured the way it is and why Christ makes him say that a legion of demons holds sway in him. It also explains why satan is portrayed here as being completely in Christ's sovereign power.

The fact that the herd of swine plunged into the sea must not be seen as a punishment for possessing swine, which to the Jews were unclean animals, for this country was mainly heathen. When Christ allows the demons to destroy the herd, we need not view this as a judgment upon sin in general.

Satan knew what he wanted. By destroying the herd he would unite the Gadarenes against the Christ. The destruction of that herd of swine touched them far more deeply than the salvation of one man. Christ let satan carry out his intention and thereby tested the Gadarenes to see whether they would recognize and acknowledge Him in His power to save.

Where the demons went after the destruction of the herd is not told us. Most likely they went out again into the country. Only while under the eye of Christ were they unable to move about freely. It is not likely that they were tormented before their time. It still gives satan a certain diversion to destroy and corrupt, although by doing that he makes his own judgment the heavier. Being bound is the perfect torment for him.

Main Thought: *Christ binds the strong one in order to plunder his house.*

In the power of the strong one. The Lord Jesus crossed the Sea of Galilee with His disciples and came to the country of the Gadarenes. He had scarcely put foot ashore when a man who was possessed went up to Him.

In that area were many cliffs in which there were caves. Many tombs had been hewn out in the cliffs. That was where this man lived. He had an insuperable strength because many demons lived in him. Many a time he had been bound with fetters and chains on his feet, but always he had broken them to pieces. During the day he could be seen on top of the cliffs screaming, and sometimes he would pound himself with stones. Then it was dangerous to pass by there. At night he stayed in the tombs.

To be in satan's power is horrible. In those days this exercise of power by satan took place under the providence of God. The case of the possessed man was not a case of madness but something entirely special. God had so ordained it in order that Christ might manifest His power over satan. This poor man, however, was robbed of his own senses and will. It is more horrible still to surrender to satan's power willfully and of one's own accord, as so many do. We are led either by the Holy Spirit or by satan.

The One with power. When the possessed man saw Jesus from afar, he went to meet Him and fell on his knees before Him. In everything this man did, he was driven by satan. Here, already, satan declared that he had met his superior in Christ and that he had to bow down before Him as before the One sent by God. With a loud voice the man shouted: "What have I to do with You, Jesus, Son of the Most High God?" The devil did not want to have anything to do with the Lord Jesus for in Him was the full revelation of God's grace. In this grace God, as the Most High, rules over all things and even uses satan in spite of himself.

What would *the Christ,* the one anointed by God, do with him now? Satan knew that he was completely in Christ's power. Now he already heard Christ saying that he was to leave that man. What would happen to him? Was he going to be bound already? That would mean being tormented right then. Satan finds a certain diversion in being able to destroy and corrupt.

The country of the Gadarenes was heathen territory. Until then satan had done pretty much as he pleased because in those olden times God had allowed the heathen to walk in their own ways. Not until after the outpouring of the Holy Spirit would God in His grace seek the heathen again. Now Christ had appeared in this heathen country. What had He come there to do? Was He going to bind satan before his time? That's why satan adjured Him by God not to torment him.

Here Christ appeared in the power of His grace and satan was in His hand. He made that very clear. He asked satan his name because He wanted to bring that whole sinister business out into the open. From sheer necessity satan answered that he was to be called *Legion*, for there was easily a legion of demons in that man. Thus it was brought out into the open what had made this man so dreadful.

The demons were completely in the power of Christ's grace. But that is also true today, of course. There is still a certain dominion of satan over the nations and over life, but Christ uncovers that dominion and brings it to light in all its hideousness. That by itself breaks down his dominion and then Christ also liberates life from his power. Someday He will wrest the whole earth from satan's hands. Didn't He shed His blood for a remission of the sins of men and thereby obtain the right to break satan's rule? Through faith in Him we, too, are free in principle.

Destruction by satan. On the hillside a herd of about 2000 swine was feeding. The demons asked permission to enter the swine. Under Christ's controlling eye they could do nothing without His permission.

The demons knew full well what they were asking: they wanted to destroy the entire herd. What would the people from the area say then? They would ascribe their loss to the Lord Jesus and would count the loss of their swine much higher than the restoration of that possessed man. They were not the kind who would value a person more highly than a sheep. And satan knew his people! Because of their loss they would all rebel against the Lord Jesus and refuse to recognize Him in the power of His grace. Thus satan preserved his kingdom in that place.

Of course Jesus saw through satan's intention. Nevertheless, He granted satan his request. The judgment of the loss of the herd would come upon that region. Christ wanted them to see that they were all in the power of corruption. The curse of satan's rule rests on this earth—in particular, on the heathen world. If they saw this, they would know the One who is able to deliver people from that curse. Thus, even in the judgment brought by this loss, Christ's searching grace was at work. He was inviting the Gadarenes to faith.

What satan had in mind he also carried out. Head over heels went the entire herd. Running madly, the swine plunged from the cliff into the sea and drowned. That's how destructively satan works.

Once the demons were out of the herd and away from the watchful eyes of the Lord Jesus, they must have swarmed off into the country again to seek other victims. The time had not yet come to bind them. Not until after the outpouring of the Holy Spirit would Christ thwart satan's plans everywhere in life. Now He had already shown His power over him.

The Gadarenes. When the herdsmen saw what had happened, they fled and told it in the city and in the hamlets. Then the whole country came to see what was going on. They saw the possessed man sitting there dressed and in his right mind. And from those who were with the Lord Jesus they learned exactly what had taken place.

How happy they should have been! There sat the man, completely cured. Now he was no longer possessed but was a temple of the Holy Spirit, for he believed in the Lord Jesus and in the power of His grace. The Holy Spirit does not bind us, as satan had bound that man. Being led by the Holy Spirit is not the same as being possessed. The Spirit of Christ leads us to serve the Lord of our own free will.

How happy the Gadarenes should have been! Instead they were only afraid. They did not dare rise up against the Lord Jesus but thought He had been sent to them in judgment. How far removed we are from Him if we regard Him in this way! And then, because of our unbelief, He does become our judgment. In their fear, they asked Him to leave their country. That is certainly the worst thing, when we beg the Lord Jesus to just go away. And how many still do exactly that today!

Still, although He did go away, He did not leave the country of the Gadarenes completely to itself and to the dominion of satan. The possessed man who had been healed asked to be allowed to go with Him. The Lord Jesus did not consent to this. The man was told to stay behind in that country and bear testimony to His name. He was to tell his family and friends about the mercy of God in the Lord Jesus.

That was no easy task for the man, but it was a marvelous calling. Evidently the Lord Jesus already trusted him with it then. He had seen much of Christ and he did indeed become an evangelist for that whole country.

The seed was sown there. Later the message of the suffering and resurrection of Christ, and also the message of the outpouring of the Holy Spirit, was brought there. Then the seed that had once been sown must have borne fruit.

CHAPTER THIRTY FIVE
THE RESTORER OF LIFE
MARK 5:21-43

Jairus came to Christ and asked Him to lay His hands on his little daughter so that she might be healed. Evidently he asked for some sort of magical power that was supposed to go out from Him. This ruler of the synagogue had not advanced beyond a faith in such magical powers. He had heard Christ preach in the synagogue many times but had not made a decision for Him. Only in his distress did he go to Him.

Christ did indeed heal people by laying His hands on them (Mark 6:5). He often touched the sick, but the object was to achieve person to person contact with them. People were not to think in terms of a magical power that would operate apart from their faith in Him. Therefore it is noteworthy that He took Jairus's daughter by the hand and talked to her. This showed that He sought the personal contact. Beforehand He cleared the crowd from the house because all the weeping and wailing would have proved distracting to the revelation of that personal contact.

We run across the very same thing with the healing of the hemorrhaging woman. She, too, only sought to touch His garments so that power might go forth from Him. Then she would disappear unnoticed. But Christ did not want it that way; He wanted to meet her.

It is evident that this woman's faith was differently oriented from the beginning, even though she herself was not completely aware of it. She did not separate His power from Jesus Himself. It never occurred to her how much she wanted Jesus Himself, even while she was looking for healing. That she did look for *Him* is clear from Christ's words: "Daughter, your faith has made you well. Go in peace." Yet the power went out from Him even before He was able to meet her and talk with her.

This did not happen unintentionally or involuntarily, however. Magical power never streams out from Him. He knew that someone was seeking Him. In obedience to the Father, He gave Himself for healing with the intention of seeking the woman who had been healed. This does not conflict with the words: "And Jesus, perceiving in Himself that power had gone out from Him" (vs. 30). Even though this power did not go out from Him unintentionally or against His will, He now gave it His full attention and connected the consequences with it. He had to find the one who was healed. This delay on the way must have been an indication to Jairus of what he could expect from Christ.

In this personal encounter Christ wants to truly set life free, to redeem it from sin and death so that it may serve God in freedom. Because He was going to make atonement for guilt and had therefore received power over all things, He held the lives of men in His hand. He could speak to Jairus's daughter and take her hand as if she were alive and He also could say that she was asleep. To Jesus she was sleeping, for He held her life in His power and returned it to her. Just as He rules over life, He also rules over sickness and health. Thus He can also cure that woman.

Main Thought: *Christ reveals Himself as the Restorer of life.*

Lay Your hands on her. After the Lord Jesus had been in the country of the Gadarenes, He and His disciples sailed back again to the western shore of the sea. Immediately a great crowd gathered around Him again on the seashore. One of the rulers of the synagogue of that city, a man named Jairus, came to Him. When he saw Jesus, he fell at His feet. This ruler had not made a decision for Jesus, but now he was apparently deeply disturbed and in great distress. No wonder, for his little twelve-year-old daughter was dying. He fell down before Jesus and asked Him if He would come and make her well.

He believed that the Lord Jesus could do this, but to him this meant that some kind of magical power went out from Jesus. Thus he asked if Jesus would lay His hands on his daughter and so heal her. The fact that Jesus was going to make atonement for sin and had therefore received power from the Father, power even over the consequences of sin and thus also over sickness and death, he did not see.

It is true that at that time nobody saw this clearly yet, not even His disciples. But the fact that He had been sent by the Father to redeem life and to restore it to freedom to serve the Lord the believers did indeed see. And they did not look for a magical power that went out from Him but for a personal contact with Him through faith.

That was not what Jairus was looking for. And yet Jesus was immediately ready to go with him. He still had to teach Jairus a great deal; He was going to show him what He wanted to be for the people.

Like Jairus, we would all like to receive a great deal from the Lord Jesus, and we all look for something special in Him. However, faith is often missing, faith in Christ who redeems life and to whom we are forever bound. Yet Jesus continues to feel the most tender compassion for this world. He wants to teach us God's ways.

Touching His clothes. When Jesus went along with Jairus, the whole crowd followed. They pressed around Him because they were going to see another special miracle of healing. The crowd was looking for sensation.

On the way something happened which Jesus and Jairus had not foreseen, something Jesus could use to teach Jairus what He wanted to be for the people.

A woman pushed through the crowd and touched the hem of His robe. This woman had been hemorrhaging for twelve years and had spent all her money on doctors without any result. Now she thought: "If only I touch the hem of His robe, I shall be healed. And then I can disappear again unnoticed in the crowd." This woman was afraid to ask openly for healing.

The woman had faith. But again it was faith in the magical power of Jesus which she believed emanated from Him. She also had to learn otherwise. Yet she did have faith. That's why, at the very moment she touched Him, strength went out from Him and she was healed. She could feel that in her body and she was already preparing to disappear into the crowd.

Saved by faith. But Jesus did not want it that way. That strength had not gone out from Him unnoticed. He had noticed that someone sought Him, and in obedience to the Father He had given healing. But He desired the personal contact so that the woman might know He was sent by the Father. And it was also better for the woman that she was aware of herself. She had indeed been ashamed to reveal her illness, but she really cared for Him and His blessing.

Therefore her deed could not go unanswered. The Lord Jesus turned around and asked who had touched Him. The disciples thought this a foolish question because the crowd was pressing all around Him. But He assured them that He knew what He was talking about because healing strength had gone out from Him. Someone had needed Him as Redeemer. Then the woman simply had to come forward and tell Him everything. Under His eyes *we* can do that too. Falling down before Him, she told Him everything.

He thereupon wanted to reveal Himself to her in His love, which redeems for all eternity. He said to her: "Daughter, your faith has made you well. Go in peace, and be healed of your illness." With this He not only told her that she was permanently healed but also gave her His peace. A faith had been awakened in her by which she truly sought Him. God's grace, which was revealed in the Lord Jesus, became known to her.

Talitha cumi. While the Lord Jesus was still speaking, some people from Jairus's house came to say that his little daughter had died. Some felt that it was too late, that he shouldn't bother the Teacher any longer. But the Lord Jesus heard their dismissal and said to Jairus, "Do not fear; only believe." He was not asking him to believe in His miraculous power but to believe in Him as the conqueror of death. He could ask this all the more readily because of what had happened to the woman. He had just shown what He wanted to be for the people. In all things we are to surrender to Him in life and in death.

When Jesus had come to Jairus's house, He did not allow anyone to go in with Him, not even His disciples, with the exception of Peter, James and John. This must have been a disappointment, especially to the other disciples. But they had to learn to submit to His will, which is also the will of the Father. The miracle which was about to happen should not be widely publicized but should rather be seen as God's grace, which had appeared in Christ to conquer sin and death. Therefore only the father and the mother were allowed to be present, together with those three disciples so that later they would be able to proclaim Christ's grace.

When He entered Jairus's house, the women and the professional weepers were already present, for in the Near East a funeral had to take place soon. But the Sovereign of life could not endure such witnesses of death. He put them all outside, saying that the girl was not dead but sleeping. They laughed at Him but He knew better. She had indeed been taken from life temporarily, but Jesus has authority over death because of His atonement for sin and He was going to bring her back. To Him she was sleeping.

Together with the father, mother and His three disciples, He went into the child's room. He did not lay His hands on the child as Jairus had asked. No magical power works in Him; instead He seeks personal contact. He took the girl's hand and spoke to her. He did all this as if she were alive. He is that powerful. After all, He conquered death by atoning for our sins. He said, "Talitha cumi!" that is, "Little girl, arise!" At once the child woke up from the sleep of death and walked soon thereafter.

Those present were astonished. He charged them not to tell anyone and said that they should give the child something to eat. At *that* time they were not to spread the news so that the people would not look upon Him as a miracle worker. Later those disciples who had witnessed this miracle were to tell it abroad and proclaim Him as the conqueror of death in order that we might believe.

By faith in Him our lives will also be restored for all eternity. He restores our lives by bringing us into communion with God today. One day He will restore our life in glory at the resurrection of the dead.

CHAPTER THIRTY SIX
THE LORD FROM HEAVEN
MARK 6:7-32

Christ is the Lord from heaven—both God and man. As such He could atone for our sins and as such He received power to persevere in His redemptive work and to overcome His enemies. Thus He conquered disease, death and the devil.

As Lord from heaven He sent out His disciples as His apostles or ambassadors. They went throughout the land. (Mark 6:30 is the only place where Mark uses the word *apostle*.) In their office as His ambassadors they could ask to be taken into someone's house and be cared for. As bearers of that office they had a right to that. If a city or a home did not receive them as coming in the name of the Lord from heaven, they were to shake the dust from their feet. By this act they banished such a city from the fellowship and declared it to be like the heathen world.

In this way, as Lord from heaven, the crowds did not understand Him. Yet they saw these unusual powers in Him and also saw the authority with which the disciples acted. They sought to explain Him as someone who had come back from the dead. Some said that He was John the Baptist. (Perhaps we should read verse 14 as follows: "And they said, 'John, who baptized there, has been raised from the dead.' ") When others contradicted this because Jesus and John had worked together, they said: "And yet He is someone who has been raised from the dead—either Elijah or one of the other prophets." The flesh cannot know Him as the Lord from heaven.

Herod could not know Him either. The thought that He might be John the Baptist found ready acceptance with him because his conscience was bothering him. His superstition made Herod afraid. He did not know Christ, nor did he acknowledge Him as the Lord from heaven, who would also be able to take away his sins. As the Idumean, he rejected the salvation that appeared in Israel.

When, on the one hand, Christ is looked upon as someone who has returned from the dead, He is greatly underestimated. He is

God come in the flesh. On the other hand, it is then not recognized that He became as one of us, that He bore our yoke.

As a result of their success and because of this idea the crowds had, the disciples were not to let themselves be brought into a state of excitement. Therefore He had to say to them, "Come away by yourselves to a lonely place, and rest for a while." How normal everything was once again when together they sailed on the lake in their boat!

Main Thought: *Christ reveals Himself as the Lord from heaven.*

Sending out His ambassadors. The Lord Jesus could not do the work alone anymore. Large crowds did indeed come to hear Him, but all of Galilee had to hear the gospel of salvation. He had to try to win the entire country for His Father. Therefore He now sent out His disciples to bring the message throughout the whole country.

He sent them out as His ambassadors, two by two. He is the Lord from heaven and in His Name they were to act with authority. They were to take nothing for their journey except their clothes, their sandals and a walking stick—no bread, no bag, no money. They had a right to be received and cared for by those to whom they brought the King's message. Those who received them received the King Himself. Therefore they were not to move from one house to another in a town; they could simply stay in the house that had received them first.

If any place did not receive them, they were to shake the dust from their feet against that place. In that way they were to give a sign that there was no communion between them and that place, that is, no communion between the King and that place. This meant that the King's message had been rejected. A terrible judgment would then come upon those people. It would be more tolerable for Sodom and Gomorrah on the day of judgment than for that city. How glorious is the King who has so much to give but whose judgment is therefore so terrible!

Thus the disciples went out two by two with the message that the Kingdom of God was at hand and that the people had to turn away from the expectation they had of themselves and turn to the grace that was freely given in that Kingdom. As His ambassadors they had also received the power to cast out demons and heal the sick. At their word demons obeyed them and left their victims. They also anointed the sick with oil. The oil was a sign of the power of the Holy Spirit, by whom the sick were made whole. By that sign the disciples elicited faith in the sick, faith that they would be made whole by the power which Jesus gave. Thus the glorious gospel of the Kingdom went out to many areas in Galilee and people there saw the saving power of God's grace.

The crowd's lack of understanding. While His disciples traveled through Galilee, the Lord Jesus Himself went on with His work as well. Great signs and miracles were taking place everywhere. Therefore the people could not help asking: "Who is He anyhow? He exceeds human standards by far!"

Did they now come to the right conclusion, namely, that He is God come in the flesh, the Lord from heaven? Because of their unbelief, they could not come to this conclusion. They no longer understood the covenant and the close bond between God and His people in the covenant. How, then, would they be able to understand the unity of God and man in the Lord Jesus Christ? God had indeed prepared them for that most glorious revelation in Christ by His covenant and by showing them His glory in the temple, but in unbelief they had closed their hearts to it. How would they now be able to recognize the Christ?

Because of this, they all had their own ideas about Him and all those ideas were lies. Some of them said: "John the Baptist, who died, has risen from the dead, and He is John the Baptist." Others disputed this: "That's impossible, for John and He worked together." Then they said, "But He is someone who was raised from the dead— perhaps Elijah, or one of the other prophets. Otherwise He would not be able to do such great miracles." Thus the sinful and erring mind was at work trying to explain what it was experiencing, but it did not come to the right conclusion—the conclusion that He is the Christ, sent from God, the conclusion that He is Himself the Lord from heaven. Only by faith can we worship Him as such.

The Idumean. The ruler of that country was Herod Antipas, the son of Herod the Great. From his father he had received rule over Galilee and Perea, and he liked to be called a king. The Herods were not Jews but Edomites. Thus their background was heathen, although they had been incorporated into the Jewish nation.

This Herod heard about the great miracles the Lord Jesus was performing, and he also heard about the rumors among the people that He might be John the Baptist, raised from the dead. That really startled Herod because he had had John killed. He knew that this had been unjust, his conscience had begun to trouble him, and he superstitiously believed that John had risen. The ministry of Jesus became an obsession to him.

The murder of John had taken place as follows. John had admonished Herod repeatedly because he had taken Herodias, the wife of his brother Philip. In the name of Israel's God, John had protested the abomination that had taken place in the house that reigned over Israel. Herod had not listened to this admonition and had not been prepared to tolerate it any longer. He threw John into prison to silence him.

That was not good enough for Herodias, who wanted John dead because she knew quite well that Herod was still impressed by John's words. Therefore she hated him with a deadly hatred. And she was right as far as Herod was concerned. Again and again Herod called for John, and each time he was deeply impressed. How Herodias must have mocked him then and how she must have tried to laugh that impression away! Yet she could not persuade Herod to kill John. Herod vacillated constantly between the words of John and the mockery of Herodias.

Herodias awaited her opportunity, and it came. On his birthday Herod gave a large banquet for his officers, his courtiers and the leading men of Galilee. Herodias had a daughter by her first husband. When the banquet was well on its way and Herod was under influence of the wine, she ordered her daughter to dance for the king and his celebrated guests. That was a degrading act: a girl in her position as princess never did such a thing. But she charmed Herod and his guests. In his drunken stupor Herod promised to give her whatever she wanted, even half of his kingdom.

Here was the opportunity Herodias had been waiting for. The girl, who was involved in a conspiracy with her mother, walked up to her and asked her what she should ask for. She was told to ask for the head of John the Baptist. The daughter was so degenerate that she did just that.

Now Herod understood that he had been lured into a trap. And he thought there was no escape—as if he should not have refused such a request! A sinful promise should never be kept. But he was ashamed because of his dinner guests, for he had sworn his promise with an oath. And besides, he did not want to disappoint the girl. The charm went on doing its work. Thus he issued the command to behead John in prison and his head was brought to her on a platter. John's disciples received permission to bury their master's body.

This blood guilt weighed heavily upon the court. Very likely Herodias did not give it another thought but it oppressed Herod. And now he heard about the miracles of the Lord Jesus and about the rumors among the people. In this revelation of grace by the Lord Jesus he did not find comfort through faith. Christ's ministry only frightened him, and in his superstition, stimulated by his disturbed conscience, he thought he saw John in the Lord Jesus.

Later, when the Lord Jesus was taken prisoner, Herod saw Him face to face and grilled Him to solve the riddle posed by Jesus (see Luke 23:8-9). However, he received no answer. This heathen, who committed horrors in Israel and rejected the grace of God, would have to bear his own judgment. The sin of Esau, who had once rejected God's promise, was continued in Herod.

Alone in a lonely place. When they had finished their journey and while great rumors about the Lord Jesus were circulating through Galilee, the apostles returned to Him, probably at a place that had been agreed on. Excitedly they reported about all they had done and learned. They had healed the sick and raised the dead. Even the demons had obeyed them.

It seemed as if the excitement of Galilee had also affected the disciples. But in such a state they would not be able to see Him as He really was—the Lord from heaven. On the one hand, He was indeed true God but, on the other hand, He was also a man as they were—really one of them. Right there was to be found the great grace which God revealed in Him. It was highly necessary that they return to the simple faith which begins to see these things clearly. Therefore He wanted to be alone with them for a while in a lonely place. Where they were now there was no rest for them. Many people kept coming and going so that they did not even have an opportunity to eat.

They went in a boat together to sail to another place on the shore. They did not go far and apparently they did not go very fast either because the crowd on the shore kept them in sight and in the meantime walked around the lake to meet them again. Hence they would not find rest on the far shore either.

But what peace they enjoyed with the Lord Jesus in their cherished boat on their familiar lake! There He was, the One in whom God had revealed His full grace, simply accompanying them in the boat. How precious that God's grace was ever so near to their ordinary lives! God's grace in Jesus also restores our everyday lives in order that we may serve and fear the Lord through them. In that boat, the disciples found rest through faith.

MARK:
THE GROWING CONFLICT

CHAPTER THIRTY SEVEN
PURITY IN THE KINGDOM
OF GOD
MARK 7:1-23

That Mark wrote for the Roman world is clear from the explanatory remarks he makes in Mark 7:3-4. There he shows Christ's attitude towards the injunctions of the rabbis. At the same time, picture the growing conflict between Christ and the leaders of the people.

It is not the law of Moses that is the issue here in the first place but the traditions of the elders, that is, of the rabbis—particularly their injunctions with regard to cleansing. You might have defiled your hands or yourself in the street by coming in contact with something ceremonially unclean; if so, you had to wash yourself, or at least your hands, before you ate. People shrank from being defiled—and shrank especially from contact with Gentiles. Thus they appeared to be very faithful to the law and to do more than the law required.

The ceremonial laws about what is clean and what is unclean, however, had been given to teach the Israelites their guilt and their lack of holiness, which had come into the world as a result of sin and which clung also to Israel. But instead of Israel's being brought to humility and confession of sin for her impurity, she prided herself on being ceremonially clean and for that reason added more manmade laws. Eventually, the ceremonial law would have to come into conflict with the moral or ethical law. As a result of this attitude, life became so superficial that if a person abused the ceremonial laws to shirk his moral or ethical responsibilities, the Pharisees would not even criticize him. For instance, someone could withhold his temple contribution presumably to support his parents and yet shirk his responsibility to support his parents. In such a case the ethical law had been shoved behind what only *appeared* to be a keeping of the ceremonial law.

From this point on, in speaking with the crowds and with the disciples, Christ went farther. He showed that in His Kingdom which, as we know, comes with the outpouring of the Holy Spirit, only the ethical law has value. The significance of the ceremonial law belongs to the past. It is not what goes into the mouth but what comes out of it that defiles a person. But at this moment in history when the Kingdom had not yet come, this way of thinking could not yet be fully realized. Christ complied with the law of Moses. But it is true that Christ's view of the importance of ethical law was already then opposed to the rabbinic view of the ceremonial law as being an end in itself.

In the second part of verse 19 we read (in the original): "making all foods clean" which must then be brought into connection with the "He said" of verse 18. With this judgment Christ declares all food to be clean. Acts 10:15 speaks of cleansing in the same way: "What God has cleansed, you must not call common." These words were addressed to Peter in his vision of the linen sheet that was let down out of heaven. It must have been a joy for Mark, who, you will remember, wrote down Peter's gospel, to be able to show that Peter's later attitude towards ceremonial impurity, particularly that of the Gentiles, had its foundation in words of Christ already spoken at the time when He walked on earth.

Main Thought: *Purity is required in the Kingdom of God.*

Ceremonial and ethical. The Lord Jesus was becoming tremendously popular. The leaders of the people, the scribes and Pharisees, watched this growing popularity with envious eyes. They understood perfectly well that He was not of the same spirit as they. Therefore they began to oppose Him and tried to catch Him deviating from the law of Moses.

One time the Pharisees were gathered around Him to observe Him. There were even some scribes there who had come from Jerusalem. Very quickly they found something to criticize: they saw that some of the Lord Jesus' disciples did not wash their hands before they ate bread.

Now, it was a rule in Israel always to wash hands before eating. This was not a regulation of the law of Moses. That law did say that you were not to eat any unclean animals and also stated that you were not to touch anything unclean, for instance, a dead body, without washing afterwards. Why, do you suppose, had the Lord commanded this? He wanted to teach His people that as a result of sin the whole creation had become unclean. The laws of Moses were to bring Israel to a knowledge of sin, so that she would long for the reconciliation of her sin through the Lord Jesus Christ, by whose atonement the world would again be cleansed.

But instead of admitting sin, Israel began to pride herself on the fact that she withheld herself from all defilement and thus was very clean. The rabbis in their schools had added many rules to the law of Moses. Without even knowing it, you might have touched something unclean. Hence you always had to wash your hands before eating, for if you touched food with unclean hands, the food itself became unclean, and if you then ate it, you became unclean yourself. Then you had lost the purity of which the Pharisees were so proud. They looked down upon everything that was unclean in the world—particularly the heathen world which in its entirety was unclean. Such blindness! They failed to see that by means of those laws regarding uncleanness, God wanted to make Israel discover her sins!

The Pharisees criticized the disciples' conduct. The Lord Jesus did not begin to defend His disciples; He attacked the Pharisees directly. "You pride yourself so much on that outward purity," He said, "but that's only a show of service to God. In your pride you only seek yourself. You live to please yourself and your heart is far from the Lord. We can only come to the Lord by confessing our sins. The prophet Isaiah already said of you hypocrites that your entire way of serving God is service in appearance only. Your manner of life displays the same pattern as that of your fathers.

"Moreover," Jesus continued, "even though you pride yourselves so much on your outward purity, you permit and even commit the worst possible sin at the same time." To illustrate His point, Jesus told them the following: "It happened that someone had to support his parents but he said 'I have dedicated my possessions to the service of the temple.' This was just an excuse because he didn't give those possessions to the temple. He shirked his responsibility, but you didn't criticize him. Doesn't the law say, 'Honor your father and your mother' and 'Whoever curses his father or mother will surely die'? With your traditions you've made the law of God ineffective. You make such a person think that he can be excused. He does not become aware of his sin or improve his life. True holiness before God, an upright life before the law, is obstructed by your traditions. The appearance of holiness has been preserved, but you really live in unrighteousness." This hypocrisy, in which the Pharisees set the example for the people, was condemned by the Lord Jesus. And He condemns hypocrisy in us, too, regardless of the form it takes.

Declaring all food clean. Jesus could not leave it at that. He felt compelled to say more on this subject to the whole crowd. Therefore He had the people come to Him again and He instructed them. Such hypocrisy is in total conflict with the Kingdom of grace, He told them. Such arrogance cannot exist in the Kingdom; Kingdom people live by the grace which God bestows on them. By grace we receive forgiveness of sin, enabling us to live in uprightness of heart with the Lord.

Besides, in the Kingdom the laws regarding cleanness and uncleanness will no longer be in force, since they were valid only for a time. Actually it is not what a man eats that defiles him; food does not affect his heart. If God gave laws regarding cleanness, it was just to point out the impurity of our hearts. The heart is unclean because of sin and is defiled time and again by all the evil that comes forth out of it—evil thoughts and desires that express themselves in sinful words and deeds. The important thing is to know and confess this impurity of the heart.

Laws regarding unclean foods, which were to teach us the lack of holiness in life, will no longer be necessary in the Kingdom. Sin is now made clear to us in another way; it is revealed especially through the suffering Jesus had to endure on the cross for our sins. Therefore we no longer need laws about unclean food, which only served as illustrations.

Through the atonement on the cross the entire creation will be sanctified, thus removing the curse from the world. We may now make use of all food, provided we give thanks to the Lord who, in spite of our sins, has made all foods available again. Similarly, all Gentiles ceased to be unclean because God will redeem all nations and invite them into His Kingdom.

These words were incomprehensible even for the disciples who, of course, were still living under the law of Moses. Therefore Jesus explained the whole matter to them once more. Again He explained that purity of heart is the important thing. That purity comes by confessing our sins before God, receiving forgiveness and then walking uprightly before the Lord and shunning sin. That is true life in the Kingdom.

Thus the Lord Jesus came into conflict with the leaders of the people. What would all this lead to? They were unwilling to abandon their point of view and He could not yield to their lies. The conflict could only increase in intensity. Let us never, by mistaking the appearance for the real thing, come into conflict with the Lord Jesus and His Word!

CHAPTER THIRTY EIGHT
A LIGHT TO THE GENTILES
MARK 7:24-30

Christ asked the Syro-Phoenician woman to acknowledge God's covenant with Israel. Only when she admitted that, in the terms of the parable, the Jews were the children and the non-Jews the dogs did Christ help her. God does not fling His benefits around at random but gives them by way of His covenant. Apart from an acknowledgement of that covenant, there can be no knowledge of Him and no hope for His blessing.

We should not say that this woman believed on behalf of her daughter. Her possessed daughter was unable to believe herself. In faith the woman prayed for God's blessing on her house, to be shown in the healing of her daughter. The woman knew that this calamity had fallen upon herself and her house. It concerned herself and therefore she struggled to have the curse removed.

Main Thought: *Christ is a light to the Gentiles.*

The children's bread. In Galilee large crowds followed Jesus, many only for the miracles He performed. The people didn't really believe in Him as sent by God to reveal God's grace. The leaders of the people opposed Him because there had already been conflicts such as the one regarding the washing of hands. Would all His work be in vain? Would He not be able to win the people for His Father? That they followed Him just for the miracles must have grieved Him deeply, because it meant the people were overlooking the real purpose of His coming.

He therefore withdrew from Israel. Israel would have to come to herself and learn to choose. With His disciples He crossed the northern borders of the land entering the territory of Tyre and Sidon. There He wanted to remain in hiding for a while.

The people would first have to decide about Him but the decision should not, He felt, be made in a whirl of excitement while feelings were running high about what they were seeing and hearing, because such a decision might not come from the heart. Hence the Lord Jesus stayed up north in a house, possibly with an acquaintance.

Still, He could not remain hidden. A non-Jewish woman of the area heard about Jesus. She was miserable because she had a daughter who was pitifully possessed of a demon. Evidently the poor girl's condition was very wretched, as the demon did with her as he pleased. The mother interpreted this as a curse upon her family. She then heard about Jesus' ministry in Israel and saw something of the grace God was showing His people in that ministry. In the light of that grace, the devil's power over her daughter became even more unbearable for her.

Now she heard that the Lord Jesus was in the vicinity. She went into the house where He was, knelt down before Him and begged Him to cast the demon out of her daughter.

She received an answer that seemed negative. Jesus said it would not do to give bread meant for the children to the dogs. By children He meant the people of Israel, people of the covenant, for whom at that time the grace of the Lord was intended. Only after salvation had been fully revealed to Israel and Israel had made its decision would grace come to all peoples.

The Lord Jesus indeed hid from Israel for a time but He did not disown His people. He could not do that because He could not deny God's covenant with them. God had first to fulfill His promise to Israel. God is eternally faithful to His covenant and grants His salvation by way of that covenant.

Acknowledging the covenant. Immediately the woman understood what the Lord Jesus meant. She displayed a surprising insight. What's more, she was not offended by the comparison of the Gentiles with dogs. She acknowledged Israel as God's privileged people and bowed humbly before God's election of Israel.

But though she did so, her expectant faith did not give up. She believed that, because He had revealed His grace to Israel, God also wanted to give a blessing to the Gentiles. She expressed that faith by saying that even the dogs eat the crumbs that fall from the children's table.

Here the Lord Jesus was confronted with a miracle, that is, with the work of His Father. Such insight, such humility, such faith could only have been given her by the Father. The Father had brought this about by the rumors about the Lord Jesus that had spread beyond the borders of Canaan.

How He must have rejoiced! He saw the Father's sign that He should help. And He could indeed help her since she had acknowledged God's covenant. When people despise and ignore the covenant, no salvation is possible because God always gives by way of His covenant.

The full number of the Gentiles. At this sign from His Father, Jesus said to the woman that she could go home because her daughter was healed. Because He spoke these words with authority, the demon was cast out. The woman believed and she did not urge Him to come with her but went home and found her daughter well.

This incident was of even greater significance to Jesus. His people, Israel, would have to make their decision. When they did, many of them would reject Him. The work the Father was doing among the Gentiles, and the blessing He had been privileged to give to the woman already, was for Him a prophecy of what would soon happen.

The gospel would go forth to all nations and faith would be awakened in many unto forgiveness of sins and redemption of life from its slavery to satan. The full number of the Gentiles would be reached (see Rom. 11:25).

This sign was undoubtedly a great comfort and joy to Him. Also, through it the disciples could learn something about the great work to which He would later send them.

CHAPTER THIRTY NINE
ALL OF LIFE IS A MIRACLE
MARK 7:31—8:26

A ll of Christ's miracles have symbolic significance. However, we have to be careful when we say this. We should not read "blind soul" for "blind eye" or "lame soul" for "lame leg" in an effort to allegorize the miracles. If we do, we start from an unhealthy division between "the natural" and "the spiritual," between "the temporal" and "the eternal." Then we are inclined to say, "This miracle applies 'only' to the material and temporal, while the spiritual and eternal is on a much higher plane."

We cannot do that. Christ redeemed *life*. By healing the deaf-mute, that is, a man who was isolated from his surroundings, He restored communion to life. That was a result of God's grace upon life as present in Him. God gave Christ that power because of the reconciliation He would accomplish.

Such a miracle is not understood by an unbeliever. For the non-elect, the unbeliever, the miracle is not an eternal blessing; it is "only temporal." But for the believer that act of healing is the revelation of God's eternal grace in Christ. The believer also sees grace in it. For him that restoration is not just temporal but has eternal significance. He may serve God again in restored communion, which bears eternal fruit. True, a believer's life and all he possessed will perish for a time in death, but it will be restored at the resurrection, sanctified and glorified. To the extent that miraculous healing is a revelation of that eternal grace, which restores all of life—and this grace has to be acknowledged in it—we can speak of the symbolic significance of miracles.

The purpose of miracles, then, is to tell us that all of life is the fruit of God's grace in Christ, the fruit of that miracle-working grace. Then *life as a whole becomes a miracle*. There is actually nothing in life which is not miraculous. For that reason it is really pointless *for the believer* to distinguish between *temporal* and *eternal*.

(To avoid misunderstanding, I should point out once again that, while God's eternal grace in Christ is for the whole world and for the whole of life, unbelievers do not benefit from the miracle of grace. Admittedly, even unbelievers receive benefits that flow from God's eternal grace for the world but those benefits are only a temporal blessing to them.)

Only by faith is it possible to believe that life—every day and in every way—is miraculous. Believing that life is totally miraculous is the opposite of living in fear and anxiety, living in unbelief. Christ pointed that out to His disciples when they were concerned because they had forgotten to take food with them.

He cautioned them against the leaven of the Pharisees and the leaven of Herod. However much the Pharisees and Herod differed, they were the same in one respect: unbelief was the source of their lives—both were unable and unwilling to live by the miracle of grace. Especially by His miraculous feeding of the multitude, Christ had taught His disciples that life was a miracle. Now He called their attention to that.

Main Thought: *Christ teaches us that life is a miracle and that we live by miracle.*

Ephphatha! Jesus did not yet want to leave the land in the north to return to Galilee. What He had revealed thus far had to settle in the minds of the people. They also had to learn to long for Him and to ask themselves what they really saw in Him.

Therefore He went far beyond Israel's northern borders and made a long journey through the heathen land where He did not reveal Himself. He traveled through Tyre and along the seacoast to Sidon where He saw the Mediterranean Sea, over which the gospel would be brought some years later to peoples who lived far to the west. What thoughts must then have gone through His mind! From Sidon He turned eastward, passed over the Lebanon and then went southward. He still remained outside Galilee, the land of Herod. He ended up on the eastern side of the Sea of Galilee, in the land where He had been only occasionally.

It was there, in the land of the Gadarenes that they had asked Him to leave their country. Yet He had not remained unknown there, because the man who had been healed of demon possession had told people throughout the whole region of the Decapolis what the Lord Jesus had done for him.

They now brought a man who was deaf and had a speech impediment. They asked Jesus to lay His hands on him. Apparently they wanted proof of His magical powers but He would not perform any healing under such circumstances.

He took the deaf man aside. How was He to make it clear to the man what was about to happen to him? The expectation of faith had to be awakened in him. Because the Lord Jesus could not reach him by speaking, He put His fingers in the man's ears. He then wet His fingers with saliva and touched the man's tongue. In this way expectation was aroused in the man. Following this, Jesus looked up to heaven and sighed to indicate to the man that the healing had to come from the Father and that it had to come through prayer. Having thus awakened the man's expectation of faith, Jesus said, "Ephphatha," that is "Be opened." At once his ears were opened and he could speak.

That man had been like a closed city with nothing going in or out. He now had been opened up and contact with his environment through hearing and speech had been restored. But how would that man have understood? Did he see that the miracle had happened so that he might serve the Lord in his community? In that case the benefit of grace became an eternal blessing for him. Then he knew God's eternal grace which had appeared in Christ and his whole life became proof of God's miracle-working grace. The miracle had not been in vain.

And how did the crowd react when they saw this man come back healed and well? Jesus again ordered them not to discuss it with anyone because He did not want to be known as a miracle-worker. But they proclaimed it all the more. They were astonished beyond belief and said, "He has done all things well. He even makes the deaf hear and the dumb speak. It's incredible. It's like a fairy tale. It's as though paradise has returned! He removes all diseases."

For most people in that crowd it remained just that—a fairy tale. They did not see God's eternal grace in it—the grace that could give them rest and restore their lives to fellowship with Him. However, it is not a fairy tale but the reality of God's grace that makes life a miracle. Very few saw that and even now there are not many who see it.

Provision for life by God's grace. For a while the Lord Jesus remained in the region of Transjordan. A large crowd had been following Him for three days. There was no food left and He was moved with compassion for them. He could not send them away without something to eat because they would collapse on the way home. He discussed it with His disciples, who told Him that it was simply impossible to provide food for a crowd of four thousand.

The disciples must have hesitated when they said this, because they had witnessed once before how He had miraculously fed a large crowd. Therefore they listened carefully to Him and did what He said. They hesitantly replied that they had only seven loaves of bread which wasn't even enough for them.

He then told the crowd to sit down on the ground. He took the seven loaves, gave thanks, broke the bread and gave them to His disciples who passed the bread around to the people. They kept handing it out and there was enough for everyone. The bread simply multiplied in His hands. The same thing happened with the few small fish which He also handed out after offering thanks and asking God's blessing on them.

What marvelous revelation we receive here! It is Christ, the Word of grace, who has power over all things. It is through Him, for that matter, that grain grows in the field. That is also the work of His miraculous grace. In this instance He caused the bread and fish to multiply in a truly miraculous way. Would anything be too wonderful for Him? Even the so-called natural growth of grain in the field is a miracle brought about by the power of His grace.

The disciples, the crowd and we also must see in this miraculous feeding how all of life is maintained and nourished by God's grace. Then our everyday life is a miracle and we also use life for the Lord. Our life is not in vain and we need not be anxious about anything!

Would the whole crowd have seen it that way? Many people must have gone home grateful for the food and amazed at the miracle but without having grasped God's eternal grace in Christ. However, the miracle spoke clearly enough: not only were they all fed, there was food left over. This apparently happened on the coast of the Sea of Galilee, where a ship was already waiting to take them back to Galilee. In that ship were some baskets which they filled with the leftovers.

If we do not see God's eternal grace in His daily mercies, we may be blessed for a time but we are not truly redeemed and our life will be in vain. But if in faith we see God's grace, we may know our lives are being cared for in every way.

The leaven of the Pharisees and of Herod. After feeding the crowd Jesus sent the people away. Immediately He stepped onto the ship with His disciples and crossed over to the western side of the lake. After a long absence He was now back in Galilee. How would the people receive Him?

The first encounter was far from pleasant. The Pharisees came and began to argue with Him. What right did He have, they demanded, to pass Himself off as a prophet and set Himself up as leader of the people? Weren't they the recognized leaders of the people? They feared He was usurping their leadership position. They admitted that He performed many miracles, but now, they felt, He should let them have a sign from heaven, a sign in which God gave proof that He had sent Him. Without such proof all those miracles said nothing to them. How fiercely the leaders of the people opposed Him already!

Was He to conclude from this that the people as a whole were opposed to Him? Were they following Him because of His miracles without acknowledging Him as sent by God's grace to redeem life? He sighed deeply. What suffering that rejection caused Him! He saw that He would have to atone for the sins of this wayward people if there was to be salvation for the core, the remnant, of that people.

In their unbelief the Pharisees had desired a sign—as if anyone is ever brought to true faith as a result of a sign! God always asks faith in His Word, after which He gives a sign to confirm that faith. But no sign is ever given to unbelievers. Therefore the Lord Jesus said that no sign would be given to that generation. He spoke of "that generation," because He saw in those Pharisees a reflection of the spirit of the entire people. Moreover, their question tempted Christ to force proof of God's favor from heaven. Had Christ responded, He would have succumbed to the devil. For Him it was a temptation from the devil, so He turned His back on them and went away.

That first encounter back in Galilee had indeed been very disappointing. Once again He withdrew from the people. He got into the ship and crossed over to the other side.

On the sea His disciples remembered that they had forgotten to buy food. They had only one loaf of bread aboard. What were they to do? At this point the Lord Jesus began to speak. He declared that they were to beware of the leaven of the Pharisees and the leaven of Herod. The disciples did not understand Him. Did He know that they had no bread with them? Did He mean that they should refuse any bread offered by Pharisees or Herodians?

Jesus meant something completely different. Leaven is yeast that permeates the whole bread. Similarly, there is also a principle that permeates our whole life. It is either the principle of faith or the principle of unbelief. With the Pharisees and Herod, it was the principle of unbelief. The disciples would have to be on guard against that principle. And wasn't that principle already at work in their lives if they stopped to worry about common bread? Did they not believe that He was able to take care of them? Wasn't their life maintained by God's grace? Hadn't they learned that yet? Were their eyes so closed and their ears so deaf? Were their hearts so hardened that they could not see it? "How many baskets were left the first time when I fed five thousand people with five loaves?" Jesus asked. "Twelve," they answered sheepishly. "And how many baskets when I fed the four thousand with seven loaves?" "Seven," they replied. "Why, then," He asked, "do you still not understand that your life is sustained by the miracle of God's grace? The miracle of God's grace will be revealed in your entire life. Then live by that miracle!" The Lord Jesus says the same thing to us. We must live by the miracle of God's grace, which sustains our whole life.

The miraculous healing of the blind man. Right after that another miracle took place, which was to confirm the disciples' faith. They did not cross all the way to the other side of the sea but headed for its northern shore where Bethsaida was situated, at the point where the Jordan flows into the sea.

There some people brought a blind man to Jesus and begged Him to touch him. Apparently they also thought He healed by some sort of magical power.

Jesus took the blind man aside and led him by the hand outside the village. There he had to awaken the expectation of faith in the blind man. He placed saliva on his eyes and laid His hands upon him. Then He asked him if he saw anything. He indeed saw something, only very indistinctly. He saw people as if they were trees walking. What joy that blind man must have experienced already! At the same time, how he must have longed for the Lord to make him completely well! Again Christ laid His hands on his eyes. When the man looked up again, he saw everything clearly, even at a distance.

He would now be able to work again in society. He could work with his hands and be useful to others. Did the man see his healing as proof of God's grace, and did he devote his life and work in society to the Lord? If he did, his healing had restored his life for all eternity.

The Lord Jesus wanted to save him from superficial gossip and bring him to reflect on God's grace. Therefore He sent him home and told him not to go back to the village. He was to tell no one what had happened.

Would the disciples see the miracle that governs and fulfills our life? Do we see it?

CHAPTER FORTY
TRANSFIGURED
MARK 9:2-13

For a few moments Christ experienced the exaltation He would obtain by His obedience for Himself and His own. Luke says He was on the mountain to pray. By surrendering in prayer to His calling, He experienced a transfiguration. It was as though He had the guilt and yoke of sin already behind Him. But this was only a temporary anticipation of what was to come at the conclusion of obedient suffering. That Peter did not understand.

(Mark 9:12 could possibly contain the following misunderstanding shared by all scribes: if Elijah is to come first to restore all things, why is it written of the Son of man that He will suffer many things and be treated with contempt? The question reflects the view held by the scribes that Elijah himself would come to prepare the Messiah's kingdom, without any humiliation for Elijah. It's no wonder that they could not see the fulfillment of the prophecy about Elijah in the life of John the Baptist, which ended in humiliation.)

Main Thought: *By His obedience in humiliation, Christ obtained glory.*

The exaltation. There came more and more tension between Jesus and the people, particularly their leaders. This made Him see the approach of His suffering all the more clearly. He withdrew with His disciples to the region of Caesarea Philippi to prepare them for that suffering. He told them very plainly that He would be delivered up, would die and rise again. But they did not understand Him at all: their minds refused to take it in. It simply went past them.

However, Jesus was thinking a good deal about His suffering those days. One day He climbed up a mountain taking only three of His disciples with Him, the three who had also been present at the raising of Jairus's daughter. Evidently He knew that something special was going to happen on that mountain.

On the mountain He prayed. Before God He struggled with the prospect of His suffering, praying for strength to remain obedient to the Father's will, even as the suffering drew nearer. His prayer was heard. He was completely one with His Father—so completely that He envisioned the end of suffering and the glory He would obtain by His obedient suffering. In spirit He already shared in this glory. This glory then began to manifest itself in His physical appearance. His face shone and His garments glowed white as snow. His disciples were amazed.

What bliss that was for the Lord Jesus! He was temporarily experiencing the glory He would obtain. The guilt and anguish of our sin still oppressed Him and He had the appearance of a slave, just as we appear in bondage under the yoke of our misery. For a moment, however, He transcended all suffering. This strengthened Him for the task that was to come.

The disciples saw a man transfigured. Thus it is possible for man in a state of humiliation to be transfigured into glory. This aroused great hopes in the disciples, hopes that were justified. Through faith we also see that glory and cherish the same expectations.

As our Head. He was not glorified only for Himself. His transfiguration foreshadowed the transfiguration into glory of all His people. The momentary transfiguration prophesied the glory in which we shall all share.

The fact that He was glorified as Head of His people could be seen from the fact that He was suddenly no longer alone. In the light that radiated from Him the disciples saw two other figures who were themselves filled with glory. The disciples knew who they were. The disciples had formed an idea of the most prominent men of Israel's history and the Spirit revealed to them that these two were Moses and Elijah. Elijah had been taken up into heaven bodily. Moses had indeed died and his body had been buried by God, but God had probably raised him from the dead. Both now appeared bodily to the Lord Jesus.

They talked with Him about His suffering and about the road through suffering to glory. They acknowledged Him as their Mediator and Head. They themselves had been two of the most prominent leaders of Old Testament Israel.

What would they have said to Him? It was probably something

like this: "We, as leaders of the people, were permitted to complete our lifework, though in weakness. We had the privilege of suffering and conquering, and we have been glorified. But everything we were privileged to do and everything we have received was because of You, because You are going to finish Your work in obedience and receive glory. You are going to make atonement for sin and give life its victory."

We should also look upon Jesus that way. It was also for us that He was willing to suffer. Through faith in Him, we will also bring our work to completion in faithfulness to the Lord and to His calling. One day we will be glorified by Him. That is sure to happen, even though we will also have to suffer humiliation.

Listen to Him! However, the transfiguration was only temporary. For a moment, it was as though He had already gained the victory, while in fact He was still facing His suffering. For just a moment He was lifted above the guilt and yoke of our sins, which He had taken upon Himself. In that brief moment He had communion with those who, because of Him, had attained their blessedness in heaven. On earth glory cannot last because the curse for sin still remains.

The disciples did not understand that the glorious moment could not last. They were amazed and enraptured, yet at the same time they were apprehensive about this heavenly glory, which was still so foreign to them. The tension it produced became almost unbearable. They had to express their feelings somehow— especially Peter.

Failing to understand, Peter told Jesus that it was a good thing the three of them were there; he suggested making a tent for each and thus continue their fellowship on earth. Indeed, that's exactly what will happen when God's glory comes to earth permanently but the earth must first be redeemed from the curse. At present it's just not possible. For the time being we keep the glory in the form of hope in our hearts. But the time will come when the life of man will be glorified.

Peter did not receive a direct answer, but an answer came in the form of a cloud which overshadowed them. It was the cloud of the glory of God's grace, which had gone before Israel in the wilderness and had filled the tabernacle or temple on occasion. God's glory was manifested in a unique way during the transfiguration on the mountain. What an experience that must have been for the disciples!

And in God's presence Peter received an answer. Human life on earth is glorified only by the favor of God, which Jesus would first have to obtain through His suffering.

Still, Jesus was fully ready to undergo that suffering. That's why the Father was so close to Him there. As token of His love the Father said: "This is My beloved Son. Listen to Him." Hearing this was a comfort to Jesus, but it was also an indication to the disciples and to us that life on earth cannot yet be glorified since it is still a life by faith in the Word that Jesus brought.

The disciples experienced the harsh truth of that immediately afterwards. The cloud was taken away, the glory departed, Moses and Elijah were gone, and they only saw the Lord Jesus as He had been before. They had to live by faith and not by sight.

The state of humiliation. The sign the Pharisees had asked for earlier had happened on the mountain. They had asked for a sign from heaven and now it had come and gone. Yet, a sign is not given to unbelief but to faith. Those who received the sign were not the Pharisees but the disciples.

Not all the disciples, however, had seen glory come down from heaven—only three of them. There was still an unbeliever among the disciples, so the sign could not be shared. Who would believe without having seen? The three disciples had themselves been confused by it. Not until the Lord Jesus had completed His suffering and entered into glory would they be able to understand it. Christ therefore charged the three, as they were coming down the mountain with Him, not to tell anyone what they had seen until He had risen from the dead (verse 9).

Although they did not understand what He said about rising from the dead, they kept this matter to themselves. Baffled, they discussed together what rising from the dead could mean.

They had yet another burning question. They had just seen Elijah. Did that have anything to do with the scribes' view that, prior to the coming of the Messiah, Elijah would first have to return to restore freedom to Israel? How could Elijah's appearance have anything to do with that? Wouldn't he have to remain on earth to restore Israel again?

They finally worked up enough courage to ask Jesus. He showed them the absurdity of the scribal view. If the glorified Elijah himself were to bring freedom and glory to Israel, what did Scripture mean when it said that the Son of man first had to suffer and through suffering redeem His people?

According to Scripture someone was to come in the spirit and power of Elijah, but his path on earth, like that of the Lord Jesus Himself, would be a road of suffering and humiliation. That man had already come, as it was written, and the people had despised and rejected Him. The disciples sensed that Jesus was referring to John the Baptist.

The way to glory for the Lord Jesus was a road of humiliation, bearing our guilt in order to atone for it. Although He made reconciliation for His people, the way to glory for them is also a road of humiliation and affliction. By following that road, their self-reliance will die and they will live by faith alone. That was the road John the Baptist had to travel, and so must we if we are privileged to serve Him.

CHAPTER FORTY ONE
FIGHTERS FOR LIFE
MARK 9:14-29

Christ's accusation "O faithless generation, how long am I to be with you? How long am I to bear with you?" was directed not to the disciples but to the crowd, the scribes and the child's father. True, the faith of the disciples was affected as a result of the surrounding unbelief. That's why Christ said at the end that this kind of devil could not be driven out except by prayer and fasting. By prayer and fasting the disciples had to fight the battle to keep their faith unshaken in the face of the unbelief that surrounded them.

Main Thought: *Christ and His Church are the fighters for life.*

The disciples' lack of power. When Jesus and His three disciples came down from the mountain on which He had been transfigured, they found the rest of the disciples in the valley, surrounded by a big crowd and by scribes who were arguing with them. The crowd saw Him coming and came to greet Him excitedly. He immediately suspected that the scribes were attacking the disciples' faith. Therefore He turned to the scribes and asked them why they were arguing with them. He wanted to intervene on the side of His disciples, that is, on the side of His Father's Kingdom, which was revealed in their faith.

He got an answer from an entirely different quarter. Someone spoke up in the crowd and told Him what was going on. This person had a son who was possessed by the devil. The devil made the boy deaf and dumb. Sometimes the devil caused him to have violent seizures and then he would lie rigid on the ground, foaming at the mouth and grinding his teeth. The father had brought his son to the disciples, asking them to cast the devil out of him, but they had been unable to do so.

This showed the Lord Jesus the powerlessness of His disciples, to whom, after all, He had given power to cast out demons. He understood very well how this situation had come about. It was not that they did not believe in Him, but they were surrounded by an unbelieving and critical crowd.

The boy's father had probably been disappointed by the fact that he did not find the Lord Jesus Himself there. Now he would simply have to take the matter up with the disciples. He did not have much confidence in them. Moreover, the scribes were there and they would love to win a victory over the disciples. Armed with their unbelief, they deliberately stood in the way of the disciples' faith. They were eager to see whether the disciples could do anything now that their Master was not present. And the crowd stood there watching to see who would be the winner. The crowd is always inclined to take the side of unbelief.

In this way the power of the disciples' faith had been broken by the unbelief that surrounded them. They were no longer able, in simple, childlike faith, to expect the power of the Lord Jesus to take effect and then perform great deeds by that power. They did command the devil to depart but the devil paid no attention. Their command was not the Word that radiated the power of the Lord Jesus, and therefore it could not bind the devil.

The disciples' faith was no match for the unbelief that surrounded them. Unfortunately, this is often the case with the Church and the believers. Today, too, God's people are to bear testimony to the Lord Jesus. If they believe in His name, their lives will be freed from sin and from the devil's control. But they, too, live in a world full of unbelief, which so often paralyzes the power of their faith. Still, it is sin for believers if they cannot withstand unbelief.

O, faithless generation! The Lord had just been on the mountain where His faith had triumphed. As a result He had been transfigured. Now He found Himself in the midst of the unbelief that surrounded His disciples.

Bitter words came from His lips about that unbelief, for He hated all unbelief that rejected His Father. "O, faithless generation! How long am I to be with you? How long am I to bear with you?" With these words He was not saying that He was tired of remaining in this unbelieving world and wanted to give up His work of redemption. He wanted to bring out the contrast between the unbelief of the world and the perfect faith by which He lived.

Thus He was shedding light on that unbelief; He was condemning it, declaring its guilt before God.

Jesus was willing to help, but first unbelief had to be exposed, also in the child's father. At His command the boy was brought to Him. As soon as he saw Jesus, the devil convulsed him, and the boy rolled around on the ground, foaming at the mouth. The child's misery was visible to all. Jesus then asked the father how long he had had this. "From childhood," the man replied. That made it all the more difficult for him to believe that his son would ever be restored.

The father, terrorized again by the awful sight, told how the devil was apparently out to destroy the boy's life, since he sometimes threw him into the fire and at other times into the water. How terrible the devil's intention is! He has come to destroy. The father now implored Jesus: "But if You can do something, have pity on us and help us." That father asked, "If you can do something . . . ." Thus there was still no faith in the man—only doubt. He was willing to give it a try with the Lord Jesus, but healing seemed all but impossible to him.

This brought his unbelief to light, together with what caused it, namely, that the boy had been possessed since childhood. The Lord Jesus did not spare anybody here but first exposed the unbelief in all its depth and put it to shame by bringing it to light. Time and again we are embarrassed and put to shame before Him, and we have no excuse left.

Healing through faith. Jesus then awakened faith. He rejected that "If You can" and said, "All things are possible to him who believes." We can obtain all things from Him through faith— that is, all things that we desire from Him in accordance with His will, all things that are in keeping with His Kingdom. Other things we can never desire in faith.

The father sensed that faith was now being asked of him. He also knew how unbelieving his attitude toward the Lord Jesus had been. Christ's dealing with him brought him to faith.

However, he was an honest man. Under Jesus' watchful eye, he could not make things look any better than they really were with him. Therefore he said, "I believe, Lord; help me in my struggle against my unbelief." This was indeed a surrender to the Lord Jesus.

And from Him would come faith and power in the battle against unbelief. So it was that faith broke through in this man.

Meanwhile, the crowd was pressing closer, eager for a new sensation. This desire of the crowd so easily interfered with faith. Therefore Jesus did not want to delay the healing any longer. He ordered the spirit of dumbness and deafness to come out of the boy. Again He addressed the devil and named the calamities he caused.

The Lord Jesus always brings the devil's shady business to light. This was no ordinary case of epilepsy, but genuine demon possession. In this case the direct influence of satan was behind the symptoms of epilepsy. At Christ's command the devil came out with a loud cry, appalled that he was conquered. But in leaving the boy he convulsed him so violently that he lay on the ground as though dead. Jesus took him by the hand and made him sit up.

The devil had been conquered again. One day the Lord will crush the devil under His feet. However, the devil had been conquered by way of the faith the Lord Jesus had awakened. Does His Word make us believers in Him, the fighter for life who one day will set life free from this dominion of death?

Prayer and fasting. When He entered the house, His disciples asked Him why they had not been able to cast out the devil. The devil who had controlled the boy had also kindled unbelief in the crowd, setting the scribes in opposition and raising doubts in the father's heart. Thus the devil established complete control. The disciples' faith had not been able to stand up against that unbelief.

If they wanted to be strong in their confrontation with all the unbelief unleashed by the devil, they would have to fast, thereby confessing before the Lord that they were worthless men. That way all false self-confidence would be rooted out. Then they would be able to pray in faith, and God's power would be revealed in their word.

By prayer and fasting they would have to exercise their faith. However, even that exercising takes place in faith. You can't produce faith by exercise alone. In faith we go to the Lord, seek communion with Him and finally through faith in Him confess our unworthiness. Thus, in communion with Him, as from His very presence, we are able to overcome the evil one.

Even though he does not manifest himself in these particular symptoms today, his reign is just as much around and in us now. Together with the Lord Jesus Christ, we shall be fighters for life.

MARK:
HIS DEPARTURE
AT JERUSALEM

CHAPTER FORTY TWO
HE CAME TO SERVE
MARK 10:32-45

The Son of man did not only serve; He now rules in heaven. Something of the glory of His reign shines on the governments of the nations. Hence there is nothing illegitimate about rulers of peoples having authority. There is even a revelation of Christ's reign in the authority of the office in the church, even though in that case we do not speak of reign.

The Son of man's serving concerns His state of humiliation. It is thus a serving in self-surrender. That's the way He Himself explained it by following up His remarks with the words "and to give His life as a ransom for many."

This serving in self-denial and humiliation is also the calling of those who are His people. To be sure, service is not for an atonement, but for redemption, the liberation of our human life from the reign of sin. Thus believers must truly serve not just in their instituted church communities but everywhere in life. Serving in self-denial for the redemption of life is the road to greatness because in that way we will bear much fruit. The grain of wheat that falls into the earth and dies bears much fruit.

A believer who, on the one hand, is called to serve in self-denial may on the other hand, have to rule as a government official or have authority in the church for supervision and discipline. However, there is no distinction between personal ethics and an ethics of office, as Luther thought. This is already evident from the fact that in Luther the distinction between the two kinds of ethics coincided with the distinction between two spheres, namely, that of the church and that of the state. But it becomes even clearer if we emphasize strongly that, properly understood, serving people is really serving God. The Son of man served God too when He gave His life as a ransom for many. The unity in man's self-denial in the service of people, on the one hand, and the exercise of authority over people, on the other hand, is found in the service of God in both spheres. In all these things we stand in our office before God. We bear the

image of the Christ in both His humiliation and His exaltation.
This viewpoint is also implied in Christ's statement that the places
on His right and left hand in the Kingdom will be given to those
for whom the Father has prepared them. During His humiliation,
Christ is nothing but the Servant of the Lord. The Father decides
about the places of honor. In the same way, we are to serve too.

Main Thought: *The Son of man came to serve.*

Prepared to be a sacrifice. From Galilee Jesus traveled to Judea and
Jerusalem. His disciples went with Him together with some others,
such as the women who served Him. On this journey He spent some
time in Transjordan and from there He got ready to go to Jerusalem.
He knew what it would lead to, namely, His suffering and death.

In going up to Jerusalem, He deliberately delivered Himself up
to that suffering. Evidently this decision moved Him deeply. The
Lord Jesus was leading His followers on the way, firmly resolved to
deliver Himself up. His disciples were amazed at His emotion, and
the others who followed Him were afraid.

He took His disciples aside on the road and told them once more,
now in detail, what was to happen to Him in Jerusalem. He would
be delivered up to the chief priests and scribes, and they would
condemn Him to death and hand Him over to the Gentiles. He
would be mocked and scourged and spit upon. He would be killed
and on the third day He would rise again. He knew all this and yet
He went. By His suffering He was to redeem His own people. By
doing so He would be serving the Father, in order to reconcile His
people again to the Father.

Did His disciples understand what He was saying? This
time, too, it passed right over their heads and failed to make any
impression. They could not imagine a Messiah who was going to
suffer. On that point they did not yet understand the Scriptures.
They only expected glory. They still had to learn to have need of
the Christ in His suffering, by seeing His suffering as an atonement
for their sins. Yet in their hearts they were already attached to Him.

Love mixed with selfishness. A bit farther along the road two of
His disciples, James and John, the sons of Zebedee, came to Him
to ask Him a question. They hadn't paid any attention to what He

had said about His suffering either. All they thought about was that they were going to Jerusalem now and that the Lord Jesus was deeply touched by that fact. Perhaps there would be tension and conflict in Jerusalem, but the reign of the Messiah was now going to begin. Hadn't they just seen His transfiguration on the mountain?

The question arose in their minds whether they would have a special place in that Kingdom. They were cousins of the Lord Jesus; their mother was His mother's sister. Moreover, several times He had shown them, together with Peter, His particular favor by taking only them along with Him.

Their love for Jesus was expressed in that question. They wanted to be close to Him in His Kingdom and share in His glory. They truly believed in Him. Yet their question suggested they were also looking out for their own interests. They wanted something special for themselves, something which also had to do with selfishness. It is so easy for love to look away from Him and begin looking to itself. Then love is off the track.

They didn't quite dare bring the matter up. At first they said that they wanted Him to do them a favor. They hesitated and tried to arouse His sympathy. When He asked what it was they wanted, they told Him—or rather, they had their mother tell Him (see Matt. 20:20-1). They wanted to sit at His right hand and left hand in His Kingdom.

Jesus saw through the selfishness in their question. Later on He would reprimand them for it, but He also recognized the love and faith present in it. For this reason He discussed the question with them further. First He said that they did not know what they were asking because the road to glory in His Kingdom was one of much suffering and self-denial. He was going to travel that road. He was going to drink the cup of suffering and be swept under by judgment as He had been by the waters at His baptism. Would they be able to travel that road of suffering with Him?

Without knowing what they were saying, they answered with a firm yes. They thought they could do anything. This was an overestimation of themselves that went hand in hand with the selfishness in their love.

When we look to Him, when He is our only concern, we also expect everything from Him and recognize our total dependence on Him. But as soon as we look out for our own interests, we rely on our own strength and think we can fend for ourselves. Then we no longer know the Lord Jesus, for His life was one of service. He did not look out for Himself but served the will of His Father. And we know Him only when we also want nothing else than to serve the Father. This was what Jesus now had to tell them.

Submission to the Father. He answered them that they would indeed share in His suffering. Of course, His suffering was totally unique in that it was to atone for our sins. No other human being's suffering is like that. Nevertheless, all who belong to Him share in the scorn and grief He suffered because He had to live in a world full of sin and misery. What grief sin brings to believers! What suffering they have to endure! Especially those who know the love of God suffer scorn and grief profoundly.

Yet in all their life believers may do nothing else than serve the Father. That's what the Lord Jesus did too. The Father alone decides what place in His Kingdom He will give to each of His servants. The Lord Jesus on earth knew Himself to be only the Servant of the Lord. One day He would receive authority from the Father, but for the present He still served in humiliation. Thus it was not for Him to say who would sit at His right hand and His left hand. The Father decides such things in His divine sovereignty. And we will only have to await His decision as His servants, submitting to Him. This is what the Lord Jesus told the sons of Zebedee.

Everyone's servant. When the other disciples found out what James and John had asked, they were terribly upset. It was as if those two disciples had wanted to get there first to reserve the highest places for themselves. But the fact that the other disciples were so disturbed showed that the same desire lived in the hearts of them all.

How little they really understood of the service of God in His Kingdom! And how little they understood that what was called for here on earth was service of one another in humiliation and self-denial. All men's lives are still caught up in sin and we are to try to free each other by denying ourselves and serving each other.

This was what Jesus now wanted to tell them. Therefore He called them together and taught them. The sovereign rulers and the prominent people on earth exercise an authority given to them by God. That's why they rule with power and demand subjection.

Something of the divine sovereignty has been put on their shoulders.

But theirs is a special calling. Not everyone has their authority and no one has it in every sphere of life. If we belong to the Lord Jesus, we must be willing to be the least, to be the servant of everyone for God's sake. We are to serve God in this respect, that we are a blessing to each other. And here on earth that is only possible by way of self-denial. Then we will bear much fruit and be great in the Kingdom of God. But God Himself will show us the way and decide what our place will be in His glorious Kingdom.

Jesus Himself is our example on this path of self-humiliation. He did not come to earth to be served. In a little while, after His suffering, He would have authority. He came to earth to serve and to redeem the lives of those who belong to Him.

He would do so by giving His life for His own. His life was like a ransom—a ransom by which slaves were redeemed. Through God's righteousness, we were handed over to the power of the evil one, but through the Lord Jesus Christ's sacrifice of Himself in death, we are set free. If in faith we know Him in His redeeming work, shouldn't we gladly give of ourselves for each other?

CHAPTER FORTY THREE
THE ANSWER TO THE QUESTIONS
MARK 12:13-44

We must guard against the idea that this portion of Scripture only shows how clever Christ was in rebuffing His questioners. Everything He says is revelation—more specifically, it is self-revelation, revelation of God's grace in Him.

Pharisees and Herodians about taxes. There is no contradiction in the words: "Render to Caesar the things that are Caesar's, and to God the things that are God's." Only if we give God His due can we give to Caesar and to our earthly rulers what properly belongs to them. When, through Christ, we give to God the love of our hearts, we can conduct our lives properly in our earthly relationships.

Sadducees and the resurrection. That God, who calls Himself the God of the patriarchs, is the God of the living implies the revelation of the resurrection of the dead. The patriarchs died and were in the realm of the dead; that is, they belonged to the dead. That's the way Scripture presents it to us. This is not to deny that they were saved but only when they are raised do they belong to the living again. Thus the fact that God is the God of the living requires their resurrection. Only then is their earthly life restored.

Main Thought: *Christ Himself is the answer to the questions.*

Taxes for Caesar. The Lord Jesus was in Jerusalem. Jubilantly the people had led Him into the city. They had honored Him as the Messiah, the Son of David. He had tolerated it, even though for many the veneration they offered was not genuine. Honoring Him was to be a proclamation of His kingship. But now He was in Jerusalem, the center of the opposition against Him.

The leaders of the people were far from happy with that honor. They surrounded Him on all sides, hoping to catch Him deviating from the law of Moses or to make Him look unacceptable to the people. Christ stood there in the midst of fire and continued to preach even though He knew what the end was going to be.

The rulers of the people sent some Pharisees and some Herodians to entrap Him. They thought they had devised an excellent trap. They began by flattering Him and saying that He was an upright man who spared no one when He spoke. That way He would surely fall into the trap. Then they came with their question: Should they pay taxes to Caesar or not? If He said they should, He would have the people against Him because they hated Roman rule. If He said they should not, they could go to the Romans and accuse Him of insurrection.

He saw through their intention at once. Angrily He reproached them for their hypocrisy, for appearing friendly while planning to set a trap for Him. Yet He wanted to answer their question. In His answer He taught them once more.

He had them bring Him a silver coin (a denarius). It was a Roman coin that was in general circulation. The coin bore the image of Caesar. He showed them the image and prompted them to say that it was the image of Caesar. Thereby He showed them that by their use of that coin, they had in fact accepted the rule of Caesar, which brought with it the obligation to pay taxes. In this way He answered them that they should give to Caesar what he had coming to him.

Could that be combined with the service of the Lord in Israel? Were they not to serve the Lord and be free of foreign rulers? Wouldn't they one day be governed by the house of David, namely, in the Messiah? Were they not to hold on to that promise in faith and resist all foreign domination?

Indeed, they were to serve only the Lord and wait for the fulfillment of His promise. Through the Messiah, He would rule them in His grace. But if they truly believed that, they would also see their sins and recognize the Roman domination as a chastisement. They might indeed groan under that domination and think of possible liberation from that yoke, but this had to happen by way of returning to the Lord with a confession of sin. Hence they were to give God what is His; that is, they were to give Him their hearts in the expectation of His salvation.

If we give the Lord our hearts and acknowledge the sovereign reign of the Lord Jesus Christ, we will also know how to conduct our lives in our earthly relationships. Then we will not be revolutionaries but will acknowledge God's hand in the direction (guiding) of history and also acknowledge the government He has given to us. On the other hand, this is not to say that we will approve of everything or passively wait for the wrong to get better. We will also fight against everything that is not in harmony with the Kingdom of God. But we may do that only according to His will and His Word.

The resurrection of the dead. The Pharisees and Herodians, sent by the rulers of the people, had suffered an ignominious defeat. The people were amazed at Him. Now there came people of another party, namely, the Sadducees. The Sadducees did not believe in angels or in the resurrection of the body. They thought they only had to accept what they could understand and what their own minds suggested to them. They were not at all open to the wonder of God's grace, which conquers sin and death.

These Sadducees made up a story to demonstrate the impossibility of the resurrection of the dead. They proceeded from a provision in the law of Moses to the effect that when a man died without a son, his brother was to marry his widow. Their first son would be considered a child of the deceased so that his name would not be blotted out in Israel (see Deut. 25:5-6). Once, they declared, seven brothers had had the same wife in that way. They then asked the Lord Jesus to whom this woman would be married at the resurrection of the dead.

By asking this question they presupposed that if we are restored to life in our bodies, life will continue as it is now, with marriage having the place it now has. First the Lord Jesus had to reproach them for their lack of understanding. Presently the glory of God's Kingdom will come. That does not just involve a restoration of the present life, except for sin. All of life, including all present relationships, will enter upon a higher glory. There will no longer be any marriage because the development and growth of the human race will have ended. In that Kingdom of glory, there will be an eternal blossoming. There God will be all in all, as He is with His angels.

Besides, the Lord Jesus wanted to show the Sadducees their unbelief. Doesn't God say in the Scriptures that He is the God of

Abraham, of Isaac and of Jacob? But that would have no meaning if the patriarchs were to be considered as belonging to the dead for good, for God is not the God of the dead but of the living. The honor of God, who is their God, demands that they be restored to earth again presently as living beings.

The Sadducees did not know the power of grace, which will bring about a complete restoration of our life. If we believe in the power of God's grace for Christ's sake, the questions will be resolved. What seemed to be impossible then becomes possible. In principle, the solution to all questions lies in faith in the Lord Jesus Christ, simply because He gives us the complete restoration of our lives.

The great commandment. One of the scribes (scholars in the law of Moses) had been present and heard the conversation. He seemed to be earnestly seeking the truth and was happy with Christ's answer to the Sadducees. He himself put another question to Him, but not to trap Him in His words. His was a question that was really bothering him. He asked which commandment came first, that is, which was the most important one and had to be kept before all the others.

That was really a question a scribe would ask. They thought that men had to earn heaven by keeping the commandments. They thought in terms of a whole lot of independent commandments which at times could come into conflict with one another. Thus the question was which one preceded all the rest—the laws regarding sacrifices, for instance, or the laws of purification, or the laws concerning the sabbath? The man was seriously concerned about this question because he wanted to act conscientiously.

The Lord Jesus had to reject this whole way of questioning. The first commandment is that there is only one God, in whom we must believe with all our heart. In that faith there is also love. Thus we must love God with all our heart. This love, then, will govern all our actions. For God's sake we will also love one another. That's the second commandment, but it is a requirement immediately given with the first; it is given with it because we are to love one another for God's sake. Hence there are not many commandments, some of which might conflict with others, but there is really just one. That commandment, which governs our whole life, is that we must love God.

The scribe was elated at the Lord Jesus' answer to his question.

That was it, all right—love God above all else, and your neighbor as yourself. That was also how the Old Testament said it and that was the way he really wanted it himself, although he had not been so conscious of that. He saw that in this way he got out of the confusion of the many commandments. He also saw something of the glory of that great requirement that governed all the commandments, even those regarding sacrifice.

Jesus rejoiced at the scribe's insight. Still, that insight was not enough because the scribe still saw love as something we have to do in order to obtain favor with God. But love for God, the love that governs everything else, is a gift too; it is an answer to the love with which God first loved us.

This love in the Kingdom is granted us by faith in the gracious love of God, the love revealed in the Lord Jesus. Thus faith in the Lord Jesus is the key to the answer to the question which commandment comes first. This the scribe did not yet see. He was more serious than the others and he probed more deeply. For that reason the Lord Jesus said to him, "You are not far from the Kingdom of God." Yet he still had to see, in faith, the glory of God's grace in that Kingdom.

David's Lord. The Lord Jesus had replied to the questions in such a way that no one dared ask Him anything further. Therefore He Himself began to ask questions. The scribes say that Christ is the Son of David. How can David himself say—and he does that under the inspiration of the Holy Spirit—that the Messiah is his Lord? In Psalm 110 he says: "The Lord said to my Lord: 'Sit at My right hand till I put your enemies under your feet.' "

The scribes were unable to answer that question. They had never faced that question although they had certainly read those words of David many times. If we do not read Scriptures in faith, that is, surrendering ourselves in faith to the Lord, who reveals Himself to us in them, we will not be confronted with the miracle of grace. Then we read right past it.

The miracle consists in this; that the eternal Son of God, who is David's Lord, also became David's Son, that is, the eternal Word became flesh. God Himself came to us in Christ for our redemption. The scribes understood nothing of that miraculous condescension of God in Christ for our salvation. They wanted to climb up to God by their own good works.

Jesus did not answer His own question. He made them think about it. Would they face up to the miracle in Scripture and find it in faith? In any case, He spoke a great deal of that miracle of God's condescending mercy. The people listened to Him eagerly. Did they understand it in faith? Perhaps in some instances their hearts were opened.

Serving the Lord either in appearance or in truth. How are we to serve the Lord? This must also have been a burning question among the people. Was it to be done in the way the scribes prescribed?

Jesus uttered a warning against the ways of the scribes. The scribes served the Lord in appearance only. In their hearts was nothing but selfishness. That was clear from the fact that they loved to strut through the streets in long robes to make themselves look important and pious, and that they loved to receive respectful greetings from others. They also liked to have the front seats in the synagogue and the places of honor at meals. They even demanded of poor widows the full fee for the service of the temple. They knew what was due the Lord! They themselves were very pious and were careful to show it in their long public prayers! They did it mainly to gain respect from men. Their judgment will be the greater because of this apparent piety. In the sincere service of the Lord we must not be self-seeking. We ought to bear that in mind always.

The Lord Jesus had an excellent opportunity to illustrate what He meant. He was sitting with His disciples in the Women's Court, where the treasure chest for the offerings of the people was located. Rich and poor deposited their offerings there.

Jesus saw a poor widow throw two copper coins into that chest. That was all she had. "Compare that with the gifts of the rich," He said. "They give out of their abundance, but this widow has given everything she has—her whole living." Very likely she had made a vow and now was paying her vow to the Lord.

We can offer all we have only when we see that we have received what we possess as a gift of God's grace. It's not necessary to give it all away, but when we put it to use, it's to serve God. We then also know how to give a proper portion for His service in His church. Everything becomes a gift of grateful love.

God has given us everything out of His grace for Christ's sake. We only give Him what is rightfully His. However, many who threw their gifts into the chest gave out of their abundance and thought that they were doing a great deal for the Lord and that the Lord then owed them a great deal in return. The scribes had taught the people they could buy God's favor.

The scribes' purpose for donating was to buy God's favor. They understood nothing at all of His grace, which gives everything freely. We accept that grace in faith.

The scribes' service was superficial, cosmetic because they understood nothing of God's grace. They lacked faith in Christ. Only by faith in the Lord Jesus Christ and in the grace bestowed on us in Him can we learn how to serve Him in spirit and in truth.

CHAPTER FORTY FOUR
LEARNING OBEDIENCE
MARK 14:32-42

In Hebrews 5:8 we are told that although Christ was the Son of God, He learned obedience from His sufferings in Gethsemane. He attained perfect obedience after going through a severe test. In Gethsemane, as the second Adam, He covered and atoned for the sin of the first Adam and for the sin we committed through Adam. By His obedience He restored the covenant that was broken by our disobedience.

Yet, His suffering in Gethsemane was only a prelude to the real suffering on the cross. In Gethsemane the Father confronted Him with His suffering and He looked it squarely in the face. This made His soul very sorrowful so that all His sensibilities and feelings were grievously affected by the thought of suffering and death (Ps. 103:1).

As early as Gethsemane the full horror of His coming suffering overwhelmed Jesus. This happened so that He would be fully aware beforehand of what He was taking upon Himself. He was being tested to see whether He would still be willing to offer Himself, just as in former ceremonial services sacrificial lambs were examined beforehand by the priest to see whether they were without blemish.

The very first words Jesus uttered in His prayer dealt with obedience and victory. He did not think of refusing the cup, but wondered only if the Father might be willing to remove it. The Father's decision was everything to Him.

How Jesus stood in relation to this suffering, is made clear by what He said to the disciples: "The spirit indeed is willing, but the flesh is weak." "Flesh" here does not mean man in his sin, because Jesus had no sin, but man in his weakness. The weakness, of course, is the result of sin but is not the sin itself. Thus the Word also became flesh, and Hebrews 5 speaks of the days of His flesh, the days of His humiliation.

"Spirit" is man in his constant communion with God as a result of being born of the Spirit (John 3:6). In this communion with God, man is to control the weakness of his flesh. The disciples, to the extent they had communion with God, were indeed willing to watch and pray. But they were also flesh and still subject to suffering and death. To this extent they were weak, unable to handle the powerful emotion and sorrow communicated by Christ to them. Luke tells us that they were sleeping "worn out by grief' (Luke 22:45, New English Bible). The spirit, or life in communion with God, did not govern their weak flesh. At the point at which their spirits failed to triumph over their flesh, their weakness became sin.

Christ asked them to watch with Him though all His people should have gathered in support of Him at that time. However, they could only have supported Jesus if they had been one with Him which, of course, was impossible. He alone gained the victory and He alone was able to undergo the necessary suffering.

Christ, too, was flesh; He was susceptible to every kind of suffering. Every emotion and horror could flood in upon His soul. The unnatural and violent element in death; the judgment in death; the abandonment in death; all these fears assaulted Him there in Gethsemane. How He must have shrunk from the prospect of dying!

His flesh, too, was weak. He had to suffer this weakness of the flesh to the full extent in the shuddering and fear of what was to come. In that fear He had to pray that the cup might pass from Him. He would not have been human if He had not prayed that; He would not really have been in the depths of our weakness.

Yet, in Him the spirit governed the flesh so that this weakness did not become sin, even for a moment. And through the mastery of His spirit over His flesh, He was able to pray during that night in which no one could pray anymore. Jesus' ability to pray already signaled the victory. He clung to His ties with heaven. By praying, He was able to gain complete victory over His fear, enabling Him to surrender in complete willingness to those who took Him prisoner. Thus it can be said in Hebrews 5 that His prayer was heard because of His godly fear. For Him His victory over fear was also an answer to prayer.

The words "Sleep on now and take your rest" were probably not ironic, but a question: "Are you still sleeping and taking your rest?"

Main Thought: *From His suffering in Gethsemane, Christ learns obedience.*

The Lamb that was examined. The tension between the Lord Jesus and the elders of the people in Jerusalem continued to rise. The elders had already decided to put Him to death. They received help from an unexpected source: one of the disciples, Judas, had come to them secretly and offered to deliver Him into their hands in such a way that there wouldn't be a riot. The Lord Jesus knew what kind of a plot was being hatched. Nevertheless, He stayed on in Jerusalem and surrendered willingly to death.

The first nights of the week in which He was to suffer He spent in Bethany, near Jerusalem. By the end of the week, the traveling back and forth apparently became too tiring. In any case, the last night He no longer returned to Bethany but spent the night with His disciples in the open air in an olive grove on the slope of the Mount of Olives. That place was called Gethsemane.

When He came to the grove, He knew that the Sanhedrin would send a band of soldiers to look for Him and that they would find Him there. Then the Father would deliver Him into the hands of sinners who would kill Him. At the entrance to the garden the terror of that suffering came over Him. He felt that in that night He would have to wrestle His way through the terror. Therefore He left eight of His disciples at the entrance and took only Peter, James and John with Him deeper into the garden.

To them He confessed what was going on inside Him. He was amazed and very troubled. God showed Him all that was going to happen to Him and He accepted it completely. He would be forsaken by God, and death would come over Him, that terrible punishment for sin. If ever there was a man who thirsted for life, for ties with this entire world, for a taste of God's loving-kindness in all of it, it was He. Death with its darkness and abandonment was so foreign to Him that He was aghast at such horror—and very troubled. To His three disciples He said: "My soul is very sorrowful, even to death." His inner awareness and feelings were grievously affected by all that is so terrible about death. His sorrow was so great that He was in imminent danger of dying from it.

Why did God permit this to come over Him? Because He first had to experience this horror fully. If He did not know this suffering, how would it ever be clear beforehand that He was prepared to take it upon Himself and be obedient unto death? He first had to fight His way completely through this horror, in order to be a willing sacrifice in His suffering. It had to be definitely established beforehand that there was nothing lacking in His obedience. Otherwise His sacrifice would have no value. In like manner, during the time of the Old Testament a priest had to examine the sacrificial lamb beforehand to see if it was without blemish. Otherwise it could not be sacrificed.

Spirit and flesh. He had to wrestle with this horror in order to conquer it completely. Therefore He left even His three disciples behind in order to be able to struggle alone in prayer. He did not withdraw far from them; they would still be able to see and hear Him. There would indeed have to be witnesses of this struggle which He, as our Head, underwent for us. He also wanted them to know Him in this struggle, to understand something of it. Indeed, all His people should have a share in this struggle. Hence He asked them to watch with Him.

How genuinely human the Lord Jesus was! With all that was in Him, He abhorred that suffering, that death. He could not help but pray to be delivered from it. To the very end, He could pray for the suffering to be taken away from Him—and had to pray that prayer. When the suffering did come, this enabled Him to bear it willingly so that it became a sacrifice of obedience. That's why He asked that this cup be removed from Him if it was possible.

That "if it was possible" was not an expression of unbelief. On the contrary, He began by saying, "Abba, Father, all things are possible with You," that is, everything that is in agreement with Your name and honor and that serves the fulfillment of Your Word. If it is in agreement with that, then let this cup be removed.

Jesus was a weak human being too, just as we are—a weak human being who would naturally suffer terribly from the thought of the death that was about to come. He was flesh, just as we are. But He was also spirit and He knew the life of communion with God.

In that communion He had to be strong and had to overcome the horror and be completely ready to be sacrificed. The spirit in Him would have to overcome the flesh completely. Thus He struggled against the horror and controlled the weakness of His flesh. Not for a single moment did the flesh in Him gain the upper hand. He did not run away from that suffering but talked it all over with His Father. The fact that He prayed was already a victory. And it was particularly a victory that He prayed that the will of God for redemption might be done. In His desire for the redemption of the world, He was in complete agreement with the Father.

By praying, He had the flesh under His control. Then He stood up and went over to the three disciples. They had not watched with Him; they had not known Him in His struggle. Instead they had fallen asleep. The emotion and distress of the Lord Jesus had communicated itself to them. They, too, were flesh; they dreaded the terrible thing that was evidently going to happen. Of course, they were also spirit and knew the life of communion with God, but the weakness of the flesh, the horror, in their case, had the upper hand. They were overcome by sadness and despair and therefore were not able to pray. Any contact with God at that moment was out of the question for them. Their sadness and despair made them fall asleep.

They should have watched with Him. They would have been able to do that only by focusing their faith on the strength of the one who was struggling for them. Of themselves they would never have been able to conquer this horror. There was only one who could accomplish this. He prayed in the night, in that hour of darkness in which no one could pray anymore. With that He conquered all weakness of the flesh. By faith in communion with Him His disciples would have been able to watch and pray, and they should have done so.

He reproached them for falling asleep—especially Peter, who had declared so strongly that he was ready for anything. And He admonished them to watch and pray so that they would not fall into a temptation from which there would be no escape, for then the horror would overcome them without their being prepared and there would be no hope of victory. They certainly were God's children. As to the spirit, they were indeed willing, but the weakness of their flesh already dominated and would presently get the upper hand.

The Lord Jesus did indeed control the flesh in Himself, but this does not mean that the horror did not repeatedly attack Him with new force or that the flesh did not threaten to become too strong for Him. Again and again He experienced that terrible anxiety. Therefore He went back to struggle alone. He prayed the same words, and by praying held down the flesh.

When He returned, He found His three disciples sleeping again. They had been completely overcome by the weakness of the flesh. They were no longer able by faith to reach out to Him in His strength. When He woke them up, they were in complete confusion, like strangers, and were embarrassed before Him. They did not know what to answer Him—that's how far removed from Him they were by then.

Once again He went back. Dreadful was the struggle. Just because the flesh in Him fought against the spirit, it rose up even stronger. The agony was hardly bearable. He sweated blood. And if an angel had not come from heaven to strengthen Him, He would have died in His agony. The angel removed nothing of the horror but only strengthened Him so that He did not perish. He underwent a terrible struggle in His agony, but He held on to His Father in prayer. His oneness with the Father's will to redeem the world prevailed in Him.

Heard for His godly fear. By praying He also gained the victory over His horror. The moment came when He could banish the anxiety from His soul and accept His suffering in complete willingness. This willingness was also the answer He received from the Father; it was an answer to His prayer. No one else has ever been able to keep on praying in such torment, and no one else has received such willingness. Only Jesus has been able to do that.

In Adam, we let go of God in completely different circumstances, when there was no question of horror but only of favor and glory. As our Head, Christ covered and atoned for our sin by struggling through in prayer to that perfect obedience in which He gave Himself for the redemption of the world, an obedience in which He was in complete harmony with the Father.

Then He returned to His disciples again and asked them whether they were now going to sleep and rest some more. The time was past. The moment had come when God would deliver Him into the hands of sinners, so that by suffering He might redeem the world. The disciples should now get up because the betrayer was close by.

How completely consciously and willingly He gave Himself! He was ready, but were His disciples ready? They were not in control of the flesh. Because of this, they would fall into a temptation which they could not resist.

The flesh is always weak, but He overcame that. By faith in Him, by being joined to Him, to the Victor, it is now possible to watch and pray even when it appears impossible to us. Anxiety sometimes seems to remove prayer far from us, for we are weak according to the flesh. But by looking to Him, we are yet able to pray, without being led into a temptation that would be too powerful for us.

CHAPTER FORTY FIVE
LIKE A MURDERER
MARK 14:43-72

For a fuller treatment of the trial by the Sanhedrin, see the corresponding section of Matthew. The question of Christ's defenselessness we will leave for our discussion of Luke's gospel. Here the arrest is in the foreground.

As Israel's ruler, Christ was also its shepherd. He said of the elders of the people that they were thieves and murderers who climbed in by another way. Now the roles were reversed as He was taken prisoner like a murderer and treated as an enemy of the state.

This happened so that the Scriptures would be fulfilled. In the Scriptures we find God's plan of salvation. That plan is fulfilled in the arrest of Christ as a murderer. As such He suffered and made atonement for the sins of His people, who repeatedly rejected Him as their ruler and shepherd and chose other leaders for themselves. For example, David was rejected in favor of Absalom. The flesh always rejects Christ as shepherd and chooses for itself leaders who confirm the pride of the flesh.

There is much to be said for the assumption that the young man who ran away naked was John Mark himself. It is noteworthy that Mark is the only one who relates this story. Then we would also have to accept the assumption that Christ and His disciples held the last supper in the house of Mary, Mark's mother.

We could picture the course of events as follows. When Judas summoned the band of soldiers from the Sanhedrin, he first went to Mary's house to see if Christ was still there. When it turned out that He was gone, he went to Gethsemane, where he was confident he would find Him. This alerted Mark to the fact that trouble was brewing. He must have gotten out of bed hastily to give Christ some warning.

All of this is indeed probable, but we cannot be certain. In any case, we may not say that this little incident is without significance because this cannot be said of anything in Scripture. Even this brief account illustrates the personal attachment and the guilelessness of Christ's followers. It brings to light all the more strongly the outrage of coming out against Him with a band of soldiers, as though He were a murderer and an enemy of the state.

Main Thought: *Christ is taken prisoner and condemned as a murderer.*

His self-surrender. No sooner had the Lord Jesus struggled through to victory in Gethsemane and told His disciples that they should get up because the betrayer was at hand, than a band of soldiers arrived on the scene, armed with swords and clubs. This band had been sent by the Sanhedrin. At its head was Judas, the disciple who had chosen to betray Him. During the night he had gone to the Sanhedrin and told the rabbis that there was now a favorable opportunity for taking Jesus prisoner without attracting attention. He knew that the Lord Jesus would probably spend the night in Gethsemane.

Yet he was not completely certain about the attitude of the other disciples. Would they offer resistance to prevent the arrest? They would have to be taken by surprise. Therefore he made an agreement with the armed band. The disciples were totally unaware of his treachery. He would go up to the Lord and kiss Him, seemingly to greet Him after his absence. Then the band of soldiers would immediately arrest Him and separate Him from His disciples. He would not be allowed an opportunity to escape in the confusion.

How poorly Judas understood his former Master! After all, the Lord Jesus is God's Son; He is the full revelation of God's grace. Either the majesty of that grace would consume Judas and his troop, or Christ would willingly surrender Himself. But what were swords and clubs against that grace? And how poorly Judas knew the disciples to whose circle he had belonged! Even though they would want to defend their Master in their own way, wouldn't His spirit govern them? Judas never knew the grace in the Lord Jesus Christ.

He went up to Him, kissed Him, and said, "Rabbi, Rabbi!" Jesus knew exactly what this meant and was not taken by surprise. Instead He surrendered voluntarily to those who arrested Him. Shouldn't He drink the cup? Hadn't He just gained a victory over the flesh? Indeed, He would surrender Himself in order to reconcile the world to God. Thus He offered no resistance to the soldiers who seized Him when Judas gave the sign.

The disciples were taken by surprise in spite of the warning from Jesus. Peter was carrying a sword because he really believed it might come to a battle of swords. How little understanding he and the other disciples had of Christ's willingness to give Himself up for the atonement of the world!

Peter drew his sword and struck out at the enemy. However, the Spirit of the Lord Jesus governed the disciples and caused Peter to stop. The Lord did not want such a defense. Instead He gave Himself up on our behalf.

That the Scriptures might be fulfilled. His arrest by a band armed with swords and clubs affected Him deeply. He even said that they had come out against Him as though He were a murderer. He, Israel's ruler and shepherd was arrested like a murderer! He certainly would not disturb Israel. Instead He would rule Israel in grace in the name of His Father and thus gather His sheep. The thieves and murderers were the leaders of the people. They were leading the people astray and doing them everlasting harm with their false teaching.

How this grieved the Lord Jesus! And how He suffered when they laid their hands on Him. Couldn't they have arrested Him in the temple, when He spoke of the grace of God? Why hadn't they arrested Him then, and why did it have to happen in this way now?

He understood why He had to suffer all this. Hadn't it been prophesied in Scripture that He would be numbered with the transgressors? (Is. 53:12). The people, through their leaders, rejected grace as something criminal and dangerous to the state.

That's how grace in Him must seem to all who themselves want to be lord and master in this life, who want to achieve their own salvation. Hereby Christ suffered and atoned for this total rejection of the grace of God by all flesh. As a criminal He was arrested in order that He might be honored one day by many in faith as their Ruler and Deliverer. Shouldn't we look, then, to what He suffered willingly?

The guileless ones. The disciples had been reduced to total confusion by this self-surrender on the part of the Lord Jesus. What was now to become of His kingship? That this road of suffering and atoning for our sins was the way to His glorious kingship in grace they did not understand.

They could have fought for Him, but now that He forbade them to do so, they did not know where they stood anymore with Him. How great the enmity was and how He would make atonement for that enmity by His willing suffering they did not understand. Neither did they understand that they, at that time, could only have been with Him by willingly surrendering along with Him.

Although Peter carried a sword, they were still quite guileless. They did not know the enmity and they did not understand their Master's desire. In confusion, they all fled. They were not ready for self-surrender. They had not struggled in Gethsemane as He had done. Now they had fallen into a temptation which they did not know how to handle. Although we do not always receive the calling to surrender without any defense, as the disciples did then, we must always be willing to suffer for Christ.

That circle of disciples was not one that would defend Him to the death with the sword. Indeed, it was in a different way that His spirit controlled them. This was also evident with regard to another follower of the Lord Jesus, a follower who was still a young man.

Evidently this young man suspected what was happening. Hastily he got out of bed, threw just a sheet around himself, and went out into the street at night to Gethsemane to warn the Lord Jesus. How guileless that young man was! Personal love drove him on, but he had nothing to defend himself with. The soldiers found him and seized him, but he left the sheet in their hands and fled home naked. He, too, left the Lord Jesus.

Thus the Lord Jesus stood there alone in His suffering. He fought the battle alone for us and made atonement. Although He was taken prisoner as a murderer, He would gather His people as a true king by means of His suffering.

Deserving of death. Bound, He was led before the Sanhedrin, which was meeting in the night. False witnesses were hired to testify against Him and many accusations were brought. Because He was against the law of Moses, He was certainly a disturber of the people, a thief, a murderer, an enemy of the state. Here, too, He had to endure these accusations. But none of the accusations could be proved.

Because they were not making any progress towards a conviction, the high priest stood up and asked Him if He really claimed to be *the Christ,* the Son of the blessed God. The high priest asked Him this under oath. The Lord Jesus affirmed that He was indeed *the Christ,* in whom God's full grace had come to them, and that one day He would reign in His grace.

For the high priest and the Sanhedrin, that was the most awful blasphemy imaginable. Weren't *they* the true leaders of the people? And did He now propose to take over in God's name—He, the one whom they, as the rightful judges, hated and rejected? Did the disturber of the people pass Himself off as *the Christi* There was but one sentence: He deserved to die.

They jeered at Him, spat on Him and struck Him. The members of the Sanhedrin joined their servants in mocking Him. Wasn't He a criminal? How difficult was the road that the Lord Jesus followed to attain His true kingship in grace!

I do not know the man! That road was made even more painful for Him by denials by one of His disciples. Peter, who had lunged out in Gethsemane and then fled, had returned. He was ashamed of himself. Because he still had not come to understand Jesus' self-surrender, he was ashamed only of having fled. He still had confidence in himself.

Because someone had put in a word for him, he had gotten into the courtyard. But his heart was trembling; he was not prepared to be with the Lord Jesus in self-surrender. He was not with Him in spirit.

What he feared finally happened. One person after another recognized him as one of the disciples. All that time in Jerusalem with Jesus, Peter had not been in the background. Three times he now denied that he was His disciple. He even declared that he did not know the man. He acted as if he didn't want to be mentioned in the same breath with that criminal.

Even His disciple, then, said he was ashamed of Him. By his denial Peter contributed to the judgment that came over Jesus. Wasn't that horrible? That, too, the Lord Jesus had to suffer. The road of atoning for our sins was indeed a terrible one!

Jesus had warned Peter that he would deny Him three times before the cock crowed twice. After the third denial Peter heard the cock crowing. How shocked he was then! He made his way out the door and went outside, where he wept bitterly. Now he was no longer just ashamed of himself. He had denied his Lord and terribly offended His grace and love. Where would he find a place to hide?

Yet, Peter knew his Master; he knew of a grace that would one day conquer everything. Therefore he did not despair unto death, even though it cost him a great deal before he got over this and was able to believe that his transgression was forgiven. Jesus also suffered Peter's denial to make atonement for our unfaithfulness.

CHAPTER FORTY SIX
REGARDED AS NOTHING
MARK 15:1-20

In this treatment of the hearing before Pilate, we focus our attention on the choice between Jesus and Barabbas. At the same time, we may not lose sight of the judge who placed the people before this choice. With a murderer like Barabbas, Pilate would never have taken the liberties he took with Christ, treating Him as a condemned man even before the sentence was pronounced. It was much less necessary with Christ, who in Pilate's mind was not even a danger to the state. As a matter of fact, Pilate, the people, Barabbas himself, and the band of soldiers all regarded Jesus as worthless.

Main Thought: *The Christ is regarded as worthless.*

By Pilate. Early in the morning the Sanhedrin met again. An official accusation was agreed upon. On the basis of the contrived accusation they could hand Jesus over to Pilate. He had called Himself the King of the Jews, thus stirring up rebellion against the authority of the Roman emperor.

They bound Him and led Him away to Pilate who took Him into his courthouse and asked Him if He was the king of the Jews. Jesus could not give a direct answer to that question. He was, indeed, King of the Jews, but not in the sense in which the Jews understood the term or the sense in which Pilate would take it. Therefore He replied, "You have said so."

After this Pilate questioned Him further. He was confronted with a real puzzle because he didn't understand the kingship of Christ. But he did understand that this man was no danger to the state and told this to the elders of the people. They then began to accuse Him of many other things. To all these charges He made no reply. This made Pilate wonder and he became even more convinced that Jesus posed no threat to his authority.

Meanwhile, the people of Jerusalem had come to the courthouse to choose a prisoner to be released. The Romans had given this privilege to the Jews; at each Passover feast, a prisoner of the people's choice would be released. In this way the Romans allowed the Jews some semblance of independence. That's probably the reason why the Passover feast was chosen; it was the feast at which the Jews celebrated their deliverance from Egypt.

When the people assembled for that purpose, Pilate thought he would surely be able to present Jesus to the people as the prisoner who was to be released. In this line of reasoning he committed the greatest injustice. After all, Jesus had not yet been convicted, but Pilate was treating Him as though He was already proven guilty. Moreover, Pilate put Him over against Barabbas, a man who had been arrested in a revolt. On that occasion he had killed someone. Pilate placed this revolutionary murderer over against the Lord Jesus, convinced that the people would surely choose for Jesus. His intentions were good but he violated all justice.

But what difference did it make, since it involved only Jesus? People thought that anything was permitted in His case. He was not counted for anything; His death had no significance. With someone like Barabbas, Pilate had to be careful, but who was Jesus?

How the Lord Jesus must have suffered under all this! No one knew Him or realized the value of His life. He was regarded as even less than a murderer. If only Pilate had known that His life, His blood, was the price with which the world was to be ransomed! But that was completely overlooked.

By the people. The elders of the people saw that there was a good chance that the people would indeed demand the release of the Lord Jesus. Therefore they moved among the crowd, stirring the people up to demand the release of Barabbas. The people allowed themselves to be led into perpetrating this travesty of justice. What did justice and a human life mean to the people?

Jesus had disappointed their expectations. All He had done through His mercy to reveal the grace of God; the way He had given Himself; all His works of healing, help and deliverance were outweighed by the disappointment the people felt when Jesus failed to liberate them from the Roman yoke. The people really didn't want the redemption of life and its restoration before God; they wanted independence and freedom from foreign rule and release from the Lord's yoke of grace.

That's the way the people still want it today—unless the Lord overcomes them by His Spirit and Word. We would sooner idealize a man like Barabbas, the insurrectionist, than submit to Christ's rule of grace.

The people cried out for Pilate to release Barabbas. When Pilate asked what he should do with the king of the Jews, the people's hatred against the Lord Jesus broke loose because of the disappointment He had caused them. They shouted, "Crucify Him!" When Pilate asked what evil He had done, they shouted all the more, "Crucify Him! "

The shame of being crucified had to come upon Jesus so that no one could ever think of Him without contempt. By means of crucifixion, a typically Roman means of punishment, He was to be removed from among the people. Nobody wanted to have anything to do with Him anymore. But the people still had expectations of Barabbas. When he was released, they may well have carried him off on their shoulders.

Jesus was despised and rejected by His own people. Yet He was the true Head of that people—even more than David or Solomon had been. He was the Head who by His obedience unto death would gather the people and bring them back to God.

One day His true people will kneel before Him and bless Him. But how Christ must have suffered when the people rejected Him and raised their banners for Barabbas! It was only along this road of suffering that He became the true Head of His people.

By Barabbas. Barabbas must have been delighted after he was set free! He had probably never dreamed of it! He had faced certain death but now he was free—and this because of that fanatic Jesus of Nazareth! How he must have despised Him in his heart and laughed at Him! He, Barabbas, who had broken society's laws goes free and receives a hero's welcome, while Jesus, who truly gives Himself to God, perishes. But that's so often the case in the life of nations and among men. Self-seeking people come to power.

Fortunately, Christ also suffered for this. But one day there will come a restoration when God will despise all who have despised Him and will honor all who have sought Him, though not because they are worthy of themselves, but because Jesus moved them to seek God. And as they have shared in His rejection, they will one day share in His honor.

By the soldiers. Pilate handed Jesus over to be crucified. The platoon of soldiers charged with the execution of the sentence took Him into the courthouse. They all gathered around to mock Him.

With a soldier's red cloak, a crown of thorns and a reed, they gave Him the appearance of a king and proceeded to ridicule Him. What could be more absurd than a man who had gone throughout the land doing good, calling himself king of the Jews but never following through and grabbing power? With such a preposterous phoney you could take whatever liberties you wanted. Those soldiers had more respect for an insurrectionist like Barabbas than for a fool like Jesus. They delighted in making Him look ridiculous.

The world still ridicules Christ's crucifixion as foolish. What on earth can be accomplished with redemption? It goes completely against the grain of our proud, sinful minds. That Christ came and surrendered to the curse and thus became a blessing for the world is something that simply doesn't fit anywhere in our proud designs. But our designs have to be converted, making the cross of Christ the cornerstone of all our thinking.

Jesus suffered the scorn of being taunted as a fool. As a result many now look up to Him in adoration, admiring the wisdom of God who gave Him up for our salvation.

CHAPTER FORTY SEVEN
POWERLESSNESS
MARK 15:21-47

Although Christ laid down His life voluntarily, since no one took it from Him against His will, we can still speak of His powerlessness. He surrendered Himself voluntarily to that powerlessness. In doing so He manifested His power over the flesh. That power showed itself repeatedly, for example, when He cried out with a loud voice at the moment He died.

His powerlessness was a result of being forsaken by God. To this abandonment He had surrendered Himself. Abandonment by God was the cause for His physical death. "Physical" refers to life in its weakness, the result of sin, the mortal element in life that must be destroyed. This mortal element or weakness of the flesh makes it possible for Him to be forsaken by God, to be subjected to final death.

Although Christ Himself was without sin, He suffered death to the full because our sin was applied to Him. As a result of His death, the mortal element within us has already been conquered to the extent that believers can no longer be forsaken by God.

Because He was abandoned by God, He could no longer have any power over life. By His suffering He gained eternal communion with God for His people, and in that communion, power over life, the right to eat from the tree of life.

Main Thought: *The Christ suffers powerlessness in death.*

Powerless in His suffering. From Pilate's courthouse the soldiers led Jesus outside the city. Criminals were always crucified outside the community. The Lord Jesus, too, was cast out of the community. He who is our Head and took our sins upon Himself was no longer judged fit for human society.

Outside the city He was crucified on a hill called *Golgotha*. First they wanted to give Him wine to drink as depressant, which He refused. He surrendered willingly to His suffering. After all, had

He not conquered the flesh? They proceeded to cast lots for His garments, already considering Him dead.

Above His head Pilate had placed an inscription stating the charge against Him: "The King of the Jews." Pilate used the pretext to frighten anyone who might similarly want to resist the emperor's authority. Neither Pilate nor the Jews understood the kind of kingship Jesus had been talking about. In any case, the glory of His kingship was temporarily overshadowed by the power of the Roman emperor.

On either side of Him they crucified a murderer. Even in death, then, He was counted with the transgressors. For our sins He was put to shame, and in the shame of our sins He was made a public spectacle.

For hours on end He was subjected to this bitter suffering and shame. He, *the Christ,* the one who was sent to redeem the world and who by His power will one day bring this world to complete redemption, hung on the cross powerless. He had surrendered willingly to His destiny and was willingly deprived of all power. On the cross He could not even move and every destructive power ruled over Him. In this way He suffered for us. Yet because of our sins we also deserve to be handed over to the powers of destruction.

Mocked for His powerlessness. Many people passed by that dreadful place. They stopped, shook their heads in false compassion and sneered at Him for His powerlessness: "Save Yourself and come down from the cross." The elders of the people followed suit with cynical jokes made to one another. He had indeed saved others, they said, but He was obviously unable to save Himself. If He would give them a sign now and come down from the cross they would believe in Him. This is how they thought to have triumphed over Jesus whom they had never been able to match in words. Even the murderers who were crucified with Him ridiculed Him.

The elders were right: Jesus had saved others but He could not save Himself. He was not allowed to save Himself if He wished to save others. By atoning for their sins through this suffering, He was able to save others. Salvation comes by the grace of God which Jesus obtained.

What an ordeal this mockery must have been for Jesus! Yet He withstood it. He had gained the victory in Gethsemane and was therefore fully prepared to suffer, even unto death.

Powerless as a result of abandonment. From nine o'clock in the morning until twelve noon, Jesus suffered on the cross. How was it possible that He was turned over to all suffering, to all the forces of destruction and ultimately even to death? It happened because God had forsaken Him. If a man has communion with God, he also has power to live, but if God abandons Him, he is subject to destruction.

God abandoned Jesus more and more. What an experience this must have been for Him, for He longed for communion with God more than any other man. No one will ever be able to fathom it. When the bond with God broke, He died a thousand deaths. Complete darkness and hell itself engulfed Him. He suffered eternal death.

Jesus Christ is the Light of the world. Only through Him come grace and light. And He is Head of the world. If He was forsaken and left in total darkness, the whole world would one day be lost in total darkness. That became clear when the sun was darkened at noon. Eternal darkness would one day have engulfed the entire world had Jesus not endured the suffering of complete loneliness.

In that darkness, concealed from every eye, He suffered for three long hours. His suffering was ultimate. Deeper and deeper He plunged. He became more and more appalled at the depth of the misery resulting from being forsaken by God. "My God, My God, why have You forsaken Me?" He cried out. "What *is* sin, anyhow, and how abysmal *is* its misery? Will I never reach the bottom of that misery?" Jesus had to explore the depths of sin and its effects on God. To that depth God cast Him down. He sank deeper and deeper, seized by unspeakable terror, in utter powerlessness. That was the price for our atonement.

When Jesus uttered that cry, He had fathomed sin's depth. He thereby removed judgment from us. Proof of that removal was the return of light. When it became a bit lighter, the mockery on Golgotha resumed. The uneasy mockery served to dispel the awful impression the darkness had made.

Because Jesus had cried, "Eloi, Eloi," they sneered that He had called on Elijah to save Him. When someone went to moisten His lips with a sponge dipped in vinegar, someone else called him back, but he insisted saying he wanted to see whether Elijah would come to save Him (see Matt. 27:48-9). He wouldn't be allowed to die just yet.

Powerless in death. But God decided otherwise. Jesus had accomplished the atonement for our sins, and was now allowed to die. That was not just to bring an *end* to His humiliation. He had been forsaken by God; now He also was delivered up to temporal death. Death, too, would rule over Him.

Temporal death came into the world because we broke the bond with God and therefore death would vanquish Jesus also. He endured the violent grip of death as though held in chains.

Yet He had willingly surrendered to all that despair, including death. Even at the moment of His death, Jesus was a willing victim. The power of all His enemies was broken because He willingly surrendered to His suffering for God's sake, in order to reconcile the world to God.

Because Jesus had been a willing victim, His suffering became an atoning sacrifice. He expressed His willingness and His victory in the spirit when He cried out in a loud voice at the moment of death. Even the centurion who stood guard over Him saw an element of victory in His death and proclaimed: "Truly, this man was a son of God."

Because His suffering and death was a sacrifice offered up to God, it would become an eternal blessing. It would bring about perfect communion between God and man. God revealed this at the very same moment, as when He died, the curtain of the temple was torn in two. Until then God had dwelt concealed behind the curtains, but now His people would be privileged to walk in full communion before God's face.

Powerless in the grave. Of all Christ's followers, only some women and a few disciples were witnesses of His death. He would have to be buried quickly, before the sabbath began at six o'clock.

God Himself took care of the burial. There was a member of the Sanhedrin who, in faith, had seen the Kingdom of grace through the words and deeds of the Lord Jesus. For fear of the Jews, he had not revealed his convictions. He now went to Pilate and asked for permission to take care of the burial. The faith of this man, Joseph of Arimathea, was genuine; when it looked as if the Lord Jesus had perished, his faith did not fail him. Rather, he declared it openly. The body of the Lord Jesus was laid to rest in a new grave owned by Joseph.

Jesus lay there powerless. They did with Him as they saw fit. They took Him down from the cross, carried Him away, and brought Him to the grave. He, too, had entered the realm of the dead and was delivered up to oblivion. And yet, He Himself had willed that. Through this He endured the judgment upon our sin. *We* are the ones who deserve to be forever forgotten. Because of His willingness, God did not deliver Him up to corruption in the grave. Instead His suffering was a sacrifice that fulfilled God's demand.

Presently He would arise. And for His sake, God will not deliver His own up to oblivion. With Christ we will one day triumph over death and grave and receive the power to live.

CHAPTER FORTY EIGHT
THE WORD OF THE KING
MARK 16:1-20

This is not the place to go into the question whether verses 9-20 of chapter 16 indeed stem from Mark. The church has accepted them as canonical. They provide a conclusion that is certainly in harmony with the intention of Mark's entire gospel. As is evident from the first verse of the first chapter, Mark meant to describe the beginning of the gospel of Jesus Christ, the Son of God, the beginning of the gospel as it was spread abroad in the Roman world. The last chapter concludes by declaring that the disciples were preaching everywhere and that the Lord worked with them and confirmed the message by the signs that attended it.

The emphasis in this last chapter, then, is on the Word that was to be preached in the name of the risen Lord. The Word of the King demanded faith and subjection. Hence it is said that he who believes and is baptized will be saved, but that he who does not believe will be condemned.

The appearances of the risen Lord are barely mentioned. They are confirmations of the Word of the resurrection. And in that connection these verses speak of the disciples' unbelief with regard to that Word.

The unbelief of the disciples is not in conflict with what Luke tells us, namely, that the disciples received the two men of Emmaus with the joyful shout: "The Lord has risen indeed and has appeared to Simon." But Luke himself says that they were really too overjoyed to believe it (Luke 24:41). That expresses it very clearly; it indicates what faith in the resurrection involves: either we do not believe the resurrection, or, if we believe, we are released from sin and death, and a new world opens to us. Thus the disciples shouted for joy at the repeated announcement, but when they were actually confronted with the fact and all its consequences, they couldn't cope with it.

Main Thought: *The Word of the King goes forth with power, for He lives.*

The Word of the resurrection. The women present at the burial had no rest in Jerusalem. They knew how hastily the internment had been taken care of. Therefore they bought more spices to embalm the body. That was not their only reason for going to the grave; they simply couldn't stay away from it. The hope of their lives lay buried there. Without Jesus and the Word of His grace, there was no life for them. Where, now, was the healing and redemption of life by the reign of grace? Jesus had perished.

On the way they remembered the stone which sealed the grave. Who would roll it away for them? But as they came close, they saw to their joy that it had already been rolled away. Evidently the grave was a whole burial chamber.

They went inside, but they did not find the body of the Lord Jesus. As a matter of fact, the first thing that met their eyes was the figure of a young man sitting on the right side, clothed in a long white robe. They looked at him in amazement.

Immediately the young man began to speak to them. No doubt they saw that he was an angel. He said to them that they should not be afraid. At the same time he told them that their search would be in vain, because Jesus was no longer under the curse of the cross or of death. He had conquered our sin and that sin, in turn, was the cause of His suffering and death. He was alive again and had power once more, this time never to lay down His life again. That right He had obtained by His death. They should simply look at the place where He had lain. If they believed what the angel told them, then seeing the empty place would confirm their faith.

They were also instructed to tell His disciples that He would appear to them in Galilee, as He had said. There they would hear the Word of the King. In speaking of the disciples, the angel mentioned Peter in particular. Peter should not think that because of his denial he was excluded from the circle of the disciples for good. There was also grace for him. How that must have comforted Peter when he heard about it later!

However, the disciples did not receive this message right away for the women fled from the tomb. Because of their fear and amazement, they did not say anything to anyone. They were unable to cope with what they had just seen and heard.

As a result of the Lord Jesus' resurrection, we, too, may enjoy perfect peace with God. Then the heavenly glory, the glory of the angels, is not strange to us anymore. But that's something so tremendous that it was still beyond the power of those women. How often it is beyond our power too!

Faith in the resurrection Word. That same day the Lord Jesus appeared to several people to confirm this resurrection Word which the angel had spoken and which He Himself had spoken earlier. First He appeared to Mary Magdalene, who was very much attached to Him because He had delivered her from seven devils. Mary brought the news to the disciples who were mourning and weeping, but they did not believe her. Afterwards the message was confirmed by two men, followers of the Lord Jesus to whom He had appeared on the road, although in such a form that at first they had not recognized Him. But the disciples did not believe these men either.

It was just so wonderful that they could not believe it. They had seen Him raise the dead several times, and they had even done it themselves. He was the ruler over death. But they did not understand it at all. If all they had seen was true, death was conquered forever, and also that which causes death, namely, sin. God is perfect peace, and there is eternal life. God's eternal blessings are right in front of us. They were not equal to all that.

Then He Himself appeared to them while they were eating during the evening of that day. He reproached them for their unbelief and their hardness of heart. We are so completely trapped in our sin and guilt, as in a prison, that we cannot believe in deliverance.

The Lord Jesus made clear that He knew them in the depth of their sin of unbelief. As a result, their sin was revealed to them and they were saved. The light of conquering grace now broke into their hearts.

Unbelief must always be chastised, for its presence shows that we keep the shutters of our hearts closed to the light of the truth. If we hear the chastisement and acknowledge its justice, then we are saved.

The King's calling. As soon as they believed and acknowledged the reign of grace and were subjected to the Christ as the King in grace, He gave them the calling to preach the gospel to the whole creation. "To the whole creation" means to men who, if they believe and submit to Him, are allowed to rule in His name over the whole creation. Through their rule the whole creation will be redeemed.

The Word that the disciples would bring, then, was the Word of the King. That Word goes forth with power. Man should submit to it in faith. Then, as a sign that they belonged to the people of His reign of grace, they would receive baptism. By being baptized they would have the evidence that they had passed through death and had left their guilt behind them. He who believes and is baptized shall be saved; for him there will be no destruction. But he who does not believe will suffer eternal judgment.

That this was the Word of the King, the Word with power, the Lord Jesus would make clear by way of the many miracles that would be performed by the disciples, and also by way of the miraculous preservation of their lives. Just as the Lord once sent Moses with miracles to Pharaoh, so the disciples now came before the world with miracles that confirmed their testimony.

Here was a display of the power of the King over life and all that threatens it. But now the gospel has gone into the world and has once for all laid its claim to life. Therefore those things that threaten life, such as guilt and death, are gone. But the power of the gospel is just as much present now, and it asks for submission in faith, for it is the Word of the King.

The course of the gospel. The resurrection was not the end for the Lord Jesus; it was only the beginning of His exaltation. After that He ascended into heaven, where He sat down at the right hand of God; that is to say, He shared in the Father's reign of grace, which He carried out in His name.

Eternally He reigns in grace. But especially for this time of conflict, He has been granted power over all enemies of God and of the life God created. Those enemies are sin, death and the devil.

He exercises this power especially through His Holy Spirit, whereby He gives strength to His Word that is preached. Thus He worked along with the disciples from the very moment they began their ministries and also supported them during that initial period by many miracles.

He is still at work today. It is by the miraculous power of His grace that a man who is imprisoned in his sins may believe and be set free. That's the way it was in the Roman world for which Mark wrote, and that's how it is today.

LUKE:
THE COMING OF THE
HOLY ONE

CHAPTER FORTY NINE
THE LORD IS GRACIOUS
LUKE 1:1-25, 57-80

It is characteristic of the gospel of Luke that the genealogy goes all the way back to Adam, the son of God. Salvation is not only for Israel but for all mankind. And salvation consists in this, that for Christ's sake men have been adopted again as children of God and are sanctified. In this connection Luke describes God's love and the mercy in the Christ for human life, which He restores to health by His Spirit.

The name John means *the Lord is gracious.* He is gracious for the whole life of mankind in *the Christ* as the second Adam, the Head of the covenant. That covenant will one day embrace all peoples.

It is clear from the above that we are not to treat the events dealt with in this section as the private family history of Zechariah and Elizabeth. For them, too, there is grace and joy in the birth of their child, but what is emphasized most in this birth announcement is the coming of the One before whose face John was to prepare the way. Later on Zechariah sang about that the most.

Zechariah went wrong in regarding it as impossible to believe the angel's promise. He had his eye fixed only on the birth of the child, which was a relatively small thing in comparison with the big news the angel had just announced. Unless he sees the little in the light of the big, he cannot believe it. If he had believed the miracle of God's coming in *the Christ,* would the birth of his child then have been too miraculous to believe? In the same way our own salvation is too miraculous for us if we do not keep our eye fixed on the miracle that God did come in *the Christ.*

Main Thought: *God gives proof of His grace for His people by sending the one who is to prepare the way before His face.*

An expectation to be surpassed in its fulfillment. For centuries God had revealed Himself to the people of Israel because in His covenant He had adopted them to be His people. God's salvation in His covenant had not been intended for Israel alone but for all people. In His mercy He would, through a Redeemer, give healing to the life that had been so terribly bruised and wounded among all peoples.

It was in Israel, however, that the Redeemer would be born. For many centuries Israel had already been hoping for that Redeemer! But He just did not come. Now the Lord had even been silent for several centuries; He had not revealed Himself to His people anew through a prophet or in some other way. Hope was bound to die in Israel. And yet there were still some who, in faith, lived with the Lord in His covenant, awaiting the fulfillment of the promise.

Finally the time had come which God had determined. Israel was still subject to the Roman empire, but a certain independence had been left to the people. For example, Rome had approved having King Herod mount the throne in Jerusalem. Thus Herod was reigning over Israel.

In those days a man and his wife, Zechariah and Elizabeth, were living in Judah. He was a priest and she was also of Aaron's line; that is, she was of a priestly family. This couple lived with the Lord in His covenant and their hope was in His grace. But they had no children. They must have prayed about this frequently, and then not just for a child but for the manifestation of God's grace in the birth of a child. If we live with the Lord, we not only pray for His gifts but ask Him to show His love *in* His gift.

They had not been given a child. They had stopped praying because they had become old. Now it was impossible that they still should have a baby. That must have darkened their life of faith. What did the Lord mean to them? Was He a God from afar?

They had to assume that their prayers had not been answered. In their disappointed expectation, those two old people were a picture of all Israel, whose hope for the Messiah had also been frustrated. Would He really come?

Yet we may not say of any prayer uttered in faith that it is not answered. The Lord sometimes answers in strange ways. There are prayers which we have long forgotten but which the Lord has not forgotten.

Neither did the Lord forget the prayers of Zechariah and Elizabeth. He would answer them in a wholly miraculous way because He had not destined for them a child with an ordinary calling in life. He was going to give them a child that had but one purpose in life, namely, to announce and point out the Redeemer. This child would be born by a miracle, and that fact itself was already an announcement of the great miracle that God Himself was coming to us in the Redeemer. Zechariah and Elizabeth could never have expected that. What God does is indeed wonderful and surpasses all our expectations. We simply have to be still and hope in God.

The announcement of God's coming. There were so many priests in Israel that various orders took turns serving in the temple. Every morning and evening a priest had to enter the Holy Place to burn incense on the golden altar of incense and offer prayers on behalf of the people. When the priest was in the Holy Place he was with the Lord. Accordingly, when he came out he blessed the people in the name of the Lord. For this aspect of the service the priests cast lots.

In the week that Zechariah's order was in Jerusalem to perform this holy service the lot fell on him. He entered the temple with the incense. Perhaps this service was difficult for him, for he had to appear before God to worship Him on behalf of all the people and to pray for them. And where did he stand with respect to the Lord? There was still that unfulfilled longing gnawing away at his heart. In the temple everything shone with the glory of God's grace, but was God really gracious?

Then came the answer. While Zechariah was doing his work there appeared on the right side of the altar of incense an angel of the Lord. In the splendor of that angel he saw the glory of the Lord's grace. Fear fell upon him. The angel told him that he was not to be afraid because God's grace was upon him. That this was indeed the case would become clear from the fact that his prayers would now be answered and he would have a son. He was to call that child *John*, that is, *the Lord is gracious.*

However, the grace that came in this child was not just for him and his wife; the child would be called to prepare the people for the coming of the Lord as Redeemer. To carry out this task, the child would be filled with the Holy Spirit from the moment of his conception. Therefore he was not to drink any wine or strong drink as a sign that he did not derive his strength from anything of this earth but only from the Spirit of the Lord. He would minister as

Elijah once had and would struggle for the return of the people to the Lord. After all, the Lord was not a stranger to the people of Israel, but their God.

The people would learn to trust again in their God. And as a result of their return to the Lord, parents and children would no longer be alienated from each other but would again become one. Sin results in estrangement between parents and children, but this child would struggle to bring about a conversion of the people, for the Lord was coming as the Redeemer.

The joy was not only for Zechariah and Elizabeth, then. Many would rejoice at the birth of this child. Salvation for Zechariah and Elizabeth had to be seen in the light of the great salvation that would be a joy to the world.

Unbelief. Zechariah did not see matters in that light. He had indeed heard that a child was to be born but the announcement of that great salvation had escaped him. Therefore he could not believe what he had heard. He considered the fact that he and Elizabeth had both become old. Surely it was impossible! If, by faith, he had seen the great miracle that God Himself was to come, he could easily have believed that God, by a miracle, would give him a child. Now he did not believe it, and in his unbelief he asked for a sign. If we have seen the full grace of the Lord in the Christ, there is almost nothing we do not dare to expect from the Lord!

Faith can ask for a sign by way of confirmation, but to seek a sign in unbelief is sin. It is rejection of the Word of the Lord. Therefore the angel said, "I am Gabriel, who stands in the presence of God, and I was sent to speak to you and bring you this good news. God is speaking to you through me."

Zechariah had not heard the Word of God in faith as God's Word. The Lord would punish him for his unbelief: he would be dumb until the child was born. The Lord is never sparing of doubt and unbelief but He reveals His wrath towards them and punishes them.

In that terrible dumbness Zechariah discovered how horrible his sin was. By putting to death the unbelief that was in him, God awakened faith in him instead. Then the fact that he was dumb, which continued to plague him, really became a daily confirmation of his faith. "What the angel talked about is certainly going to happen, for I am dumb. I do not have the right to speak, for I did not believe the Lord." All our speaking should be a speaking in faith.

The people outside wondered why Zechariah delayed so long. At last he came out but he was unable to pronounce a blessing on the people, for he was dumb. Also, he was too much in a state of consternation and too engrossed in what had happened. He motioned with his hand and the people understood that something unusual had occurred. He must have seen a vision. Obviously that thought was alive among the people again. Evidently God was already drawing closer.

The fulfillment. When he got home Zechariah must have communicated to Elizabeth in writing what the angel had said to him. Together they believed, though they were also ashamed because of the abiding sign of dumbness. By way of their faith the fulfillment came. God always fulfills His Word to us by way of the faith He awakens. For months they kept their secret to themselves. Then, finally, the child was born.

The whole neighborhood talked about it. It was a miracle that people at that age still had a child—a miracle of God's grace. Was God about to reveal Himself again, and was His salvation near?

On the eighth day many relatives and friends came to the house of Zechariah and Elizabeth. On that day the child was to be circumcised, thereby receiving the sign of his incorporation into God's covenant. Then he would also be given a name. Everybody wanted him to be called *Zechariah* after his father, but Elizabeth said that his name was to be *John*. Then they said, "There is no one in your whole family with that name." But Zechariah wrote on a tablet that his name was to be John. They were all surprised.

God was claiming the whole life of that child for the special calling He had in mind, and therefore He gave the child a name that corresponded to that calling, a name that departed from the family's tradition. God acts according to His good pleasure and has the right to lay His claim on us according to His will.

Now the promise had been fulfilled. In assigning the child's name Zechariah showed that in faith he had obediently accepted the Word of God concerning the calling and lifework of his child. Therefore the sign of dumbness could disappear. His tongue was loosed and his heart opened in a song of praise.

In that song, the so-called "Benedictus," it was clear that Zechariah no longer overlooked that great salvation for Israel and for life. It was of this that he sang first and most. God was bringing honor to His people in restoring the house of David.

Living under this display of grace according to the promise, the people would again serve God in freedom. The glory of God's covenant would be revealed in its new Head. After that Zechariah sang of his child—but in the light of that great salvation. He sang of the calling and lifework of his child, namely, to announce that the Lord was coming who would grant forgiveness of sins and peace and shine as a light upon Israel and thus establish her life. The Lord in His grace—and He alone—was great for Zechariah.

Should we ever see anything we receive from the Lord in any other way? Everything is put in the light of the great miracle that God has appeared. Thus we are to see everything in faith. If God had not come to us in the Lord Jesus Christ, there would not be any salvation or any gift at all. But now our whole life can stand in the light, bathed in the shining luster of God's wonderful grace.

How they all marveled at what had taken place! What would become of the child? Indeed, much more than the people suspected, and also much less; John's life was soon over. Because of the task to which God called him, however, he had greater significance than anyone could have suspected. He pointed to *the Christ!*

Very early he began to prepare himself for his calling. He withdrew from ordinary life into the wilderness where he sought communion with God. There he discovered that without God, life is a desert of loneliness. He also learned that God offers His communion purely out of grace. This is what he would later preach to Israel.

CHAPTER FIFTY
HOLY IS HIS NAME
LUKE 1:26-56

As the Holy One God seeks Himself and has Himself in focus in everything He does. As the Holy One He maintains Himself over against any creature that does not want to belong to Him but seeks its own independence over against Him. He maintains Himself in His judgment and punishment. But also as the Holy One He seeks out His fallen creature, turns him towards Himself again and enlists his service in His own cause thereby saving him. He, who is holy is also gracious.

In this redemption He sanctifies Himself* in that redemption proceeds from Him alone—no one was His counselor—and is effected solely by Him. This is especially the case with the central miracle of the incarnation of the Word, the birth of the One who was not of the will of the flesh. In His works He puts to shame all the expectations and pride of men; He pulls down the mighty from their thrones and exalts the humble ones.

---

*To understand phrases like "to sanctify Jehovah" or "Jehovah sanctifies Himself," we must be aware that the word *holy* when applied to Jehovah in the Old Testament does not have a primarily ethical meaning. The *International Standard Bible Encyclopaedia* presents the following explanation: "Jehovah's holiness is His supremacy, His sovereignty, His glory, His essential being as God. To say the Holy One is simply to say God. Jehovah's holiness is seen in His might, His manifested glory; it is that before which peoples tremble, which makes the nations dread (Ex. 15:11-18; cf. I Sam. 6:20; Ps. 68:35; 89:7; 99:2, 3). Significant is the way in which 'jealous' and 'holy' are almost identified (Josh. 24:19; Ezek. 38:23). It is God asserting His supremacy, His unique claim. Therefore, to sanctify Jehovah or to make Him holy, is to assert or acknowledge or bring forth His being as God, His supreme power and glory, His sovereign claim . . . . The sanctification of Jehovah is thus the assertion of His being and power as God, just as the sanctification of a person or object is the assertion of Jehovah's right and claim in the same" (Vol. IV, p. 2682). —TRANS.

The Christ is God's Son in three senses. Firstly, He is the eternal Son of the Father. Secondly, as man, He was conceived by the Holy Spirit. And finally, as *the Christ,* as Office-bearer and Head of the covenant, He was appointed to be the Son. Thus, behind the appointment to be the Son who does the work of God on earth, there lie the other two relations of sonship. As *the Christ* He is the Holy One, the one devoted solely to God.

Mary did not fall prey to unbelief the way Zechariah did. Immediately she saw the great miracle of grace in the birth of the Redeemer. Therefore she was able to believe. In that faith she was holy to the Lord and God sanctified Himself in her. Only when we subject ourselves to His Word are we holy to the Lord. When Mary asked, "How can this be?" it was not unbelief on her part but a question as to how God would perform His miracle. In faith she sought to understand.

In the meeting between Mary and Elizabeth God sanctified Himself in these two women. He anointed the unborn baby John with His Holy Spirit, thereby consecrating John to Himself, and He made a prophetess of his mother Elizabeth. Nowhere do we read that Mary first told Elizabeth what had happened to her; Elizabeth knew it through prophetic illumination.

Mary, too, became a prophetess at this meeting. What Elizabeth said took her by surprise, just as God's grace is always ahead of us and surprises us. Then she broke out in her song of praise. The dynamic which until that moment had filled her soul and was almost oppressing her now broke loose so that she could speak out.

We must never discuss this meeting between Mary and Elizabeth as though it was just a charming family scene. God is great and mighty in this story.

Main Thought: *God sanctifies Himself in the conception of the Redeemer in the flesh.*

Blessed among women. Let's go back a few months in history. The son of Zechariah and Elizabeth was not born yet. In the sixth month after the angel foretold the miraculous birth of Zechariah's son, the Lord again sent out the same angel, Gabriel. This time he was to announce the great miracle of the birth of the Redeemer.

This miracle of redemption, that God Himself, God's own Son

would come into the world and be born as a man-child, proceeded from God alone. It would never have occurred to the mind of any man. In fulfilling His promise God thus sought ways of His own that were completely different from what we would have expected.

The angel was sent to a very simple maiden, this time not in Judea but in the somewhat despised area of Galilee, in the humble little town of Nazareth. The maiden's name was Mary, and she was engaged to a young man named Joseph. Joseph, though he was of the house of David, was not a person of any standing or esteem, any more than Mary was. He was simply a carpenter.

The Redeemer was going to be born to Mary. God did seek out the house of David because David had been given the promise that *the Christ* would be born of him. Yet God did not seek out any persons of standing; He chose very simple people unknown in the land.

When the angel appeared to Mary and greeted her, he addressed her as the one most favored and told her that the Lord was with her and that she was blessed among women. The Lord was about to grant her an extraordinary gift of His grace. He had chosen her for this not because she was anything special or any better than others but because it was God's good pleasure.

If it pleases the Lord, He works faith in us directly by His Word. That was what happened to Mary. At once she understood by faith what the special tidings meant and she thought about them. Indeed, it became too much for her. She saw something of the holiness of God's grace which was going to take possession of her, and she was afraid.

The angel therefore said that she was not to be afraid. He assured her anew that God's favor rested upon her. Then he explained further what his words meant: she would have a son and would call Him *Jesus,* for He would be the Redeemer. In Him the promise given to David would be fulfilled. He would rule over His people just as David once had, but then still more gloriously. He would bring them deliverance from all their enemies—from sin and death and the devil. As King He would be called God's Son, but that was only possible because He was God's Son in a still higher sense. Because He was God's own Son, His reign could be an everlasting one.

Further revelation to faith. Mary heard and believed. In Mary's faith the Lord's glory was reflected. Yet, she was puzzled. How could she have a son if she wasn't even married? In faith she asked the angel this question so that she might better understand God's will with her. If we ask our questions in faith, the Lord has an answer for us.

The angel said that the child would be born to her by a miracle. That miraculous birth would be the exclusive work of the Lord. He would be the Holy One and He would sanctify Himself in His Son's birth. No one would have the honor of the world's redemption but God alone.

Because the child would be conceived solely by a miraculous deed of God, even considered as a human being it would be God's son. It would be holy. While all other children are conceived and born in sin, He would be the Holy One from the moment of His conception. In Him there would come a new beginning, a new chapter in the life of the human race. He would be worthy to take the guilt of men upon Himself and make atonement for it. Throughout His work Jesus would be devoted to the Father.

It was in faith that Mary asked and understood. She received a sign in confirmation of her faith. The angel told her that a child was going to be born to Zechariah and Elizabeth by another miracle. When she saw this fulfilled, this would confirm her faith that a still greater miracle would take place in her.

Submission in faith. Mary bowed her head and said, "Behold, I am the handmaiden of the Lord. Let it be done to me according to your word." What the angel had told her must have been beyond her understanding. When will we ever perceive the fullness of God's grace in the Lord Jesus Christ?

It must have bewildered and confused her, but it also became an unspeakable joy to her that God wished to make use of her in order to give the world the Redeemer. God should do with her life as was His good pleasure. She would be His servant in everything. If only His name was sanctified and glorified! For that she would give herself completely.

Of course, Mary was given a very special privilege. The Lord made her serviceable to His grace in a very special way as the mother of the Redeemer. But the Lord also is pleased to glorify His grace through us, in order to sanctify Himself through us. We must all believe that. We will then surrender ourselves to Him in faith and desire to be His servants in any way that pleases Him.

Elizabeth as prophetess. Once the angel had departed there was no rest for Mary in Nazareth. She wanted that sign for her faith; she wanted to hear about the miracle that had taken place in Elizabeth's life. Hastily she journeyed from Galilee to the hill country of Judea where Zechariah and Elizabeth lived.

The visit also represented a miracle of grace for Elizabeth. Immediately the Holy Spirit revealed to her what had happened to Mary. In the spirit Elizabeth saw the great salvation that was coming. A miracle had taken place in her too, but what was that miracle in comparison with the tremendous event that was going to happen to Mary?

By faith Elizabeth saw that the miracle in her life was to be viewed in the light of the great miracle that had come upon Mary. She was completely taken by surprise by the greeting Mary gave her and by the illumination she received. At the same time she was comforted. Her ecstasy intensified when she saw her joy in the light of the joy that would fill the whole world. The Lord Himself came upon her through His Holy Spirit.

As a result her child was sanctified and qualified even before birth for a special calling. And Elizabeth herself became a prophetess. She blessed Mary and the child that was to be born to her. She expressed her bewilderment and delight at this meeting; it was almost too much for her. She assured Mary that what the prophecy had foretold would surely be fulfilled.

The sign that Mary received from Elizabeth to confirm her faith did not lie. Elizabeth, the older of the two, blessed and anointed Mary with the joy of faith.

Of course Elizabeth had seen much of the Lord's miracles before this meeting. Yet, when the Lord comes to us with the fullness of His miraculous grace, it surprises and delights us and catches us off guard time after time. It is so much greater than we could ever imagine.

Mary as prophetess. Mary had a similar experience. Her life had been filled with faith and expectation. The miracle had been fulfilled in her through her faith. But when she heard Elizabeth declare the blessing and sing in praise, it still surprised and delighted her.

Faith and joy had been within her all along, but she had not been able to express it. Her pent-up emotions had become almost oppressive. At Elizabeth's greeting and blessing, her tongue was loosed and she burst out in a song of praise.

She praised the Lord who had chosen her to be a servant of His grace in such a special way, a way for which she would be called blessed down through the ages. She exalted the richness of His mercy which would always be available for those who fear Him. She saw that God alone had accomplished this and that He was glorifying Himself in it and would glorify Himself forever. "Holy is His name!" she exclaimed.

Because the birth was of Him alone, He followed ways of His own choosing. He had chosen Mary, the humble maiden. In His grace He always puts to shame the proud expectations of men. He upholds His simple people and makes them rich, but those who are satisfied and rich in themselves He sends away empty. All this the Lord has done in accordance with the promise He once gave to Abraham.

Mary stayed with Elizabeth for three months. They talked together about the wondrous things God would do, thereby further glorifying the Lord. It's possible for us to sinfully abuse God's miraculous gifts of grace by thinking they're of our own making rather than seeing them as God-given supports for our lives.

Both these women were prophetesses, having seen the Lord and His greatness. In a similar way we can also be prophets. Through the Spirit of the Lord, God revealed His holiness in both these women.

Mary returned to her home before Elizabeth's baby was born but their experiences were of lasting significance because they had recognized the Lord's sovereignty in their lives.

CHAPTER FIFTY ONE
CHRIST THE LORD
LUKE 2:1-20

The angel said to the shepherds, "To you is born Christ the Lord," that is, the One who was sent by the God of the covenant, the One who has been appointed *Lord*. And Christ Himself is also the God who through His covenant is united with the world in grace and love.

The most intimate union was established in the coming of the Word into the flesh. Thus the birth of the Christ was the fulfillment of the promise given in the covenant. It is true that this union of God and man in *the Christ* far transcends the communion of the covenant, but the covenant fellowship is firmly secured in this union.

The birth of Christ brought a new beginning, a new starting point. The fatal chain indicated by the words "who can bring a clean thing out of an unclean?" (Job 14:4) was now broken. This was possible in the case of Christ because His birth was of the Spirit. What happened was of God alone; it was a perfect miracle of His grace.

In a certain sense there were no points of contact here in life on earth, that is, in the sense that apart from grace nothing would be attuned to God or would seek Him. As far as the direction of life is concerned, there is a complete opposition (antithesis) between the Spirit and the life of the flesh.

Yet it was possible for God to be born in the flesh. That's because the purpose of the creation was anchored in man's communion with God. In His covenant God wished to give Himself to His people. He wanted to be glorified in that covenant fellowship. That's why He created man and the entire world. Thus the birth of heaven and earth was a birth out of the Spirit of communion. At that time the communion was still provisional; man could still withdraw from it, as in fact he did. Because of the fall, the life of the flesh now forms a contrast with the Spirit, but the original disposition to the communion of the Spirit has not been lost. In His work of redemption God could attach His efforts to that. This life of ours could again know the communion of the Spirit and thus become spirit—and not provisionally but forever, for it became spirit. Because the original disposition to the communion of the Spirit was not lost, it was possible for God to be born in the flesh.

The communion between God and man is the purpose of the whole creation of heaven and earth. Accordingly, it is in that communion that man is lord of heaven and earth, and thus also of the angels. Now that this much closer union of God and man has been established in Him, Christ is also the Lord. Because this communion between God and man was the purpose of the creation, the existence of the world and also of the angels depended on that communion. Thus scripture can say in Colossians 1:20 that in Christ all things have been reconciled, whether they are on earth or in heaven.

Through the restoration of the communion between God and man in Christ, the angels have also been brought back to the right relationship with God. The purpose of their existence, too, lay in the communion between God and man. We must not regard the angels who sang in Ephratah's fields as disinterested spectators at the miracle of Christ's birth. They themselves had a very great interest in that birth. Because communion between God and man has been restored, heaven and earth are joined together again in Christ, and men and angels are able to understand each other again.

By becoming flesh, Christ also entered the history of this life. Therefore this history does not remain alien to God but becomes covenant history. It is noteworthy that Luke, who so much emphasizes that the birth of Christ was of the Spirit, brings out so strongly that Christ was born in Bethlehem, the city of David. When he tells us that, he speaks to us in the language of covenant history. This event attaches to everything that happened earlier in the covenant; in other words, everything that happened earlier and would happen later is linked to this event in Bethlehem. This event governs all of history; to say *covenant* is to say *history*.

David was lord, as was Solomon. The bond between God and them had been given in His covenant, and by that bond they possessed the earth. But they were what they were through Christ.

Main Thought: *Christ is born as Lord.*

310

To Bethlehem. After her visit to Elizabeth Mary returned to Nazareth. With whom could she discuss what had happened there except with Joseph, her fiancé, to whom the angel also had revealed the miracle? But between the two of them the angel's birth announcement remained a secret which they would not reveal to anyone else.

In general the world takes a strange attitude towards the miracle of God's grace. God's grace has indeed come into the world, but who knows anything about it and who lives out of that grace? Who lives by the miracle? (See Chapter 39 above.)

But Joseph and Mary became caught up in the swirl which in those days carried the whole world along with it. The emperor in Rome had issued a decree that the whole world should be enrolled. All the people in the empire had to be registered on lists and their property assessed. In this way the emperor could get an idea of the power he could command. How foreign is this life where people boast of their own power, when compared to that other world of living by the miracle of grace, the world in which men glory only in God's mercy!

The enumeration of the Roman empire must have greatly inconvenienced Joseph and Mary as it forced them abroad and upset their normal lives. Joseph was not from Nazareth; he had come there as a stranger. His people were from Bethlehem, for he was a descendant of David. And it was required that each person be enrolled in the city from which his family had come. Thus Joseph had to go to Bethlehem. But he did not dare leave Mary behind alone since it was about time for her child to be born. What did the people in Nazareth know of the marvelous secret of this birth? Thus they journeyed together from Nazareth to Bethlehem.

How little those two suspected that the grace of God was governing this course of events in the history of the Roman empire and in their own lives! God had willed that the Redeemer would be born in Bethlehem, in the city of David, where David's family had lived. In His providential governing of history, God picked up this connection. Hadn't He given deliverance to His people in David?

David lived in communion with God, and God in communion with him. That's what had made David lord over his people and over his land. And with David the people had been privileged to possess their land. To David the promise had been given that *the*

Christ would be born of his line. In *the Christ* a far more intimate communion would come between God and man, for He Himself was both God and man. Therefore He would be Lord not only over Israel and over the land of Canaan but over all peoples, over both heaven and earth. And His people would again possess heaven and earth with Him. The promise given to David would be fulfilled in a much more wonderful way than anyone could ever have imagined. But it was the fulfillment of the promise to *David*. Therefore Christ had to be born in Bethlehem; God was directing things that way.

Born in the flesh. When they arrived in Bethlehem, Joseph and Mary could not find accommodations. Because of the general registration many people had come to the city, and the inn was full. Finally they found a place in the stable. How strange they must have felt there! In their hearts was an ecstasy too great for them to bear. There was no one to share it with; indeed, to an outsider it would have appeared as if God was no longer a partner with them in it since He had allowed them to end up in such a place.

There the little child was born. Mary herself wrapped Him in cloths and laid Him in the manger. What a wonder of joy that must have been for Mary! The love of a mother gilded it all over. But there was more than motherly love at work here; her faith and that of Joseph must have seen the greatness of the event. That little child was God's Son, the Redeemer of the world. At the same time it was *her* little baby, her own flesh and blood. Wasn't it amazing? It was far beyond them both.

They must have been speechless from ecstasy when Mary wrapped the baby up. Joseph, too, took the baby in his arms. Was God that near to them—in their own flesh? Indeed, that's how near He has come to us. And woe to us if we do not recognize Him in His love and do not wish to know Him. Could God have come any closer to us than to be born in our own flesh? Shall we not lay our hands on Him now and say, "You are mine"?

Yet Joseph and Mary must also have been puzzled. That little one was God's Son in our flesh. Why, then, was it born under such circumstances? Mary must surely have dreamed her dreams too. The circumstances must have been a great disappointment to her.

No doubt she understood it better later. That little child was the Son of God, born by a miracle of the Holy Spirit. Was that possible?

Was it possible that God would be born in our flesh which was so burdened with guilt and so completely corrupted by our sin? Then He had to be born to atone for that guilt; He had to be born for suffering. This humiliation at Jesus' birth was already a prophecy of His suffering.

Later Mary must have seen a prophecy of the cross in that stable and in the manger. But He had to be born to sanctify our flesh. He was born holy in our flesh. If we believe in Him who came to atone for our sins, He sanctifies us too and we come to share in His holiness. We are then born again. For us, too, this birth is of the Spirit. We should be overwhelmed that it was possible for God to be born in our flesh.

Glory to God in the highest heaven! The birth of God in our flesh concerned not only the earth but also heaven. Christ is also Lord of the angels. If a man has communion with God, he is lord in God's name over all things, over heaven and earth. And surely the One who is both God and man is Lord of the angels. Heaven and the angels rejoiced at His birth. That same night something else happened: the praise of angels was revealed to us.

That night there were shepherds in the fields near Bethlehem keeping watch over their flocks. Those shepherds were not thinking about angels. Do we think about them very often? It is as though angels do not belong to life on earth. Holy angels mingling with this sinful, dark life? Angels? It sounds almost like a fairy tale. Do we really believe they exist? Such spirits, which are wholly light, communing with this dark life of ours? They are completely foreign to us. And we are by nature anything but ready for an appearance of angels.

Those shepherds weren't ready either. Yet, suddenly, there they were! First there was only one angel in the brilliance of heavenly glory. That's the splendor of the glory of God's grace. That glory is nothing that should cause us to fear because it shows us that God wishes to clothe our lives with it. But often we don't believe that. How far we are often removed from such glory because of our unbelief! Therefore that glory gives rise to fear. We are, after all, sinful people who simply cannot see the glory. Thus the shepherds were similarly filled with fear.

The angel said that they should not be afraid, for he brought them joyous news, namely, that the people's fear of heaven was removed since Christ the Savior was born. Christ would obtain heaven and earth for God through His blood and thus reconcile heaven and earth, angels and men, to each other. He had been born in Bethlehem, in the city of David. The promise, made to David, would be fulfilled in Him in a much more glorious way than it had in David's day. All God's people would rejoice in Him.

Their faith would also receive a sign. If they went to Bethlehem they would find the baby wrapped in cloths and lying in a manger. That was indeed a strange sign. They must have imagined the Lord of heaven and earth in quite different circumstances. If, on the other hand, they found it just as the angel said, it would confirm their faith in the angel's word.

Faith, which accepts the miracle, also has its miraculous signs. And this particular sign certainly became very meaningful for our faith. In His humiliation, in those cloths and in that manger, He was available to all. Having been born in a stable the Lord of heaven and earth was not too remote for even the lowliest on earth.

Suddenly the shepherds saw a whole host of angels in that heavenly brilliance. And they heard words that sounded like music. The meaning of the words also reached them. They heard the angels praising God and saying, "Glory to God in the highest heaven, and on earth peace among men with whom He is well pleased." The angels sang of harmony between heaven where God is glorified, and earth where men, sharing in God's good pleasure, have peace. It may not seem as though men, even when aware of God's good pleasure, have much peace with themselves, with each other and with life in general. Yet the angels, in their song of praise, pointed the way to that peace. If we are one with the angels in praising God for the miracle of salvation, that peace is in us.

The shepherds had never experienced anything like it before and nothing like it was ever experienced on earth again. The angels went away again into heaven. Ever higher they soared in praise of the Lord. Yet, by faith we go with them.

If we praise the Lord for the miracle of His grace in Christ, we go just as high as the angels went. There is no longer any opposition between the life of angels and our life of faith. Angels are not a fairy tale anymore but belong to our life on earth, even though our eyes do not see them.

314

The adoration of the shepherds. The shepherds must have seen the contrast between angels and themselves for just a moment. They had seen a heavenly light and heard heavenly music. Then, suddenly, it was all gone. There they stood again, with their feet on the ground. It was dark all around them. And in the world it was pitch black because of sin. Had they been hallucinating or was it real after all? But that wasn't possible. Their faith still wrestled with the darkness of the world.

However, they did receive a sign, proof of which they could find in Bethlehem. Therefore they hurried to Bethlehem and found Mary and Joseph and the baby lying in the manger, just as the angel had said and their faith rallied, for there lay the Savior who would remove the opposition between heaven and earth—Christ the Lord, the Possessor of heaven and earth. In Him God's full favor was with men.

Could they really believe it? It was true! This child was the one expected. They jostled one another at the manger to have a good look. They may even have touched Him for a moment and taken His tiny hand into their coarse hands. That was the Savior! They believed and wanted to be a part of Him. He belonged to them because God had given Him to them, and they belonged to Him.

And we must believe because He who is God, the fullness of God's grace, is of our own flesh and blood. He belongs with us; God gave Him to us. Woe to us if we should wish to undo this act of God!

The shepherds couldn't get enough of it but finally they had to leave. Still, they couldn't keep quiet about it. To anybody who cared to listen they told what the angels had said, namely, that the little baby was the Savior, the Lord. All the people lodging in Bethlehem, many of them of the house of David, heard about it along with all of Bethlehem. God saw that the news was given to the house of David first. What did they do with it? Later we hear nothing more about their response.

Joseph and Mary heard it all from the shepherds. Mary still wasn't able to express her feelings. For her that salvation, that miracle, became greater and greater. Heaven had been opened by her little child and the glory of heaven was meant for the world. She couldn't think about it enough. She saw endless possibilities. She could not yet foresee or understand everything, but she did believe, and she experienced immeasurable joy. Many people refuse to believe what they cannot fathom—but not Mary.

The shepherds had to return to their flocks but they returned with a song in their hearts and carried the joy of adoration with them. They really felt they could take care of their flock again because the praise of God no longer conflicted with their earthly occupations.

Through this link with heaven, we are sanctified to the Lord in everything, and this enables us to carry out our task on earth also. Thanks to the Christ, our whole life and work may be seen in the light of heaven.

CHAPTER FIFTY TWO
THE CONSOLATION OF ISRAEL
LUKE 2:21-39

The presentation of Jesus in the temple must have taken place before the wise men from the East arrived in Jerusalem. After the coming of the wise men it would not have been safe for the little child in Jerusalem.

Through Simeon and Anna, His presentation became known in the circle of those who were awaiting consolation for Israel. Yet, at the time of the arrival of the wise men, nobody seemed to know anything about it. How removed from official Jerusalem this circle evidently lived! Just as in Bethlehem (see above, p. 33), the connecting threads break off in Jerusalem.

Later Christ was revealed out of Nazareth. Luke tells us nothing about the coming of the wise men or the flight to Egypt. From Jerusalem Joseph and Mary must first have returned to Bethlehem again, which was only a distance of eight kilometers.

Christ was born under the law (Gal. 4:4). His circumcision, like His baptism, was a prophecy of His suffering. He underwent that suffering as the one who bore our sins. That He was the bearer of our sins is also evident from the fact that His mother, too, was ceremonially unclean at His birth (Lev. 12:2). Furthermore, the fact that He would bear our sins was evident from His presentation in the temple. That presentation, you will recall, was related to God's curse on the people's sin at Sinai, which meant that their oldest sons could not be priests. The tribe of Levi had taken the place of the first-born sons (see Ex. 13:2, 11-15; Num. 3:1113; 18:15; Lev. 12). Even Christ participated in that rejection. He bore the sins of His people.

We should not think of Simeon as someone who was tired of living and wanted to die. That desire to die is contrary to Scripture. It was not characteristic of believers.

Simeon could die because he had finally seen the salvation God had prepared for all peoples; that is to say, he knew that through the Messiah the resurrection of the dead and the restoration of life before God would come. Therefore he could lay down his life for a time. Accordingly, it is curious that he used a word for *Lord* that brings out strongly the relation of master and slave. He knew his life to be the Lord's property, and he knew that God would surely restore it to His service presently.

In connection with the words "and for a sign that is spoken against," the expression "for the falling and rising up of many in Israel" has to be understood in this sense: for the falling of some, and for the rising up of others.

Anna, the prophetess, "professed" God. *Professed* is used here in the sense of "responded to what God revealed to her." To all who were looking for the redemption that would take place in Jerusalem, she made known the consolation of Israel.

Main Thought: *The Christ is revealed in the temple as the consolation of Israel.*

Born under the law. Although Israel largely drifted away from awaiting the Messiah, cherishing the expectation only in appearance while in fact relying on itself, there were still pious Jews who looked forward in hope to His coming. Especially in Jerusalem there was such a circle. To that circle, too, God wanted to make it known that the Savior had come. For their consolation they would have to look upon the child. The Lord used the obedience to the law displayed by Joseph and Mary to reveal the Lord Jesus to this circle in Jerusalem.

These two kept the law faithfully. To begin with, the child had been circumcised in Bethlehem on the eighth day. Like all boys in Israel, He received the sign of putting to death the sin in Him. That sign had meaning for Him only because He bore our sins. Those sins would be removed from Him through His suffering on the cross. Thus His circumcision was already a prophecy of His suffering on the cross. At His circumcision He received the name which the angel had spoken of: He was called Jesus, which means Savior.

When a son was born a mother had to bring a sacrifice of purification in the temple at Jerusalem forty days after the birth. Joseph and Mary could easily do this because Bethlehem was only eight kilometers from Jerusalem. And there was something else that had to happen to the child. All Israel was a people of priests. It had been the Lord's intention to have every eldest son function as a priest but Israel had forfeited this honor by its sin at Sinai. The

318

tribe of Levi was then called instead of the entire people of Israel represented by their eldest sons.

Still, every eldest son, when he was thirty days old, was to be presented to the Lord in the temple in order to be redeemed from special priestly service. This also had to happen with the Lord Jesus; He, too, was rejected for the priesthood.

In this He bore the scorn of all His people. But by His obedience He would obtain the right to offer Himself to God in place of His people as an atoning sacrifice. Thereby He became the priest and the sacrificial lamb at the same time.

By His sacrifice He would fulfill the whole meaning of that priestly service in the temple. With His sacrifice would come the end of that service, and also of the law of shadows. Then the people would no longer serve the Lord in shadows or types which in Old Testament times had represented true service of the Lord. Instead they would be privileged to serve God in spirit and in truth. No one at this time understood that the Lord Jesus, even as a child, was still subject to all those shadowy laws in order that He might free the people from them and thus bring people to the spiritual service of God. In this way the people would pass from childhood to adulthood.

What Simeon saw. When Joseph and Mary came into the temple to present their child to the Lord, one of the circle of people looking for the consolation of Israel, Simeon, came up to them. The Holy Spirit revealed to him that the little child was the Redeemer. Inspired by the Spirit he had come to the temple at just that moment. The Spirit often moved him so that he received prophetic illumination. Here was further evidence that the Lord was beginning to speak to His people again after four centuries of silence.

Simeon lived with the Lord in His covenant. He communed with the Lord in prayer and showed himself to be a servant of the Lord. He longed intensely for the fulfillment of the promise. And the grace of God had been marvelous upon him: the Lord had revealed to him that he would live to see the fulfillment. That was a consolation to him and to all who looked for it with him.

How the Lord wanted to kindle hope within these people, hope for the coming of the Redeemer, so that He would be received by them with great joy! But this promise made to Simeon did not penetrate very far. The hearts of the people were closed to the grace of the Lord in the Redeemer and therefore also to His Spirit and Word.

Simeon now experienced the high point in his life. The Spirit revealed to him that the child was the Redeemer. By the Spirit he then saw the entire salvation, the complete redemption, the perfect bliss that would come. He praised the Lord.

Simeon was the first to state clearly that this salvation was not only for Israel but for all peoples. The dark, sinful life among the heathen would be illumined by the light of grace which was beaming in the Redeemer. Along with all nations, the true Israel which believed in the Redeemer would rejoice and be glorified.

How Simeon's heart leaped for joy! Through the Redeemer the dead would one day be raised up. Then His people, without sin, would be privileged to serve God in glory. Because he saw all that he no longer dreaded death. He had seen God's salvation and one day, as God's servant, he would serve Him in glory. Now he could depart and relinquish his life for a time.

Simeon took the little child in his arms while he praised the Lord. In his ecstasy Joseph and Mary were again confronted with a revelation from the Lord. So much had been revealed to them already and they themselves had already experienced great bliss and ecstasy. Yet, when they experienced this they marveled all over again. The salvation of the Lord, if we see it, surprises us time and again.

A sign spoken against. But how would the Redeemer be received in Israel? Illumined by the Spirit of the Lord, Simeon foresaw that too. Many would reject Christ, denying the one who was a sign and revelation of God's grace. Thus He would not only be a blessing and a hope for Israel; for many He would be their downfall. Because they would reject Him, He would become a curse to them. What would He not bring out in the people—love, longing, faith, but also opposition, unbelief, and hate! Through Christ the things hidden in the hearts of men become public before God.

How much Christ would have to endure! How would all that affect Joseph, and especially Mary? Simeon blessed them. They were certainly unspeakably blessed in this child. But how Mary would have to suffer when the child was rejected by Israel! A sword would pierce her soul. This, too, Simeon foretold. Fortunately, there was something else implied in his blessing: Mary would also live by faith and glorify her Redeemer in her child. By that faith she would be restored.

Mary did indeed have to suffer in a very special way because she was the mother of the Redeemer. But everyone who loves the Lord Jesus suffers rejection, also in our own time. To live with Him in this world always means suffering. There is also much in us that has to be put to death, but there is another side as well: we are conquerors in our suffering through faith. By faith we may behold God's salvation for all peoples and for all of life.

Professing the Lord. A second person from the circle of people awaiting Jerusalem's redemption came up to them—a very old woman whose name was Anna. She had been married for seven years, and after her husband's death had lived another 84 years. Thus she was well over a hundred years old. But she was still in the temple every day.

She was there early in the morning before the morning sacrifice, and also in the evening for the evening sacrifice. The thought never entered her mind that she was earning something for herself by performing this temple service. In all those sacrifices as well as in the temple itself, she saw the gracious forgiveness of sins and the Lord's gracious nearness. She longed for the presence of the Lord and marveled at His grace. She, too, was a prophetess. Through His Spirit, the Lord revealed Himself also to her.

She also recognized the Redeemer in that little child. And, like Simeon, she also professed the Lord. She professed that the Lord is faithful in fulfilling His promise, and explained the meaning of Christ's birth to the whole circle that was awaiting the redemption of Jerusalem. Evidently she had a special position in that circle.

To that circle the Lord revealed that the Redeemer had come. Unfortunately, this knowledge remained within that circle. Israel did not open its heart to receive the glad tidings. And with the passing of the years that circle died out.

Joseph and Mary left Jerusalem to return to Nazareth. It was impossible to keep in touch with them and so the ties with the circle were broken. When the Lord Jesus began His public ministry in Israel thirty years later, He was unknown.

How little the world is suited to receive the message of salvation! Yet it comes anyway, and through that message God overcomes the world!

CHAPTER FIFTY THREE
IN HIS FATHER'S WORK
LUKE 2:40-52

Jesus is *the Christ*, the Anointed, the Office-bearer, the Mediator. In that He is *the Christ*, we recognize Him as true God and as a true and righteous man (see Lord's Days 5 and 6 of the Heidelberg Catechism).

As such Christ must have known Himself from childhood. He knew Himself in His oneness and His communion with the Father. As a child He must already have seen the contrast between His communion with His Father and the life around Him. Gradually, but at a tender age, He must have understood His calling to set that life free.

From the very beginning, the guilt of our sin was laid upon Him. Isn't that in our confession, that He bore the burden of God's wrath for us from the beginning of His incarnation? It is also in what is written in Luke 2:40, where we read that He was made strong in the spirit. In His life of communion with God He became strong so that He would be able to bear the burden.

Even when Jesus was only a child, He knew that He was the Redeemer. What His mother told Him about the circumstances surrounding His birth must have contributed especially to this self-knowledge. As His mother who was to train Him for His special calling—to the extent that this could be done by a human being—she could not keep the facts of His birth from Him. The fact that Jesus was filled with wisdom made it all the easier for her to talk with Him about these things. And when He became conscious of His special calling, the meaning of His miraculous birth must have become clearer to Him.

Because Jesus recognized His special calling, He did His Father's work every day of His life—and not only in the temple in Jerusalem. In other words, He was occupied with His calling, and therein He knew the communion of the Father. In this communion the grace of God was upon Him.

Doing His Father's work was not in conflict with His obedience to His parents. On the contrary, when He submitted to His parents, He was fulfilling God's calling for us in that regard too. As the One specially called, He became like us in *all* things.

When we consider what happened in the temple, we cannot say Jesus disobeyed His parents because He felt prior obedience to His Father in heaven. Parental authority is never absolute; its task is only to train each child so that he is prepared for the special calling he receives from God. Mary and Joseph had to keep that in mind particularly with regard to the child Jesus. The reproach He addressed to them was that they were not keeping it in mind.

They should always have been prepared for the revelation of the special element of His calling. It is not lack of consideration on the part of the child Jesus that He did not warn His parents that He was staying behind; it was not a neglect that would have been sin. We could better speak of negligence on the part of Joseph and Mary. They let Him be on His own as someone who was in a certain sense independent. All the more, then, they should have taken into account the uniqueness of His calling.

Main Thought: *Christ is always busy in His Father's work.*

Strengthened in the spirit. Joseph and Mary returned to Nazareth with their little child. He grew up in that quiet, humble little town. We do not know much about His youth in Nazareth, and it's doubtful whether our imaginations will help us much. God did not reveal these things to us because it's nothing that we need to know.

We do know that He grew strong in His spirit, that is, in His life of communion with God. That was what He needed more than anything else. He lived in this world differently than we do, for He was born holy. All sin was alien to Him, an abomination. We often do not notice the sin in ourselves and in others simply because, sad to say, sin has become pervasive like the air we breathe. We don't experience living in the midst of sin particularly grievous.

How Jesus must have suffered when He saw sin around Him and also in those who were dearest to Him! As a child He must have wondered about this world and about His place in it. In His home He heard what His parents told Him about God's covenant and promise, and in the synagogue He heard the Scriptures read. In this way He came to understand that He was the Redeemer who was to free this world from sin. Already then He took upon Himself the yoke of the guilt of our sins. What a burden He bore, even as a child, and how sin pained Him! Indeed, He needed to be strengthened in the spirit more than anything else.

It must have been very difficult for Him to determine His place in the world and His relation to others, particularly His parents. He saw them as full of sin and yet as His parents to whom He owed obedience. But God gave Him the wisdom He needed. He was obedient in everything to His Father in heaven and therefore He found, seemingly naturally, the way He had to go. Because of His obedience, God's favor was upon Him and God's peace was in His heart.

When we think of what the Lord Jesus did for us, we often think only of the latter part of His life on earth. But He suffered for us from the very beginning. All His life He was obedient in our place. *We* have ruined our lives from the beginning, but *His* total life of obedience and suffering is a substitution for that. By His life He freed us from God's wrath.

Conscious of His calling. Already at a very early age Jesus went with His parents to Jerusalem for the major feasts. When He was twelve He also came under the obligation of the law to do that. From the very beginning He was subject to the law in order that He might free His people from the bondage of the law. The law in the Old Testament still carried with it a certain servitude, because atonement had not yet been made for sin and the Holy Spirit had not yet been poured out. The people in the Old Testament had to be instructed in the law to await God's glorious redemption. In this sense He delivered His people from the bondage of the law because He Himself fulfilled the law in obedience.

As a twelve-year-old, Jesus assumed a responsibility of His own toward that law. Evidently His parents took that into account. When He celebrated the Passover feast in Jerusalem with them that year, they allowed Him a certain amount of freedom. The temple service must have fascinated Jesus, yet that whole priestly service would be fulfilled by Him as the true High Priest. Besides, He Himself was to be the lamb for an atonement of sin. Because of His sacrifice God would no longer dwell hidden behind the curtains. Instead there would be open access to the Lord. How He must have absorbed the revelation that came to Him there in God's temple!

When the feast was over and Jesus' parents returned in the company of many other celebrants, He stayed behind in Jerusalem alone. Not until the end of the first day of travel did His parents realize that He was not with their group. The next day they went back, asking about Him all along the way. He was with none of the other groups. The third day they looked everywhere in Jerusalem. Finally they found Him sitting in the front court of the temple, listening to the instruction of the scribes and asking them questions.

Everyone who was sitting there was amazed at His insight into the Scriptures, which was evident from His questions. He heard and understood Scripture differently than anyone else because He was the Messiah of whom the Scriptures spoke. Through Him would come complete salvation.

Mary's anxiety had upset her and she reproached Him: "Son, why have You done this to us? Why did You make us look for You in fear?" But Jesus was taken aback and had to correct His mother for being worried. Didn't she know that He had a special calling from the Father and always had to be busy doing His Father's work? Certainly she knew that He walked in the way of His Father and would not cause them needless trouble! Surely they could rely on that! God pointed out His way on earth.

The stay in Jerusalem had been very significant primarily for the Lord Jesus Himself who was strengthened in the awareness of His calling. He subsequently faced life in Nazareth differently than before.

He also encountered the doctrine of the scribes and their blindness to the Scriptures. Their great learning notwithstanding, they did not see God's grace. A great conflict would arise in the future between Him and the scribes. For the scribes this contact was also important. They were confronted with a wisdom from above, a wisdom that understands grace.

Mary must have been even more prepared to respect His special calling. He was first of all the Redeemer, the Head of His people. In that calling He was engaged daily in His Father's work.

Under His parents' authority. Jesus returned to Nazareth with His parents. As before, He subjected Himself to their authority. Yet His obedience was different now. Because He saw His calling clearly before Him, He knew even more clearly that He was rendering this obedience on *our* behalf. In being subject to His parents, Jesus was also being obedient to the Father in heaven and was fulfilling His special calling for our sakes. While He was Lord over every creature He nevertheless submitted willingly to God's demand on His life. By His obedience He sought to atone for our disobedience in a wide variety of relationships.

Mary and Joseph did not understand the significance of what He told them in Jerusalem. But Mary did remember them, as well as everything else that had happened. All these things she pondered in her heart, awaiting the full light of the Lord upon them.

The Lord Jesus increased in wisdom as He grew older and people were amazed at Him. Although He fully shared our life, He was special in everything. He did not withdraw from life. Hadn't He come in order to make atonement for life and redeem it? Increasingly He realized that God's favor was upon Him. He also enjoyed the favor of the people of Nazareth. He gave Himself to them and entered sympathetically into their life as no one had ever entered into people's lives before. From the very beginning He bore our griefs and carried our sorrows.

LUKE:
THE MERCIFUL HIGH PRIEST

CHAPTER FIFTY FOUR
EXODUS
LUKE 3:1-20

The prophecy of Isaiah cited here reminds us of Israel's return (exodus) from the Babylonian captivity. Like another Joshua, John the Baptist led the people out of the land of bondage. In this case it was out of the bondage of seeking self-righteousness into the freedom of life by God's grace. He was to announce that the Lord was coming to redeem His people. Thus John was to bring the people to meet the Lord.

God's warning that He was able to raise up children to Abraham even from stones, should not lead us to conclude that while in the Old Testament the covenant community stood in the foreground, the New Testament emphasizes *personal* responsibility. To do that would be to overlook the fact that God raises up those children to Abraham and thus incorporates them in the covenant community. (See the remarks in the first outline of this Volume.) We already find something of a magical view of the sacraments in those people who sought John's baptism in order to escape the coming wrath, and also a failure on their part to understand the covenant with its promise and claim. John protested against these things.

Main Thought: *John the Baptist brings the people to meet the Lord.*

All flesh shall see the glory of the Lord. The child of Zechariah and Elizabeth had grown up and was now thirty years old. The time had come for him to begin his public ministry in Israel. In the wilderness where he stayed God spoke to him, probably through an inspiration in his heart. He was to call the people back to the Lord. The grace of the Lord would appear gloriously in the Messiah. The people should turn away from their sin and their trust in self and turn to the Lord in faith. The Lord would then show Himself to them as a God who forgives sin.

As a sign of their repentance the people were to be baptized by John. They were to go down under the waters of the Jordan as a sign that they had died to their life of sin and then come up out of the water as a sign that a new life with the Lord had begun. The Lord wanted to confer that benefit upon His people in His covenant. Washing with water signified the washing away of their sins. At the Word of the Lord John entered upon this ministry. He did so in the desert, near the fords of the Jordan River where he would meet many people.

The time of his ministry seemed anything but favorable for his appeal for repentance and for faith in the grace of the Lord. Israel was subject to the Romans, who governed a large part of the land through the governor, Pontius Pilate. The Romans were complete strangers to the promise of Israel. Another part of the land in the North was governed by Herod Antipas the tetrarch, who ruled under Roman supervision. Because of his sinful life, Herod was hostile to the idea of Israel's election and to the Lord's grace in His covenant with Israel.

What was worse, the spiritual leaders of the people, the high priest Caiaphas and his father-in-law Annas, hated the gospel. They hated the good news that God in His grace wanted to be everything for His people. Those men thought that they could bring it off themselves by their own religiousness.

Yet the Lord knew what He was doing. The gospel of grace, as John would be preaching it and as it would be taken over by Jesus Himself, had to join battle with all those hostile powers. God did not want to abandon His people to their sins.

This ministry of John's, by which the people were to be brought to meet the Lord, God had already promised in the Old Testament. At that time God had said that a voice would appear in the wilderness crying that the Lord would be coming in His grace. And assuming they believed that message of grace, the people were to prepare the way for Him, that is, everything in people's lives hindering the coming of the Lord would have to be removed. Sins were to be confessed and put away in the strength of faith in the Lord's grace. The coming of the Lord would see the salvation of the Lord provided to all flesh, old and young, free and slave, Jew and Gentile. Salvation was not limited and no one would be rejected beforehand.

Bringing them out of their false confidence. John ministered in the desert, preaching that wonderful message. He also baptized. Many came from the surrounding countryside to be baptized. John's ministry made a deep impression. He said that the Messiah's kingdom was at hand and everyone knew that the Messiah had come to execute judgment. John painted a vivid picture of that coming judgment so that the people might see their sins and confess them.

But many did not faithfully confess their sins before the Lord's grace. Many just became afraid. They wanted baptism out of fear for judgment and wrath upon their sins, as though that baptism would provide protection against the coming of that wrath. Thus they saw baptism as a magical charm.

People often act that way. They see the church and their "religion" as a means of protecting themselves from the judgment. In anger John directed himself to these people and asked them who had taught them to see baptism that way. They had made a magical charm of that wonderful sign of God's grace for His people, as people so often do. For them baptism offered no protection but the judgment would hit them doubly hard. Those people really thought they would have a good chance of escaping the judgment. Didn't they belong to the covenant people after all? Thus they thought they had a right to God's blessing.

People of the covenant indeed have a right to the Lord's blessing but only because He has graciously promised it. But how is a man to receive that blessing if he does not want to know the God who has promised it or if he does not believe in God's grace or confess and avoid his own sin? That they were children of Abraham according to the flesh did not protect them. They had to be one with Abraham in faith. Then they would truly be Abraham's children.

The Lord would make such children of Abraham out of the Gentiles. They would be taken up into the covenant and would inherit the promise made to Abraham. God would do this according to His own good pleasure or according to His election. Would that be too wonderful for the Lord? He could even make children of Abraham out of stones if He so pleased. Israelites were not to boast of their descent from Abraham or of their status in the covenant. They were to glory in the grace of the Lord who had placed them in the covenant.

Escaping from judgment was out of the question. The Messiah

had His ax in His hand and the blow was about to fall. Every tree that did not bear fruit would be cut down, separated from the people of the covenant and cast into the fire.

Bringing them out of their sins. What then, they asked John, were those fruits which were the result of faith? What did the Lord desire of them? Among those who asked these questions were people who had genuine faith in the grace of the Lord. They wanted to be instructed by John. What answer would John give to them? Would he ask them to live such a life as he himself lived in the wilderness? Was that the nature of life in the Kingdom of God?

To their amazement John gave quite a different answer. They were to remain in the midst of life, and in those everyday relationships know and love one another in faith. Their love would become evident from sharing their possessions with those in need.

Further, the justice of the Kingdom of God was to govern their lives. To the publicans, the tax collectors who had put themselves at the service of the foreign tyrant, he did not say that they should leave their posts but that they were not to commit theft. To the soldiers of Rome he did not say that they should give up their military service. They were not to rob or commit violence but be content with their wages.

Life in the Kingdom of God is really quite simple. It is true that through the Kingdom, conditions in the world will also have to be changed, but we must begin to know one another in love and to give ourselves to each other for God's sake.

The Mighty One is coming. John's ministry made such a deep impression on people that they began to ask themselves whether he was the Messiah. John understood their questioning and said to them that he too had been sent by God. However, his baptism was nothing but the sign of God's grace in His covenant. He who came after him, the Messiah, would impart grace itself. He, who awakens new life, would baptize with the Holy Spirit and with fire that purifies from sin and brings about the battle between those who fear the Lord and those who do not. The Messiah would be so much greater than John. He is the Lord from heaven. John, who was only a sinful man, was not worthy to untie the laces of His sandals. How could people think that he was the Messiah? When

334

Jesus came—and His coming was imminent—the sifting among the people would begin like the sifting of the chaff from the grain. He would burn the chaff with unquenchable fire. Great is the grace which the Messiah brings but terrible also is His judgment.

Enmity. Enmity against John and his message was bound to come. The leaders of the people were afraid of him. They feared that they would lose their hold on the people. John spared no one. He did not even spare Herod the tetrarch, whom he reprimanded in the name of the Lord for his ungodly life. But Herod refused to listen to reason and finally threw him into prison.

Thus John suffered the shame of the gospel and in that bore something of the suffering of the Lord Jesus Himself. That was a great trial for him. All who confess Jesus Christ will suffer something of this and it will be for their purification. By means of their suffering, the victory of the gospel of grace will come. John too had to make way for the Lord Jesus and for His ministry in Israel. It is Christ alone, not His servant John, who saves His people.

CHAPTER FIFTY FIVE
THE LORD'S ANOINTED
LUKE 3:21—4:30

For Christ's baptism and temptation see the corresponding sections in Matthew and Mark. Luke barely mentions His baptism. For him all the emphasis is on the anointing.

Chapter 3:23 should probably read: "He was the son of Joseph, who was thought to have been son of Heli." In that case Luke gives the genealogy of Mary, who must have been a daughter of Heli. The genealogy goes back to Adam to show that the Christ is not only of Israel but of the whole human race.

There is a knowledge of Christ according to the flesh. Such a knowledge is present whenever men want to glory in Him without knowing His grace by faith. That's how it was in Galilee where people praised His great deeds. This danger existed especially for Nazareth, the place where He had grown up.

Today too it is possible for people to join Christian political parties, colleges and other Christian organizations, especially when these are prospering, without believing in Christ for the forgiveness of their sins, that is, without knowing Him according to the Spirit. This knowledge according to the flesh stands in the way of the knowledge according to the Spirit.

Thus, especially in Nazareth, Christ had to join battle with that knowledge that is according to the flesh. He revealed Himself there as the Lord's Anointed according to prophecy. What great opposition that prophecy would encounter in Nazareth!

Main Thought: *The Christ reveals Himself as the Lord's Anointed.*

The anointing. While John was baptizing, the Lord Jesus, who was only a few months younger than John, had also become thirty years old. For Him too the time had come to reveal Himself to the people as the Redeemer. He went from Nazareth to Judea, into the wilderness where John was baptizing and had John baptize Him too. John was gathering His people together so He too had to be there, one with His people in baptism, because He was also one with them in their sins. Thus He acted as the Head of the people.

Then He prayed. Now the Father could give Him an assurance of His calling and fill Him with the Holy Spirit for His task. In answer to His prayer He saw the Holy Spirit descend upon Him in the form of a dove, an event witnessed only by John. That event signified His anointing for office. Prophets, priests and kings of old were anointed with oil in Israel. Thereby the Lord appointed them to their office and gave them the sign that He would qualify them through the Holy Spirit. Through the Spirit all their gifts and powers would blossom so that they could give themselves to the Lord's work. In the same way the Lord Jesus received His anointing with the Holy Spirit. This prepared Him too, with all that was in Him, for God's work. Everything that was in Him thus accommodated itself to His redemptive work which was dedicated to God's service.

Moreover, the Father's own voice from heaven said that He was the One called to the work of redemption because He was the Son, in Whom God revealed all His love. "You are My beloved Son," God said, "in You I have been well pleased." Once God had had good pleasure in Him when He had destined Him for this work. Now, because of His obedience in that work, God's good pleasure rested on Him continually.

The Spirit which He had received continually urged Him on in the work. First the Spirit led Him into the wilderness where He stayed for forty days and was tempted of the devil. At the beginning of His ministry He had to conquer the great enemy. Afterwards the Spirit led Him to Galilee where He began to preach in the synagogues of various towns and villages. He preached as they had never heard before, quite differently from the preaching of the scribes. He did not tell them what they should do to save themselves, and thus be saved, but always pointed out the grace of God, through which God bent down to His people. Moreover, by the many signs and miracles He performed, He confirmed that through Him God's grace had returned to His people.

All the people talked about Him. Rumors about Him penetrated beyond the borders of Canaan. From all sides they came to hear Him or be healed by Him. He was praised by all. They had never seen or heard anything like this. Why did they praise Him? Did they hear and see that God's grace had come to them in Him? For most people that was not the case. His Word did not take hold of them unto eternal life; they just found it exciting. And His deeds did not set them free from the guilt and the power of sin; they admired Him for His miracles. The way to their hearts was thus cut off for Him.

Knowledge according to the flesh. The danger that they would praise Him without believing in Him for their salvation must have been greatest in Nazareth where He had grown up and played in the streets. In Nazareth they heard what He was doing everywhere in Galilee. Why didn't He come to His own town to do the same things there? How proud they were of their townsman who had gained such fame! Jesus also must have thought about Nazareth in those days and seen the danger that their hearts would be the most resistant to the Word of grace. Resistance would bring conflict and struggle in Nazareth. Prospects of conflict must have made Him reluctant to go there while at the same time He must have longed to reveal the grace of God in Him there too. Would He be victorious and would Nazareth want to acknowledge Him as the One anointed by the Holy Spirit for the work of redemption?

Finally He knew that He should go. He entered the town before the sabbath. Of course, everybody knew it immediately but what they were expecting did not happen. The many miracles failed to materialize. There were sick people in Nazareth too, and the Father gave Him the opportunity to perform many miracles. But it would not happen there because of their unbelief. Certainly, He had performed many miracles in Galilee but here He was simply one of them, an ordinary citizen of Nazareth. He should not, they thought, let it go to His head! Not only did they not believe in Him for their own salvation, but they did not even believe in His power to perform miracles and thus could not be healed.

"Today this scripture has been fulfilled in your hearing." The sabbath began to dawn. Like old times, He went along the familiar streets and passed through the door of the synagogue He knew so well. There He seated Himself, just as He had done so often in the past. Yet it was different now. Great tension could be felt among the people in the synagogue. Was He now going to speak here too? What would He say?

The reader read the selected portion from the books of Moses. Next in the order of service was the reading of a portion from the prophets. That portion could be freely chosen and anyone could do the reading. At this point He stood up and went forward. An attendant gave Him the scroll of Isaiah. He rolled it open to chapter 61 and began to read that the Servant of the Lord says He has been anointed to preach of sin and its consequences. People who had been held captive by the fetters of sin would be released from their prison. The sick would be healed. The fulfillment would come of what had been promised in the Year of Jubilee as in a sign, namely, the complete liberation of life.

When He had finished reading, He gave the scroll back to the attendant and sat down to teach. "Today," He said, "you are experiencing the fulfillment of this prophecy, for I am this Servant of the Lord, the Anointed One, and I have been sent to set you free from your sin and from its consequences." He concealed nothing but placed the people of Nazareth immediately before the demand to believe in Him as the promised Redeemer, as the anointed Servant of the Lord.

The people listened breathlessly. When He stopped for just a moment they looked at one another and said, "Have you ever heard anything like this?" They thought it was wonderful. Nobody else could speak like that. They had never expected this of the boy who had played in their streets and whom they had so often seen in Joseph's carpenter's shop. They were amazed.

But their amazement meant that while they were indeed proud of Him, they had not heard the content of His words, because they were not willing to bow before them. They did not acknowledge Him as the Lord's Servant. They found it all very thrilling and were greatly astonished but yet they rejected Him. How often that also happens in our day when the Word of God is heard!

Unbelieving Israel. The Lord Jesus saw that in their astonishment they rejected Him. Would He then not gain any access to their hearts? He therefore began to talk to them differently. He no longer announced the grace of the Lord; He wanted them to discover both their own unbelief of previous days when He had not performed many miracles, and also their present unbelief in the synagogue.

He said, "Doubtless you will quote Me this proverb, 'Physician, heal yourself,' and say 'What we have heard You did at Capernaum, do here also in Your own country. Why can't You do those same miracles here? Heal Yourself of that powerlessness.' But that," He said, "is because you do not believe in Me. No prophet is acceptable in his own country. His home town, where he is so well known, will not honor him as a prophet. So you will not subject yourselves to My Word and will not acknowledge Me as the anointed Servant of the Lord, who was sent for your redemption."

"But be warned. In this way salvation will pass you by. That is how it went in the days of Ahab. Truly, I say to you, there were many widows in Israel then, but Elijah was not honored in Israel as a prophet. So he was sent by God to a heathen widow in Zarephath, in the land of Sidon. There was salvation for her. Likewise in Elisha's time, many lepers in Israel were not cleansed, because Elisha was not acknowledged as the prophet of the Lord. Salvation was for the foreigner Naaman, the Syrian, who submitted in faith to the Word of grace in the prophet. So now salvation will pass you by too."

Christ's majesty. Jesus spoke sharply to them in order that they might yet turn around and receive salvation. But even these words did not bring them to repentance. His reproach of their unbelief had only filled their hearts with anger. Who did He think He was, they fumed, that He could say this to them? Wasn't He just an ordinary boy from their town? Such presumption!

The quarrel degenerated to the point that they threw Him out of the synagogue. Once outside they pushed Him to the brow of the hill on which Nazareth was built to throw Him down headlong. But when they reached the top, He turned around and straightway the crowd fell back. All at once a majesty went out from Him which frightened them. This opened up a path among them by which He went away.

They still had seen something of the majesty of Christ even though they had not acknowledged Him as God's Anointed. One day all men will thus behold Christ's majesty. If they have not bowed before the majesty of His grace here, they will one day tremble before His majesty in the judgment.

CHAPTER FIFTY SIX
FISHER OF MEN
LUKE 5:1-11

W e do not have to take up the question of whether what is told here is the same as what we read in Matthew 4 and Mark 1. In any case there is a very close connection. In the first period of Christ's ministry we see that the office of disciple had three aspects: a) in Judea He asked several of His later disciples to follow Him on His return to Galilee (see Gospel of John, chapter 1:35-51); this was not yet decisive for their special discipleship; b) thereupon followed the calling of Peter and Andrew and the sons of Zebedee by the lake of Gennesaret; c) after this came their appointment to be apostles (Luke 6:12, 13).

However, in Luke 5:1-11 the calling of the disciples to be fishers of men is not the central issue, with the miracle of the extraordinary catch of fish having only symbolic significance. Here we have again the revelation of the grace of God in Christ. Christ comes first. He also controlled that miraculous catch of fish. The miracle of the Kingdom of grace is in all things, in all the ordinary things of life and in this unusual catch. This is what we must learn to see. To that end He spoke to the crowd on the shore and ordered Peter to put out to sea. In all of this He is the Fisher of men who would have them see the Kingdom of God. Only when the disciples see the Kingdom can they in turn become fishers of men in His service.

Christ is the Fisher of men. This is evident to the crowd, in His command to Peter to push off from the shore, in the miraculous blessing on the net, in the amazement of Peter, and in the calling of the disciples.

Main Thought: *Christ reveals Himself as the Fisher of men.*

Preaching to the crowd. After His visit to Nazareth Jesus again preached throughout Galilee. But the center of His activity was Capernaum by the Sea of Galilee where He also lived for a while.

He could not appear in Capernaum or the crowds would press around Him.

So now He was once again in Capernaum by the sea. A large crowd wanted to hear Him. Along the shore lay two boats in which the fishermen had been fishing during the night. They were now busy washing their nets alongside the boats. One of those boats belonged to a certain Simon who already earlier had come in contact with the Lord Jesus and believed in Him. After the Lord Jesus had gotten into his boat He asked Simon to put out a little from the shore. Then He sat down in the boat and from there He taught the crowd on the shore. There would be no danger of their pushing Him into the water and at the same time everybody could hear Him.

The lakeshore was a peculiar place for preaching. The Lord Jesus sat in the boat; the fishermen stood beside Him with their clothes still dripping wet; the waves lapped against the boat; the crowd, not in their Sunday best but in their work clothes, was lined up along the shore.

The Lord Jesus spoke to them just as He always did. He might tell them of the field, of a household, of a shepherd with his sheep or of the catch of fish. But always He proclaimed the Kingdom of God's grace. He could do that because everything in the whole wide world is not merely a picture of the grace of the Kingdom, but a result of it as well. That God's blessing still rests on fields, on households, on cattle businesses and on fisheries is a result of His grace shown to us in Christ. In that everyday life the grace of the Kingdom is manifest. That is where people including ourselves must see it. For that reason He pointed it out to them. Then we see that our whole life becomes a miracle of God's grace.

In this way He was busy catching men. He was the great Fisher of men. And, like every good fisherman, He looked for them where they were, that is, in their daily activities. Right there He pointed them to the Kingdom of God.

Put out into deep water. When He had finished speaking He asked Simon to go out to sea to cast out his nets. Simon must certainly have been surprised at that. They were used to fishing at night, not during the day, and they had fished the whole night without result. So there would surely be no chance of their catching anything now during the day. Simon might have thought: the Lord Jesus doesn't know anything about catching fish; shouldn't He keep out of it? But Simon had already seen the Lord Jesus before and had noticed that the grace that is in Him governs all things. And so, while He did say that they had caught nothing all night, he immediately added that at the command of the Lord Jesus he would cast out the nets.

So there Simon went with his boat out to sea with his nets and with Jesus in the boat. Experienced fishermen on shore must have looked upon this scene with a smile. Had Simon gone daft? But this was the Lord Jesus' way of catching him. He had to learn to surrender unconditionally by faith to the Word of grace that the Lord Jesus speaks. And the Lord brought him to that point. That is how the glory of the Kingdom is revealed to us.

Blessing on the net. Far from shore the net was cast overboard. They dragged it along and when they were going to draw it up they couldn't get it on board. The net was tearing apart; that's how full it was. From a distance they motioned to the fishermen in the other boat, James and John, the sons of Zebedee, to come to help. When they had come up close, they carefully drew up the net and filled both boats with their catch, so that they both almost sank.

That was tremendous. But in this the power of grace was revealed which also governs fishing. Apart from God's grace there isn't any blessing in life. This abundant catch pointed especially to the riches of grace that are in the Lord Jesus. That abundance is overwhelming. That's how the glory of the Kingdom was revealed.

Depart from me, for I am a sinful man. It was fortunate that Simon and those who were with him in the boat, and John and James as well, saw it that way. They also could have looked upon that rich catch without their eyes being opened to the grace of the Lord which was revealed in it. We often go through life with closed eyes. We do not see God's Kingdom in life's miracles, and then we say, "What success we have had!"

With Simon it was different. He walked to the stern of the boat, fell down at the Lord Jesus' feet and said, "Depart from me, for I am a sinful man, O Lord." Amazement had seized him, and all who were in the boats. It was amazement at the power of grace in the Lord Jesus. God Himself was close to them in the greatness of His grace. As a result Simon saw himself as a sinful man. We may tremble before God's power, but if we see the power of His grace we are brought to confessing our sins. Simon and the others were overcome by the power of God's grace.

The calling of the disciples. "Do not be afraid," the Lord Jesus said. There was nothing to fear because God's grace was near in Him, God's grace which forgave guilt and by which they were adopted to be God's children.

When they had seen God's abundant grace and were taken captive by it, they could also go out and preach it and thereby catch others. To that work the Lord Jesus called especially Simon and his brother, Andrew, and the sons of Zebedee. They were to follow Him always and they would catch men for God's Kingdom.

In so doing they would always have this catch of fish before their very eyes. The work of preaching would sometimes seem just as impossible to them as going out to fish in broad daylight. But in that work too the power of grace would remain just as great for them. And one day there will be with the Lord Jesus a multitude of redeemed which no one can count.

CHAPTER FIFTY SEVEN
THE APOSTLE OF OUR CONFESSION
LUKE 6:12-49

Christ called twelve of His disciples individually and also named them apostles. *Name* or *naming* simply means appointing: He *appointed* them to be apostles. Thus we have the *institution* of the apostolic office. And when we consider that all later offices in the church, including the ones we have now, originated from the apostolic office, we can say that Christ's appointment of the twelve constituted the foundation of the instituted church in the New Testament. Christ did not proceed with this before He had spent the night in prayer. This should keep us from all indifference with respect to the church as an institution. Through His apostles and through the church as institution He goes on working in spite of the sins of that institution. Christ, the apostle of our confession, is faithful over all of God's house. (Read Hebrews 3.)

The crowd sought to touch Him, for power went out from Him and He healed them all. This was healing on a big scale where all personal contact, all seeking for the personal restoration of the sick which accompanied His earlier healings seems to have been excluded (see section 35 above). But let us; not forget that these healings are followed by the Sermon on the Mount in which Christ calls those who are miserable, blessed. This means that they are blessed not because they are healed, but because they endured life's sufferings in communion with the Lord.

Having discussed the Sermon on the Mount at some length in our treatment of Matthew, we shall not discuss it here. Here we will deal only with the themes we have pointed out above. This is not the place to discuss whether Luke, who does not speak of "poor in spirit" but of "poor," was thinking of those poor in material goods and those physically hungry. Bu: it may be said that by his more general expressions Luke leads us to think of "the poor according to the world," those who only by way of exception occupy a position of leadership in life and in general are pushed aside by those who elbow their way forward. This not only characterizes discipleship, but also provides the necessary chastening in a disciple's life.

Main Thought: *The Apostle of our confession is faithful over His whole house.*

Appointing the apostles. During the time of Jesus' activity in Galilee, large crowds were constantly following Him. They came from all over the country and even from far beyond its borders. Often they stayed around Him day and night. Frequently they would spend the night in the open fields. One evening Jesus was again surrounded by a crowd. But towards nightfall He withdrew from everybody and went up into the hills alone. That night He did not sleep but prayed all through the night. He was frequently in prayer for a very long time. In prayer He sought and held on to communion with His Father, that in all His work He might be one with the Father. He did that also for us. He held on to communion with His Father for us in this sinful world.

On this particular night there was a special reason for His praying. Already there was a great crowd of disciples in His following. Among them were twelve whom He had called to follow Him daily because He had a special calling for them. To twelve of His disciples He wanted to give a special charge for the future. Jesus Himself was the Father's ambassador in this world. These twelve were to be ambassadors in Jesus' name, to preach His Word with authority and thus to gather His people, His Church. Something of the power of the office that He Himself occupied He would lay on them. They were to preach His Word and also write it down, so that it might be preserved for all times and His people might be saved by faith in that Word. For when those twelve died, others would again be called who would receive a portion of their task and power and spread their word everywhere. These are the office-bearers of the church today.

That night He prayed for those twelve and for their Word as well as for all who later would proclaim that Word in the church. He prayed for all the work that would be done and for the gathering and guidance of His church. He asked God's blessing upon it and asked forgiveness of everything that would be sinful in it, for also in the church and its office-bearers there would be much sin.

The next morning He called to Him twelve of His disciples and appointed them to be His apostles, His ambassadors. These twelve He chose in accordance with the will of the Father. He knew that the Father had given them to Him. Among them were very different kinds of people. First there were the four to whom, after the miraculous catch of fish, He had said that He would make them fishers of men. There was a tax collector among the twelve, a former tax official who had put himself at the disposal of the foreign tyrants and was therefore hated by the people. Then there was a zealot, a passionate national partisan, the extreme opposite of the tax collector. Christ could use them all if they only believed His grace and submitted to His Word.

First and foremost, they were to live out of faith in that Word. Not all of them did that. There was one among them who said that he accepted this calling, but for whom the Lord Jesus and the Word of His grace meant nothing. That man sought only himself and his own advantage. In the long run he would come in conflict with this calling. Later he even went so far as to betray the Lord Jesus. That such a person was among the twelve should be a warning to us that service of the Lord Jesus demands our all and that we cannot live for ourselves and at the same time hope to serve Him.

Healing the sick. With these twelve He came partly down the hill to a level place. There the twelve stood with Him, together with the great crowd of His disciples and the even larger throng of people who had come from all parts of the country and beyond to hear Him and to be healed of their diseases. There the Lord Jesus showed to the full the mercy of God which had appeared in Him. There He healed many sick people all at the same time. They just touched Him and were healed, because power went forth from Him.

He did not do this often. He had always sought people out personally and tried to bring them to faith in the grace of God. Did these sick people not need this personal touch? Indeed they did, which was why He spoke to them presently. But first He wanted to show them how wonderful it was going to be on earth as a result of the grace of God. All sickness and all results of sin would one day be overcome. One day He would show the glory of His grace.

Blessed are you who are poor. But He did not leave them without guidance. Immediately He began to speak to them. And He said to them that if they believed in Him they would be oppressed by the world. Over and over again they will have to yield to those who have another goal in life, namely, to get ahead in the world, and who therefore are prepared to trample everyone else under foot.

Christ's faithful are not to be of that spirit. They want to serve God in this world. They want to give all their strength and develop their talents but only for God's sake. They do not want to trample upon others but as a result will have to suffer blows and contempt. They have to bear all this for His sake. They will then inherit the glory of God's Kingdom. But woe to those who are self-seeking and seek to get ahead in this world. They are blind leaders of the blind, falling headlong into the abyss. At the end of their lives they will meet destruction because they have not built on solid ground. Only when we build on the Word of grace are we secure. Thus He sends all His own into the world, as He Himself was sent by the Father.

CHAPTER FIFTY EIGHT
HE HAS BORNE OUR GRIEFS
LUKE 7:11-17

Raising the young man of Nain occurred under different circumstances than raising Jairus's daughter in that the former was done not just in the presence of a few people but on a public road. Desire for sensation played no role here; it was a case of genuine sympathy with the grief of this widow. "A large crowd from the city was with her." The Lord Jesus Christ entered into that sorrow. In the words of the prophet Isaiah, "Surely He has borne our griefs" (53:4).

Also, the reaction of the people after the miracle was more genuine than on other occasions. The crowd was seized with fear and they glorified God saying, "A great prophet has arisen among us," and "God has visited His people." Especially in that latter testimony was a grateful acknowledgement of the Lord's faithfulness in His covenant.

Main Thought: *Christ bears our griefs.*

The ties severed. Again the Lord Jesus was going through Galilee. Many of His disciples were with Him and also a great crowd followed Him. They were coming to a town called Nain. From the city a funeral procession came towards them. The crowd in the procession was exceptionally large because they were mourning an exceptional loss. A widow had lost her only son, her sole support and hope. The whole city grieved for her.

That's how life is. Even life's deepest ties are not immune from death. Why could this young man not have been spared? He could still have meant so much to his mother. And what was the mother's life without her son? Death is so cruel. Nevertheless, it is a result of our sin. We must not therefore rise up in rebellion against God but seek to understand the weight of the guilt we have laid upon ourselves by our sin.

In her great loss, the widow's only consolation was the compassion of the crowd. Human compassion is one of God's blessings; it enables us to share one another's grief. It enabled the crowd to share the sorrow of the mother who was following her son's bier.

Moved with compassion. Yet the sympathy is only slight comfort. They can never enter fully into our sorrow nor can they take it away. But with the Lord Jesus that's different. As soon as He had approached the procession and heard how a great a loss had been suffered, He was moved with compassion towards this woman. He knew much better than any of us the consequences of sin and He was able to take that burden fully upon Himself. He did that time and time again. He could bear the cross of our grief because He had taken upon Himself the cause of our grief, namely our sin, and would make atonement for it.

This means a great deal. By faith we may know that there is someone who shares our burdens and feels its full weight. We are not alone in our sufferings. In His mediatorial work He takes our yoke upon Himself. This also explains the sympathy we encounter among our fellow-men. Jesus has given all of mankind something of His compassionate spirit. Our fellow human being's imperfect sympathy convinces the believer of Jesus' perfect sympathy. To Him we can express ourselves completely. What would it have been like had we been left alone in grief?

Taking away the grief. Yet He does more than merely sympathize with our grief; He can also take it away. One day He will do just that. He will restore all the ties which have been sanctified in Him. One day, when He restores His people in His glorious Kingdom on the new earth, He will wipe away all tears from our eyes. Then we shall see that our ties on earth were not just temporal and meaningless but we shall discover their sanctified, glorious meaning.

He wanted to show that He restores and saves the ties between people. He told the mother not to weep and placed His hand on the bier. The bearers came to a stand-still and He said, "Young man, I say to you, arise." And the dead man sat up on the bier. Then the Lord Jesus gave him to his mother; He restored the tie that had been broken.

352

He could do that because He was going to atone for sin and thus conquer death, the consequence of sin. If that mother and her son acknowledged Him as the Redeemer, the restoration to life would not just be temporary. They will have served the Lord in love throughout their lives. The restoration of life here would be followed by an eternal restoration. This is what the Lord Jesus prophesied in raising this widow's only son. In Him we may mean something to one another. The tie will remain because one day we shall find it again. Then all that is sinful and imperfect will be removed from our relationships. Then we may forget all sin and imperfection because God casts it into the sea of oblivion.

God has visited His people. The crowd was seized with fear and they glorified God saying "a great prophet has arisen among us," and "God has visited His people. " No wonder the crowd was fearful. They has seen the revelation of God's glory – the glory of His grace, which conquered sin and death. Thus it was not a timid fear on the part of the crowd but a fear that prompted them to glorify God.

Faith was at work among the people, perhaps not in everyone, and not in full clarity, yet many eyes were opened. The people thought of the Lord and His covenant. They said that the Lord was visiting His people, was seeking them out in His grace, as in the days of old. They believed that He was a prophet sent by God to tell them that God's grace was near, confirming His words with such signs as these.

Jesus indeed revealed that God visited us with His grace and has given us the Holy Spirit, in whom He is always close to us. Seek the Lord while He may be found; call upon Him while He is near.

CHAPTER FIFTY NINE
FORGIVENESS
LUKE 7:36-50

It is not necessary to believe that the woman described by Luke as a sinner was a common prostitute. It is also possible that she had left her husband and lived with another man, or had even committed some other sin.

She did not come to Christ as a penitent asking forgiveness of sins. Her adoration was an expression of grateful love for earlier forgiveness. She must have seen and received forgiveness before. That need not have happened at an earlier meeting between Christ and her; it is not necessary to assume such a previous encounter. On the contrary, from the story we receive the impression that this was their first meeting. However, the Word of God is a living word. She could have heard the Word of reconciliation either directly from Jesus in the synagogue or outside of it, or it could have been transmitted to her by others. In any case, the Word of grace had set her free.

It is not an argument against this view that Christ said to her at the end of this meeting, "Your sins are forgiven." This simply places a seal on her faith which had liberated her. The words of verse 47 cannot give rise to any misunderstanding. Her sins, which were many, were forgiven her but not because she loved much; rather, her great love is proof that much was forgiven her. God's love and forgiveness came first; she thereupon reciprocated.

Main Thought: *He to whom much has been forgiven loves much.*

The unwelcome guest. In a city in Galilee lived a Pharisee named Simon. This man invited Jesus to have dinner at his house. This showed that he wanted to be his own man, for the other Pharisees had already chosen sides against Jesus and would not have received Him in their homes. Simon wanted to form his own opinion of

Jesus. And how could he better observe Him than during dinner in his own home?

Simon had no intention of surrendering to Jesus. From his own standpoint he wanted simply to observe Him. Is it ever possible to know Jesus that way? On the contrary He is known only to those who wish to receive grace from Him. Although the Lord Jesus knew the spirit in which the invitation had been extended, He accepted it. He seized every opportunity to sow the seed of the gospel.

Yet Simon was a bit embarrassed with his own invitation. Jesus should not in the least think that Simon honored Him. Therefore Simon was reserved and he kept at a distance. He would let Him feel that it was a favor to sit at a Pharisee's table. So Simon did not even show Him the usual courtesies. He did not provide water to wash the Lord Jesus' feet. He wouldn't think of greeting Him with a kiss as a friendly welcome. And he certainly did not have His head anointed with oil, as was the custom with an honored guest. The Lord Jesus saw and understood all of this. He suffered it all. Perhaps here too He might set life free from this sin of pride.

The adoration of love. There also lived a woman in the city who was publicly known as an infamous sinner. We don't know what sin she was guilty of. However, she had heard the Word of redemption as the Lord Jesus had proclaimed it. Therefore she had come to see her sin in the light of God's grace and had become aware of her guilt before God. She had also come to believe that there was forgiveness for her with God even while people still looked down on her. With grateful adoration she thought of the Lord Jesus who brought the Word of redemption in a way that made all Old Testament Scriptures come alive for her!

When she heard that the Lord Jesus was in the city having dinner in Simon's house, she simply could not restrain herself. She was eager to show Him her adoration. She did not care what people would say about it and how Simon and the other Pharisees at the dinner would regard her. She would tell Him all about her love. She could not do that with words, but she would show it with a sign.

Uninvited, she pushed her way into Simon's house. She had brought with her an alabaster flask of expensive ointment which she wanted to pour out over Jesus' feet. But when she stood behind Him, bent over His feet, she broke down and tears fell on His feet.

When she saw that, she undid her hair and with it dried off His feet. Then she also poured the ointment over His feet.

How did she dare? Not only was she risking being shamed in front of the others, but Jesus might also know her reputation and sin. Yet that did not hold her back. She knew that He, who had been sent by God, judged differently than men because with God is much forgiveness. She could show Him that she believed the forgiveness which He preached. What could be more pleasing to Him than such faith in the Word of God's grace? She truly knew the Lord Jesus because she surrendered to Him, while Simon would not know Him.

Confrontation. Simon thought he had Jesus on the run. He had observed the Lord Jesus and noticed that He was not a prophet. If He had been a prophet, He certainly would have known who this woman was and would not have had anything to do with her.

Jesus knew what was going on in Simon's mind but He still wanted to make an effort to have the Pharisee discover who He really was. He told a parable of two debtors and at the end asked which of the two would love more, the one to whom much had been forgiven or the one to whom little had been forgiven. Arrogantly, Simon answered that, in his opinion, it would be the one to whom much had been forgiven.

At that the Lord Jesus confronted Simon with this woman. Simon had shown Him no honor or love but the woman had been all gratitude and adoration. Should He then not come to the conclusion that much had been forgiven this woman? And had anything been forgiven Simon who showed no love at all? In his pride, Simon had never desired forgiveness. He was no object of God's merciful good pleasure. He therefore knew nothing of a love that shows adoration. Our love will be as great as our perception of God's mercy. Thus Jesus tried to bring Simon and the others to self-discovery. But they did not let themselves be put to shame; they maintained themselves over against God.

Sealing her forgiveness. While Jesus was speaking with Simon, He turned toward the woman, pointing to her and said, "Your sins are forgiven." Formerly she had believed the Word of forgiveness. How well she must have known what struggle was! Was it true that there was forgiveness? Now she might hear it from His own lips. Thus she was confirmed in her faith.

Undoubtedly, the Pharisees were annoyed at His pronouncement of forgiveness. They said among themselves, "Who is this, who even forgives sins?" They did not know Him as the One sent by God and did not hear His Word as the Word of God. They therefore could not admit that He had power from God to forgive sins. In this they did not know Him because they did not submit to Him.

Against this doubt and unbelief, which always tried to wipe out the Word of God and break its power, the Lord Jesus maintained the power of His Word. Once again He spoke to the woman and said, "Your faith has saved you; go in peace." The Word of grace prevailed in Simon's house. In the same way it will have power in the world against all unbelief and doubt, and time after time it will liberate men and women and confirm them in their faith.

CHAPTER SIXTY
GOVERNED BY THE KINGDOM
LUKE 9:49—10:24

Although Luke's gospel generally does not follow a chronological line, yet we see a change in Christ's ministry. The preaching in Galilee had come to an end. In verse 51 Luke writes that the time approached when He was to be taken up to heaven and that He set His face resolutely towards Jerusalem. In this period Jesus spoke especially about discipleship. To be a citizen of the Kingdom also means to be a worker in the Kingdom. That Kingdom must govern us in everything.

The man who cast out demons in Jesus' name was evidently a believer. There is no question here of the use of Jesus' name as a magical formula, as later was the case with the sons of Sceva (see Acts 19:14). That John and his fellow disciples forbade the man sprang from a wrong idea of their office. They thought that they alone had received the Spirit for the salvation of life. The grandeur of their office had affected them. They did not see the blessing which the Spirit also gives to others to spread abroad. We have a situation here similar to what happened in Moses' days when it was Joshua's wish that prophesying be forbidden to everyone but the seventy who had been set apart (see Numbers 11:16-30). John and his fellow disciple were still seeking their own interest and not just that of the Kingdom.

By condemning the wish of John and James that fire consume the Samaritans, the Lord Jesus did not condemn what Elijah had done. Indeed, Christ Himself will one day cause fire to come down from heaven. The proclamation of the Kingdom is also an announcement of judgment upon those who do not believe. In that sense they were indeed to be Boanerges, sons of thunder. But here their pride had been hurt. They were not concerned only about the Kingdom and about the gospel of the Kingdom, otherwise they would have understood that the time for judgment had not yet come, especially not for the Samaritans who had not all heard the gospel and who were irritated by the national pride of the Jews.

When, at the end of this section, Christ said that His own should rejoice not because the spirits are subject to them, but because their names are written in heaven, He did not preach a spiritual egoism, an exclusive occupation with their own salvation after this life. That our names are written in heaven means that we are citizens of the Kingdom. As citizens, in the name of the Lord we may once again use the earth and its fullness in peace. This is the essence of the Kingdom. Because this Kingdom is not yet fully realized on earth, but must push its way through with force, these remarkable phenomena, such as controlling the spirits, were necessary. But the disciples saw these special signs as more valuable than that which is the very essence of the Kingdom, our use of the earth in the name of the Lord. And, alas, that is still the case today. We seek the Kingdom in all kinds of signs and not in our everyday life in the fear of God.

Main Thought: *The Spirit of the Kingdom of God governs its workers in all respects.*

He who is not against us is for us. The Lord Jesus could not do the work in Galilee all by Himself. So He sent His twelve disciples to preach the gospel of the Kingdom everywhere in His name. To that end He gave them power to perform many signs. With great zeal they preached and performed many miracles. The Lord greatly blessed their work.

Would they have done all that work exclusively for the Lord and His Kingdom? No, they also sought their own interests. This was evident from the fact that when they returned to Jesus again, they argued about which of them had accomplished the most and which was the greatest in the Kingdom. The Lord had to put them to shame. Our importance lies not in what we think we have accomplished but in our adoption by God as His children. A child that is adopted by God is of great worth in the Kingdom. As His children we must see our adoption by God through His love as the greatest blessing.

When Jesus spoke about adopted children, John remembered what he and his fellow disciples had encountered on their assignment. They had seen a man casting out demons in the name of the Lord Jesus. He did not belong to the twelve, so they had forbidden him. As Jesus spoke about adopted children serving the Kingdom exclusively, doubt came up in John as to whether they had been right in thus forbidding him. He asked the Lord Jesus about it.

And, sure enough, He said that they had been wrong. That man had been casting out demons in faith. He was not trying to compete with the Lord Jesus and His disciples. He was not against them or against the Kingdom of God. And if he was not against them, then he was for them and for the Kingdom. The power of the Spirit is not bound to the office or limited to those to whom the Lord has given a special position in the Kingdom. If they had only been able to focus on the Kingdom they would have rejoiced in what that man was doing. How fortunate that God's work is so manifold!

He came to save. The Lord Jesus and His disciples had worked in Galilee a great deal but Galilee had not accepted them. The time for His work there had come to a conclusion. The days of His suffering were approaching. During that time of crisis Jesus instructed His disciples especially in the meaning of kingdom service.

From Galilee He journeyed to Jerusalem to suffer there. On the way He still had much to do. He went through the country of the Samaritans. At the end of a day's journey He sent James and John ahead to the nearest hamlet to find lodging for the night both for Him and for the large crowd which followed Him.

There was jealousy between Samaritans and Jews. The proud Jews looked down at the Samaritans, and this irritated them. Moreover, the Samaritans had heard of the public ministry of Jesus. Now He was coming into their country, only not to preach or to perform miracles but simply to stay overnight on His way to Jerusalem. That irritated them even more and they flatly refused to accommodate James and John.

Disturbed, James and John came back to Jesus and asked Him whether they should perhaps have called down fire from heaven to consume the Samaritans, as Elijah had once done. They did not ask Him that because the gospel of the Kingdom had been rejected. If the gospel had been uppermost in their minds they would have realized how little the gospel had yet been preached to the Samaritans and how the Jews had irritated Samaritans by their pride. Instead James and John asked it because their pride had been hurt. Only, that hadn't been Elijah's reason for calling fire down from heaven....

Consequently, the Lord Jesus rebuked them saying that they did not understand what kind of spirit made them say these things. It was the spirit of the flesh and of the evil one, the spirit that has its own interest in mind. That spirit destroys everything. But the Son of Man had not come to destroy the life of man but to save it by restoring it to fellowship with God. Only after men have rejected the gospel in unbelief will Christ bring judgment upon them. The motive for the judgment, however, will not be wounded fleshly pride but the spurned love of God which had been revealed in the Kingdom.

The Lord Jesus was going to suffer for man's salvation. The time for judgment had not yet come. Therefore He went on to another village to spend the night. How willingly He bore the scorn! By His suffering He would make atonement for this insult from the men of that Samaritan hamlet.

Following Jesus. On the way a man came to Jesus who said he would follow Him wherever He went. Here was someone who voluntarily offered himself for His service. Should the Lord Jesus not have rejoiced at this? However, He saw that this man had not realized what discipleship involved. He therefore put him to the test by saying: "Foxes have holes and birds of the air have nests; but the Son of man has nowhere to lay His head." Christ was a stranger on earth where sin reigns. He had indeed come to atone for that sin and to see that grace prevailed and by His Spirit He would again open up life for His own and give them a place on earth where they might serve the Lord in freedom. Yet Jesus Himself was forced to wander and roam to obtain that freedom for those who belong to Him. Whoever wanted to follow Him at that time had to be willing to share His life of humiliation. Besides, because of sin, so much on earth is hostile that every believer must, in this respect, feel himself a stranger on earth. We must be willing to share that alienation with the Lord Jesus. And whoever is truly His disciple must feel that he is a stranger to the reign of sin in this present age. Consequently, a believer must sacrifice everything for the benefit of his discipleship.

Jesus called yet another person to follow Him, but this man's father had just died and he asked permission to bury his father first. The burial had to be done properly, according to custom. The man calmly accepted the fact of death and did not see that the Kingdom of God, the Kingdom of life, means victory over death. In his heart there was not a single protest against death. This is how those who are spiritually dead accept death because they do not see death as reward for sin. Jesus felt that if the man were not spiritually dead himself, he'd do better to leave the burial to those who were.

That this was how he looked at death was evident from the fact that he first asked permission to see to the burial. He saw the burial as something that had to be finished first, a part of his former life which needed to be dealt with. In the Kingdom of God we bury our loved ones too, but with a vigorous protest in our hearts against death as result of sin and with the certainty of ultimate victory over death. So even while engaged in burying we can still be busy in the Kingdom of God.

Still another man came to Jesus, saying that he wanted to follow Him. But he asked for the opportunity to bid his family farewell first. Once Elisha had also said farewell to his parents when he had been called by Elijah, but he had done it prophetically, with a heart full of joy for the task which he was about to accept (see I Kings 19:19-21). This man, however, saw it as a great sacrifice that he was reluctant to make. His heart was more attached to the life back home than to fulfilling his calling in the Kingdom.

Following the Lord Jesus then becomes a matter of merit by which one obtains a place in glory. Such a person is always looking back to what he has left and is therefore unfit for his work in the Kingdom, just as someone is unfit for plowing if, instead of looking ahead to plow a straight furrow, he keeps looking back. To serve in the Kingdom we need not abandon everything, unless we originally obtained it apart from the Lord and His Kingdom. We may glory in our possessions only if they are used to serve the Lord.

Workers in His harvest. Jesus and His disciples had worked hard in Galilee but He had only been in the other provinces sporadically. He still wanted to work in sections of Judea and the Transjordan. But how was that possible in such a short time while He was traveling only through villages and cities? For that reason He designated seventy of His followers to go two by two and work in the villages and cities where He Himself was about to come. A brief stop would then have to suffice.

To the seventy He gave the same instructions and authority He had earlier given to the twelve sent out in Galilee. They were to take nothing along for the journey. Since the worker is worthy of his wages, those who would believe the gospel would welcome them into their homes and provide the necessities of life. They should not hesitate to accept hospitality because they came in the name of the King, who has a right to all of earth's bounties. They should not tarry along the way with idle chatter and ceremony. The work of the Kingdom could not wait and the workers were few. A short greeting of peace was to suffice and then they were to proceed with their work immediately. There would be those who would accept their peace in faith as spoken in the name of the Lord. If their peace was not accepted, it would return to them but their own peace of mind would not be disturbed by it because they knew that they were doing the work of the King and could leave the results to Him.

Jesus told them they would encounter much hostility. He sent them out as lambs in the midst of wolves. Fellowship with those who rejected the gospel had to be broken by symbolically shaking the dust from their feet. Despite rejection they were to persist and say that the Kingdom of God's grace had come near. Judgment upon rejection would be severe, more so than the judgment on Sodom. He also reminded them of the cities in Galilee, Chorazin and Bethsaida and especially Capernaum, where He and His disciples had worked so much.

As Jesus sought all Israel He now seeks the whole world. He extends His mercy everywhere. Yet judgment upon rejection of that mercy is sure, for the person who rejects His messengers rejects both Jesus and the Father who sent Him. But we, as His messengers, may not focus on our own glory lest we obscure the cause of the Kingdom.

Joy in the Kingdom. With joy the seventy returned saying that even the demons were subject to them. What made them happy was the success they had had. They did not see that their success was due to the fact that the power of satan had been broken. It had been broken when Jesus had assumed His office, had been anointed with the Holy Spirit and had conquered satan in the wilderness. This He told them now. He had seen satan fall like lightning from heaven. They were to pay attention especially to His work, not to their successes.

The Lord Jesus admitted that in those miracles the Kingdom of God was pushing its way through, but He said that that was not the essential element. The essence of the Kingdom is that we once again live and make use of the earth's goods in the Lord's name, that in our daily lives we are citizens of the Kingdom and that our names are registered in heaven as citizens of that Kingdom. We must rejoice most in our communion with God in all we have and do, as the Lord Jesus rejoiced in His communion with the Father. All things have been delivered up to Him by the Father in order that He should redeem the world. Only the Father knew the Christ as Redeemer of the world and no one, save Jesus, knew the Father's will to redeem the world. Only Christ could reveal the Father. Only then would men see the glory of the Kingdom.

To see that glory is not for the wise and understanding of this world but for babes and for the humble. To them the glory of the Kingdom has been revealed. The disciples were blessed to see it and so are we. Old Testament prophets and kings desired to see and hear the essence of the Kingdom but did not. They did not see the totality of life and the whole earth opened up to God's people as we may see it. What joy there ought to be in the life of believers of this age!

CHAPTER SIXTY ONE
MY NEIGHBOR
LUKE 10:25-37

A scribe asked Jesus, "What must I do to inherit eternal life?" The Lord Jesus answered, "Do this and you will live." Christ's answer made it clear to the scribe that earning salvation as he had in mind was impossible. There is indeed eternal life in keeping the commandments but only faith in Christ can enable us to keep them. Faith-led obedience will strengthen eternal communion with God.

A life of earning salvation and rewards, as the scribes saw it, always creates loneliness. Such people think only of their own salvation; they no longer acknowledge their neighbor. Hence the question, who is my neighbor, was a serious one for the scribe. A man who lives by faith is restored to fellowship with others. For him it is no longer a question who his neighbor is. He is bound to his neighbor and makes himself answerable for him.

Notice how the Samaritan made himself answerable for all the expenses of the victim's care. Notice also the Lord Jesus' words at the end. He did not say that the victim was the neighbor of the Samaritan but that the Samaritan was neighbor to the victim. The Samaritan proved himself the neighbor, knew himself to be the neighbor. He demonstrated that he knew what fellowship with others was.

We should not make a believer out of that Samaritan. Also, it was not Christ's intention to recommend philanthropy. There is a kind of charity practiced from afar, without personal communion. But this Samaritan understood what fellowship, dedicating oneself to another, was all about. Because of God's goodness, something of this charity can also be found among unbelievers. But then the flower is cut off from its root. The root of that fellowship is faith in Jesus Christ, in Whom fellowship was restored. Thus the mercy of the Samaritan points to the restorative work of Christ. He is the really merciful One; He restores fellowship and practices it. Through Him we can again practice fellowship and charity. In that fellowship and mercy is eternal life, but not in the sense of the scribe who thought eternal life could be earned.

Main Thought: *By faith we know ourselves to be the neighbor of everyone whom God places in our path.*

The way to life. While the Lord Jesus was speaking about the glory of the Kingdom of God a scribe came forward and interrupted Him saying, "Teacher, what shall I do to inherit eternal life?" His intention was to catch Jesus deviating from tradition. Was He not teaching something completely different than the scribes? They said that men were to keep the law and thereby earn eternal life. But just what was it that Jesus was teaching? It was something entirely different, yet no one had succeeded in identifying the heresy. Now this scribe wanted to lure Him into a trap. What answer would He give to this question?

Jesus answered with a question of His own: "What is written in the law? How do you read it? What do you see in the law?" The scribe's answer to this question was quite correct. He did not sum up several commandments but said that the law requires that we love God with all our heart and actions, and our neighbor as ourselves. He had seen the deep meaning of the law. Therefore the Lord Jesus said that he had answered correctly.

Jesus thereupon instructed the scribe: "Do this, and you will live." The scribe must certainly have been dumbfounded! After all, this was what they taught. Did He teach the same thing too? Yet it was not the same. The scribes said that by keeping the law men had to earn eternal life. It was as though the Lord Jesus wanted to trap him in his own words: Go ahead, try it! For deep in the scribe's heart he must have sensed that he could not do it and that he could never make himself deserving of eternal life. But if we believe God's grace and He grants us His favor, He will teach us how to live according to His will. We will then have communion or true life with God in obedience to His will. This is what Jesus meant when He said, "Do this, and you will live." Faith, not merit, therefore, is the way to life.

Who is my neighbor? The scribe was somewhat embarrassed by Jesus' answer in front of the crowd. He had meant to trap Jesus but Jesus had turned the tables on the scribe by answering him in his own words. Yet he understood that the Lord Jesus' words had another meaning. He, the scribe, had been thrown into disorder. Now he would have to save face before the crowd and show that his question was not all that foolish. So he asked, "Who is my neighbor?"

Scribes always debated whether they were to regard only a fellow Jew or also a Gentile as their neighbor. But in this question a deeper defect came to light. This man did not know who his neighbor was. And he really didn't have any neighbor, did not recognize anyone as his neighbor, and had no relationship with another.

How had he come to be so alone in life? It had come from his wanting to earn his own salvation. In that predicament we only think egoistically of our own salvation and have no room for anyone else. If we live by faith, and expect everything from God's grace, we create room in our lives for others and know ourselves to be one with others. We know we share guilt together but also know that, through Christ, we can be saved together.

The community. Jesus wanted to show the scribe what he still lacked, so He told him a parable. Once, He said, a man was traveling on the lonely road between Jerusalem and Jericho when he was suddenly attacked by robbers who stripped and beat him, leaving him half dead. A little later a priest came past, having just performed the priestly service in the temple at Jerusalem. Why had the priest done that? For this priest the service was not a service done out of faith, thankfulness, or praise, because the whole service was meritorious. His egoism in seeking merit dictated all he did. He saw the victim lying on the side of the road but he turned and ran. A Levite who came past the spot a little later did the same thing.

Shortly thereafter a Samaritan came by. When he saw the beaten man lying there, he did not think of himself or of the danger that also threatened him. He didn't argue with himself at all but recognized his oneness with that man and was moved with compassion. He cared for the man, brought him to the inn and the next morning gave the innkeeper two denarii and made himself responsible for any further expenses. He took care of that man as if he were his own brother. He knew that he was bound to him and made himself responsible for him. And yet it never occurred to him that he would be doing a work of merit. Perhaps the priest and the Levite, had they seen it as a work of merit, would also have helped. But the Samaritan gave of himself spontaneously, out of a sense of solidarity.

Go and do likewise. When Jesus had told this parable He asked which of the three had shown himself a true neighbor. When the scribe answered that it was the one who had shown mercy on him, He said, "Go and do likewise." Mercy like that of the Samaritan can fortunately still be found here and there in the world. Something of the sort can also be found among unbelievers. That is a gift of God's goodness. But if the scribe, who had learned to think first of himself, would begin to practice mercy, it would have meant his conversion. The Lord Jesus made that point very clear by picturing the priest and the Levite as the ones without mercy. The Samaritan, who had not been influenced so much by the idea of deserving something for one's own work, could still show mercy. How wrong and corrupting was the whole view of life of Pharisees and scribes! Conversion from their view could only come through faith in God's grace in which He gives us all things without deserving. Christ Himself is the Merciful One; He restores fellowship and has given Himself for others. Through Him we again know ourselves one with others and learn to practice community. That community is the revelation of the true life with God.

CHAPTER SIXTY TWO
ONLY ONE THING IS NEEDED
LUKE 10:38-42

Sitting at Jesus' feet is not necessarily better than serving in His Kingdom. That's not the point of the passage. Whether sitting at His feet or otherwise serving Him, the only thing that's needed is for His Word to dwell in us and we in Him. That can happen in any and all areas of kingdom service. By contrast, it's possible to sit at His feet and be proud of it, thus making it meaningless because we lack His indwelling.

Main Thought: *The one thing needed is to abide in Christ.*

Getting lost in too many things. Once Jesus was in the neighborhood of Jerusalem. He came to Bethany, a small town just three kilometers from Jerusalem. A family He knew well lived there consisting of two sisters, Martha and Mary, and a brother, Lazarus. His followers must have stayed overnight somewhere nearby but He, possibly with several of His disciples, stayed at Martha's house.

Much work had to be done to serve all the guests. That kept Martha very busy while Mary sat by the Lord Jesus listening. She had taken her place at His feet in adoration.

At first Martha probably did her work out of love for Jesus because she loved Him too. Thus in spirit she still stayed close to Him despite her duties. But after a while her thoughts began to move in a wrong direction. She prided herself in doing so much for Him! Wasn't that much better than what Mary was doing? Once her thoughts started along that line, they began to shift. She began to feel sorry for herself that she was so busy. And then she no longer did her duties out of love for Him. That is when she became angry with her sister who was not lifting a finger to help her.

Finally she could not suppress her feelings any longer and angrily exploded before Jesus and her sister, "Lord, don't You care that my sister has left me to do the serving alone? Tell her to help me." She not only gave her sister a lecture but the Lord also.

The one in the many. Gravely the Lord Jesus pointed out Martha's mistake to her. She was anxious and troubled about many things. She had to think of many things, of course, but if she did them out of love for Him they should not make her feel anxious or troubled. In spirit she should still be able to remain with Him and do her tasks easily and joyfully. Then she would not be jealous of her sister either.

Jesus had to defend Mary against Martha. What Mary did was not better in itself. If Mary had thought that her listening was better than Martha's service, she would also have lost touch with Jesus even as she was listening to Him. But Mary listened for Jesus' sake. This is the central thing in life: to remain close to Him. This was the part Mary chose, and no one, not even the jealous Martha, could take it away from her.

We too must always seek one thing only, that we abide in Him in spirit. That is always possible, no matter what we do. Whether we listen quietly to His Word or are busily engaged in life for Him makes no difference. Even though we may have many things to do, we can still seek to be with Him in spirit. No man can rob us of that. Then we also acknowledge the calling of others who do something else; we then refrain from jealousy but are one with them in Him.

CHAPTER SIXTY THREE
PRAYING TO THE FATHER
LUKE 11:1-13

It would be wrong to suggest that the parable encourages impertinent prayer. The parable, as appears from the context, says something about God the Giver who gives. Therefore, it should not be called the parable of the presumptuous friend, but the parable of the friend who gives because he is under obligation to give. "Friend" here is not a passive, but an active concept; it does not indicate someone to whom friendship is shown, but someone who shows friendship.

To bear the name of "friend" brings obligations with it. Even though the friend would not give spontaneously out of friendship, he would still have to give because of the obligation of friendship to which the petitioner makes an appeal.

The inquirer does this boldly and even unashamedly. He does not allow himself to be turned away by his friend's unwillingness. He doesn't say: If he will not help, there is no true friendship, friendship cannot be forced; no, on the contrary, he forces him to show his friendship.

Such an obligation to help out is also characteristic of God's fatherhood. While with men obligation and spontaneous desire to help are not always identical, there can be no question of a conflict between these two in God. The obligation which God in His covenant took upon Himself by becoming our Father for Christ's sake, He fulfills with the complete willingness of His divine love.

Main Thought: *Because God is Father we are to pray in bold confidence.*

Christ's prayer life. Several times Jesus prayed for a long time all by Himself. The disciples had become used to that. Now too He had withdrawn Himself from them and prayed a long time.

He needed that. There He found the strength for His work. He surrendered in prayer to the Father and His Name. The grace of

God had to be exalted, even though that would bring Him suffering and death. When He thus surrendered to God and became one with Him, He also could pray God to supply all His needs. Through such prayer He would take up His task again with renewed strength.

But He also prayed like that as our Head. To pray in that way is really to acknowledge God as Father. He did that, while all flesh had rejected God as Father. He would continue to acknowledge God as His God even when God rejected Him on account of our sins. By doing that He would make atonement for our sins and obtain for us once more the right to call God our Father. We would be allowed to do that again. And by the Spirit we would be able to surrender completely to God again and thus be able to pray boldly for the supplying of all our needs.

Our fellowship with Him in prayer. The disciples certainly were eager to understand the secret of the way He prayed. Should they not have fellowship with Him in prayer? Had not John the Baptist also taught his disciples how to pray? So when the Lord Jesus returned to them, again one of His disciples asked Him if He would teach them to pray, as John had done.

What a joy that question must have been for the Lord Jesus! Therefore He immediately satisfied their desire; He therefore shared his prayer-life with them and taught them to pray as He prayed. They too would first surrender to the Lord's name and cause saying, "Hallowed be Your Name, Your Kingdom come, Your will be done, on earth as in heaven." And then they too could boldly pray for all their needs. First for their bodily needs: "Give us this day our daily bread." This was the most basic petition, but it was also a test. If they could surrender that physical concern to the Lord in faith, they could also pray for their spiritual needs: "And forgive us our sins; for we also forgive everyone who is indebted to us. And lead us not into temptation, but deliver us from the evil one."

Throughout they acknowledged God as Father. For that reason they were also to address Him as Father. They were free to do so because He would obtain that right for them. And He also gave them the boldness to do it by His Word and Spirit.

Obliging friendship. He urged them to pray in bold confidence. Confidence should result from the fact that through Jesus, God had again become their Father. They ought not to reject that fatherhood for lack of confidence. He illustrated this with yet another parable.

Suppose, He said, that late one evening an unexpected friend came to spend the night and you had no bread in the house and it was too late to buy any. You would not want to violate the rules of hospitality and leave your friend uncared for. You would go to one of your friends in the village, knock on his door to wake him up and ask him for three loaves, for your guest, yourself, and "for good measure." Imagine if he refused in the first instance because he was already in bed, the children had finally quieted down and he simply couldn't rouse everybody again. Suppose you persisted, whereupon he would finally help you, even if it was not from spontaneous friendship, but only because you continued to knock and boldly reminded him of the obligations of friendship.

If it is true that obligations of friendship will persuade men to help each other even though they may not feel like it, will not God help as a result of the obligation He took upon Himself when He became your Father? And He will not do it grudgingly because nothing ever holds Him back; He will do it with all the love of His heart. Thus we must always dare ask and appeal to His fatherhood. The fact that God is our Father again for Christ's sake and has adopted us as His children demands boldness and persistence on our part.

The Father's giving. We can then be assured that God will give. If we appeal in Christ's name to God as Father, God will respond. Jesus assured His disciples and He assures us of that. Pray, and it will be given to you.

If we thus ask as children we shall better understand what we should ask for. Just as a child receives from his father what he needs and is not deceived by his father, we will also receive what we need. It may often appear that God sends us bitterness and troubles instead of the good we ask of Him, but then we must not think that God disappoints us in our prayer-life. He gives us just what is good for us. A father will not give a stone to his son when he asks him for bread. His first gift, our greatest need, will be the Holy Spirit through whom we grow increasingly in sonship. We must simply surrender to God and expect every good thing from Him. Through the Holy Spirit God will then grant us all things.

LUKE:
THE DISCLOSURE OF
LIFE'S NEED

CHAPTER SIXTY FOUR
SECURITY
LUKE 12:13-21

Christ came to preach the gospel of the Kingdom and so to move men to faith. He refused to function in the place of the government. That is not to say that the exalted Christ has no authority in all areas of life and that governments do not exercise their proper authority in His name. The righteousness of the Kingdom of heaven applies to every area. But while He walked on earth Christ kept strictly to His calling to preach the gospel. This means that the church (institute), which has as its calling the preaching of the Word of God, is not to take action in any area outside its jurisdiction.

In itself it was probably not wrong for the man of verse 13 to want to receive a portion of the inheritance. But the motive of his desire was greed for money, security in life, and the desire to preserve his own rights, not the right of God. He wanted to "use" Christ and His influence for his own ends.

Main Thought: *Security for man lies in the grace of God.*

Legal security. While Jesus was speaking to the crowd, someone stood up and asked Him to tell his brother to divide the inheritance with him. The man was apparently being defrauded by his brother. Certainly, he thought, the Lord Jesus who ministered in the name of God, would show His anger at this injustice. And if He would speak to his brother His word would probably have the desired effect.

The man's reasoning didn't appear to be so faulty at that. What had prompted him to interrupt the Lord Jesus? He felt that he had been wronged. His sense of personal rights had been injured and this drove him to ask his question. It did not grieve <u>him</u> that his brother was violating divine justice, but he was embittered because his own rights had been violated. And that feeling caused him to lose all perspective. Jesus had certainly not come to resolve legal disputes between people. For that God had instituted government. This is why the Lord Jesus turned this man down. He would not allow His calling to preach the gospel of the Kingdom to be obscured in any way. He remained faithful to His Father's assignment and refused the temptation to go beyond it. There is always the temptation for a person or for the church institute to go beyond the limits of their competence. We are to be obedient to the Father in all things.

Even if this man were to seek a ruling by the courts, the purpose should still be to maintain God's sovereign right which secures the interests of men, not simply to preserve someone's individual rights. To maintain God's right is the government's calling. In carrying out that task it is to serve God and His Kingdom. We may also request a ruling from the courts, but above all we must see that God Himself will uphold His right.

Life's security. The man acted not just because his sense of personal rights had been injured. If his portion of the inheritance should escape him, he also feared that his future would be anything but secure. He sought his security in his possessions and not in God. This always goes hand in hand with seeking one's own rights. The man lived out of fear and not out of faith. He desired to have many possessions in order to feel secure.

Jesus warned the whole crowd, who had heard the man's question, against love of money; it was not true that a man's future was secure only if he had many possessions. God can take it all away from him. We never have an all-risk life insurance except through trust in the Lord who will care for His own. Our security in life rests in God's favor and that favor becomes our portion through the Lord Jesus Christ.

Security of possession. The man did indeed desire goods in order to make his life secure but he also loved money itself. His treasure was his possessions, not God's favor. How can we have a treasure apart from God's favor? It's not really a treasure we possess because it is not our eternal portion, the promise of the eternal portion we shall possess on the new earth. Neither can we really enjoy our earthly treasure, for our real treasure is that we enjoy God's favor in everything we possess.

Again the Lord Jesus made this plain with a parable. Once, He said, there was a rich man whose harvest in a particular year was so huge that he could not store it in his barns. He decided to pull them down and build larger ones. Then, when the harvest was in, he would say to himself that he had accomplished much and henceforth could enjoy a carefree life. But God said to him: "You fool," and took his life from him that very night. What would happen to that huge harvest and all that he had possessed? The man's entire life and cherished treasure would be in vain. He would have no eternal possession.

Jesus' warning was addressed to everyone who places his trust in his treasures without acknowledging them as tokens of God's favor. He is not rich in God and does not share God's favor and love. We can only be certain of what we possess if we see it in the light of God's favor, the favor which was obtained for us by Christ. Christ sanctifies all our possessions and makes us rich in God.

CHAPTER SIXTY FIVE
THE DISCLOSURE OF LIFE'S NEED
LUKE 13:1-17

When we live by our own righteousness we are blinded to the common guilt. This leads us to look for particular guilt in the victim behind particular catastrophes. But the Galileans perished as a sign of the common guilt of all Israel. We cannot ask ourselves whether there might not have been among those Galileans, believers who were saved for eternity. The disaster which came upon them revealed the judgment upon all Israel. That judgment can strike at one place or another according to God's decree; thus it can also strike believers. The purpose was to bring all the people to their senses.

That certainly applied in the first place to the Israel of those days which had forsaken the covenant of the Lord. See, for example, the parable of the barren fig tree. Yet where there is no question of a general forsaking of the covenant, we may not say that such a calamity was not meant to bring the people to their senses. Always, and in an increasingly deepening sense, there must be the confession of Paul: "Wretched man that I am."

On the other hand there is the confession of redemption. Redemption also shows us our misery in its deepest sense. The healing of the woman who was bent over from her sickness thus revealed life's need. It is striking to read here of a spirit of infirmity, and that the Lord Jesus said that satan had bound her for eighteen years. Behind the sickness was the guilt, not a personal guilt but the communal guilt and the reign of satan. The deliverance of this daughter of Abraham, of this child of the covenant, disclosed Israel's need and the need of the human race in general.

The ruler of the synagogue, who lived by his own righteousness, did not see life's need nor did he know deliverance and therefore didn't know the sabbath as a sign of redemption in the covenant. He saw in keeping the sabbath a meritorious act.

Main Thought: *Christ reveals life's need.*

Communal guilt. Some people told Jesus that Pilate, the governor of the country, had had a group of Galileans killed in the front court of the temple where they had been sacrificing, and that their blood had been mixed with the blood of sacrificial animals. They were evidently nationalistic zealots who constantly raised Pilate's ire. In violation of every law, his soldiers had penetrated into the front court of the priests, where Gentiles were never allowed to come, and had there slain the Galileans. That their blood had been mixed with the blood of the sacrifices had made a deep impression on the people. People saw in it a divine judgment upon them and suspected the Galileans of some particular sin. Apparently those who brought the report to Jesus wanted to hear what the Lord Jesus would say about it.

His answer was entirely unexpected. This was indeed a judgment of God, yet they were not to think that those who had been slain were worse sinners than other Galileans. In this judgment God revealed His anger against all Israel for having forsaken the covenant and having rejected the words of John the Baptist and of Jesus Christ. If His hearers did not stop boasting of their own righteousness, repent of their sins, and expect only God's grace, they too would all perish.

It was the same with a disaster in Jerusalem which was still fresh in their memory. A tower near the Siloam tunnel had collapsed and eighteen people had been killed. Those eighteen were no worse sinners than others in Jerusalem. God's judgment on all Israel was revealed in it and if the people did not repent they too would all perish.

Whenever we hear of particular calamities, we must not suspect particular sins in the victims. If we do that we have no knowledge of general sin, as it also shows up in our life. Then we have not arrived at the redemption of sin either and then our life becomes a life of anxious and superstitious fear. Whenever calamities come, God's wrath is revealed against sin in general. His wrath can strike in one place or another according to His sovereign good pleasure. God's intention is that we ask ourselves how sin, which reigns everywhere, works in our life. Our confession must show a deeper and deeper understanding of the presence and the nature of sin. But we also know of grace and redemption which deliver us from fear and set us free.

384

Postponing of judgment. If those disasters do not fall on us or on all Israel, we must not conclude that there is no guilt in us or in the nation as a whole. It is possible that sin is present in our own lives but that God as yet postpones judgment. This is what He did in those days with regard to Israel which continued to reject the covenant.

Jesus made that clear with a parable. Someone had planted a fig tree in his vineyard. Since it was the only fig tree he watched it with great interest. Three years running he looked for fruit during the summer, but found none. He told the gardener to cut it down. The gardener, however, asked for an extension of one more year. He would give the tree some special care and fertilize it. If that didn't help, then it would just have to be cut down.

These words were intended primarily for Israel which had heard the words of John the Baptist and Jesus for three years and still did not repent. But none of us must come to the conclusion that his life is completely in order if judgment does not come. We are all deserving of judgment. If we realize that each day anew and grow in our awareness, we continuously learn to live by faith out of grace. We will then truly bear fruit which we sometimes may not see, but which is seen by the Lord.

The power of satan. One sabbath day He was teaching in one of the synagogues. There was a woman bent over by disease, unable to straighten up. For eighteen years she had already been in its grip. It was a power that governed her life. It was a manifestation of satan's power, as is every sickness. For through our sin satan obtained the power to destroy life. It is true that in his use of this power satan is in God's hand, and God can use the scourge of satan to sanctify His children but it is nevertheless satan's power at work in our diseases.

This was immediately clear in that woman, so deformed that she could not straighten up at all. It was as if the hand of satan pressed down upon her. Her misery touched Jesus and He saw His enemy. In His grace Jesus immediately went into action against him. He called the woman to Him and said to her that she was healed from her illness. He proclaimed His victory even before He had done anything. He then laid His hands on her and immediately she straightened up and praised God. What joy for the Lord Jesus that He might redeem life from satan's power!

Shouldn't all rejoice with Him? But that was not the case. A self-important ruler of the synagogue took it very ill of Jesus that He had healed on the sabbath. But he did not dare speak to Him personally. So he said to the crowd that there were six days in which to work and that people should come to be healed on those days, but not on the sabbath. For this man keeping the sabbath was a work of merit. If that's how we keep the law, it will enslave our life.

Just as the Lord Jesus was setting life free, the ruler came dragging his chains. Should He not protest that? How could people, such as this ruler, enjoy reducing life to slavery? They did it because they did not see the real chains which hold life in bondage, namely, the power of satan. Otherwise, before everything else, they would have wanted to be free from those bonds to let life blossom again, also on the sabbath day. Didn't they all untie their oxen or donkeys to lead them to water on the sabbath? And should Christ not set this woman free, who was a child of the covenant, a member of the covenant people, and who, according to God's promise, had a right to life having been bound for eighteen years by satan? The ruler, however, had never seen the power of satan, even though it was so obvious in this woman. That was because he had never had an insight into what sin really is.

All Christ's opponents were put to shame by His answer. And all the people rejoiced at the wonderful things He was doing. Had they all understood His purpose, and had they all seen the power of satan, from which He had delivered them? And did they all confess their sins, through which satan obtained his power?

CHAPTER SIXTY SIX
SPIRIT AND LIFE
LUKE 14:1-14

Jesus was still "making His way towards Jerusalem" (13:22). As is clear from chapter 13:31, He was in the territory of King Herod, but no longer in Galilee so that we must think of Perea, in Transjordan. Very likely it was there that the meal was held of which we read in this section. The hostility was a bit less fierce there than in Galilee. In many places people were still meeting Him for the first time.

Evidently the man who had dropsy and was healed had been stationed there by the scribes and Pharisees. That is clear from verse 2 and from the fact that Christ immediately entered into their thoughts. They were watching Him to see if He would heal on the sabbath. On that issue Christ had already made His position clear in Galilee but in the Transjordan it was still a live issue.

Throughout the dinner Jesus showed that the law of the Kingdom is spirit and life. Over against this is placed the materializing of life by the self-seeking scribes and Pharisees.

Main Thought: *The law of the Kingdom is spirit and life.*

The call of life. While Jesus was on His way to Jerusalem and staying in the country on the other side of the Jordan River, He was invited one sabbath day to have dinner at the home of a prominent Pharisee. Many Pharisees and scribes would be sitting at that table. They wanted to learn to know Him better because He had not been in that region often.

Before dinner was served there suddenly stood before the Lord Jesus a man who suffered from dropsy. That man had been ordered there by the leaders who wanted to watch whether Jesus would heal on the sabbath. To entertain at a rather large dinner was permitted; to heal was not. How did they establish criteria for that? It can be explained by their search for merit, for their own righteousness. For then the law begins to enslave life. Men no longer see how life lies imprisoned in sin and sickness and death, how God in His Kingdom delivers life from these enemies and how the sabbath is a sign of this deliverance. Then men no longer hear the sighs of God's creation.

The Lord Jesus understood what they were thinking, so He asked whether it was lawful to heal on the sabbath. He would like to hear their opinion on that. But they kept silent; they were not going to be caught by Him. He then took the sick man to Himself, drew him out of that sphere of distrust and so awakened faith in him, healed him and let him go, sending him away from an atmosphere in which he, as a believer, no longer belonged. How powerful is the grace of the Lord Jesus! He pulled that man, who had allowed himself to be used as a guinea pig, out of that climate and taught him the redemption of life.

Those who were standing around had serious objection to this act of healing on the sabbath. That's why Jesus now answered His own question in His own way. If your ox or your donkey falls into a well on the sabbath, you immediately pull him out. In that case you still understand the call of life in distress. But you do not understand the call of life which is in need because of sin and sickness and death. You have become so insensitive to the world's misery that you would use this sick man as a guinea pig for your own purposes. You no longer protest against the yoke that has been placed on life because of sin.

Jesus wants us to rediscover the distress of life and have us hear the groaning of the creature. He does this by redeeming life. Then He points us to the day of rest as a sign of that redemption, as a sign of God's covenant with life.

Exaltation. The scribes and Pharisees were not able to answer Him. After this incident they were going to sit down at the table. Jesus noticed how they all rushed to get the most important places. They all wanted a place of honor. Everyone wanted to be exalted in the eyes of others. They were all seeking themselves. They sought to capitalize on everything, even a dinner.

Life is full of lies and duplicity. These people went to a dinner and were self-seeking even there; they did not go in gratitude for the invitation or to share their host's festive mood. Jesus wanted to make them aware of this lie in their lives. He said that if invited to dinner you don't sit down at the place of honor. It might just be that the host wishes to honor someone else and asks you to move.

You would then be embarrassed. Why not go and sit humbly at the lowest place? To receive honor from your fellow-men should not be your goal. The object is to have fellowship with your host. Imagine that your host, seeing you at the foot of the table, invites you to a better place to show you his favor; that would raise your esteem in the eyes of your fellow-guests. At least then the honor has value because you did not seek it yourself, but it becomes clear to everybody that you are favored by your host. It always happens that he who exalts himself will be humbled, and he who humbles himself will be exalted.

The lie in our lives whereby we seek ourselves and our own glory is defeated when we are thankful for the position we have in life, and thankful that we may serve in that particular place. This is what happens when we have beheld the Kingdom of God, in which God governs all things well. Simply wait to see where He calls us. We do not seek our own honor, but seek to have fellowship with Him in all things. In His fellowship He will exalt us. That is true honor because it is the honor of a favor freely given. This exaltation certainly does not always come in this life, but God is prepared to give everything to those who serve Him!

Hospitality. Jesus saw clearly that not only the guests but also the host were at fault. Why were so many honored guests invited? It certainly was in his own self-interest and not in order to share himself or do good and show kindness. Even in extending the invitation the host had his own interest at heart. To have a man of high position at his table was an honor in itself. In addition, there might also be a return invitation. One never knew what advantage might sometime come from those relationships.

How miserable we have become as a result of sin! We are always thinking of our own interest and never spontaneously give of ourselves without hoping for some reward. Addressing Himself to this problem, Jesus said, "When you give a dinner, do not invite your family and friends and your distinguished acquaintances but rather the poor and wretched from whom you can expect nothing in return." His point was not to forbid social life and making friends. He simply wanted to encourage inviting the poor and wretched because it's easier to give of oneself. It's the acid test of true hospitality.

We can do it if once we've seen God and His Kingdom. In His Kingdom He gives us Himself, without being able to receive something in return that He had not first given us. If we have thus become imitators of God, we shall indeed receive in return but not from men. In His favor God will exalt us on the day of Christ's return, at the restoration of all things. That honor is real because it's the honor of His favor.

CHAPTER SIXTY SEVEN
THE TIE TO THE LOST
LUKE 15

In these three parables we must pay special attention to the third point of comparison. The mercy or the love of God by which He seeks the lost is not what stands in the foreground here. Such mercy is not involved in the parable of the woman who was looking for the lost coin. She was simply looking for something that belonged to her. The world and humanity, also what is lost therein, belong to God according to the covenant of His grace in Christ in whom He embraces the world and the human race. As long as people are still in this life He makes His claims felt on them. For the sake of His covenant He is not done with them yet, even though for a time He allowed the heathen to walk in their own ways (Acts 14:16).

These parables deal in the first place with those who have wandered away from the covenant people, the tax-collectors and the sinners. With a certain amount of justification many have also applied these parables to the heathen. There is always a tie between God and the lost for the sake of His covenant. It is in the name of the Father that Christ maintains His search for the lost, over against the Pharisees.

With God this tie always implies a certain love. The covenant is never a business-like arrangement. Thus we must tell about the love of God, especially in the case of the first and the third parable. Yet it would be wrong to tell of the mercy and love of God and forget the covenant which governs the whole situation. God seeks that which belongs to Him, that which is rightfully His according to His covenant.

Therefore we must be careful not to engage in speculations about pity for the lost sheep or to emphasize the wretched condition of that sheep. *This is not the parable of the lost sheep, but of the tie of the shepherd to his sheep,* also and particularly to the one that is lost. That this is what the parable is all about is clear also from the emphasis Christ puts on the joy when the sheep is found. The shepherd has recovered what belongs to him. That is the motive for the joy. It's the same way in the third parable. The father's own son is back. The family too is governed by a covenant. In it each member has his own place, even the grownup sons. And the father gives himself to his family with his whole heart. The oldest son never understood this. He was never truly a son but always a servant, as is evident from what he said about the young goat that had never been given to him. All that the father had was his; the father's heart was his. He overlooked all that for a single gift. He had been serving all the time for wages and never seen the covenant in which people give themselves. In the covenant relationship we belong to each other before we *do* something for each other.

Main Thought: *For the sake of His covenant the Lord is still bound to the lost in this world.*

The tie of the shepherd to a lost sheep. Just as in Galilee, the Pharisees and the scribes in the region where the Lord Jesus was now staying were embittered because of the kindness He showed to tax-collectors and other people who were social outcasts. He even accepted invitations from them and ate with them. The Pharisees didn't want to have anything more to do with these sinners who had broken with their idea of the nation. God, so the Pharisees thought, had abandoned them and they looked down on them with contempt. The Pharisees never doubted that they themselves deserved God's favor.

The Lord Jesus knew what He was doing when He sought the lost. He did that at His Father's command because God had not yet broken with those who were lost. They originally belonged to the covenant people. By their public sins they had indeed rejected the covenant but God still claimed them because of His covenant, and He wanted to assert that right. That is why He and the Lord Jesus sought them.

Once again He made this plain with parables. A shepherd who tends a hundred sheep and loses one does not abandon that lost sheep to its fate. He knows it to be his sheep, part of the flock of which he is the shepherd. Although that sheep obstinately wandered away from the flock, it is still bound to him. He bears the responsibility for it and has a claim to it and therefore does not leave it a prey to wild animals.

The shepherd thinks especially about the lost sheep, more so than about the ninety-nine which are safe with him. The tie to the one that is lost he feels the most. He therefore leaves the flock in the wilderness to seek the one that is lost until he finds it. Then he joyously lays it on his shoulders and carries it back to the flock. When in the evening he returns home with his flock, he calls his friends and neighbors together to celebrate for having found what was lost.

Similarly, there are people who have become lost. They do not want to have any more to do with God's covenant and church. They have completely lost sight of the flock, of God's people, and no longer hear the voice of God, their Shepherd. That was the case with the tax-collectors and sinners of those days. But God does not let go of them and He does not forget them. After all, they belong to Him—He has a right to them; He is the Shepherd. He seeks them by the Word which He causes to be proclaimed to them and also by the many life circumstances in which He leads them. He asserts His right to them. That is what the Lord Jesus did then; it is what God does now.

How God rejoices when again He lays His hand on one of those who was lost and hears him acknowledge God's right to him, the right to his love! Heaven is filled with that rejoicing. And he who was lost but found again shares in that joy. He knows that he is borne up by God as the lost sheep was carried back by the shepherd. God recovers the sinner who was lost and is drawn to him *because* he was lost. Hence, there's more joy for the return of one wayward sinner than for the rest who never strayed.

The woman's tie to a lost coin. A similar case, the Lord Jesus said, was the woman who had ten coins and lost one of them. That single coin was very precious to her. She therefore turned on the light and swept the whole house until she found it. She then invited her friends and neighbors to celebrate because she had recovered part of her treasure. She was overwhelmed by the fact that her lost coin had miraculously turned up!

God is similarly affected when He loses His precious possession. When people become so uncharitable that they will have nothing to do with tax-collectors and sinners and all those who are ignorant of God's covenant, then they no longer know God either, for God still asserts His claim on these outcasts. Imagine how angels in heaven will rejoice when God has successfully reclaimed what was His. The angels are one with God in such celebrations and so are we.

The tie between a father and a lost son. Jesus wanted to reinforce the value of a sinner returned and therefore told the people yet another parable. Once there was a father who had two sons. He loved them both, although each had a special place in his heart. Each has his own place and worth and yet all are one in the father's love. Such a family is a covenant in which all are bound together by that single love.

With his elder son the father had no difficulty. He appeared to be willing in everything. The younger had a more fickle nature. He sometimes longed for a change and far-away pastures. He knew that his older brother, according to Israelite custom, would receive two-thirds of the inheritance including the homestead, while he would receive one-third. With his portion he wanted to establish his independence now, and at the same time see something of the world.

In itself his desire for independence was not wrong but behind it was a lack of appreciation for his father's house and for the family tie. Such an attitude always goes wrong. We should strive to become independent by appreciating that family tie which is a gift of God. When a young person slams the door of his parental home behind him with the words, "I'm never going to come back here," he will certainly become lost in life. That's what happened to this young man. He failed to become independent and squandered all his money.

When all his money was gone, a famine broke out in the country where he was. Finally he ended up with a man who hired him to take care of his pigs. He earned so little that he was glad to eat the pigs' food. What a humiliation for a Jew who considered pigs unclean!

In his misery he thought of his father's house and remembered how the hired help were treated there. His father also had a heart for his servants. Would love for his sons not be greater? But he had spurned that love and broken the tie. He felt he no longer deserved to be a son; at most he could ask to become a hired servant. He decided to return and admit that to his father. He had crushed his father's heart and God had witnessed it.

There are many people who have similarly forsaken the circle of God's covenant, the fellowship of His love. How can they see the error of their ways unless they begin to see the glory of God's love which binds us all together in that covenant and in that fellowship? God can lead them in ways of misery to bring that awareness home to them.

Meanwhile, the father had thought about his son every single day. Every day he looked for him. After all, he was *his* son. No matter what his son had done wrong, he was still his son. And now he had lost him. With him he had lost part of his life. Now that he had lost his son, he was even more wrapped in his thoughts. Would his son ever return? Would he ever be able to enjoy receiving him back again? He could overlook and forgive everything.

The father's anxiety explains why he saw him returning from afar. Moved with compassion, he ran to meet him, embraced and kissed him. It was *his* son, and he had him back. He had not just returned because he couldn't do better for himself elsewhere; he had seen the value of the house and of his father's love. That was clear from his confession of sin. But the father didn't even let him finish. When he heard that the heart of his son had come back, he arranged a banquet in his honor. For, he said, this son of mine was dead and is alive again; he was lost and is found. He had recovered his own possession.

Similarly God in His fatherly love and in His covenant has for Christ's sake not finished yet with the lost in this world and with all who live outside the circle of His fellowship. They have forsaken Him, or perhaps their ancestors had already rejected His covenant; often they have not even been baptized. Yet He continues to look for them. He was looking for the tax-collectors and sinners of those days because He has a claim to all of them according to the covenant of His grace. His love has a right to them and He wants to assert that right.

How God rejoices when a person lost is found, when a person who was dead to God becomes alive again, when one who had wandered away comes back. There is no reproof but only forgiveness for his sins and restoration in the Lord's covenant for him; he may enjoy God's fatherly love.

At the time the younger son returned, the older one was in the field. When he approached the house he heard celebrating.

One of the servants told him what had happened. It aroused great resentment in him and he refused to welcome his brother home and take part in the festivities.

His father heard about it, went outside and pleaded with him to come in and share the joy. The older boy then poured his heart out. He had served his father now for so many years and his father had never let him throw a party with his friends. But when his younger brother who had squandered a fortune returned, a great banquet was given.

The older son betrayed a poor relationship to his father. He had been as a servant, working for wages in his father's house. He had never understood his father's love, the spiritual covenant that exists in a family, through which the father gives himself to his children and the children are united in their father's love. In such a covenant the members completely belong to each other with all they possess. He had overlooked that; he complained that he had never been given a young goat. How spiritually poor he was! What lack of understanding of what love is all about! Was that ever a disappointment to his father! Here was his older son who never had given him any trouble, but who had evidently never known his father's heart. "Son," he cried, "you are always with me, and all that is mine is yours. Isn't there perfect fellowship between you and me? Your younger brother had been cut off from this fellowship but now has come back to it. Shouldn't you also be filled with joy at this?"

This is the story Jesus told. In the latter part of this parable He was thinking especially of the Pharisees who were displeased that tax-collectors and sinners returned to fellowship with the Father. They showed that they had never understood the Father's love, had never known the covenant in which God gives Himself to us along with everything else. They had not been children of the Father; they too had served for wages. They were servants who wanted to earn their own salvation. The mystery of the love God freely gives in His covenant they had never enjoyed. And how many there are still who are not children but servants working for wages. However, such an attitude implied a rejection of God's fatherly love in Christ.

CHAPTER SIXTY EIGHT
BUILDING THE ETERNAL
COMMUNITY OF THE SAINTS
LUKE 16:1-13

This parable is connected with the preceding one. The older son in the previous parable had never truly been a son but only a servant, and so had lived for himself and for his possessions. The disciples are not to be like that. They are to build the eternal community of the saints.

The master commended the dishonest manager even though he had been wasting his possessions. But he understood him in his shrewdness. He had appreciation for his smart move. The children of this world understand one another in such things.

The children of this world or, as the text actually reads, the sons of this age, are the unbelievers. Believers too live in this age but they live here in the light of the coming age which began with the coming of Christ. They are not "children" of this age; their life doesn't arise out of it nor is it lived just for it.

A person does not make a friend of the unrighteous mammon by, for example, giving a gift to the deacons' fund. We are to be building the new eternal community of the saints in Christ. To that end we must also use our money. When we build such a community we shall also be its eternal members in the age to come.

Christ calls money the unrighteous mammon because it is generally worshiped and served. When a man serves mammon he is driven to injustice. For the believer, if he lives out of faith, money is not mammon, certainly not the unrighteous mammon.

Main Thought: *The eternal community of the saints is being built in this age.*

Children of this age. The older son in the parable which the Lord Jesus had just told lived for himself and for his possessions. He was a servant of money. The disciples were not to live that way. Of course, they also had to handle money but they had to use it for an entirely different purpose than to enrich themselves. The Lord made this clear to them in yet another parable.

There was once a rich man who had an estate manager. He received reports about this manager—and they were supported with evidence—that he was wasting his master's possessions and that there was a considerable shortage. His master gave him notice. He had to hand over the books so that someone else could take his place.

This manager realized he would soon be out on the street. He therefore decided to do the following: he summoned his master's debtors, returned their IOU's and had them sign another, discounted by 20% or even 50%. He calculated that in a little while those debtors would receive him and come to his aid because he had been so obliging.

When the master learned how his manager had robbed him, he could still appreciate his shrewdness. That manager had made friends for himself and thus secured his future.

The children of light. Jesus drew His disciples' attention to that manager, not that they should follow his example of fraud, but that they should be aware of his cleverness in making friends for himself. The disciples, and believers in general, should show the same kind of foresight. They too should make friends for themselves, but only in a higher sense. They should build up the community of the saints. To that end they should also use their money and all their possessions. Money, which the unbelieving world worships as a god and with which so much injustice is committed, believers should put to use to build the eternal community of the saints. And if in this life they have worked at building that eternal community, then in the future life, when the Lord Jesus has returned, they will be received with joy as members of that community.

This was the only right way for them to use their money. And money was the least important. If they could not properly use it, God certainly could not entrust them with the higher gifts of spiritual powers. For they too served to build the eternal community of the saints.

If they couldn't use their money in this way, they would also become servants of their money; their money would become their lord and master in whom they would put their trust. Man cannot serve two masters, God and mammon; he will have to choose for one or the other.

CHAPTER SIXTY NINE
THE TRULY RICH MAN
LUKE 16:19-31

The rich man was not lost because he was rich and Lazarus was not saved because he was poor. We may also not picture the rich man as a brutal criminal. We read of him only that he "feasted in great magnificence every day." However, the rich man was a possessor who, in his opinion, was a rightful owner who makes his demands on life. Over against him is Lazarus, the outcast, who has no material share in this life. That was his grief, a grief which had its root in faith. For as a true child of Abraham he had a right (because of grace) to fellowship with his people and to the possession of life and land. But in this life he suffered deprivation. It is striking that, unlike other parables, Christ gives this poor man a name. Forgotten by his own people, the man has a name with God.

We have to keep in mind that this is a parable. Conclusions about life after death can not be drawn from the details in this parable. Our main concern here is the third point of comparison. (See Section 67.) Christ paints a picture of life after death with strokes borrowed from this life in order to make His main point clear. Thus we are not to draw any conclusions from Abraham and the rich man's talking to each other, nor from the fact that the lost man still feels mercy for his brothers who are on earth.

Main Thought: *Believers are the truly rich.*

The apparent possessor. With the parable of the unjust estate manager Jesus had said that we are to use our money to build the eternal community of the saints. The Pharisees, who were greedy for money, had taken offense at this. They did not spend their money that way. They used it for themselves. They thought that they were lord and master here on earth. Thus they really lived apart from God while belonging to the covenant people. They weren't going to take any advice from the Lord Jesus; on the contrary, they scoffed at Him.

Again He wanted to warn them, and He did so with a parable. Once, He said, there was a rich man. He was clothed in purple and fine linen and feasted in great magnificence every day. He did not indulge in excesses but lived well, and because he was rich there was an aura of greatness around him. He fancied himself lord and owner of life. With his class of people he was the man who really had the rightful claim upon this world. He forgot God from whom are all things. He knew nothing of the humility of faith which sees everything as a gift. The world is still full of such presumably rightful owners today.

Every day there lay a poor man, named Lazarus, at the gate of his luxurious estate. Lazarus lived from the left-overs in the rich man's house. But the rich man hardly even noticed him when he passed Lazarus going out of his house. A poor man like that simply did not count. No one paid any attention to him. Besides, he was too dirty to look at, for he was covered with sores. Only the street dogs paid any attention to him, for they licked the man's sores.

Life is still that way. There are people who think that they can order everybody around. There are others who just do not count. God's judgment could well be different. If those who do not count here acknowledge God as the only One who has authority over all of life, they certainly count with God. So it was with this man Lazarus. The rich man was also a descendant of Abraham but knew nothing of faith, of the expectation of faith, of what it meant to be a stranger here on earth. Lazarus, however, was a true child of Abraham because of his faith.

In Abraham's bosom. Lazarus died completely alone and forsaken. Yet he was not alone. God was with him and he was carried by the angels to Abraham's bosom. At the banquet of God's love he was privileged to recline at the table quite close to Abraham. There he enjoyed communion with his people and with the father of his people, a fellowship for which he had thirsted in vain here on earth.

The rich man also died, surrounded by many. His funeral was magnificent; the body was followed by a long procession. Yet this rich man was alone in his death and he opened his eyes in hell. His possessions on earth had all been an illusion. Only the man who possesses what he has as a gift from God and enjoys God's love in having it truly possesses it.

The rich man saw Lazarus at Abraham's side and asked Abraham to send Lazarus to cool his tongue. He was tormented because he was deprived of everything. There were burning desires in him which were not fulfilled. But Abraham refused. All the desires of that rich man had been fulfilled on earth. He had desired nothing but what he could possess only temporarily. He now had to suffer agony. Lazarus had lacked what he had so fervently desired, to be a part of life and to have fellowship with his people for God's sake. Such a desire will be eternally fulfilled. Besides, there is no communion possible between the saved and the lost. Between them lies the chasm of God's judgment.

The Lord Jesus introduced this parable in order that we should determine the purpose of our possessions. How can they best be used?

The Word of the resurrection. The rich man asked if Lazarus could not be sent to his five brothers on earth to warn them, since they were living the same kind of life he had lived. Abraham pointed out to him that they had the Word of God in the Scriptures of the Old Testament. They had the Word of grace, the Word of promise that called them to repent from their apostate lives. For the Word of the Lord calls us to be rich by faith in the love of God. That is indeed the resurrection.

The rich man thought that if only someone would rise from the dead his brothers would surely repent and mend their ways. But Abraham answered that if they did not believe the Word of God in the Scriptures, neither would they believe if someone were to rise from the dead. They were deaf to the Word of life. Has Christ not risen from the dead and is His Word not being proclaimed? How many hear that Word of resurrection and are rich in God?

CHAPTER SEVENTY
THE FEAR OF THE LORD
LUKE 17:1-19

In verse 5 the disciples are called apostles. Evidently they were engaged in their apostolic calling in connection with what the Lord had said to them. With an eye to that apostolic calling they asked for an increase in their faith.

They literally asked for something to be added to their faith. That is the wrong view of faith and Christ rejects it. Faith does not consist of a certain quantity of something or other. Faith is awakened by, and is dependent on, its content. By faith we know God and we know Him as the Absolute Sovereign. What then is impossible for us? The power of faith is limitless.

Just as limitless as the power of faith is our calling, faith's task. Christ points that out in the parable of the servant who comes in from the field. With body and soul we belong to Him who, as the Absolute Sovereign, demands everything we have.

The nine lepers who failed to return to give thanks accepted their healing as something to which they felt they had a right. Here we have another example of people who are always claiming their rights. They were Jews, were they not? They did not know the fear of the Lord as the Absolute Ruler. They did not belong to the little ones whom the Lord protects. These nine lepers are an example of so-called miracle-faith, faith in the Lord's power to work miracles, while faith in *Him* as Savior of the world is lacking.

Main Thought: *Faith has to do with God as the sovereign Ruler.*

Earth's humble. In the narrow circle of His disciples Jesus also began to sound a note of warning. He not only had something to say to the Pharisees but also to His disciples. Believers are those who are humble before God. They are concerned with God in His glory and majesty. He is the only One who has rights and in everything they are dependent upon Him. By contrast, there are the people who pose as lord and master in this world. Undoubtedly, people like that will also appear in the congregation of Christians, among the disciples. These will cause believers to sin, so that they too will begin to feel themselves as having rights in themselves. These believers will come to repentance again, but it is terrible to cause a believer to fall, to bring him to the point of sinning against his God. God will judge such a tempter. It would be better for him if a millstone were hung around his neck and he were cast into the sea.

Believers were to look after one another, to see that no one became arrogant. If someone submitted to temptation, they were to rebuke him earnestly and forgive him if he repented. Even if he were to sin seven times a day they were to forgive him. If they did not they would themselves not be humble before God. Their lack of humility would be evident from their pride towards their brother.

In this way the Lord Jesus warned His disciples. If we live by faith, we see the Lord in His greatness and know the fear of the Lord. We become humble and small before the Lord and seek to be the least among Our brothers.

Faith's power. The disciples understood something of what Jesus had told them. The life He preached and demanded of His followers was to be completely different from the life that most men lead. His principle was squarely opposed to that which governs life in the world, where everyone desires to be first and uses his elbows to get ahead. In the world people trample upon the humble and inconsequential. The disciples would have to give guidance for living out of Jesus' principle. The task overwhelmed them. Would they be equal to it? That is why they asked Jesus to increase their faith.

The question arose from lack of faith. Their view of faith was certainly very wrong. They saw it as a kind of power with differing degrees of intensity. But the power of faith is not contained in faith itself but in God, whom we know by faith. If we trust in God, there is nothing we cannot do.

Therefore, Jesus answered that if they had faith as small as a mustard seed, they would be able to order a mulberry tree to be uprooted and it would be done. By faith they would do things which were impossible with men. God, in whom they put their trust, would work the impossible. For with God all things are possible.

Faith cannot be understood in unbelief. Faith will never be powerless; for God can do all things. If only there is faith and we expect only Him, we will not long for any miracles but simply do all that is necessary for the coming of His Kingdom. And there is no need to fear.

Faith's task. When we see God in faith, we can do everything but we also have a never-ending task. He who gives all also demands all. He has a right to everything because He created us and we belong to Him body and soul. When we have done something for Him we must not pride ourselves on it because we have only done what we were sworn to do. We are not indispensable servants.

Our relation to God, said Jesus, is like that of a slave to his master. The slave is also completely the property of his master. Jesus did not condemn slavery but simply used a factual situation to illustrate our relation to God.

Suppose a slave came home from working in the field. He did not have the right to sit down at once to his meal. The master could still order him to serve him at the table. The master need not show his gratitude for that service because it's the slave's duty to do all those things. In the same way, we have to give ourselves completely to the Lord, every day again. The Lord is not obliged to thank us for such service. His calling is without limit because He is the Lord!

Faith's thankfulness. The Lord Jesus continued on the way to Jerusalem. He had so much to say and to do. He was traveling along the border between Galilee and Samaria. In Samaria, remember, the people had been unwilling to provide accommodations for Him.

As He entered a certain village He was met by ten lepers. These outcasts stood at a distance and cried out in a loud voice, "Jesus, Master, have pity on us." When He saw them, He only said that they should show themselves to the priests. He evidently meant that they would be healed when they arrived at the priests.

Away they went, showing great faith because at that moment they were still lepers. They all believed in His miraculous power. Whether they also believed in Him as the One sent by God for our salvation would become clear later. On their way they were healed and when they discovered that, they hastened to the priest. There was only one who returned, praising God with a loud voice. He fell at Jesus' feet and gave Him thanks. And he was a Samaritan.

Jesus said to him, "Rise and go your way; your faith has made you well." Evidently the Samaritan not only believed in the miraculous power of the Lord Jesus, but also saw Him as sent by God for salvation. That man was saved for all eternity. He was healed and reentered society where he served the Lord. That was the salvation of his life.

How did the other nine react to their healing? From their lack of thankfulness it would appear that they thought they had a right to be healed. Were they not Jews, after all? They did not see that we have not only forfeited everything by our sins, but we also can never establish any right over against God except the right that rests in His promises. God is the sovereign; we have come forth from His hand. He is in no way obligated to us. He who knows God in this way and has become humble before Him sees every blessing as a gift of His favor and is thankful.

CHAPTER SEVENTY ONE
THE CRY FOR JUSTICE
LUKE 18:1-14

No one would dare do what Christ does here, namely, to compare what God does with the act of an unjust judge. There is a difficulty which remains unsolved as long as we think of the relation between God and the present world in terms of an absolute dualism (two utterly distinct "worlds"). There must be some similarity between God and this judge otherwise Jesus would not have made the comparison.

The judge was compelled by his office to do what at first he did not want to do. He feared that the widow would finally come and wear him out. In the end, she would get the better of him because he could not shirk the demand for justice which he had to protect. Justice compelled him even though he feared neither God nor man.

Note the peculiar language usage. In connection with God there is only mention of fear, of being afraid, while in connection with men mention is made of having respect for, of looking up to, a certain majesty. That describes the spiritual attitude of this judge: he never so much as thought of having respect for the majesty of God or of the fact that men might fear His name. Yet he is unable to maintain his position. In the final analysis there is something of reverence for the majestic justice of God, a certain awed hesitation before that justice, of which he is reminded by the widow's constant pleading. The demand for justice reaches him through appeals men make of him. Thus he has fear after all. This respect for justice, this bowing to its demands, is still present in unbelievers in spite of themselves. It is still a fruit of the covenant of grace, and applies in the first instance to His people, but also manifests itself in the lives of unbelievers.

In this respect a comparison between the unjust judge and God is possible. Because of His righteousness God will surely do justice to His chosen ones. But in God's case, justice is not some compelling power above Him; it is something that proceeds from Himself, it is the justice of His covenant. That justice is never at odds with the will of His love, but is in harmony with it.

God will speedily do justice to His chosen ones although He is long- suffering to them. That He is long-suffering means that He still puts off the decision for them; He does not give His help in everything immediately. By means of this delay He wishes to allow the faith which He put into His chosen ones to develop. Through this test their faith must come to open expression. Thus, while on the one hand He delays coming to their aid, on the other, He hastens to their aid. He will help as soon as the development of their lives allows it.

(That He will bring about justice for His elect must not lead us to ask, Am I one of the elect? Everyone who sees the honor of God's calling in his life and responds to the call is one of the elect. I'm not suggesting a doctrine of election on the basis of faith which God has foreseen. The election is indeed the cause, and the faith the result. But this election is not proclaimed as a theory. The revelation of election has to drive us from our place. Everyone is elect who day and night cries out to God and thus shows that he has heard God's call. The call of God is His call in His covenant.)

It is undoubtedly true that the parable urges us always to pray and not give up. But we would be wrong to pass on this urging without placing in the foreground the basis for that urging, namely, that because of God's justice He will surely hear us. What God does is the ground for what we do.

Thus the following parable (of the Pharisee and the publican, actually it is only an example) is connected with this one. The tax-collector made an appeal to God for justice. But it is the justice of His covenant, justice according to His promise to which he appealed. For God will do justice to His own over against everything that opposes them because He has chosen them. Thus that justice is not based on their own works, as the Pharisee imagined. Noteworthy in this connection is what the tax- collector prayed. "O God, have mercy on me"—that is, be reconciled to me. That was a prayer on the basis of the Word of reconciliation which was particularly typified in the temple. The publican appealed to the justice of the covenant. Thus he was one of the elect.

Main Thought: *Because God works justice according to His covenant, we are to appeal to it unceasingly.*

A judge's obligation. The Lord Jesus had spoken (ch. 17) of the end of the world and of the oppressions that were to come. What injustices the believers would have to suffer and how many attacks they would have to endure! In that conflict they are to appeal to God unceasingly. They are to appeal to justice. Had God in His covenant not chosen for them and adopted them as His people? Therein rested the promise that He would deliver them and give them the victory. They had a right to the fulfillment of that promise. Would God not work justice?

That God will surely effect justice Jesus assured us by way of a parable. There was once a judge who neglected his office. He also did not seem to worry about the consequences of his negligence. Not being one to tremble before the majesty of God, he was not at all afraid of divine punishment. Nor did he shrink from the power of men's curses. In his city lived a widow who was suffering injustice. She came to the judge to ask him to look after her rights. But capricious as he was, he did not bother about her complaint and sent her away. But she persisted.

The judge then became fearful. Though he neither feared God nor cared about man, he nevertheless felt that he could not refuse her indefinitely. To begin with, the widow's whining wore him out. But he especially feared the justice for which the woman was asking and which he was neglecting. If he didn't do something about it, this woman's case could just possibly be his undoing. At last he sensed that he could not let the injustice go unpunished, otherwise justice might rise up against him. For that reason he finally helped her.

If in the end, said Jesus, this unjust judge was compelled by the threats of justice to himself to come to the widow's aid, will God, in whom all justice has its origin, not do justly? He has given His promise to His people, and thereby the right to hope in Him. He will surely cause justice to be done to them.

Therefore believers must continually appeal to Him. God may put off the deliverance for a time. He may want to put believers to the test, and through that test mature their faith. Yet He hastens to their aid. As soon as their maturity will permit He will help. According to His promise they are entitled to that. He has put His seal on that promise to His people. Everyone who hears that promise in faith and holds God to His Word by appealing to His justice belongs to His people.

The basis for the "rights" of God's people. We must bear in mind that we are entitled to God's blessing only because God has promised it to us. The only basis for that "right" is the promise God made in the covenant of His grace; it is not because of our own works. Even the circle of the disciples was constantly threatened by the sin of self-trust. The disciples had admittedly broken with the Pharisees, yet there still was in them that special Pharisaical sin of trusting in themselves. Accordingly, the Lord Jesus warned them by way of an example.

Once a Pharisee and a publican went up to the temple to pray. Both sought God in prayer. But how differently they did it! The Pharisee thought that he had earned God's favor by his works; thus his prayer sought the reward for his life. The publican knew that he had forsaken God's covenant and that he was unworthy of God's favor. He knew that God's favor was a free gift and that God gave it with the forgiveness of our sins. Yet even though he had broken God's covenant, he still dared to go up to the temple to pray. His prayer took hold of the Word of grace.

In his prayer the Pharisee thanked God that he was not like other men, like a public sinner, or even like the publican who had also entered the temple. He completely overlooked the sin of his uncharitable, selfish and unbelieving heart. He apparently knew nothing of the Word that promises grace to sinners. On the contrary, he summed up all his good works; he had even done more than the law required of him. It didn't even enter his mind that God does not recognize merit or that we can only serve Him if we belong to His covenant with body and soul. He thought he had done what the law required of him. Only the law is the will of the Father and he did not know God as Father; he hadn't even *begun* to do the will of the Father.

The publican stood at a distance and didn't even dare lift up his eyes to heaven, but beat his breast and cried, "O God, be merciful (reconciled) to me a sinner!" God could forgive the sin of breaking the covenant and be reconciled to him again. Did he not have the symbol of reconciliation in front of him in the temple? Had God not promised that reconciliation in His Word? Thus the basis for the publican's praying was not his life, his conversion, his earnest repentance, or even his faith or his prayer, but solely the Word of God. So he too appealed to what was his right; it was the right which God in His grace has given to His people, to all who put their hope in Him.

We so easily slip from trusting in God's Word to trusting in ourselves. That's what Jesus was warning His disciples against. The publican went down to his house justified. God had been reconciled with him and he enjoyed God's favor and fellowship. The Pharisee was a stranger to all this. He knew neither the grace of God nor the wonderful communion with Him which, in His grace, becomes our portion. Let us appeal for justice, also when we ask for the forgiveness of our sins, but for the justice which He has granted us through His Word!

CHAPTER SEVENTY TWO
TO RECEIVE THE KINGDOM
LUKE 18:31—19:27

Luke relates the healing of Bartimaeus on the entrance to Jericho; Matthew and Mark, on leaving the city. Perhaps the solution is that Bartimaeus learned of Jesus' presence when He entered the city and saw to it that he was on hand when Jesus left Jericho.The parable of the ten pounds is very similar to the parable of the talents in Matthew; we will deal with it very briefly here. The first part, about traveling to a far country to receive a kingdom, is quite different. We find a clue to the idea that governs this whole section. Although Jesus was going to suffer, He was going to inherit the Kingdom. In that light He still had to reveal Himself to Israel. That revelation took place at His triumphal entry amid the cheering crowds, but here we see the prelude to it. Now He found it no longer dangerous that the blind man called Him the Son of David. The blind man followed Him, glorifying God. And all the people gave praise to God. The Christ allows Himself to accept that.

In His power He also had a claim to Zacchaeus's house. Zacchaeus rendered to Him, Israel's King, an account of his conduct and his intentions. The righteousness of the King, the righteousness of the Kingdom of heaven, had won the victory over him and had set him free.

Main Thought: *Christ goes up to Jerusalem to receive the Kingdom.*

The way of the cross. Little by little Jesus and His disciples were approaching Jerusalem. Already earlier He had said to them that He was going to suffer, die and rise there. Now that all this had come so much closer He told them again, but in greater detail. Everything that had been written of Him by the prophets would be fulfilled. Israel would betray Him, deliver Him up to the Gentiles. Yet He was Israel's King! To receive the eternal Kingdom He would have to endure the betrayal. He would be reviled and put to death, but on the third day He would rise again.

The disciples understood about as much now as they had before. They didn't expect it and didn't like it. They did not understand that the Kingdom of grace was identical with the Kingdom where righteousness had first to be conquered. He would conquer by His suffering and death. Only afterwards could He reign in righteousness.

The beginning of the jubilation. In the vicinity of Jericho a blind beggar was sitting at the side of the road. When Jesus approached surrounded by a large crowd, the blind man asked what was going on. From the passers-by he heard who was coming. At once he saw a chance of being healed. He had heard of the miracles. Did God specifically send Christ his way so that he too might be healed? Faith was at work in that man. In a loud voice he cried out: "Jesus, Son of David, have mercy on me!"

The people in the crowd told him to be quiet. They had already seen several miracles; there was nothing sensational about it any more. Moreover, everyone understood that it was now a question of getting to Jerusalem. Suspense was in the air about what was going to happen there. They didn't want to be distracted. But the mercy of the Kingdom of God is different. The blind man didn't pay any attention to them; he cried all the louder. The Lord Jesus stood still and commanded that the blind man be brought to Him.

He made him repeat his question so he could show his faith. He had to forget about everything else and place his trust squarely in Jesus. That happened when he said, "Lord, let me receive my sight!" What he desired was no trifling matter. Probably he desired the healing of his life as a healing before God, so that, with his sight recovered and being thus restored to full communion with this life, he might serve God in that communion.

Jesus saw the faith that the Father had given to this blind man. He said, "Receive your sight; your faith has made you well." As King He restored his life to him. And the man, healed, glorified God. As a result of that miracle and because of the man's joy the crowd was greatly moved and all the people gave praise to God. By now all the shouting began to accompany Jesus, but He permitted it, because before He underwent His suffering Israel had yet to see who He was. He was going to reveal Himself as King. In the instance of healing the people could see how His Kingdom brings a full restoration of life. With eyes open to the full communion with the life He created, we shall live under His scepter.

I must stay at your house today. In Jericho there was a large customs office. The chief tax-collector was a man named Zacchaeus. He was a wealthy man. But he had not come by all his wealth honestly.

When the rumor circulated that the Lord Jesus was coming, all of Jericho turned out to see Him. Zacchaeus also went out into the street. Perhaps his subordinates mocked him for it. Christ was for the Jews and they, the publicans, had betrayed the national interest. The Pharisees and almost everybody else despised them. Moreover, they were far from honest in their dealings. What did they care about *the Christi*

But Zacchaeus did not allow that to hold him back. He had heard about Him. He had also heard that Christ could not tolerate injustice. Yet the righteousness He preached was different from the righteousness the Pharisees prided themselves in. The Pharisees despised Him and His associates for their supposed self-righteousness. The Christ proclaimed a righteousness that is a gift of God's grace, which is accepted by faith and is thus a calling. His proclamation of righteousness offered promises and made demands at the same time. The scribes' preaching of righteousness had closed and hardened Zacchaeus's heart; he had clenched his teeth at their contempt. But he had been touched by Christ's proclamation of righteousness. So he couldn't stay home.

For a time he had walked along with the crowd, hoping that he would get to see Him. But he saw nothing because he was so short. Then it occurred to him to run on ahead and climb a fig tree. He was determined to see Jesus. When Jesus came to that spot He saw him sitting in the tree. The Father showed Him Zacchaeus as someone who had to be saved. For it was God who led everything in this way.

Stopping, He said that Zacchaeus should hurry down since He intended to stay at his house that day. Zacchaeus couldn't believe it! Jesus Christ in *his* house! The Man of righteousness was coming to him, the unrighteous one. Yet it was possible because the Lord Jesus was going to suffer in order to obtain righteousness for all who are unrighteous. Righteousness had become a gift in such a way that we, once reconciled, can begin to live in righteousness again.

Zacchaeus did not yet see any of that, but he was ashamed and overcome by this word of the Christ. The crowds and the Pharisees didn't know what they heard either. If he was looking for a place to stay, why settle for the home of a chief tax-collector? By doing that He compromised Himself at a time when the crowds had such high expectations that He was now going to become their king. They still didn't know that in His Kingdom righteousness is a gift that God gives to whom He pleases and that people who pride themselves in their own righteousness cannot receive.

Like a king, the Lord Jesus laid claim to Zacchaeus and his house. He had not received an invitation from Zacchaeus but claimed his house for Himself. He had much more to give than He received. Yet He also demanded much. He gave everything but He also demanded everything—Zacchaeus's whole life. That became very clear from His words in Zacchaeus's house.

Jesus' words took hold of Zacchaeus. The righteousness of the Kingdom of heaven won the victory over him. He acknowledged that publicly to Jesus. He said he would give half of his goods to the poor. He who had always lived for himself would henceforth give himself to others for God's sake. He also promised to restore fourfold whatever he had taken fraudulently from others. The law in such cases demanded only restitution with a twenty percent fine. But Zacchaeus recognized that his sins demanded a fourfold return. He confessed openly that he was a sinner. That's how the righteousness of the Kingdom seized him. His words and deeds were the result of a thankful heart, for the grace of Christ had redeemed him and he had received forgiveness.

Jesus said, "Today salvation has come to this house." In His grace He had taken possession of it. That had happened on account of the covenant since Zacchaeus was also a son of Abraham. The Son of man came to seek and to save what was lost. God continued to reach out to what was lost and Christ was privileged to restore it to the fellowship of His covenant and Kingdom. There was rejoicing among the angels.

The King's judgment. For many it would be different than it was for Zacchaeus. He had acknowledged Christ as the King of righteousness and as his King. Many would not do that because they were expecting the immediate establishment of the kingdom in Jerusalem. They did not expect a Kingdom of righteousness established by Christ's atoning death for unrighteousness. They would reject Him because of their false hopes.

It would be with Jesus as with the nobleman who traveled to a far country to receive kingly power over his own country. (That was the way the Roman emperor appointed the kings of the various countries.) This nobleman gave one pound to each of his ten servants for them to trade with during his absence. His fellow- countrymen, who hated him, sent ambassadors to the emperor to say that they did not want this man to reign over them.

When he returned as king, he demanded an accounting of his ten servants. He rewarded those who had worked faithfully and punished-the one who had been unfaithful. Afterwards he had his enemies, who had sent the ambassadors, brought before him and slain in his presence.

Similarly, Jesus was going to receive the Kingdom. But there were many who did not wish to receive Him as the King of grace, the King of righteousness, although right now they were crowding around Him. One day He will pronounce judgment on them. He received His Kingdom at His resurrection and ascension. His Kingdom came at the outpouring of the Spirit on Pentecost. And it will come in glory upon His return. We must live in expectation of Him, and in the meantime work righteously with what is His, as Zacchaeus and the faithful servants did. Then we shall also reign in righteousness.

CHAPTER SEVENTY THREE
ISRAEL'S KING
LUKE 19:28-48

More than once the people wanted to proclaim Christ as their king. Every time He evaded them. Now He accepted their praise willingly. The prelude to this had already taken place during His journey through Jericho. He had to be revealed as Israel's King. That is the proclamation of His victory over all of life's need.

The entry into Jerusalem still lies between the reality and the shadows. On the reality side, Christ is the fulfillment of the prophecy which was symbolically present in the procession of Israel's kings and of the ark of the covenant to the mountain of the Lord. On the other hand, His entry is still a shadow: the hosannas of the crowd were to a large extent false; yet in them He heard the praise which would be brought to Him eternally by His own. Thus Christ's entry is a prophecy of His ascension to the heavenly throne amidst the songs of praise by the angels and, further, a prophecy of His entry by His Spirit into the hearts of all His people and of His coming into the glory of His Kingdom at His return.

Luke tells us that He entered Jerusalem weeping. That the Jerusalem of shadows would be replaced by the service of God in spirit and in truth was in itself no reason for sadness. But Jerusalem would be destroyed, it would come under judgment because of its sins, particularly the sin of glorifying itself. Jerusalem is pictured as a city of flesh. But He entered Jerusalem to reconcile the sins which He took upon Himself. He thereby restored the true service of God.

The cleansing of the temple is related to that. That too is a prophecy of the restoration of the true service of God. The temple, then, represents not only our hearts, or the church, but the whole world. He shall make the entire creation a temple of God again.

Main Thought: *Christ reveals Himself as Israel's King.*

Amidst Israel's songs of praise. Jesus was approaching Jerusalem. It was Sunday morning and He was ready to enter the city. The roads were busy because it was just before the feast of Passover and crowds of guests were coming into the city. Among them were a large number from Galilee who knew Him and knew of His miracles. The last miracle in Jericho too had aroused great enthusiasm. There was a great deal of suspense about what He was going to do and what was to become of Him.

Jesus knew that this was His last journey to Jerusalem, and that now He was entering the city in order to suffer there. Before that happened He wanted to reveal to Israel who He was. Although the crowds and even His disciples had a mistaken notion of it, He was still Israel's King. The people now had to see Him claim that honor for Himself, even though the way to His throne would be an entirely different one than they imagined.

So when they drew near to the Mount of Olives at the village of Bethphage, He ordered two of His disciples to go into the village and fetch a donkey's colt they would see standing on the side of the road. God's Spirit illumined Him so He knew that. If anyone should ask why they were taking the colt with them, they were to say that the Lord needed it, and it would immediately be handed over to them. Evidently the colt's owner was also a confessor of Christ. The disciples found everything exactly as He had said and brought the colt to Him.

The disciples understood now just what it was He was doing. For so long they had wanted Him to reveal Himself as King. Now He Himself was encouraging them in that wish. He wanted this too, though it was in a different way than they. They threw their garments on the colt and set Jesus on it. Then they spread their garments on the road for Him to ride over them. At that point a shock went through the crowds. They saw what was happening and understood that now He was going to have Himself proclaimed King. The crowd too began to spread their garments or branches from the trees on the road in front of Him, praising God for all the mighty works that they had seen and saying, "Blessed is the King who comes in the Name of the Lord! Peace in heaven and glory in the highest!" It was as though they were taking over the praise that the angels had once sung at His birth. God's Name would be praised to the highest heavens and there would be peace with God for His people, because the King who had been given from God had come. David and Solomon and all the redeemers of the people had only been Old Testament types of Him.

Indeed, that is how the Lord had meant it. Here was the fulfillment of all the promises in the history of the Old Testament. Now the true King was coming. And yet this was still not the actual fulfillment. Many in the crowds did not truly know Him. Their shouts of joy were only excitement at His mighty works, not a recognition in faith of the Redeemer. Yet He permitted all this jubilation. For Him it was a prophecy of all the jubilation that would surround Him at His ascension, and when down through the ages He would come to dwell in the hearts of His own by His Spirit, He would return in glory. Now through all the centuries there is a festive procession surrounding Christ. Are we in *that* crowd shouting our joy?

Jerusalem! Jerusalem! Not everyone joined in the praise. There were some who were bitter, and kept silent. These were the Pharisees. Was He yet going to usurp their rule? If His Kingdom, the Kingdom of grace, were to come, it would be the end of theirs. They still wanted to try to prevent this by taking advantage of His previous dislike for the praise of the crowds. They therefore asked Him to reprimand His disciples. But the Father's appointed time had come, now it had to happen. So He said that if the disciples were to be silent, the very stones would cry out. The praise of all creation had to be brought to Him from the lips of men.

Reflected in the Pharisees' request was Jerusalem's hostility. When He had come near the city, He wept over it. His tears fell on the colt. Jerusalem did not see its true salvation. There would be peace for her only through faith in God's grace. Now she boasted in herself and rejected the Lord and His covenant of grace. Judgment would have to come. The city would be besieged and captured and its inhabitants slaughtered; it would be leveled. Had God not visited the city once again with His grace? But it had not been willing to recognize Him.

That was His lament. This entry was also a suffering for Him. But thereby He took the guilt of sin upon Himself in order to atone for it Himself. By His atonement He would receive authority to create a different kind of life, a life in which men would serve the Lord truly and look for His grace. That was the purpose of His coming and that was what He wished to show the people during those days in Jerusalem.

The sanctity of the Lord's house. When He had entered the outer court of the temple, the court of the Gentiles, He saw some money-changers and merchants who sold animals for the sacrifices. The money-changers did, of course, have to be near the temple, for the temple money could only be paid in a certain currency. And those who sold animals for the sacrifices or doves for the sacrifices of the poor also had to be nearby. But that they carried on their business in the temple court showed that they didn't give a moment's thought to the holiness of the Lord, who revealed Himself there. They were only mindful of their own interest; they looked out only for themselves. That was the result of the service of self-righteousness. In that service each one looked out for himself. These people did not take notice of God or give any thought to the holiness of His grace.

In holy anger the Lord Jesus lashed out against them. He drove the salesmen out and overturned the tables of the moneychangers. He was zealous for the sanctity of the Lord's house. It ought to be a house of prayer, but it had been made into a den of murderers. For where men look out only for themselves, true life, which seeks God, is put to death. There He stood as Israel's King, who cleansed the temple. And no one dared resist Him.

This zeal of Christ is still at work. He wants to restore our hearts together with all of life and the whole world to a holy temple (see Vol. I, p. 34 bottom, pp. 310-11; Vol. II, pp. 202-3). By atoning for our sins He obtained authority from the Father to do that. He does not tolerate unholiness. His will is that all of life be dedicated to God. One day He will cleanse the whole creation. Let us in faith acknowledge Him in His authority! Then He will cleanse our lives too.

LUKE:
THE LAMB THAT WAS SLAIN

CHAPTER SEVENTY FOUR
DEFENSELESS
LUKE 22:35-53

For a fuller discussion of the agony in Gethsemane see the treatment in the Gospel of Mark (p. 265). A different relationship now comes into view than when Jesus sent his disciples out to preach in Galilee. Now they must expect resistance. This applies to the time when they will preach the gospel to Israel and to the world. While they are never to stand up for themselves, they *are* to defend the Name and the Word of the Lord. He earned us the right to stand up for His Word by His own defenselessness, by His voluntary surrender for the atonement of our sins.

Main Thought: *Because of Christ's defenselessness we now may be spiritually on the offensive.*

The summons to defend His Word and name. After His entry into Jerusalem on Sunday, that week Jesus spoke in the temple every day and was attacked on all sides by the elders of the people. Thursday evening He ate with His disciples, knowing that it would be His last meal with them before His suffering. During that meal He said goodbye and prepared them for the meeting with Him after His resurrection. At the point of going out into the night, He gave them a glimpse into the future.

"You remember," He said, "that I sent you out in Galilee to preach. You were to go without money or bags, for I told you that the people would receive you and provide you with all the necessities. And you were to accept that because you came in My Name. Did you lack anything at all on that journey?" They answered that they had not. Many had received them because they had come in the name of the Christ.

"From now on," He said, "it is going to be different. Now you will go out into a hostile world. Often people will not receive you. Therefore you must see to it that you have with you everything you need. Provide for money and luggage, and if you do not have a sword, you must sell your cloak and buy one."

In this way He prepared His disciples for the great opposition which they were going to encounter in the world. But they were never to defend themselves, only His Name and Word. That would also determine the means they had to use in that struggle in the world. If it concerned themselves, He had said that they were not to resist the evil one. But they were to stand up for His Name.

That tension in the world would be determined by what would now speedily overtake Him. As it had been prophesied of Him, He would be reckoned with the transgressors because His present life was coming to a close. He would be known as the rejected one. Therefore men would scorn and hate Him, and also hate His gospel.

The disciples said to Him, "Look, Lord, here are two swords." Perhaps they meant the big knives which some of them carried with them to prepare food. The disciples had again taken His words wrongly. They thought that they had to arm themselves against the danger that threatened Him. How often had He not told them that He would have to suffer in accordance with the Scriptures and in order that God's grace might be shed upon us? But now He no longer contradicted their mistaken notion. The events would just have to teach them. He therefore put an end to the conversation by saying, "It is enough." It was a form of dismissal. They were not to defend Him; for He was going to suffer as an atonement for our sins.

His victory over Himself. After this conversation He left with His disciples for the Mount of Olives. He had been there so often! He had withdrawn there many times to be alone with His disciples, or to pray.

When He had come to the place where He wanted to be, He told His disciples to pray that they might not fall into temptation that would be too strong for them. He Himself withdrew about a stone's throw beyond them. He wanted to pray for all the suffering that was to come over Him. The horror of death under the wrath of God fell upon Him. And more than any man, He, who thirsted for life and for fellowship with God, shrank from such a death. This suffering went against His whole human nature. His human nature prayed that the Father would remove the cup of suffering from Him.

But He knew that, for the sake of atonement, He had to suffer. In His obedience of faith He wanted to be one with the Father. Therefore, He went on, "Nevertheless not my will, but thine be done." With that same obedience of faith He now had to conquer His own nature so that it too would accept the suffering willingly. Jesus wrestled in prayer that demanded so much of Him that He threatened to succumb under it. An angel appeared to Him who strengthened Him that He might not die. It did not make the struggle any easier. It was so grievous that His sweat fell down on the ground like great drops of blood.

There Jesus struggled to accept willingly with His whole nature what His Father had decreed. There He covered and atoned for the refusal of both Adam and us through Adam to render obedience to God. And after a long struggle He won the victory. He was ready to surrender Himself up to His enemies in total surrender that He might fulfill the Father's mission for our salvation.

Rising from prayer, He came to His disciples and found them sleeping for sorrow. They had seen something of the perplexity of the Christ and shared His astonishment and grief. But they could not cope with that deadly struggle. They could not struggle along with Him but instead left Him to struggle alone. If He had not seen it through, if He had not obediently decided for us, none of us would be able to struggle and win the victory over ourselves any more. That doesn't alter the fact that His disciples should have struggled along with Him through His strength. Therefore He reproached them that they had fallen asleep and told them to rise and pray that they not fall into a temptation which might swallow them up. But they were unable to do it. No one of His people was with Him during His moment of crisis. And yet by His grace we may be with Him in His victory.

Spiritual defenselessness. While He was still speaking with His disciples, there came a crowd led by Judas who had become a traitor. Judas came forward and kissed Him to tip off his fellow conspirators. He submitted to that despicable treason. How He must have abhorred that kiss. He uttered only one reproach to try to bring the traitor to his senses: "Judas, do you betray the Son of man with a kiss?"

The disciples understood that this was the moment. Therefore they asked whether they should defend Him with the sword. And before He could answer, one of them struck out and cut off the right ear of the high priest's slave. How little the disciples understood

His self-surrender, His total defenselessness, for our sake! What is the meaning of a love that does not understand? Actually, their insights were very limited. He therefore disclaimed their behavior, even touched the wounded ear and healed it. Even in that night of betrayal there was still the power of His grace to heal. Should it not have been clear to all that He simply surrendered Himself up defenselessly in order to obtain power for the victory over sin and its consequences? He stressed His defenselessness by pointing to the crowd's swords and clubs. Had He not been teaching in the temple every day? Now they looked for Him in the dead of night and in this dark place, for this was the time and the place for their works of darkness. Yet He did not resist them but gave Himself up into their hands.

By His defenselessness He earned for us the right to go out in defense of His Name. We may defend only His Name and Word, His right and honor. Sometimes it may also be necessary for us to give ourselves up defenselessly for Him. We may pursue only what serves the coming of His Kingdom. We cannot do what He did because He gave Himself up for our reconciliation. Yet our intention, just as His, must be none other than the coming of the Kingdom of God in which He reigns supreme.

CHAPTER SEVENTY FIVE
FROM PILATE TO HEROD
LUKE 23:1-25

The expression has become proverbial: he was being sent from Pilate to Herod, or driven from pillar to post. That is what happened to Christ, because no one knew what to do with Him. It was His peculiar suffering that Christ had become an embarrassment to all. The world did not know Him. He did not fit in anywhere. By that suffering He had to obtain a place for Himself in the world. He had to obtain power to pour out His Spirit that men might receive Him.

Main Thought: *Christ suffers vicariously in being sent from Pilate to Herod.*

Pilate's dilemma. When He had been taken prisoner, Jesus was brought before the Sanhedrin. That body was already at a loss what to do with Him. He could not answer the questions put to Him there, for no one understood Him. When He finally had confessed that He was God's Son, that the fullness of divine grace had come to us in Him, they had said that there was no need to talk any further. His confession was enough to condemn Him. Thus among His own people He did not find understanding and acceptance. What then would the situation be among the Gentiles?

The Sanhedrin led Him to Pilate, the governor. They wanted Pilate to sentence Jesus to death. Before Pilate they accused Him of proclaiming Himself *the Christ,* the king, and of stirring the people up against the emperor.

To Pilate's question, whether He was the king of the Jews, He only answered: "You have said it." He was indeed the king of the Jews though not in the sense Pilate understood it. Pilate didn't understand the charge, but he saw clearly that Jesus was not a danger to the state. Therefore Pilate said that he found no fault in Him (the equivalent of our verdict of "not guilty").

The leaders of the people persisted, and said that He had begun to stir up the people in Galilee and that He continued to do so in Judea. When Pilate heard that He was from Galilee, He saw a way out for himself. Herod, king of Galilee, was in the city for Passover. He had better pass judgment on Him, Pilate decided. So he sent Him and His accusers to Herod.

Jesus was an embarrassment to Pilate. If the Jewish council couldn't even do anything with Him, what was this Gentile to do? It was clear to Jesus that no one in the whole world understood His grace. What suffering this caused Him! Truly, satan was the lord of the world. All of life was estranged from communion with God. It had come to be that way because of our sin. For that sin Christ made atonement, that there might again come room in the world for the grace and communion of the Lord.

Herod's dilemma. Matters worsened when the Lord Jesus stood before Herod. This criminal and superstitious king had long desired to see Him. Herod had killed John the Baptist and, when he heard of the Lord Jesus' miracles, he thought that John had risen from the dead. He could not see the power of grace in faith, but superstitiously imagined and feared a super mundane power. He would now question Jesus and try to discover the secret of His life. For the worst thing, surely, is fear of the unknown.

But Jesus did not accommodate Herod because He cannot reveal Himself in that fashion. He is known only by those who subject themselves in faith to His Word. Accordingly, He did not answer any of Herod's questions. This is how He still deals with those who will not subject themselves. Still, how He must have suffered under the foolishness of this superstitious interrogation! Superstition has nothing in common with faith in Him, and the superstitious do not know Him at all.

Before Herod too the chief priests and the scribes brought their charges against Him. But Herod was as baffled by their accusations as Pilate had been. Deeply embarrassed, but also annoyed by Christ's silence, Herod delivered Jesus up to the mockery of his soldiers. The grace in Jesus Christ remained a mystery to him. What could he possibly do with Him? To mock Him was at least a way of saving face. Mockery is also helpful in suppressing inner fear. Back to Pilate, Herod sent Jesus, dressed in a gorgeous white mantle.

Before this the relationship between Pilate and Herod had been strained, but from that day on they were friends. They delivered Christ up to each other. Pilate paid homage to Herod and Herod recognized Pilate as judge. They felt a certain kinship in that they both found Christ an embarrassment. Spiritually they were united in common ignorance. They were both capable of the same treason towards Him and the same travesty of justice.

Thus hostility towards Christ and His church brings people together who first seemed to be strangers to each other. All polarities will one day be subordinated to the great polarity between believers and unbelievers.

Delivered up to death. Thus Pilate was again faced with the necessity of passing judgment on Christ. Three times he declared Him not guilty. Nevertheless he already treated Him as a criminal by proposing to have Him chastised and then released and by placing Him alongside Barabbas. In so doing he had already abandoned justice. He could then not escape the demand of the elders of the people. They began to call for the crucifixion of the Lord Jesus. Their cry grew louder and louder. The hostility to the grace that is in Him flared up. And Pilate, embarrassed by the whole affair, decided that their demand would be met. Something was happening among the Jewish people that he did not understand. He resignedly washed his hands of the whole affair.

It was true that the gentile world was utterly estranged from Christ, from the grace of God in Him. The gentile world no longer knew the Lord. In His suffering Christ saw that. He endured the suffering of that estrangement of humanity. He experienced it in the injustice that was inflicted on Him in order that He might atone for the sins of that estrangement. One day the heavens would rejoice at the entry of the Gentiles into the covenant. The strangers to the covenant would become members of the household of God.

CHAPTER SEVENTY SIX
ALONE
LUKE 23:26-31

On Simon of Cyrene's carrying the cross, see our discussion on the gospel of Matthew. The women of Jerusalem did not know Christ in His suffering. Their sympathy with Him must have meant further agony on His part. It showed Him all the more clearly that He was alone.

Main Thought: *Christ suffers all alone, that His people may know Him again.*

Empty tears. After Pilate had pronounced judgment, Jesus was led away to be crucified. He was led out of the city gate. He was being banned from the community of His people. No one knew Him or wanted to know Him. A certain Simon of Cyrene had to be forced to carry His cross for Him. But Simon didn't want anything to do with Jesus either.

In the procession that followed Him were also several women of Jerusalem. They wept for the Lord Jesus. When they saw that He almost succumbed under the weight of His cross, that someone else had to take it over from Him, and how He was being led as a lamb to the slaughter, they broke out in a loud weeping: Just look at Him, poor man! What do they want of Him anyhow? He hasn't done anything wrong!

What were those women weeping about? They were only very superficially affected by what they saw. It was superficial pity that moved them. There was something human in their lamentation as opposed to the inhuman thirst for revenge on the part of the chief priests and scribes.

Yet those women did not perceive what was really going on. Their eyes were not only blind to the injustice, but, more importantly, they did not see that He who is the Truth of God, the Truth of God's grace upon His people, was being banned from the community of the people. They ought to have seen that; for He had preached the truth of grace also in Jerusalem. Now they were prevented from seeing it by their overriding feeling of pity. That feeling made them all the more blind. Often our feelings are so badly corrupted that they can keep us from seeing the truth. It is not true that tears never lie. Sentimentality can prevent our true feelings from being aroused at the rejection of the Lord and of the grace of His Kingdom. Our feelings, too, have to be redeemed and healed by the grace of the Lord.

Jesus suffered anew from this emotional outburst of the women. If someone feels pity but does not understand the true nature of suffering, then the pity itself becomes a source of suffering. And these were the women of Jerusalem, the women of His own people! They should have known Him. Thus the women's tears were yet another drop in the cup of His agony. This, too, He had to endure. He had to atone for all those false and sinful emotions, in order that He might heal our feelings and we might truly know Him both in His suffering and in the joy of His victorious reign. On that road He was the Unknown, the One who stood alone, so that His people might have eternal communion with Him.

Genuine sorrow. Jesus halted and turned to the women. All at once it was quiet; everyone wanted to hear what He was going to say. He addressed them as daughters of Jerusalem, the daughters of His people. What they would have to go through! They should be weeping for themselves and for their children, because the time would come when women with no children would be considered fortunate. How intense would be the sufferings of mothers forced to see the agony of their children! They would call on the mountains to fall on them and on the hills to cover them, so that they would not have to see such misery.

Jesus was alluding to the horrors in connection with the destruction of Jerusalem, which was soon to come. They should weep about *that*, though not just out of pity for themselves and for their children. Those who would perish there would be the daughters of Jerusalem, together with their children, members of God's people. They would be lost to God's Kingdom, though they belonged to the people on whom He had put His claim. Because of the people's sin God would be deprived of what properly belonged to Him. If they would weep for that loss and acknowledge the right of God's grace to His people, their feelings would be more accurately focused. Then, whatever might happen, they would be saved for God's Kingdom.

They would know Christ then and understand what He meant by His statement, "For if they do this when the tree is green, what will happen when it is dry?" He was the living tree, linked to God and would therefore bear fruit. They were the dry branches which could not produce any fruit. They must see that they deserved the suffering that fell on Him. His suffering was indescribably severe, more severe than that of any man, but when He came through it, He would rise from God-forsakenness to eternal communion with God. If they, however, did not know Him, they would be lost eternally under God's wrath. From that He wanted to save them.

How alone the Christ was on this road! Even the feelings of the women were an illusion. One day judgment would come on their failure to understand and on all untruth, including misguided feelings, first in the destruction of Jerusalem and then in the destruction of the world. But He embraced this all in His suffering that He might heal our feelings and restore the right fellowship among His people and thus save that people in the day of judgment.

CHAPTER SEVENTY SEVEN
HIS SACRIFICE
LUKE 23:32-56

Christ gave Himself as a sacrifice for sin. His suffering may also be looked at as His self-sacrifice. That's the way it appears, especially in Luke's gospel. When the dying Christ said, "Father, into thy hands I commit my spirit," He laid His obedient life as a sacrifice in His Father's hands. This too was the act of a mediator.

In the sin of men, and thus in the sin of the leaders of the people, there is always an element of ignorance (Acts 3:17). The elders did not know what they were doing because they did not know Christ as the Lord of glory. But ignorance is no excuse for sin; for ignorance, not knowing the grace of God which reveals itself to us, is itself sin. Yet this ignorance is sin that can be forgiven. In satanic sin and in the sin against the Holy Spirit that element of ignorance is not present. Christ, praying for the forgiveness of this ignorance, took the guilt of that ignorance upon Himself. Thus the intention of that petition was that the elders might see and know what they were doing, might come to know the Christ and thus be saved.

The criminal on the cross prayed for salvation in the eternal Kingdom, about which he as a Jew had some knowledge. For him, however, the coming of that Kingdom perhaps lay in a still distant future at the resurrection of the dead. His faith showed great insight when he confessed that Christ, who was dying on the cross, would be King. In answer he received a promise, the fulfillment of which lay much closer at hand: that very day he would be with Christ in paradise. With the word "paradise" Christ was obviously alluding to the blessed communion with Him that believers will enjoy between death and the resurrection of the flesh. Paradise and Kingdom each has its own glory. "Paradise" is being oriented to Christ, to our hidden communion with Him, something that continues after the resurrection of the flesh. "Kingdom" promises the sovereign rule in His Name over all the works of God's hands. In His promise Christ adopted that criminal and offered Himself as a sacrifice for a life that was spent in crime.

Main Thought: *Christ offers Himself as a sacrifice for the salvation of life.*

A sacrifice to atone for ignorance. Along with Jesus two criminals were led away to Golgotha. These were crucified with Him, one on His right and one on His left. While they crucified Him, Jesus prayed, "Father, forgive them; for they know not what they do." He was not thinking so much about the soldiers who were carrying out their orders, as about the elders of the people who had delivered Him up to be crucified.

But did these elders really not know what they were doing? Had He not confessed that He was *the Christ*? He had indeed confessed that but they had not known Him as *the Christ*, because we can only know Him in faith. Their eyes were blinded. Only satan fully knows who *the Christ* is. Satan is not ignorant; he commits sin solely out of hatred of God. Because of this element of ignorance among the leaders, Jesus could still pray for those who were responsible for His death. But that ignorance is itself sin. It is a terrible thing that we do not know God's grace when it comes to us. The Lord Jesus could only pray for forgiveness for this sin because He took the guilt of that ignorance upon Himself. In that petition He offered Himself as a sacrifice to atone for their guilty ignorance.

Of course it meant that they could not remain in their ignorance. If God's grace is revealed to men because He wants to grant them forgiveness, they must come to see both the guilt of their ignorance and the sins they have committed in their ignorance. Christ's prayer for forgiveness may not have been efficacious for all the leaders involved but some may later have come to repentance. Christ still intercedes on behalf of the ignorant because He once took their guilt upon Himself that they might come to knowledge.

How little the people and their elders realized what they were doing was apparent from their mockery and jeering. Even the soldiers in their ignorance joined in. Occasion for the mockery was found in the inscription that had been written above His head. He endured the suffering of that guilty ignorance to effect its atonement.

A sacrifice to atone for a wasted life. One of the criminals began to join in the mockery. In the shadow of death, he bitterly sneered, "Are you not the Christ? Save yourself and us!" All his cynical disbelief of goodness and pity in life spilled out in this cry. Such a person drives salvation away with his mockery and sinks into eternal darkness.

At first perhaps the other criminal played along, hoping to suppress his fear. However, the revelation of the Lord Jesus, His petition for those responsible for His death, and His demeanor in suffering struck him. He came to see Christ as the One sent from God, the Redeemer. In the crucified Christ he saw the King. In Jesus' suffering he saw the magnificence of God's grace. For him that was a revelation from the Father; the Holy Spirit opened his eyes. He reprimanded his fellow-criminal, confessed that they were suffering their sentence justly, and expressed his opinion that Christ was innocent. He saw His righteousness and must have sensed something of the fact that *He* was undergoing this suffering voluntarily for the sake of others.

He then directed himself to Jesus and asked if He would remember him when He came into His Kingdom. He confessed Him as the King, who one day would reveal the glory of His Kingdom and raise the dead, including him. What a confession concerning Christ, who at that point was sinking into death!

How great must have been Jesus' joy as He listened to this sign of His Father's work in the heart of the criminal! He saw a life entirely wasted in crime. Would He accept such a life? If He did, He would be taking all that guilt upon Himself. He did not hesitate for a moment but offered Himself as an atoning sacrifice by accepting the criminal.

The man had asked for mercy at the resurrection of the dead when Christ came into His Kingdom. To him that probably meant some event far into the future. Christ promised him that he would be with Him in paradise that very same day. For a time he would be hidden in blessed communion with Christ, to rise again at the resurrection.

Christ's joy at the prospect of paradise showed how much He longed for that paradise. His soul was being scorched in the wilderness of God-forsakenness and He thirsted for relief. This also gives us a glimpse of what He suffered for our sake. He offered Himself as a sacrifice for even such a life of crime. That such a life was saved was to the greater glory of the Father's grace. Therefore, even that life had not been entirely in vain. The criminal confessed the crucified Jesus as the King and rebuked the criminal who was crucified with him, thus breaking with the emptiness and blasphemy of a godless life.

The sacrifice offered up to the Father. He was utterly forsaken by the Father, especially during the darkness that covered Golgotha from noon until three o'clock. These were the hours of His most intense suffering: He suffered the very fires of hell. All that time He continued willingly to offer Himself as a sacrifice for our sins, thereby fulfilling what all Old Testament sacrifices had foreshadowed. With His sacrifice all previous sacrifices and the entire service in the temple had come to an end. As a sign, the curtain of the temple which separated the "holy place" from the "holy of holies" was torn in two.

Finally the moment of His death had come. He offered His entire obedient, God-oriented life to His Father as a sacrifice. All the fruits of His life and suffering He placed in the hands of His Father when He cried, "Father, into Your hands I commit My spirit." When He had thus called out with a loud voice, He died.

His victorious death made a deep impression on the bystanders. The Roman centurion acknowledged, "Truly, this was a righteous man." He beheld the innocent suffering of Christ and, without realizing it, showed the vicarious nature of His suffering as sacrifice for the sins of men. Thus the officer glorified God. The crowds returned to Jerusalem, beating their breasts and unwittingly testifying to the real significance of His suffering, which to them was a mystery.

Waiting for the sacrifice to be accepted. Jesus had offered His life and His suffering to His Father as a sacrifice for our sins. The Father's answer that Christ's sacrifice freed us from sin would come a few days later when the Father raised Him from the dead.

For three days He was concealed in the grave. Joseph of Arimathea, a member of the Sanhedrin, had seen to it that He was buried in a new grave. In his heart Joseph also confessed Christ as the King and expected His Kingdom. The honorable burial at the hands of friends also showed that He had suffered as a righteous man, as an atonement for others. At the burial, besides Joseph, were the women who had accompanied Him from Galilee.

In the grave Christ awaited the Father's answer. Yet the burial too spoke of forsakenness. He had vanished from the earth and darkness covered Him. He had willingly offered Himself up to that indignity in His suffering and death. It would have been just judgment upon our sins had that darkness buried us eternally. The Father's answer to His sacrifice would come. He would presently return to the light of eternal communion with God, and we with Him.

CHAPTER SEVENTY EIGHT
THE REDEMPTION OF LIFE
LUKE 24

Luke describes Christ as the true Man. In Him human life was redeemed. This redemption was seen especially in His resurrection. The angels reproached the women for seeking the One who was alive among the dead. For now He had obtained eternal life and stood on the other side of sin and death. He also was the dispenser of life and of all the treasures in life. He showed this when He acted as host in the house and at the table of the men from Emmaus. That is exactly when they recognized Him as *the Christ*.

To believe in Him in this way always means that we ourselves have life, and that we too stand on the other side of sin and death. A merely historical faith in the resurrection is not possible. To believe in Him for their life was, at first, too much for the disciples. They considered the women's message utter nonsense. And when the Christ appeared in their midst, they were so overjoyed that they still could not believe it.

Belief in Christ's resurrection must not depend on His appearing to us but in the Word of God, or, what is the same thing, in the Word of Christ. It is noteworthy how often we are referred to the Word of Christ in this chapter, and to the Word of God in the Old Testament. Moses and the prophets had foretold this resurrection of life. If it was to come to that, the Christ would have to pass through suffering and death. That had been prophesied about Him. But then He was the same after His resurrection as before His death. Human life had been truly victorious.

Only, He was no longer subject to the laws of our universe. He could, for example, disappear suddenly and He could ascend into heaven. He could also reveal Himself in another form (Mark 16:12), because He now had a spiritual body (I Corinthians 15:44). Yet He still ate right before their eyes. Furthermore, He also visited with them at the sea of Tiberias. Was this glorification of His body only partial, to be completed at His ascension?

Main Thought: *Christ arises as the Redeemer of life.*

Delivered from the bonds of death. On Friday evening the Lord Jesus had been buried in some haste. Afterwards, the women who had been accompanying Him had prepared spices to embalm the body. Very early Sunday morning they went to the grave and found the stone rolled away. They saw that the body was not there. What else could they think but that the body had been stolen?

Suddenly they saw two men in clothes gleaming like lightning. They were very frightened, for they understood that these men were no mere human beings. There they stood with their sadness, their darkness and their sin in the light of God's grace as it was revealed to them by the angels. They bowed their faces to the ground.

They heard the voice of the angels: "Why are you looking among the dead for the One who is alive?" The angels informed them that He had risen. Had He not foretold His suffering, death and resurrection when they were still in Galilee? They suddenly remembered His words which at first they had not understood and could not have believed. Now they were faced with the fulfillment when they heard the angels' words. They began to live in the Word of the Lord Jesus Christ, which now became a Word of life to them. All at once it became clear to them how He had stood above all these things and had Himself willed them all along. It was all part of the work the Father had given Him to do. Therefore they believed, although time after time they found it difficult to accept that everything they experienced was true.

Returning to Jerusalem, the women told these things to the eleven disciples and to the others. The disciples simply didn't believe it. They took their words to be pure nonsense. The women were obviously overwrought and the one got the other stirred up. That's how little even the disciples had previously understood the words of the Lord Jesus. That He was risen was simply impossible for them to accept.

We are all confronted with the seemingly unconquerable power of death. All of us go down to the grave. Every day that goes by is buried in the grave of the past. And no one can make our life rise up again. If Jesus was risen, it meant that the power of death had been broken and that their lives would also not perish; it meant that they had eternal life, that their lives had value for God. The power of death lies in sin, in our guilt. If death had been conquered, the power of sin had been broken and the guilt removed, freeing us to live in God's favor. That was all contained in the resurrection of the Lord Jesus. However, that was something the disciples could not believe. Often we do not believe it either. We so often still think of the unbroken reign of death.

Peter, however, went to the tomb and saw the linen cloths lying by themselves. He could not believe it either. But he went away greatly astonished at what had happened. He was confronted with the miracle of God's grace though it still was not clear to him. Jesus had yet to gather all those crushed and lost people and bring them to a life in God's favor through faith in Him. He did that in His own way.

Israel's Redeemer. On that Sunday evening two followers of the Lord Jesus were walking from Jerusalem to their home in Emmaus. That was a walk of two to three hours. They were engaged in an animated discussion of all that had happened. The name of the one was Cleopas; he may have been an uncle of Jesus and a brother of Joseph.

While they were walking together someone came up behind them. It was the Lord Jesus. However, they did not know Him. His appearance was different than before and, moreover, God kept them from recognizing Him. They should not believe that He was risen only on the basis of His appearance but they should acknowledge that God had said it. They were to believe the Word of God. God's Word is the ground of all our certainty.

The stranger asked them what they were discussing. Was he the only stranger in Jerusalem, they wondered, who did not know what had happened there? When he asked what they were referring to, they told him of Jesus and of their expectations. He was a prophet, mighty in deed and word. He lived before God, for all the people to see. Now He had been put to death by the elders. Everything lay buried with Him: their hopes for their life, their hope for the restoration of Israel, and their hope for the blessing which was to come upon the nations through Israel.

Yet, because of their expectations, they could not let go of Him. He had said that He was Israel's Redeemer. They had believed Him, but now He had perished. It was already the third day since He died and He had not returned from the dead, neither had He revealed Himself to the whole nation to raise the dead from their graves. Some women had indeed reported that angels had told them that He was alive and some of the disciples had also found the tomb empty, but they had not seen Him. If He was alive, He certainly would have shown Himself to the whole nation of Israel.

At that point the stranger began to speak. He reproached them for their unbelief and said to them, "Did the Scriptures not say that the Messiah would have to suffer and die and so enter into His glory?" He had to suffer death in order to destroy the power of death for all His people. He would thus enter into His glory, which, however, would not immediately be revealed to all men. Those who believed in Him would see His glory by faith. He supported what He said with Scriptures. They didn't know what they were hearing. The Scriptures were being opened up to them. They had never seen Scripture in that light before. Could it be true that He was risen? Hope burned in their hearts but in their joy they couldn't believe it. His resurrection would mean the complete redemption of life!

Meanwhile, they were approaching Emmaus and the stranger acted as if he had to go on. They urged him to stay with them since it was already late. They could no longer do without his words; they meant life itself to them.

Once in the house, they sat down to eat. Immediately, their guest took charge. He gave thanks and prayed, broke the passover bread and gave it to them. Instantly they saw who He was. It was the Lord Himself! For by His resurrection He had all things in His power. He gives life and provides for its needs. He distributes His favor and the favor of His Father. In life He is the Host. To their amazement they recognized Him. We never know the Christ other than in wonder.

At that same moment He vanished from sight. After His resurrection the Lord Jesus had that power over Himself; He appeared and disappeared at will. They looked at each other and said: Didn't it sound very familiar when He opened the Scriptures to us in that way? It was just as if we heard Him speak again. And yet we did not recognize Him. How was that possible? We could not believe yet.

Why did Jesus disappear so suddenly? He did not want to give Himself here and there to isolated individuals, but He wanted to gather together His own circle, the community of His people. And He succeeded because those two men did not have a moment's rest in Emmaus. Immediately they hurried back to Jerusalem. Before they had been able to utter a single word, the circle which was gathered there called out to them, "It's true! The Lord has risen and He appeared to Simon!" Whereupon *they* told what had happened to them. The circle of believers was once again assembled in faith. Within that circle we must take our place.

It is I. While they were still talking together Jesus stood in their midst and greeted them with His salutation, "Peace be with you!" That startled them and they were afraid, thinking that they were seeing a ghost. After all they had heard, that's how little they were ready for the victory over death. Let's not forget, however, that we are also cowed by the reign of death. He told them that they could see and touch Him, as He was really a man and not a ghost.

Delirious with joy they still could not believe it. Amazed, they marveled at this great happening. Was it really the Jesus they had known before? If so, the life which He had in common with them had been delivered from death. It meant that they were saved too! They still couldn't believe it! As proof He ate a piece of fried fish and a honeycomb which they had brought to Him.

Then they believed. It was Jesus Himself! The life He had in common with them had passed through death; He had led it to victory. How different life had suddenly become! They were free from the guilt and power of death. They were living in the light of God's eternal favor. They were now above death. Admittedly, they still had to die, but their life on earth was not in vain. Life could not be destroyed forever. Life had value in God's eyes because they were privileged to live in communion with Him. One day it would be restored when Christ would raise the dead unto glory.

Witnesses of life. Jesus talked about the Scriptures and showed them how Scripture had foretold all these things. He based their faith firmly on the Scriptures. To that end He opened their minds so that they understood what Scripture taught. For years they had known those Scriptures, but they had never before seen their meaning. They had not been able to see the breadth and depth of the grace of God which redeems life. Now the Holy Spirit so enlightened their minds to understand the Scriptures.

He also showed them how it was foretold in the Scriptures that this redemption of life was to be preached everywhere. Life was redeemed because people repented, because they turned to God and lived in communion with Him, and because they shared in the forgiveness of sins. All this was made possible through Him, the risen Lord. This message had to be preached to all the nations, beginning at Jerusalem.

That was to be the content of the disciples' witness regarding Him. To enable them to witness they would receive the Holy Spirit, which He had promised to them. They were told to wait for that Spirit in Jerusalem. And witness they did; through their testimony we may believe today. As a result, we may also see and experience the victory of life, enabling us to become His witnesses also.

The reconciliation of life in heaven. Forty days after His resurrection Jesus again appeared to His disciples in Jerusalem. He led them out of the city in the direction of Bethany. There on one of the hills He stopped, lifted up His hands and blessed them. And while He was blessing them, He left them and was taken up into heaven.

What was He going to do there in heaven? On earth He had given His life as a sacrifice for His own. Now, as the Priest, He went to present that sacrifice to the Father. On the basis of that sacrifice He is able to bring about a lasting communion between God and us. In that fellowship we are blessed. For that reason He ascended into heaven while He was blessing His disciples.

Life is currently being redeemed by Christ's blessing. The disciples were privileged to be its messengers. Should it amaze us then that, although He had departed from them, they returned to Jerusalem with great joy? They were continually in the temple, praising and thanking God. They finally saw the complete redemption of life that is given in Christ. And if we see it, shouldn't we also be full of joy since we know that He is constantly occupied on our behalf in heaven?